Introduction to European Social Security Law

In the series Studies in Social Policy this book
Introduction to European Social Security Law
is the second title.

The titles published in this series are listed at the end of the book.

STUDIES IN SOCIAL POLICY

Introduction to European Social Security Law

Frans Pennings

second edition

1998
Kluwer Law International
The Hague - London - Boston

Published by Kluwer Law International
P.O. Box 85889
2508 CN The Hague, The Netherlands

Sold and distributed in the USA and Canada by
Kluwer Law International
675 Massachusetts Avenue
Cambridge, MA 02139, USA

Sold and distributed in all other countries by
Kluwer Law International
Distribution Centre
P.O. Box 322
3300 AH Dordrecht, The Netherlands

A C.I.P. Catalogue record for this book is available from the Library of Congress

Printed on acid-free paper

Cover design: Alfred Birnie bNo

ISBN: 90 411 1033 X

© 1998 Kluwer Law International

The first edition of this book was published as volume 2 in the 'Kluwer Sovac Series' on Social Security in 1994.

Kluwer Law International incorporates the publishing programmes of Graham & Trotman Ltd, Kluwer Law and Taxation Publishers and Martinus Nijhoff Publishers

Preface

As from 1 January 1993, free movement of workers has become a reality in the internal market of the EC. This development raises several questions. To what extent is freedom of movement realised? What are the effects of cross-border movement to the social security position of the workers concerned? What has still to be done in this field?

These questions are, however, not new. From the first days of the European Community (1957) regulations have been made in order to enable workers to be employed in another Member State and measures were taken in order to avoid their benefit rights being negatively affected. In addition, the Court of Justice of the European Communities was required to give rulings on questions from national courts on the interpretation of Community law. The judgments of the Court on the coordination of social security systems have been very relevant to the realisation of freedom of movement.

In addition, there were some harmonisation initiatives by the Council of the EC. These involved, in particular, directives on the equal treatment of men and women. The case law on these directives has been very important as the Court left very little room for Member States to avoid the full implementation of these directives.

In this book, we will describe the coordination law for migrant workers in Part I. This concerns Regulation 1408/71 and the judgments of the Court of Justice. We will analyse the contributions which these made to the development of coordination law and to the realisation of the objective of free movement of workers.

The second part of this book is dedicated to harmonisation initiatives. Harmonisation instruments are described in general, so as to give a good insight into the possibilities and impossibilities of a 'social Europe'. Secondly, the judgments of the Court on Article 119 and the directives on equal treatment of men and women in social security are analysed.

Mel Cousins (Dublin) made an indispensable contribution to this book by editing the text and by his suggestions for clarifications and additions. Ann Musters gave a finishing touch to the lay-out. The responsibility for this book is, of course, entirely mine.

The book is the second edition of the *Introduction to European Social Security Law*. The text of this edition has been revised completely. I am grateful for the comments on the first edition.

At the end of this book can be found an index on the case law of the Court, and a subject index.

Frans Pennings   Tilburg, April 1998
Postbox 90153
NL 5000 LE Tilburg

Table of Contents

Abbrevations

AAW	Algemene Arbeidsongeschiktheidswet [Netherlands law on general disability]
ABP	Algemene Burgerlijke Pensioenwet [Dutch social security act for civil servants]
AG	Advocate-General
AKW	Algemene Kinderbijslagwet [Netherlands law on child benefits]
AOW	Algemene Ouderdomswet [Netherlands law on old-age pensions]
AWW	Algemene Weduwen- en Wezenwet [Netherlands widows and orphan's law]
BTSZ	Belgisch Tijdschrift voor Sociale Zekerheid [Belgian magazine]
CMLR	Common Market Law Reports
CMLRev	Common Market Law Review
COM	proposal of the European Commission
CRvB	Centrale Raad van Beroep [Netherlands Court of Appeal for social security)
EC	European Community
ECR	European Court Reports
ECU	European currency unit
EEA	European Economic Area
EEC	European Economic Community
EFTA	European Free Trade Association
ELR	European Law Review
EP	European Parliament
ESC	European Social Charter
ILJ	Industrial Law Journal
ILO	International Labour Organisation
ILR	International Labour Review
IOAW	Wet Inkomensvoorziening Oudere en gedeeltelijk Arbeidsonge-schikte werkloze Werknemers [Netherlands Law on an income provision for the older and partially disabled unemployed persons]
KB	Koninklijk Besluit [Royal Decree]
LIEI	Legal Issues of European Integration
NCIP	non-contributory invalidity pension
NCJM	Magazin of Netherlands Comitee for Human Rights
NJB	Nederlands Juristenblad [Dutch magazine]
NLG	Dutch guilders
NYIL	Netherlands Yearbook of International Law
OJ C	Official Journal of the European Communities, Information and Notices
OJ L	Official Journal of the European Communities, Legislation

PS	Periodiek voor sociale verzekering, sociale voorzieningen en arbeidsrecht [Dutch magazine]
RMC	Revue du Marché Commun
RSV	Rechtspraak Sociale Verzekering [Dutch magazine with law reports]
RTDE	Revue Trimistrielle de Droit Européen
RV	Rechtspraak Vreemdelingenrecht [Dutch magazine]
RvB	Raad van Beroep [former Netherlands social security court]
SDA	Severe Disablement Allowance
SEW	Tijdschrift voor Europees en economisch recht [Dutch magazine]
SGB	Sozialgesetzbuch [German social security code]
SMA	Sociaal Maandblad Arbeid [Dutch magazine]
SR	Nederlands tijdschrift voor sociaal recht [Dutch magazine]
Stb	Staatsblad [Netherlands Official Journal]
SVB	Sociale Verzekeringsbank [Netherlands administration of national insurances]
Trb.	Tractatenblad [Netherlands official journal of treaties]
WW	Werkloosheidswet [Netherlands unemployment law]
WWV	Wet Werkloosheidsvoorziening [Netherlands unemployment provisions]
WAO	Wet op de Arbeidsongeschiktheidsverzekering [Netherlands law for benefits in case of incapacity for work]
YEL	Yearbook of European Law

PART I

COORDINATION

Chapter 1

Introduction: Why is Coordination Necessary?

1.1. General

At the beginning of the 20th Century, when employees' insurance schemes were established, it became clear that social security gave rise to special problems in cross-border situations. Such problems arose, for instance, in the case of employees who worked in a State other than the State of residence and who claimed an occupational accidents benefit. In such a case it could happen that an employee was insured for occupational accidents benefits in both States, or in no State at all. Such problems had to be solved and therefore coordination provisions were inserted in bilateral trade treaties. This location of coordination provisions in trade treaties reflects the fact that such rules were, in particular, seen as necessary in order to avoid unfair competition; it was necessary to prevent a situation whereby one State had to pay for gaps in an insurance record of workers, whereas other States would not have such costs. Without such regulation, there would be a distortion of competition. In the treaties it was agreed that nationals of a State which has signed the treaty have to be given the same advantages as apply to the nationals of the State where the advantage is required. This provision is sometimes called the 'reciprocity condition'.[1]

In 1957 the European Economic Community (EEC) was created and promotion of the freedom of movement of workers was one of the pillars of the Community. Impediments to the freedom of movement were held to be unfavourable to 'the economy', whereas with the free movement of workers Member States would be able to benefit from the effects of an optimal allocation of labour.

Ensuring the freedom of movement of workers across national borders requires active measures. For the main part, these measures will have to be taken in the field of social security, since workers cannot be expected to go abroad if this has negative effects on their benefit rights. Negative effects are bound to occur when a person is employed in a foreign country, for, as we will see later on, national social security legislation often makes a distinction between claimants on grounds of nationality. Under such systems, only persons who are nationals of the country in question are eligible for benefit.

---

[1]   An example of a treaty containing the reciprocity condition is found in the *Frilli* judgment (Court of Justice 22 June 1972, Case 1/72, [1972] *ECR* 457), *see* Section 7.5.

Another rule, which can be found in many national systems, and which is disadvantageous to migrants, is that which provides that benefits are only paid to persons residing in that country. Migrants, who often go or return to foreign countries, do not receive such benefits. A third category of provisions causing problems to migrants, arises where a country makes the acquisition or calculation of benefit is conditional upon the completion of periods of insurance, employment or residence, where only periods completed under the legislation of that country are taken into account. In such a system, a migrant worker may not be entitled to benefit or may receive a smaller benefit than he[2] would have, had he stayed in his native country.

In view of these provisions, disadvantageous for migrants, international social security rules have been adopted. These rules are based on the assumption that a worker will not be prepared to go abroad, if this would have negative effects on his right to benefit. To a certain extent, this assumption is of an abstract character: often workers will not be conscious of the negative effects until a certain risk actually occurs. In making their decision to go to work abroad, they will usually not consider the social security effects. Coordination problems with, for instance, old age pension schemes will not be apparent until after retirement. However, this is no excuse for not removing the causes of loss of benefit rights as a result of a change of country of employment. Having heard of bad experiences, future generations are likely to take such effects into account. Moreover, it is difficult to conceive of an alternative approach to removing these impediments to the freedom of movement. Hence social security coordination rules are directed at national regulations as such in order to remove social security problems for migrants.

This argument draws a direct link between the freedom of movement of workers and social security and as a result the protection of workers who change their country of employment is an important part of European social security. So, as soon as the EEC was founded, there was a great need for a rapid formulation of coordination rules.

Besides promoting the freedom of movement of workers, another important aspect of international social security is the combating of poverty. This subject has a long history, as can be seen from, for instance, the initiatives taken by the International Labour Organisation (these will be discussed in Section 20.2). Preventing poverty on an international level has recently received more attention with a view to the European unification process. For some time, an unfounded enthusiasm existed for the process of creating a single EU market.[3] This euphoria is now tempered by, among other things, the sense that economic measures and developments without a supporting social policy will have serious negative effects for large groups of the

---

[2]   Where the pronoun 'he' or 'his' is used, the reader is asked to read, where relevant, also 'she' or 'her'.

[3]   When referring to the present European Union, as created by the Maastricht Treaty we use the term EU; when referring to the European Community, which existed before this Treaty, we use the abbrevation EC. The Treaty and Court of Justice are still called EC Treaty and Court of Justice of the EC.

population. The European Commission has also recognised that, especially during the first stage of the process towards a single market, important restructuring may occur, which may cause extensive unemployment in certain sectors.[4] In addition, it is to be expected that the Member States will be inclined to lower their labour costs in order to strengthen their competitive position. One of the (few) possible ways of achieving this is to lower social security contributions, as this will reduce labour costs. However, the result of this is that there will be less funds available for benefits and this will lead to a cut back of benefit levels. Such a development would lead to a decrease in the welfare level for large groups of employees.

This book focuses on both aspects of international social security (promoting free movement of workers as well as social policy). These two types of rules do not have the same target groups. The first group consists of persons changing their country of employment. The second group concerns the entire population, not only migrant workers.

In Part I of this book, the coordination problems in social security, which occur or will occur in a unified Europe, will be identified. In Part II, the activities of the EU in the field of social policy will be described.

1.2.   Why is Coordination Necessary?

It is a general phenomenon that a State restricts its responsibility in the area of social security to its own territory and/or its own nationals. The linking of the social security system to the territory of a State is called the *territorial principle*. This principle is no legal principle, but a term which explains some phenomena. According to this principle, social security law only applies to facts which happen within the national borders of the own State. An example of the effects of this principle is the condition that a person is entitled only to benefit if the risk materialised on the territory of a State. Another example is the condition that a person must have worked or lived for specified periods on the territory of a State in order to be entitled to benefit. A third example is the condition that benefits are paid only on the territory of the State where the right to benefit was acquired. In other words, a relationship is made between, on the one hand, the territory of the State, and on the other hand, the group of persons, contributions, benefits and/or risks that are governed by the legislation of that State.

The territorial principle is an impediment to the realisation of free movement of workers. When each country uses territorial criteria to define the field of applications of its social security system, this will lead to problems in the case of cross border movement of workers. The criteria which States use to define the field of application of their social security systems are called national *rules of conflict*. Examples are where persons are insured who *work* in that State or who *live* in that State. Rules of conflict define the persons or facts to which a national legal system

---

4   Opinion of the Commission as appears from *e.g. OJ C* 163/3, 22 June 1991, *see* also Chapter 21.

is confined. In social security law the following criteria related to the territorial principle may be chosen as rules of conflict: the place where the worker *works*, where he *resides*, or where the *employer* has his registered office or place of business, or, for seamen, the flag under which they sail.

The problem with the national rules of conflict is that the rules belonging to public law (including social security), have a one-sided character. To understand the problem better, it is useful to look first at *civil law* rules of conflict. In civil law, rules of conflict have a two-sided character. This means that rules of conflict of the law of one State determine a field of application not only to national law but also to foreign law. For example, national law can provide that the place where the agreement was made is decisive for the choice of a legal system; this means that in case of a conflict on an agreement made in a foreign country, the court has to apply foreign law.

Rules of conflict of public law are, however, of a one-sided character. This is because public law is not concerned with relationships between individuals, but with relationships between States. The logical consequence is that a national government cannot decide that its legislation is also applicable outside its territory. Belgium can, for instance, not decide that a person is entitled to a German passport or to German unemployment benefit.

We call the rules of conflict of public law unilateral rules: they can establish only that a particular subject is either within the competence of a particular State or beyond the competence. For instance: persons are insured under national insurance, if they are resident of the Netherlands; if somebody is not covered by this rule, it is not clear to which law he is subject.

The importance of the fact that rules of conflict of public law are unilateral appears, for instance, in situations where rules of conflict of one State are contrary to those of another State. This may happen, because, as was mentioned above, national legal systems do not always use the same (territorial) criteria in their rules of conflict: *e.g.* a State may use the criterion of the residence of the worker for the applicability of its law, whereas another State uses the criterion of the place of work, and a third State uses the criterion of the place of business of the employer.

As rules of conflict of public law have a unilateral character, a State can only decide whether or not to adopt rules on a particular subject, but cannot adopt a regulation in which the exact role of foreign and national law is set out. As a result it may, for instance, occur that a person working in another State than the one in which he lives, falls under two legal systems at the same time, or under none at all. For instance, State x provides that people who work on its territory are insured for old-age pensions and State y provides that residence is the decisive criterion. In the case of a person who works in State x and resides in State y, he is covered in two countries; if he resides in State x and works in State y he is insured in neither State. In other words, when a State applies criteria different from those of another State, *conflicts of law* are likely to occur.

When a migrant worker falls under the legal systems of more than one country at the same time, this is called a *positive conflict of laws*; when a migrant falls under no system at all, this is called a *negative conflict of laws*.

These conflicts can, precisely because of the unilateral character of the national rules of conflict, only be solved by a supranational coordination regulation.

The effects of the territoriality principle can also be see in rules of *substance*. Rules of substance concern the conditions and provisions of a national scheme which determine which facts lying outside the territory of a State are relevant to its own benefit rules. For instance, a national scheme may provide that periods of residence abroad are taken into account for the acquisition of a right to benefit in the host country. A provision that persons of a State which signed a reciprocity agreement are treated in the same way as the own nationals is an example of a rule of substance.

Rules of substance can have, unlike rules of conflict, a multilateral character, as they can refer to facts occurring in other countries.

Differences in national rules of substance can lead to conflicts. This may be the case if a person receives benefit from in country x and country y. Country x will be inclined to deduct the benefit of country y from its own benefit. But country y will also do so. Also these discrepancies make clear the need for a common regulation, for *coordination*.

1.3.   What is Coordination?

In the previous section the term 'coordination' was used. In this section we will give a definition of this term.

> *Definition.* Coordination rules are rules of international social security law intended to adjust social security schemes in relation to each other (as well as to those of other international regulations), for the purpose of regulating trans-national questions, with the objective of protecting the social security position of migrants workers, the members of their families and similar groups of persons.

This definition contains a normative element: coordination concerns the protection of migrants. This is an essential element of coordination.

The definition also comprises the coordination of issues which are only indirectly related to migrants, such as the co-operation of (benefit) administration offices.

The definition mentions not only adjustment of national social security rules, but also involves adjustment to international regulations. Coordination must pertain to the coordination of international treaties, since, for instance, in addition to the EU coordination regulations, the European Interim Agreements, ILO Conventions and bilateral treaties (*see* Chapter 2) may contain coordination rules applicable to the same persons.

The definition of the term 'coordination' is important, in particular, where the question arises whether a particular measure is a coordinating or a harmonising one. We will discuss harmonisation in Part II.

Definition. Harmonisation is the sum of international provisions directed at States which have the objective or obligation that these States adjust their national law to the requirements of the harmonisation provisions.

Coordination leaves the rules of national schemes intact, which implies that the differences between the national schemes remain. It supersedes, however, those national rules, and only those, which are disadvantageous for migrant workers and self-employed persons. Harmonisation on its turn involves changes of national legislation for all employees (sometimes for all residents), not only for migrants.

An example to illustrate the difference between coordination and harmonisation: an important objective of coordination rules is to assign the national social security scheme applicable. In addition, coordination rules have to ensure that periods abroad count to satisfy the conditions of the scheme assigned as applicable. Coordination rules overrule national provisions contrary to them. Despite such coordination rules, it can happen that a migrant worker appears to have no right to a particular benefit under the scheme assigned as applicable, since he does not meet the conditions of that scheme (even if the periods fulfilled abroad are aggregated). Another reason may be that under the scheme assigned as applicable a particular contingency is not covered. It may be that in the State of origin this person would have been entitled to benefit or to a higher benefit; coordination does not remove such differences between States. Harmonisation would, on the contrary, have the effect that differences were removed.

As regards EU law, it can be said that neither Regulation 1408/71 nor the EC Treaty provide a definition of coordination. Neither has the Court of Justice given such a definition in one of its rulings. In several decisions the Court held that the Regulation leaves the Member States the powers to determine the type, and the content, of the provisions of their benefit schemes.[5] When discussing the scope of coordination, the Court even uses this concept in a negative sense: 'coordination does not preclude the powers of the Member States to determine the benefit conditions and the type of benefits, nor does it forbid differences between Member States'.[6]

On the other hand it should be remembered that the Court is not concerned with discussions on coordination in general, but with coordination as it is made possible by Article 51 of the Treaty and Regulation 1408/71. Thus, in some decisions, the Court speaks of 'the mere coordination at present practised'.[7] Therefore, it is an open

---

[5] For example in Court of Justice 15 January 1986, Case 41/84, *Pinna*, [1986] *ECR* 1.
[6] Court of Justice 13 October 1977, Case 22/77, *First Mura judgment*, [1977] *ECR*1 169
[7] *See Mura* judgment, previous note.

question what the approach of the Court would be if the Community legislator introduced a Treaty or regulation with a broader coordination objective.[8]

1.4.   Tasks of a Coordination regulation

Protection of social security rights of migrant workers implies that at least the following essential problems have to be solved:
1. conflicts of law;
2. unequal treatment on grounds of nationality;
3. occurrence of breaks in the career of a worker resulting from cross border movement, which are disadvantageous to the fulfilment of the conditions for benefit and/or the calculation of the amount of benefit;
4. territorial requirements for payment of benefit rights.
These issues are discussed in the following sections.

1.4.1.   Solving Conflicts of Law

In section 1.1. we already mentioned, that if an employee goes to work in another State, it must be clear which social security system is applicable to him.

There are, in theory, several different ways for the international legislator to determine the criteria for deciding the law applicable. The first way is to offer employers and employees a choice as to which scheme is applicable. In such a system, employers and employees are free to designate a national legal system as applicable to their situation. In this option, it is also conceivable that parties could designate the law of a third country. Such options exist, for instance, in civil law. If such an option exists, regulations have to be made for the case where parties have not designated a particular legal system in their contract. This approach does not prevent provisions requiring that at least rules of public order (*e.g.* rules on minimum wages) of the State of work are always applicable, even if parties have designated the law of another State (with no minimum wages).

A system giving the possibility of opting for a particular national system seems less obvious for coordination of social security. This is because a third party, not the employer or the employee, but the State would be responsible for the expenses of the designated social security scheme. Freedom of choice would cause problems, especially when a national system is not cost-effective and receives State subsidies.

A second system for drafting the rules for determining the law applicable could be that persons who lived or worked in two or more countries are entitled to the most *favourable* solution. As opposed to the previously described approach, this system does not provide the opportunity of choice. Binding coordination rules instead

---

[8]   In Chapter 19 we will go on to discuss the concept of coordination as practised by the Court, having discussed Regulation 1408/71 in the following chapters.

determine this outcome. Suppose that a person worked for ten years in country x, ten years in country y, and twenty years in country z. In this system, the law of the State where forty years of work result in (for instance) the highest old age pension would be designated. However, in case of large differences between national schemes, this method would result in disproportionate benefit charges for the country with the most favourable scheme. In addition, improper use would be possible: workers would try to spend at least a short period in the most favourable country. Another problem which might arise is that it not always that easy to determine which scheme is the most favourable. What should be done when, for instance, country x has the most attractive disability benefit, whereas country y has the most advantageous old age benefit system?

In comparison to the coordination treaties preceding the present EU coordination regulation, the present system marks a development in coordination. Initially, bilateral coordination conventions contained the possibility of the option between either separate application of national legislations or the application of the system of coordinated assimilation of pensions. In a later stage, multilateral treaties abandoned this option.

Currently the rules of conflict given in international conventions do not leave freedom of choice and are binding. This is at present the most obvious method in social security and this method is followed in Regulation 1408/71 on coordination of social security.

Characteristics of Rules for Determining the Legislation Applicable.
Rules which assign which legislation is applicable are an essential part of coordination. These rules have to prevent workers from being, as a result of cross-border movement, insured in two States or not insured at all. They affect the national rules of conflict.

An important question as regards the rules for determining the legislation applicable is whether they have *exclusive* and *binding* effect.

If these rules have *exclusive* effect, this means that as a result there is only one national legislation applicable at the same time. Such a rule overrules national rules of conflict.

Suppose that the rules for determining the law applicable provide that for a person the legislation of State x is applicable. He has also a relationship with State y, for instance, he resides in that State. The exclusive effect of the rules for determining the legislation applicable in this example means that the *national* rules of conflict of State y which may provide that this person is covered by the social security scheme of State y are overruled.

Rules for determining the legislation applicable have *binding* effect, when they determine that national legislation is applicable in a particular situation, even though the rules of conflict of that national law system provide the opposite.

An example arises where the coordination rule provides that a person falls under State x, and the national conflict rules of State x entail that this person does not satisfy the territorial criteria laid down in the national legislation (for instance, he does not reside in State *x*). *Binding* rules for determining the legislation applicable overrule that specific national rule. It means that the person is insured in State *x*, despite the national rules of conflict.

The exclusive effect of the rules for determining the legislation applicable avoids a positive conflict of laws, where the negative effect serves to prevent a negative conflict of laws.

1.4.2. Unequal Treatment on the Basis of Nationality

Equal treatment of migrant workers and nationals is fundamental for each coordination scheme.

An important distinction is that between *direct discrimination* and *indirect discrimination*.

By *direct discrimination* is meant a situation where a distinction is made between persons on the basis of a forbidden criterion, *e.g.* nationality.

We describe a rule as *indirectly discriminating* if it, although not containing a forbidden criterion, leads to disadvantageous effects for specific categories of persons who can be defined by the forbidden criterion (such as 'migrant workers'). As in the case of indirect discrimination there is no forbidden criterion mentioned, it is much more difficult to prove indirect discrimination than direct discrimination.

A case of indirection discrimination starts with the suspicion that a rule is indirectly discriminatory. This is the case if the rule predominantly affects a particular category, such as migrant workers. It is not relevant whether the author of the rule had the intention to discriminate against this group.

Sometimes this suspicion has to be supported by statistical data. This does not have to be always the case, see *Commission EC v. Kingdom of Belgium*.[9] In this case the Belgian government stated that the Commission has not proved that its regulation affected a relatively higher percentage of persons with the nationality of a Member State other than Belgium. The Court answered that a provision of national law must be considered indirectly discriminating, if it affects by its nature migrant workers more than national employees and threatens to affect the former group negatively. Consequently, statistical proof is not required.

If there is an alleged case of indirect discrimination, the person or organisation who made the rule or applies it, has the opportunity to show grounds of justification, which must not relate to discrimination. If the person or organisation succeeds in proving such grounds, there is no indirect discrimination. This approach means that the person accused of indirect discrimination has to prove that he is innocent; this is a reversal of the burden of proof.

It is difficult to say in general whether a particular provision can serve as an objective ground of justification. *See*, for the case law, Section 10.3 and, for indirect discrimination on the basis of sex, Section 23.5.5.

---

[9]   Court of Justice 12 December 1996, Case 278/94, [1996] *ECR* I-4307.

1.4.3. Territorial Requirements for Acquiring Benefit Rights

Some national schemes provide that a person is entitled to benefit only if he or his family members live in that State. This is a clear elaboration of the territorial principle. Another example is where a scheme makes the receipt of an industrial accident benefit conditional on the fact that the accident happened on the territory of that State. The right to certain types of benefits is often subject to the condition that the person in question completed periods of residence, or periods of contributions or periods of work. When periods completed in other Member States do not count for the fulfilment of such conditions, cross border movement leads to serious problems. Without further rules, it might happen that a worker does not satisfy such conditions and will not receive benefit.

It may also happen that, although an employee succeeds in satisfying the benefit conditions, the periods completed in a foreign country do not count for the calculation of the amount of benefit. This worker receives a lower benefit than he would if these periods were aggregated. Therefore, an important objective of coordination is that migrant workers, who have been insured in more than one State, do not suffer the disadvantages caused by breaks in their career as a result of cross border movement. It is important that the periods completed in a foreign country and those completed under the regulation of the State where benefit is applied for, are aggregated.

This requirement does not mean that all periods of insurance of migrants must be assimilated. It requires, however, the possibility of aggregating these periods. Aggregation needs coordination and hence rules for assimilation have to be given. This is because the national schemes vary to a large extent. There are, for instance, systems in which the right to benefit is conditional on the periods in which contributions were paid; other systems require periods of residence. Other systems do not have requirements on periods of residence or work, but only demand that a person resides on the territory of the State in question at the moment the risk occurs for the first time. Aggregation of periods completed under such different types is not a *sine cure* and neither is it clear at first sight how such aggregation is to be effected: how can periods completed abroad be 'translated' into those periods required by the schemes of another State?

Coordination regulations have to solve these problems, they can affect the character of national systems drastically. *See*, for instance, Chapter 15.

1.4.4. Territorial Requirements for Payment of Benefit

Some national regulations require that a person who applies for benefit (or the person on behalf of whom the claim is made) resides in that country. This is, of course, a problem for the free movement of workers, as a worker who has acquired a right to benefit will be disinclined to go abroad, if he does not actually receive this benefit. Therefore, a coordination regulation must make it possible for migrant workers to receive the benefits they are entitled to, regardless of the fact that they no longer reside on the territory of the country which is due to pay these benefits. Often workers will return to their State of origin in case of serious disablement or retirement. In these cases, the principle of equal treatment does not require the payment of benefits under all circumstances, as the scheme in question may provide the same for its own nationals. Hence, a separate principle of coordination is to be invoked, which requires that territorial requirements with regard to payment of benefit are removed. This is an essential coordination principle.

Chapter 2

A Brief Overview of non-EU Coordination Instruments

2.1.   General

Alongside with the EU coordination regulations, which are the main topic of this book, there are supranational coordination schemes of other organisations. These will be discussed in this chapter

2.2.   International Social Security Initiatives of the International Labour Organisation

The end of the First World War effected an important break-through in the international development of standards in the field of social security. The Treaty of Versailles, which concluded this war, contains provisions for the foundation of the International Labour Organisation (ILO). Among other things, the ILO is responsible for preparing and adopting treaties and recommendations and the supervision of the observance of existing international labour standards. Besides representatives of the governments of Member States, representatives from employers' and trade unions sit on every board. The creation of this organisation brought about an institutional framework for harmonisation initiatives, which has the powers and the authority to draw up coordination and harmonisation treaties.[1]

A limited number of ILO Treaties are specifically devoted to the *coordination* of the social security schemes of signatory States. Furthermore, a number of ILO Conventions contain coordination rules alongside other provisions. Coordination under the ILO progresses with difficulty and as a result it is still in a rudimentary stage. The reason is that world-wide conventions with extensive coordination rules run the risk of being ratified by only a small number of countries. Hence it is natural that the Convention holding the largest number of ratifications (Convention 118), contains

---

[1]   *See*, for a historical overview of the ILO, Tamburi (1983) and Perrin (1969). *See* for the texts of ILO Treaties relevant to social security, F. Pennings, 'Codex' in R. Blanpain (ed.), *International Encyclopaedia of Laws, Social Security Law* (looseleaf). This work also mentions the ratifications of these treaties.

only one imperative coordination rule, viz. the equal treatment of the nationals of any other Member State in which the Convention applies.

An ILO Convention specifically devoted to coordination is Convention 48. This Convention provides for extensive rules for the maintenance of rights in the course of acquisition and acquired rights under invalidity, old-age and widows' and orphans' insurance schemes.[2] This Convention has a limited significance, as it has been ratified by only a small number of States.[3] Generally, the Convention was considered to be too much detailed and too inflexible. Therefore, negotiations were opened for a new Convention, Convention 157, which is eventually to replace Convention 48.[4]

Now that the EU coordination rules have gained in importance (being binding on all Member States and some associated States), the ILO coordination rules have faded to the background. Yet, the ILO was able to offer considerable technical support in drawing up EU coordination rules.[5]

2.3. International Social Security Initiatives of the Council of Europe

While the First World War led to the foundation of the ILO, the Second World War resulted in the *Congress of Europe*, organised in The Hague in May 1948. During this Congress, propositions were made for a Unified Europe with freedom of movement of persons, of opinions and of goods, as well as a Human Rights Convention and a Court of Justice for Human Rights. This resulted in the Statute of the Council of Europe, which was signed on 5 May 1949. Currently, all West European States and some Middle and East European States are a member of this organisation. The aim of the Council of Europe, as laid down in its Statute, is to achieve greater unity between its members for the purpose of safeguarding and realising the ideals and principles which form their 'common heritage' and of facilitating their economic and social progress. This also includes social justice and the promotion of the freedom of movement of workers.

From an institutional point of view, the Council of Europe is not strong. The Council of Europe is an organisation of a purely intergovernmental character, based on voluntary co-operation between States not willing to give up their sovereign power.[6] These characteristics of the Council of Europe place it in a position somewhere between the EU and the ILO and its importance with respect to international social policy initiatives has decreased in the past decades.

---

[2]   Convention of 22 June 1935.

[3]   After cancellation by Poland and Czechoslovakia, this Treaty only holds for Hungary, Israel, Italy, the Netherlands and Spain.

[4]   Convention of 23 June 1982.

[5]   *See* Perrin (1969).

[6]   *See*, for the Council of Europe, Driessen (1992) and Wiebringhaus (1983). The Council of Europe also established the European Convention for the Protection of Human Rights and Fundamental Freedoms, which is relevant to social security (as Article 6 requires due process, which is relevant to social security adjudication).

The current low-key position in the field of social security is in contrast with the initial stage of the Council of Europe. During this stage, the Council started with great elan to prepare conventions to promote social progress. These activities fitted in well with the above mentioned general objectives of the Council; these objectives implied the task and objective of coordination and harmonisation of social security law of the Member States. In order to encourage the freedom of movement of workers, three agreements on social security were signed in 1953, which were called the Interim Agreements.[7] These agreements were meant to be a temporary provision for the period until the European Convention on Social Security of the Council of Europe had been signed and ratified by the Member States. The latter Convention was signed in 1972.[8] This Convention, for which the Interim Agreements served as a prelude, was aimed at a multilateral coordination of social security systems of the Member States. Due to the small number of ratifications of this Convention, this objective was not achieved.[9]

In addition to both Interim Agreements, the European Convention on social and medical assistance was signed in Paris on 11 December 1953.[10] This is the only multilateral Convention on *public assistance* and this Convention received many ratifications, viz. of sixteen Member States of the Council of Europe. It has taken over the role of the earlier bilateral treaties on public assistance.

Article 1 of this Convention provides that the contracting parties undertake to ensure that nationals of the other signatory States who are lawfully resident in the territory of one of the States and who are without sufficient resources, are entitled like the own nationals and on the same conditions to social and medical assistance provided by the legislation in force in that part of the territory. The Convention provides that the costs of assistance to a national of a contracting party are borne by the State that has granted the assistance.[11] It can be seen that this Convention does not require States to refund the costs to the State where benefit has been granted to their nationals, as is the case in some other bilateral agreements. The second basic principle of this Convention is that a national of a signatory State who is lawfully resident in the territory of another signatory State, shall not be repatriated on the sole ground that he is in need of assistance.[12] In Chapter 20 we shall discuss some of the harmonisation instruments of the Council of Europe.

---

[7]   European Interim Agreement on social security schemes relating to old age, invalidity and survivors; European Interim Agreement on social security other than schemes for old age, invalidity and survivors; signed at Paris, 11 December 1953 (Pieters 1987: 106 ff. English versions).

[8]   Convention on Social Security of 14 December 1972, text can be found in Pieters (1987: 200).

[9]   *See*, for the coordination rules of this Convention, Urbanetz (1991).

[10]   *See* Pieters (1987: 132), for an English version of this Convention.

[11]   *See* Article 4 of this Convention.

[12]   Article 6 of the Convention. More extensively on this Convention, Vonk (1991).

Chapter 3

The European Union and the European Economic Area

3.1.   General

The European Union is currently of most direct importance to the coordination and harmonisation of social security in Europe. Primarily, the EC was designed for economic purposes, but from the very beginning, social justice was indirectly one of the objectives of this organisation. An important aspect of European integration is the promotion of economic and social progress and the continuous improvement of living and working conditions. This is also stated in the Preamble to the EC Treaty:

"-   (..) determined to lay the foundations of an ever closer union among the peoples of Europe
-    resolved to ensure the economic and social progress of their countries by common action to eliminate the barriers which divide Europe
-    recognizing that the removal of existing obstacles calls for concerted action in order to guarantee steady expansion, balanced trade and fair competition
-    anxious to strengthen the unity of their economies and to ensure their harmonious development by reducing the differences existing between the various regions and the backwardness of the less favoured regions (..)
     the (signatory parties) have decided to create a European Economic Community."

These general objectives proved to be important in the case law of the Court of Justice, as can be seen in the *Second Defrenne* judgment, *see* page 230.[1]

3.2.   Some Institutional Aspects of the EU

Since this book is mainly concerned with EU regulations, it is useful to mention some important institutional aspects of the EU.

The EC Treaty serves as the 'Constitution' of the EU. In the decision-making structure of the EU as recorded in this Treaty, national governments play an important role. This is because in the EU, the legislative power is not given to the European

---

[1]   Court of Justice 8 April 1976, Case 43/75, [1976] *ECR* 455, considerations 8-11.

Parliament, but rather to the Council of Ministers, which consists of government representatives.[2] Furthermore, the Council can only make decisions on the initiative of the European Commission. Since the national governments were unwilling to give up their sovereignty when the EC was founded, the Treaty articles which gave decision-making power to the Council, provided that a decision of the Council had to be unanimous. As a result, each Member State had a veto right. Since the move towards a common market became a tedious process, the Single European Act[3] amended the Treaty of 1957, so that for a specific number of decisions only a qualified majority of votes is required. Articles of the Treaty provide whether a decision based on that specific article is to be made unanimously or by a majority of votes. As we will see later on, the regulations concerning social security usually require unanimity; this is one of the fields in which the Member States are reluctant to give up their national power.

The Court of Justice in Luxembourg has the task of ensuring a uniform interpretation of EU law in all Member States. When an applicant states, during a procedure before a national court, that a national rule is contrary to EC law, this court, when in doubt as to the interpretation of the rules of European law, *can* refer this question to the Court of Justice and ask for a so-called preliminary ruling under Article 177 of the Treaty. When a question concerning the interpretation of the Treaty, the validity and interpretation of acts of the institutions of the Community, or on the interpretation of the statutes of bodies established by an act of the Council, is raised before a court of a Member State, that court may, if it considers that a decision on the question is necessary to enable it to give judgment, request the Court of Justice to give a ruling thereon. When any such question is raised in a case pending before a court of a Member State, against whose decisions there is no judicial remedy under national law,[4] that court *has* to bring the matter to the Court of Justice. It is only after the ruling of the Court, that the procedure before the national court is to be continued.[5] Hence, the Court has an indirect function; individual subjects cannot appeal to this court, unless a certain rule is specifically directed at them.

The Treaty provides for several different types of EC legislation. One of these is a *regulation*. As is provided in Article 189 EC Treaty, a regulation has general application, it is binding in its entirety and directly applicable in all Member States.

---

[2]   Article 145 of the Treaty.

[3]   Signed at Luxembourg on 17 February 1986.

[4]   So this need not be the highest court in a hierarchy, but the highest court which can decide on an issue in a particular field of law.

[5]   The decisions of the Court are published in the *European Court Reports* (hereafter abbreviated as *ECR*). It is published in all languages of the Community; in all language editions of a volume the text is printed in a parallel lay-out. This rather uncommon typography is meant to maintain a uniform lay-out for all publications (which enables reference to a particular consideration or ruling of the Court regardless of the language it is published in). In the *Official Journal C* a short excerpt is given of the judgments of the Court. There is also an internet homepage of the Court. This page enables readers to retrieve documents and recent judgments of the Court in the eleven languages of the Community. The internet address of the homepage is: http:/europa.eu.int/cj/index.htm.

Therefore, the character of a regulation differs from that of the *directive*, as a directive is binding as to the result to be achieved, upon each Member State to which it is addressed. However, the national authorities retain the freedom of the choice of forms and methods to achieve this result. This does not mean that a directive is less binding than a regulation. After all, Member States are obliged to adjust national rules which are not in accordance with a specific directive. Provisions of a directive may sometimes offer but little discretion to the Member States as to the execution of the rules; if, for instance, the directive requires equal treatment of men and women in social security, national provisions contrary to this rule have to be repealed. Furthermore, the Court of Justice has consistently held that if a Member State does not implement a directive within the period prescribed by that directive, the directive has, under certain conditions, direct effect and individuals can rely on it before a national court.

These conditions are:
- the provision contains an explicit obligation on the Member States;
- the provision is unconditional and sufficiently precise;
- additional implementation rules are not required; and
- the provision is meant to restrict the discretionary power of the Member State.[6]
If these conditions are satisfied, individuals can rely on a directive before the national court. Examples of such a direct effect of a directive are given in Chapter 24.
Directives do not have a horizontal effect. The State has to guarantee that individuals can realize the rights awarded to them in the directive.

Regulations can have horizontal effect, Regulation 1408/71, for instance, can be invoked when defending benefit claims against benefit administrations and employers.

A third instrument mentioned in Article 189, the recommendation, is the weakest among Community legislative instruments. However, recommendations are not completely without consequences, since the national court is obliged to take recommendations into account when 'interpreting' national provisions.[7]

In 1992 the Council issued a Recommendation on the convergence of social security schemes. In addition, a Recommendation on minimum benefit schemes was published. These recommendations will be discussed in Section 21.3.

In 1997 the Amsterdam Treaty was adopted, which is still in the process of ratification. This treaty gives a few more possibilities for making directives in the area of soical policy. The Treaty will be discussed in Chapter 21.

---

[6]   Court of Justice 19 January 1982, Case 8/81, *Becker* [1982] *ECR* 53.
[7]   Court of Justice 13 December 1989, Case 322/88, *Grimaldi* [1989] *ECR* 4407.

3.3.   The Power of the EU to make Coordination Rules

The following articles of the EC Treaty are relevant to social security. Primarily, Article 48 and Article 51 of the Treaty are to be mentioned. These form part of Title III of the Treaty, entitled 'The Free Movement of Persons, Services and Capital', and more specifically of Chapter 1 of this title, called 'Workers'. This position of the articles is important with regard to their interpretation; it means that, primarily, these articles are meant to secure the freedom of movement, especially of employees.[8]

Article 48 of the Treaty prohibits any discrimination on grounds of nationality between workers of the Member States as regards employment, remuneration and other conditions of employment. This article does not apply to employment in the public service.[9]

Article 51 provides the legal basis for a coordination regulation. This allows for a supranational coordination regulation, an instrument which never existed before in international social security law.

> Article 51 provides that:
> 'The Council shall, acting unanimously on a proposal from the Commission, adopt such measures in the field of social security as are necessary to provide freedom of movement for workers; to this end, it shall make arrangements to secure for migrant workers and their dependants:
> *a)* aggregation, for the purpose of acquiring and retaining the right to benefit and of calculating the amount of benefit, of all periods taken into account under the laws of the several countries;
> *b)* payments of benefits to persons resident in the territories of Member States.'

In the case law the phrase 'necessary to provide the freedom of movement of workers' plays a large role. The Court refers, when questions of interpretation of the Regulation are raised, to the objective of Article 51. The question of interpretation is answered taking this objective into account.[10] This is the case where the interrelationship of national social security rules leads to a situation which is unfavourable for the migrant worker, but this problem is not foreseen in the Regulation. An example concerns the rules on children allowances: the Regulation gives a rule for the case where one parent works and lives with the child in the same State while the other parent works in another State. There was, however, no rule designed for the situation where the child lives in a third State.[11] In this case not all impediments in the field of social security had been taken away by the Regulation and a gap

---

[8]   This is explicitly considered by the Court when answering questions of interpretation concerning the Regulation; *see*, for instance, the Decision of 9 June 1964, Case 92/63, *Nonnenmacher*, [1964] *ECR* 1261, and Decision of 21 October 1975, Case 24/75, *Petroni*, [1975] *ECR* 1149.

[9]   *See* Section 7.4.

[10]   *See* the case law mentioned in note number 8.

[11]   *See* Court of Justice 14 December 1989, Case 168/88, *Dammer*, [1989] *ECR* 4553.

existed; then the Court was required to find a solution. In such a case the Court will decide to apply an article of the Regulation by analogy to cases such as the contested one: 'If it were not possible to adopt that solution, it could even be said that the Council had failed to carry out completely the duty incumbent upon it, by virtue of Article 51 of the Treaty, to adopt such measures in the field of social security as are necessary to provide freedom of movement for workers'.[12]

Article 51 does not give the powers to take measures which are desirable for a 'social Europe' in general. Instead, the measures have to be necessary for ensuring *freedom of movement* of workers. As we will see in Chapter 6, the personal scope of Regulation 1408/71 has been extended to self-employed persons.

Measures are deemed necessary if a worker suffers disadvantages in his social security position when he crosses national borders.

As a rule, the Council has to decide whether a measure is necessary, but prior to this decision, the Commission will already have considered this question, as the Commission has the right of initiative. If the Court of Justice found, in a preliminary reference or in an infraction procedure, that a measure was not necessary in this sense, this could mean that the Council did not have the power to make that particular rule and therefore it would be void. So far, the Court has not yet come to such conclusions. Neither is this situation likely to occur because when a measure is not deemed necessary, it would not survive the voting procedure in the Council. Because of the general reluctance against taking social measures, measures which are 'not necessary' are not likely to be adopted.

In the Amsterdam Treaty, adopted in 1997 (not yet ratified), Article 51 is not changed apart from a reference to the new Article 189b, which gives rules on the cooperation with European Parliament, and is thus of 'mere' procedural relevance.

The measures required by Article 51 are elaborated in Regulation 1408/71, the full title of which is 'Regulation (EEC) No 1408/71 of the Council of 14 June 1971 on the application of social security schemes to employed persons, to self-employed persons and to members of their families moving within the Community'. In addition, the so-called implementing Regulation is relevant, *i.e.* Regulation 574/72 'laying down the procedure for implementing Regulation (EEC) 1408/71'.[13] Regulation 1408/71 replaced Regulation 3,[14] which was drawn up in 1958. As the co-ordination of social

---

[12] *See* Court of Justice 19 June 1979, Case 180/78, *Brouwer*, [1979] *ECR* 2111 at page 2121. This consideration is somewhat surprising, as the Court uses an argument for its interpretation of the law that if another approach were followed the duty of the *Council* would not be fulfilled. *See*, for another example, Court of Justice 21 February 1991, Case 140/88, *Noij*, [1991] *ECR* 387. This decision is discussed in Section 14.9.

[13] Regulation 1408/71 was published for the first time in *OJ* 149 of 5 July 1971 and since then it was revised several times. A consolidated version of Regulation 1408/71 and Regulation 574/72 was published in *OJ L* 28 of 30 January 1997.

[14] *OJ* 30 of 16 December 1958.

security for free movement of workers was essential, Regulation 3 was one of the earliest EC regulations.[15]

Regulation 1408/71 must be seen in the light of Article 51 of the EC Treaty. This means that this Regulation serves to promote the free movement of employed persons. In order to ensure this free movement the Court has an active role in interpreting terms of the Regulation in a way which most favours this mobility. In order to do so the Court is consistently and also creatively in search of such interpretations and, if necessary, will give additional rules to guarantee that negative effects of migration will be removed.

Examples are the interpretations of the terms *employed person* and *self-employed person* in respectively the *Unger* case[16] and the *Van Roosmalen* case[17] (discussed in Chapter 6 of this book). In respect of the material scope of the Regulation, the interpretation of *social security* is an example of this attitude of the Court (*see* the *Frilli* case[18] in Chapter 7 of this book).

3.4. The Extension of Coordination to the European Economic Area

Initially, the agreement on the European Economic Area concerned the EC and the Member States of the European Free Trade Association (EFTA), Finland, Norway, Liechtenstein, Austria, Iceland and Sweden. Later Austria, Finland, and Sweden entered the EU. Consequently, the European Economic Area concerns the remaining EFTA countries. Many EU rules are extended to these States by the Agreement on the European Economic Area. This agreement is important, from the point of view of social policy, as it realizes the free movement of employees and self-employed and the coordination of social security.

The Treaty provides that important parts of EU law in force on 1 August 1991 became applicable to the participants of the Free Trade Association who signed the Agreement. The Agreement contains a number of provisions which are also part of the EC Treaty and has a number of annexes in which the regulations and directives which are applicable are mentioned. In one annex Regulation 1408/71 and Regulation 574/72 are mentioned as being applicable.

---

[15]   As a matter of fact, Regulation 3 was prepared before the EEC itself was established, because by 1958 the text for a European Convention on social security for migrant workers was just completed (Convention of 9 December 1957). This Convention was related to Article 69(4) of the Treaty of the European Coal and Steel Community. After the EEC was established, this text was used for drafting the regulation required by Article 51 of the EC Treaty. Thus, the regulation was to govern the future EC coordination instead of the Convention. The reason for this was, that regulations can be issued by a much faster procedure than conventions, as no ratifications are required for regulations (and these are generally binding as well).

[16]   Court of Justice 19 March 1964, Case 75/63, [1964] *ECR* 369.

[17]   Court of Justice 23 October 1986, Case 300/84, [1986] *ECR* 3097.

[18]   Court of Justice 22 June 1972, Case 1/72, [1972] *ECR* 457.

An European Economic Area council, which consists of members of the Council of the EU, members of the European Commission, and one member of each of the participating EFTA States, has to ensure the actual realization of the agreement (Article 90).

The provisions of the Agreement must be interpreted in conformity with the corresponding rulings of the Court of Justice of the EC (Article 6). This is true as far as the rulings were given prior to the date of signature of the Agreement.

A problem is that EU law which was created after that date does not apply directly in the law of the EFTA States. This is because the Agreement is an agreement of governments with the EU; it is not a newly created uniform economic order as the EU is. Therefore new law has to be inserted into the Agreement and the annexes of the Agreement each time when it is created.

Article 28 of the Agreement provides that freedom of movement for workers shall be secured among EU Member States and EFTA States. Such freedom of movement entails the abolition of any discrimination based on nationality of EU Member States and EFTA States as regards employment, remuneration and other conditions of work and employment. This article corresponds with Article 48 of the EC Treaty.

Article 29 of the Agreement corresponds with Article 51 of the EC Treaty. It is more modern than Article 51, as Article 29 refers to the self-employed. Also the survivors and members of the family are referred to, whereas Article 51 is silent on these groups. The contents of both provisions are, however, the same, as Regulation 1408/71 covers the members of the family and survivors as well.

In Annex VI the relevant EU law is mentioned, *i.e.* Regulation 1408/71 and Regulation 574/72. In Annex VI provisions are given in order to take account of the systems of the EFTA States.[19]

---

[19]   For the text of the Agreement, *see* F. Pennings (looseleaf).

Chapter 4

The Structure of Regulation 1408/71

4.1. The Framework of Regulation 1408/71

Regulation 1408/71 starts, as is usual with international treaties, with a Preamble. This Preamble consists of considerations of the Council which led to this Regulation. These considerations are sometimes relevant to the interpretation of provisions of the Regulation and can be regarded as an Explanatory Memorandum. It is the view of the Council that considerations are relevant to the interpretation of the Regulation; later Regulations which amended Regulation 1408/71 sometimes contain amendments to previous Considerations.[1]

Title 1 of the Regulation contains Articles 1 to 18. In Article 1 the meaning of some terms used in the Regulation is given. Some of these definitions are quoted in Section 4.2 below.

Article 2 defines which categories of persons are covered by the Regulation ('the personal scope'); this subject will be discussed in Chapter 6. Article 4 refers to the type of legislations within the field of application of the Regulation ('the material scope'), discussed in Chapter 7.

Article 3 forbids discrimination on grounds of nationality (*see,* Chapter 10).

Article 5 of the Regulation requires or allows respectively Member States to define, for the purpose of the application of some specific articles of the Regulation, which of the national regulations (benefits) are covered by those articles.

For instance, the first and second section of Article 4 mention the types of benefits covered by the Regulation and Member States must mention in declarations the national schemes which correspond to these benefits. Also the national minimum benefits to which Article 50 applies and the benefits referred to by Articles 77 and 78 must be mentioned in declarations.[2] In respect to these articles, Member States have the possibility to decide whether their national benefits fall under the scope of that article of the Regulation or not, and consequently their declarations on this issue are necessary.

Of course, one may wonder whether Member States have a complete discretion whether or not to mention a particular national legislation in a declaration. This issue was one of the questions in the *Beerens* case.[3] It was not clear whether the benefit

---

[1] For a recent publication of the present considerations in force, *see OJ* 1997 *L* 28.
[2] These declarations are published in Annexes to the Regulation, *see OJ* 1997 *L* 28.
[3] Court of Justice 29 November 1977, Case 35/77, [1977] *ECR* 2249.

scheme at issue, the Dutch *Wet Werkloosheidsvoorziening* (WWV - Unemployment Provisions), was within the material scope of the Regulation. The Court considered that Article 5 of the Regulation provides that the Member States must mention in declarations the regulations referred to in Article 4. To fulfil this duty, the Netherlands made such a declaration and one of the benefits mentioned was the WWV benefit. The Court held that if a certain benefit is not mentioned in a declaration according to Article 5, this is not sufficient to decide that such benefit will not be covered by the Regulation. If such benefit satisfies the material characteristics for benefits falling within the scope of the Regulation (as developed by the Court - *see* Chapter 7) it falls within the material scope, despite the fact that it is not mentioned. If, however, the *Wet Werkloosheidsvoorziening* is *positively* mentioned in the declaration, it is, according to the Court, certain that it is covered by the Regulation.

Article 6 concerns the relationship of the Regulation to international treaties. As we saw in Chapter 1, several international treaties may be applicable for West European States. An important question is, therefore, what the relationship is between such a treaty and Regulation 1408/71 if a Member State is bound by both. According to Article 6, Regulation 1408/71 generally has priority over such international social security Treaty. Of course, this priority exists only within the personal and material scope of Regulation 1408/71. Consequently, if such a Treaty contains provisions lying outside the field of application of the Regulation, these are not made void by the Regulation. The impact of this rule is discussed in Section 15.10.

Article 7 provides that this Regulation shall not affect obligations arising from any convention adopted by the International Labour Conference (*i.e.* ILO Conventions) which, after ratification by one or more Member States, has entered into force. This is also true for obligations ensuing from the European Interim Agreements on Social Security of the Council of Europe of 1953.

Article 10 gives rules for waiving residence clauses in national regulations. This is one of the measures required by Article 51(b) of the Treaty, which enables payment of benefits outside the national territory. In other words, this article ensures that benefits are paid to persons not resident in the territory of the Member State under whose regulation these benefits were acquired. This export facility exists only where the migrant person remains within the territory of the EU (or EEA). Article 10 applies to some specific types of benefits only: invalidity, old-age or survivors' cash benefits, pensions for accidents at work or occupational diseases and death grants.[4]

Waiving of residence clauses in respect of other types of benefit can be found in the sections of the Regulation concerning these benefits. Examples are Article 69 for unemployment benefits, and Article 19 for sickness and maternity benefits.

Title 2 of the Regulation gives the rules for determination of the legislation applicable (Article 13 to Article 17). This subject is dealt with in Chapter 8 of this book.

Title 3 contains more specific rules for the various types of benefits. In this title, the requirements of Article 51 of the Treaty on the coordination rules are elaborated

---

[4]   *See*, on this article, Chapter 12 of this book.

in separate chapters for each type of benefit. These chapters contain, among other things, rules on the aggregation of periods of insurance for qualifying for benefit entitlement and rules for the calculation of benefits. The respective chapters are:

Chapter 1 Sickness and maternity benefits
Chapter 2 Invalidity benefits
Chapter 3 Old age benefits and death pensions
Chapter 4 Benefits in case of accidents at work and occupational diseases
Chapter 5 Death grants
Chapter 6 Unemployment benefits
Chapter 7 Family benefits
Chapter 8 Benefits for dependent children of pensioners and for orphans

Finally, Article 80 must be mentioned. This article concerns the Administrative Commission. The Administrative Commission consists of government representatives. The task of the commission is, *inter alia*, to deal with all administrative questions and questions of interpretation arising from the provisions of the Regulation. The duty of this Commission is also to submit to the European Commission proposals for the revision of Regulation 1408/71 and Regulation 574/72 and subsequent regulations. The decisions of this Commission have significant value in the management of administrative practices. However, the legal force of these decisions is of a relative nature only. This follows from Court's decisions. In one of these decisions[5] the Court held that a decision of this commission can be a useful instrument for social security institutions, but it can not oblige these institutions to follow a particular method or interpretation of Community legislation. In the following chapters, the decisions of the Administrative Commission will sometimes be referred to.

4.2. Extract from the Definitions in Article 1 of Regulation 1408/71

Below we will reproduce some definitions of the Regelation. These can be found in Article 1.

Employed person or self-employed person
'By *employed person* or *self-employed person* is meant respectively:
i   any person who is insured, compulsorily or on an optional continued basis, for one or more of the contingencies covered by the branches of a social security scheme for employed or self-employed persons;
ii any person who is compulsorily insured for one or more of the contingencies covered by the branches of social security dealt with in this Regulation, under a social security scheme for all residents or for the whole working population, if such person:

---

[5]   Court of Justice 14 May 1981, Case 98/80, *Romano*, [1981] *ECR* 1241.

- can be identified as an employed person or self-employed person by virtue of the manner in which such a scheme is administered or financed, or
- failing such criteria, is insured for some other contingency specified in Annex I under a scheme for employed or self-employed persons, or under a scheme referred to in (iii), either compulsorily or on an optional continued basis, or, where no such scheme exists in the Member State concerned, complies with the definition given in Annex I;

iii   any person who is compulsorily insured for several of the contingencies covered by the branches dealt with in this Regulation, under a standard social security scheme for the whole rural population in accordance with the criteria laid down in Annex I;

iv   any person who is voluntarily insured for one or more of the contingencies covered by the branches dealt with in this Regulation, under a social security scheme of a Member State for employed or self-employed persons or for all residents or for certain categories of residents:

- if such person carries out an activity as an employed or self-employed person, or
- if such person has previously been compulsorily insured for the same contingency under a scheme for employed or self-employed persons of the same Member State.'

Frontier Worker

According to Article 1(b) *frontier worker* means 'any employed or self-employed person who pursues his occupation in the territory of a Member State and resides in the territory of another Member State to which he returns as a rule daily or at least once a week; however, a frontier worker who is posted elsewhere in the territory of the same or another Member State by the undertaking to which he is normally attached, or who engages in the provision of services elsewhere in the territory of the same or another Member State, shall retain the status of frontier worker for a period not exceeding four months, even if he is prevented, during that period, from returning daily or at least once a week to the place where he resides.'

Legislation

The meaning of this term can be found in Article 1(j) of the Regulation. This Article provides that in respect of each Member State, *legislation* means 'statutes, regulations and other provisions and all other implementing measures, present or future, relating to the branches and schemes of social security covered by Article 4(1) and (2) or those special non-contributory benefits covered by Article 4(2a).

This term excludes provisions of existing or future industrial agreements, whether or not they have been the subject of a decision by the authorities rendering them compulsory or extending their scope.

However, in so far as such provisions

i   serve to put into effect compulsory insurance imposed by the laws and regulations referred to in the preceding subparagraph; or

ii set up a scheme administered by the same institution as that which administers the schemes set up by the laws and regulations referred to in the preceding subparagraph,

the limitation on the term can at any time be lifted by a declaration of the Member State concerned specifying the schemes of such a kind to which this Regulation applies.'

Competent State

Article 1(q) provides: 'The Competent State is the Member State in which territory the competent institution is situated.'

Article 1(o) defines the *competent institution* as:

'i   the institution with which the person concerned is insured at the time of the application for benefit; or

ii the institution from which the person concerned is entitled or would be entitled to benefits if he or a member or members of his family were resident in the territory of the Member State in which the institution is situated; or

iii the institution designated by the competent authority of the Member State concerned; or

iv in the case of a scheme relating to an employer's liability in respect of the benefits set out in Article 4(1), either the employer or the insured involved or, in default thereof, a body or authority designated by the competent authority of the Member State concerned.

(Which State is the competent State is defined by the rules for assigning the legislation applicable - *see* Title 2 of the Regulation).

Family benefits and family allowances

According to Article 1(u)(i) *family benefits* means 'all benefits in kind or in cash intended to meet family expenses under the legislation provided for in Article 4(1)(h), excluding the special childbirth allowances mentioned in Annex II';

Article 1(u)(ii) defines *family allowances* as 'periodical cash benefits granted exclusively by reference to the number and, where appropriate the age of members of the family.'

Member of the family

Article (1)(f) provides:

'i   Member of the family means any person defined or recognized as a member of the family or designated as a member of the household by the legislation under which benefits are provided or, in the cases referred to in Articles 22(1)(a) and 31, by the legislation of the Member State in whose territory such person resides; where, however, the said legislations regard as a member of the family or a member of the household only a person living under the same roof as the employed or self-employed person, this condition shall be considered satisfied if the person in question is mainly dependent on that person.

ii where, however, the benefits concerned are benefits for disabled persons granted under the legislation of a Member State to all nationals of that state who fulfil the prescribed conditions, the term 'member of the family' means at least the spouse of an employed or self-employed person and the children of such person who are either minors or dependent upon such person.'

Chapter 5

The Territorial Scope of Regulation 1408/71

Regulation 1408/71 is relevant to the territory of all Member States of the EU. A question arose in the case law as to whether schemes concerning a (former) colonial territory of a Member State were also covered by this definition. This issue in fact concerns the territorial scope of the Regulation. The question was answered in the *Bozzone* judgment.[1]

> Walter Bozzone was an Italian national who worked in former Belgian Congo, from 1952 to 1960. He then applied in Belgium for an invalidity allowance and settled in Italy. His claim was based on the Colonial Decree 1952 governing invalidity insurance of colonial employees. He was granted this allowance until 31 January 1961, but he was informed by a letter of 29 December 1960 that since he did not actually and habitually reside in Belgium, payment was not continued. Bozzone wished to rely on the Regulation, as Article 10 of this Regulation provides that invalidity benefits shall not be subject to any suspension by reason of the fact that the recipient resides in the territory of another Member State (*see*, Chapter 12 of this book).

The Court considered that Regulation 1408/71 applied, according to Article 2(1) of the Regulation, to workers who are or have been subject to the legislation of one or more Member States and who are nationals of one of the Member States. In view of that provision it must first be considered whether the applicant can be held to be or have been 'subject to the legislation of a Member State'. In case of a negative answer, his situation is not subject to Community rules.

In answer to this question, the Court quoted Article 1(j) of the Regulation and remarked that this definition is remarkable for its breadth. The Court considered that the person concerned first enjoyed the benefit of the Colonial Decree of 1952 governing the sickness and invalidity insurance of colonial employees, pursuant to which he was granted an invalidity pension. That insurance scheme was guaranteed and rights acquired thereunder were affirmed by a Belgian Law of 16 June 1960 ensuring the continuity of this scheme. Moreover, that Law supplemented the decree by providing for the grant of additional benefits and adapted it to the costs of living according to the rules in force in Belgium. As a whole, the Court concluded, those

---

[1]   Court of Justice 31 March 1977, Case 87/76, [1977] *ECR* 687.

provisions therefore constitute 'national legislation' within the meaning of Article 2(1) of the Regulation.

The Court was, in another case, requested to answer the question whether a scheme which applied to a person who worked outside the territory of a Member State, including the (former) colonies, falls within the scope of the Regulation. This was the *Van Roosmalen* case[2], in which the Court remarked that the main criterion of the term 'legislation' is not the place of the occupational activities, but the relationship between the person - regardless of the place of activities - and the social security scheme of the Member State under which he completed his periods of insurance. Thus, it is not relevant that the insured person performed his activities within or outside the territory of the Community; a national scheme which extends its field of application to persons working outside the Community must be considered as legislation within the meaning of Article 2 of the Regulation.[3] This case law is confirmed in the *Buhari Haji* judgment.[4]

According to Article 2, it is only necessary in the case of stateless persons and refugees that they live in the European Union. This condition does not apply for employed and self-employed persons. Many provisions of the Regulation are worded, however, in such a way that for the application of the provision concerned they require that the employed or self-employed persons live in the territory of the Community. Article 3, for instance, provides that the prohibition of discrimination on grounds of nationality applies only for persons who are resident in the territory of one of the Member States (see also Chapter 6).

With respect to the rules for determining the legislation applicable the system is somewhat different. Article 13(2) assigns the legislation of a Member State applicable *even if the employed person resides in the territory of another Member State.* This formula seems to restrict the applicability to persons who reside in the territory of one of the Member States. The Court has decided, however, *not* to restrict the applicability to the territory of the Community. This appeared in the *Aldewereld* judgment.[5]

Mr Aldewereld was a Netherlands national, who took a job with an undertaking established in Germany. This undertaking posted him immediately in Thailand, where he worked throughout 1986. On the basis of that employment the German authorities charged social security contributions under German law. The Dutch benefit administrations also required contributions for their national insurance schemes.

---

[2]   Court of Justice 23 October 1986, Case 300/84, [1986] *ECR* 3097.

[3]   *See*, for the same approach, the judgment of the Court of Justice 14 October 1990, case 105/89, *Buhari Haji,* [1990] *ECR* 4211, described in Section 6.2.5.

[4]   Court of Justice 14 October 1990, Case 105/89, [1990] *ECR* 4211.

[5]   Court of Justice 29 June 1994, Case 60/93, [1994] *ECR* 2991.

The question was whether these double charges could be prevented. The Court considered that the mere fact that the activities were carried out outside the Community is not sufficient to exclude the application of the Community rules on the free movement of workers. This is the case as long as the employment relationship retains a sufficiently close link with the Community. The Court remarked that in a case such as this one, a link of that kind can be found in the fact that the Community worker was employed by an undertaking from another Member State and, for that reason was insured under the social security scheme of that State.

The subsequent quesion was which legislation was applicable. The Court answered that the applicable legislation must be determined on the basis of the tenor and the aims of Title II of the Regulation. The Commission proposed that a worker such as Mr Aldewereld should be able to choose the legislation applicable. The Court rejected this point of view. It considered that, except in special cases such as employees of diplomatic missions, the applicable legislation is derived objectively from the provisions of Title II. In a situation such as that of Mr Aldewereld, the only factors connected with the legislation of a Member State are, on the one hand, the worker's residence and, on the other hand, the place where his employer is established. The choice of criterion to determine the legislation applicable to that situation must therefore, the Court reasoned, be made from those factors. According to the system of the Regulation, the application of the legislation of the Member State in which the worker resides appears to be an ancillary rule which applies only where that legislation has a link with the employment relationship. Accordingly, when the worker does not reside in any of the Member States where he works, the applicable legislation is normally the legislation of the Member State where his employer has its registered office or place of business. It follows that, in the absence of a provision dealing expressly with the case of a person in Mr Aldewereld's situation, such a person is covered by the legislation of the Member State where his employer is established. It follows that only the German legislation could be applicable, and the Dutch authorities were not allowed to collect the social security contributions.

Chapter 6

Persons covered by Regulation 1408/71

6.1. Introduction

The Regulation is - as set out in its title - meant to apply to employed persons or self-employed persons *moving within the Community*. This implies that the Regulation is only applicable if someone moves across the borders of a Member State to another Member State or a Member State of the Extended European Area; if he stays within the territory of his own State he cannot make invoke the Regulation, even if he is confronted with national rules with discriminatory effects. An example of such a situation is found in the *Petit* judgment.[1]

> In this case an employee was confronted with conditions on the use of language to be used in legal procedures in Belgium (the required language not being his native tongue). This employee could not, as his situation concerned exclusively national facts, rely on the non-discrimination clause of the Regulation.

The criterion that the Regulation applies only in the case of cross-border mobility is applied neutrally: in general, the *reason* for the movement of a worker is irrelevant. Movement need not be for economic reasons: visiting one's family in another Member State is, for instance, sufficient to have the Regulation applied to one's case.[2] If an employed person moves across the border for the first time *after* having ended his working life, the Regulation is also applicable.

Even if the employee has never crossed the borders before he is retired, he can invoke the Regulation.[3]

Members of the family and survivors of employees and self-employed persons also fall under the personal scope of the Regulation. For members of the family and survivors it is not necessary that the employed person crossed the borders in order to rely on the Regulation. The provisions concerning members of the family (*see*, for instance, Article 19(2) of the Regulation) are applicable as soon as the members

---

[1]   Court of Justice 22 September 1992, Case 153/91, [1992] *ECR* I-4973.
[2]   *See*, for instance, the *Unger* judgment, Section 6.2.
[3]   *See*, for instance, the Court of Justice 25 February 1986, Case 284/84, *Spruyt,* [1986] *ECR* 685; Court of Justice of 24 September 1987, Case 43/86, *De Rijke-Van Gent,* [1987] *ECR* 3611.

of the family live in a Member State other than where the employed or self-employed person lives.

Article 51 of the EC Treaty gives the power to make co-ordination regulations which have a limited field of application only: i.e. to employed persons. Regulation 3, the predecessor of the present Regulation was limited to rules concerning employed persons. The personal scope of Regulation 1408/71 had also been limited to employed persons for a long period. In 1981 the scope of the latter Regulation was extended to the self-employed. This extension was based on Article 235 of the Treaty, as Article 51 does not give the powers to give rules on the free movement of the self-employed.[4]

Freedom of movement has not yet been achieved for all citizens. In 1991, the Commission presented a proposal to broaden the personal scope to all residents of Member States.[5] Of course, the power to make this extension could also not be derived from Article 51 of the Treaty and it was proposed that the Regulation to amend Regulation 1408/71 should be based on Article 235 as well. This proposal has not yet been adopted.[6]

At present, the personal scope of Regulation 1408/71 is defined as follows. The Regulation is applicable to (Article 2):

1. employed or self-employed persons who are or have been subject to the legislation of one or more Member States and who are nationals of one of the Member States *or* who are stateless persons or refugees residing within the territory of one of the Member States;
2. the members of the family and the survivors of the persons referred to under (1);
3. the survivors of employed or self-employed persons who have been subject to the legislation of one or more Member States, irrespective of the nationality of such employed or self-employed persons, where their survivors are nationals of one of the Member States, or stateless persons or refugees residing within the territory of one of the Member States;
4. civil servants and to persons who, in accordance with the legislation applicable, are treated as such, where they are or have been subject to the legislation of a Member State to which this Regulation applies.

---

[4]   The scope was extended to self-employed persons by Regulation 1390/81 of 12 May 1981. The Court has accepted this extension, *see* Court of Justice 23 December 1986, Case 300/84, *Van Roosmalen*, [1986] *ECR* 3097.

[5]   COM (91) 528 final of 13 December 1991, *OJ* 1992 *C* 46.

[6]   Actually, this proposal intends to extend the scope to two categories: to civil servants and to all nationals. For the category of 'all nationals' (*i.e.* the extension to persons not engaged in work) the effect of the extension is limited to a few special provisions (such as equal treatment on grounds of nationality). For civil servants, the relevance is considerably larger, since this category will be subject to the normal rules of the Regulation (in their case especially the aggregation of periods worked in other states and under other types of schemes is relevant). Therefore, the opposition of the Member States is directed towards the extension to civil servants (and not to the extension to the category of all nationals).

In order to invoke the application of Article 2, it is required that one is an employed person or self-employed person (Section 6.2.1 and 6.2.2. respectively) and that the legislation of one of the Member States is or has been applicable (Section 6.2.3). The legislation meant here is the social security legislation of one of the Member States, and, more specifically, the social security legislation falling within the material scope of the Regulation.

In addition, it is required that one is national of a Member State (Section 6.2.5.). If the employee or self-employed person is not national of one of the Member States (nor a stateless person or refugee) he is outside the personal scope of the Regulation.

According Article 2(3), in order to be able to rely on the Regulation, refugees and stateless persons are required to live in the territory of the EU. This requirement does not exist for employed persons and self-employed persons. An employed person or self-employed person who is a national of a Member State and who lives outside the territory of the EU, but who has been insured under the pension schemes of two or more Member States, can require that his pension be calculated in accordance with the provisions of the Regulation.[7]

6.2. Employed Persons and Self-employed Persons

6.2.1. The Meaning of 'Employed Persons'

In order to be covered by the first section of Article 2, it is required that one is (a) an employed or self-employed person, and (b) is or has been subject to the legislation of one of the Member States. Condition (b) means that persons who, although in search of work, have not (yet) been engaged in employment are not covered by the Regulation.

The third condition is that one is (c) a national of a Member State. Thus, if the employed person or self-employed person is not a national of one of the Member States (nor stateless nor a refugee) he is excluded from the personal scope of the Regulation. As a result, a worker with Turkish nationality who first worked in Germany, and subsequently in the Netherlands, cannot make use of the Regulation, for instance, for the aggregation of his periods of work or the calculation of his pension rights. This is a serious gap in the protection of the Regulation.[8] This gap has been strongly criticized, because so-called third-country workers may have made significant contributions to the economy of Member States and adequate protection of their social security rights would be no more than appropriate.

The meaning of 'employed person' and of 'self-employed person' can, first of

---

[7]   *See* Van Limberghen (1991: 23).
[8]   *See* Feenstra (1990) for criticism on this exclusion.

all, be found in the definitions set out in Article 1 of the Regulation, *see* Chapter 4 for the full quotation of this article.

Even with the extended definition of Article 1, the question has to be answered how exactly is it to be determined who is an employed person and who is not. Is it required, for instance, that a person has a contract of employment? This question is relevant, as in some social security systems for employees, persons without a contract of employment are equated with employees covered by that social security system for employees. One example is that many national social security systems treat home workers, even when they do not have a contract of employment, under some conditions as employees. Sometimes also musicians, sportsmen and insurance agents working without a contract of employment are covered by compulsory employees' insurance.

The *Unger* judgment is relevant to this issue. In this case the Court held that the term 'worker' (or 'employed persons') has a Community meaning.[9]

> This judgment was given under Regulation 3, but from various later judgments of the Court it appeared that the Court considered this decision still relevant to the interpretation of the term 'employed person' in Community law. The *Unger* Case concerned an employed person who resigned and who was subsequently admitted to the continued voluntary insurance scheme provided for by that law. During a family visit to her parents in Muenster (Germany), she fell ill. Her state of health required immediate medical treatment. After her return to the Netherlands, she claimed payments of sickness benefit and the costs of expenses of treatment in this period. Benefit was refused, however, for the period she stayed in Germany. Mrs Unger wished to rely on Article 19(1) of the co-ordination Regulation then in force (Regulation 3).[10] In order to be able to rely on this Article, the question had to be answered whether Mrs Unger belonged to the personal scope of the Regulation.

The question posed by the national court was whether the term 'wage-earner or assimilated worker', as used in the Regulation, is defined by the legislation of each Member State or by Community law as having a supranational meaning. The reply to this question essentially depended upon the scope, whether Community or otherwise, of the provisions of the Treaty from which the concept of 'wage-earner or assimilated worker' was drawn in this Regulation. Article 51 is included in the Chapter entitled 'Workers' and placed in Title III ('Free movement of persons, services and capital') of Part Two of the Treaty ('Foundations of the Treaty'). The establishment of as complete a freedom of movement for workers as possible, which thus forms part of the 'foundations' of the Community, therefore constitutes the

---

[9]   Court of Justice 19 March 1964, Case 75/63, [1964] *ECR* 177.

[10]   Regulation 3 did not contain a definition of 'worker', as Regulation 1408/71. Under the latter Regulation Mrs Unger would fall under the personal scope on the basis of Article 1 (a) (i) also mentions persons who are 'insured on an optional continued basis'.

principal objective of Article 51 and thereby conditions the interpretation of the Regulations adopted in implementation of that article, the Court argued. By the very fact of establishing freedom of movement for 'workers', Articles 48 to 51 of the Treaty, have given Community scope to this term. This term must therefore be interpreted in such a way as to ensure free movement of workers throughout the Community. This means that the term 'wage earner' (used in Regulaiton 3 instead of 'worker' or 'employee') is not to be determined by national legislation alone; if the definition of this term were a matter which falls within the competence of national law, it would be possible for each Member State to modify the meaning of the concept of 'migrant worker' and to eliminate at will the protection afforded by the Treaty to certain categories of persons. The Court argued that Articles 48 and 51 would be deprived of all effect and the objectives of the Treaty would be frustrated if the meaning of such a term was to be unilaterally fixed and modified by national law. The expression 'wage-earner or assimilated worker' used in Regulation 3 is intended to clarify the concept of 'workers' for the purposes of Regulation 3 and has therefore a Community meaning.

This decision does not define what this Community meaning is supposed to be. It is clear, however, that it is not decisive that Mrs Unger was not an employee according to the rules of national law. On the other hand, the Court did not follow the case law concerning Article 48 of the Treaty, which concerned the labour law interpretation of 'employed person'. Therefore, the labour law position of a worker is not relevant. However, it is relevant that a person is or has been subject to a social security scheme for employed persons. This implies that a person who is assimilated with employed persons under a national social security scheme (as has been the case with Mrs Unger) belongs to the personal scope of the Regulation, even if this person is not called 'employed' under national law.

The conclusion we can draw from this, is that it is up to the national legislators to decide whether a person is insured under a social security scheme for employees. If a Member State decided that only persons with a contract of employment are to be covered under an scheme for employees, Community law does not forbid this. If, however, a Member State also includes persons without a contract of employment in such scheme, these are 'employees' for the Regulation.

The rules of Article 1(a)(i) make it possible to determine that persons who fall under a s specific employees' social security scheme are under the personal scope of the Regulation. There are, however, also Member States which have general social security schemes which are not limited to employees. These schemes cover, for instance, residents. It is important that it can be specified which categories of persons covered under such schemes are employees and which are not, otherwise everybody covered under such a scheme would fall under the Regulation.

With respect to these schemes Article 1(a)(ii) provides that: whether a person is compulsorily insured for one or more of the contingencies covered by the branches of social security dealt with in this Regulation, under a social security scheme for all residents or for the whole working population, must be derived from the following criteria: the first is that the manner in which such a scheme is administered or financed can identify a person as employed or self-employed.

An example of the application of the first criterion is that if a scheme has varying contribution rates, for instance for employees, self-employed persons and others respectively, it is possible to define on the basis of these differences who is employed or self-employed and who is not. It is also possible that a general scheme has different funds for the contributions of employees, self-employed and others. These differences enable us to differentiate between employees, self-employed persons and others.

The second criterion is that, (ii) failing such criteria, a person is under the personal scope if he complies with the definition given in Annex I of the Regulation. Annex I provides the definitions of employed person or self-employed person for the respective schemes of the various Member States. For the Netherlands, for instance, the Annex provides that any person pursuing an activity or occupation without a contract of employment shall be considered a self-employed person within the meaning of this part of Article 1 of the Regulation. The Annex provides, in respect of the United Kingdom, that the meaning of the terms 'employed earner' and 'self-employed earner' in the legislation of Great Britain or Northern Ireland is relevant.

Section *iv* of Article 1(a) concerns the application of the Regulation to the *voluntarily insured*. If a person is voluntarily insured for one or more of the contingencies mentioned in Regulation 1408/71, he is considered to be an employed person or self-employed person for the purpose of the Regulation in two situations. The first is where such a person carries out an activity as an employed or self-employed person. The second is where such a person has previously been compulsorily insured for the same contingency under a scheme for employed or self-employed persons of the same Member State.

6.2.2.   The Meaning of 'Self-employed Persons'

In the *Unger* judgment the Court based its decision to apply a broad interpretation of the term 'worker' on the principle of the freedom of movement of workers. Because of Article 51 of the Treaty the free movement of workers must have a maximum scope. It could be expected that the Court would also follow this approach with respect to the meaning of the term 'self-employed person'. This was confirmed in the *Van Roosmalen* judgment.[11]

Van Roosmalen was a Dutch priest, who was sent to Belgian Congo, where he stayed until 1980. In 1977, he applied for voluntary insurance under the Dutch General Disability Act (AAW). After his return to Europe, he was found to be disabled because of back troubles which he had incurred in Zaire. In 1982, he returned to live in Postel (Belgium). His AAW benefit was suspended on the grounds that a person is only eligible for AAW if he has been disabled for at least fifty-two weeks in the Netherlands. If the Regulation were applicable this territoriality condition were not allowed. It was therefore important to him that

---

[11]   Court of Justice 23 december 1986, Case 300/84, [1986] *ECR* 3097.

he could be qualified as a self-employed person. Van Roosmalen did not receive an income from his order, but was supported by his parishioners.

The Court took into consideration that by means of Regulation 1390/81 the personal field of application of Regulation 1408/71 was extended to self-employed persons. As Regulation 1390/81 was adopted in order to pursue the same objectives as Regulation 1408/71, it follows that the term *self-employed* also has a broad meaning.

Van Roosmalen was voluntarily insured. It follows that the rules of Article 1(a)(iv), discussed in the previous section, are relevant. The Court considered that a self-employed person falls under this article if he is voluntarily employed and he is not engaged as an employed person. The scheme involved was a national insurance scheme which did not differentiate between employees, self-employed and others. Therefore the Court had to answer the question whether he was an employed person or a self-employed person. The Court applied the rules of Article 1(a)(ii) by analogy in order to interpret Article 1(a)(iv). Article 1(a)(ii) provides as we have seen, that the mode of administration or financing or Annex 1 are decisive. The Annex defines a self-employed person for the Netherlands as 'a person who pursues an activity or occupation without a contract of employment'. It follows, according to the Court, that in a general voluntary insurance scheme a person who performs activities without a contract of employment is a 'self-employed person', provided the activities are occupational activities. The term *occupational activities* must be interpreted in a broad sense: activities for which a person receives direct consideration. Contributions from parishioners count for this purpose if they enable the priest to support himself partially or completely. Therefore, Van Roosmalen is a self-employed person for the Regulation.

6.2.3. The Legislation is or has been Applicable

The condition that the legislation of one or more Member States must have been applicable is mentioned in Article 2 (1) and concerns the question of whether a person is or has been subject to a social security scheme of a Member State. In order to know whether a scheme qualifies as a social security scheme for the purpose of bringing a person covered by this scheme under the personal scope, it is important to look at Article 4 of the Regulation, as this concerns the material scope. Thus, a person who has been subject to a civil servants scheme does not fall under the personal scope, as civil servants scheme are excluded from the material scope of the Regulation.

The question whether the legislation of one or more Member States has been applicable, depends not only on national rules, but also on the rules for designating the law applicable, which are given by the Regulation. It is possible that, under the national legislation, a person does not fall under the social security scheme of the country where he works (for instance, because he resides in another Member State). If the rules of the Regulation concerning the legislation applicable could be applied, he would fall under the legislation of the country of employment. It is, however, necessary in order to invoke the rules for determining the legislation applicable, to be within the personal scope of the Regulation.

This issue led to the *Zinnecker* judgment[12], where the question was raised: in which order do the provisions of the Regulation have to be applied in order to determine whether a person is under the personal scope of the Regulation: the rules for determining the legislation applicable or the rules concerning the personal scope?

The case concerned Mr Zinnecker, who was a resident of Germany and carried on his activities as a self-employed seller of foodstuffs with approximately one-half of his business in the Netherlands and one-half in Germany. He was not insured, either compulsorily or voluntarily, in Germany. Neither was he insured for the Netherlands national insurance scheme as he did not reside in the Netherlands. Nevertheless, the Netherlands benefit authorities decided that he had to pay contributions for the national insurance scheme.

Zinnecker wished to invoke Article 14*a* of the Regulation, which provides that 'a person normally self-employed in a territory of two or more Member States shall be subject to the legislation of the Member State in whose territory he resides if he pursues any part of his activity in the territory of that Member State'. This meant that if Zinnecker were under the personal scope of the Regulation, the legislation applicable in this case was that of the Member State where he resided, *i.e.* Germany. In that case he would not have to pay the Dutch contributions. it is decisive, therefore, whether he falls under the personal scope.

The Court considered that the definition of the Regulation of the personal scope requires that an employed or self-employed person is or has been subject to the legislation of one or more Member States. For this purpose, all the countries where the person is working are relevant, not only the State which is designated by the rules for determining the legislation applicable. This meant that Mr Zinnecker had been subject to the personal scope if one of the two legislations relevant to him, either the Netherlands or the German law, had been applicable to him. As regards the Netherlands law, it appeared that he was not insured on a compulsory basis; neither was he insured under the national insurance scheme, as he had not been a resident of the Netherlands. The Court considered that Annex I of the Regulation provides with respect to the Netherlands: 'any person pursuing an activity or occupation without a contract of employment is to be considered a self-employed person within the meaning of Article 1(a)(ii) of the Regulation'. It decided that this provision applied to Mr Zinnecker as it did not require that he resides in the Netherlands. Consequently, despite the fact that Mr Zinnecker did not satisfy the residence requirements of Netherlands law, he had to be regarded as a self-employed person, and was therefore within the personal scope. In this case, the rules for determining the legislation applicable assigned the German social security scheme as applicable, because he worked and resided in this country.

---

[12]   Court of Justice 13 October 1993, Case 121/91, [1993] *ECR* I-5023.

The conclusion from this judgment is, that first one had to investigate whether a person satisfies the conditions of the personal scope for the country where he is employed. It is not required that this is the country which is designated by the rules for determining the legislation applicable. In other words, the rules on the personal scope have priority in solving this problem, The advantage of this approach is, that positive or negative conflicts of law can be avoided.

The definition of 'employed person' in Article 1(a) reads that an employed person is any person who is insured, compulsorily or on an optional continued basis, for one or more of the contingencies *covered by the branches of a social security scheme* for employed or self-employed persons. For some time there has been a dispute whether an employee who was covered by only one branch of a social security system (for instance, for sickness benefits), has also to be considered as an 'employed person' for the complete Regulation, i.e. also for other types of contingencies.[13] The *Van Poucke* judgment clarified this topic.[14]

Van Poucke was working as a military doctor in Belgium and as a self-employed docter in the Netherlands. As he worked as self-employed in the Netherlands he had to pay contributions for the Belgian insurance for the self-employed (*see* Chapter 8). Van Poucke had the Belgium legal status of civil servant and was therefore, in principle, not covered by the Regulation. The Belgian compulsory sickness and invalidity insurance for employees was, however, extended to civil servants. As Van Poucke had the legal status of civil servant, he fell under the employees insurance scheme only with respect to the contingency of sickness and invalidity.

Article 2 (3) of the Regulation provides that the Regulation is applicable to civil servants where they are or have been subject to the legislation of a Member State to which this Regulation applies. The national Court sought an answer from the Court on the question whether the persons mentioned in this section are actually subject to the legislation within the meaning of this provision, if the persons concerned were only subject to one branch of social security. The Court answered that if somebody is subject to one branch of social security, he actually falls under that Regulation, provided the branch concerned of the social security system is part of legislation to which the Regulation applies according to Article 2(3). The *Van Poucke* judgment means that the relevant rule for determining the legislation applicable (in this case Article 14 (c)(a) - see Chapter 8) also applies to Van Poucke. Belgium was allowed to collect contributions for the self-employed scheme from him.

---

[13] The disputes were caused by interpretations of the *Brack* judgment (Court of Justice 29 September 1976, Case 17/76, [1976] *ECR* 1429).
[14] Court of Justice 24 March 1994, Case 71/93, [1994] *ECR* I-1101.

6.2.4. Part-time Workers

An interesting question is, whether in order to be considered as an employee it is required that a person is engaged for a minimum number of hours a week. This was one of the questions asked in the *Kits van Heijningen* judgment.[15]

> Mr Kits van Heijningen, who was resident in Belgium, worked as a teacher at a Dutch institute, teaching for two hours on Monday and Saturday (four hours in total). He claimed child benefit for his two children for the first quarter of 1984 from the Dutch authorities; this claim was rejected, as under the Dutch legislation relevant to this issue, a person is only entitled to family allowances during a calendar quarter if he was insured at the first day of that quarter. Since the first day of the first quarter of 1984 did not fall on a Monday or Saturday, it was decided that he did not fulfil the conditions for child benefit. The Dutch authorities argued that he was only insured for the days on which he taught.

The Court pointed out that neither Article 2 nor Article 1(a) of the Regulation contain provisions which exclude certain categories of workers who only work part-time from its scope. Therefore, the Court ruled that Regulation 1408/71 applies to all persons satisfying the conditions of Articles 1 and 2, irrespective of the number of hours they work.

This ruling enables persons who wish to do so, to influence their social security position: if they accept just a small job - even after retirement age - in another Member State, they are covered by the social security system of the latter State. The consequences of this for retired persons will be discussed in Chapter 8.

6.2.5. The Requirement on Nationality

One of the requirements for falling within the personal scope of the Regulation according to Article 2, is that a person must be national of one of the Member States. Nationals of one of the European Economic Area countries are assimilated with nationals of EU Member States. The question was raised at *which moment* a person has to satisfy the nationality condition.

> *Example.* A person with Iraq nationality works from 1980 to 1990 in Belgium and changes to Belgian nationality in 1989. If he subsequently moves to Germany to work in that country as an employed person, but he becomes disabled within one month, can he rely on the Regulation in order to fulfil the waiting conditions of the German disability benefit?

---

[15] Court of Justice 3 May 1990, Case 2/89, [1990] *ECR* 1755.

It appeared from the *Belhouab* judgment[16], that the periods in which a person worked, or pays contributions or acquires benefit rights are relevant and not the moment of the claim. This approach implies that periods in which a person has not yet acquired nationality of one of the Member States are not relevant to the application of the Regulation; the Iraqi in the example given above cannot invoke the Belgian periods for the time when he did not have Belgian nationality.

The situation is different if a person has worked as a national of a State, but lost this status before this State entered the EC, *see* the *Buhari Haji* judgment.[17]

> Buhari was born in 1914 in Nigeria and had British nationality until 1964. At that time, he acquired Nigerian nationality. From 1937 until 1986, he worked in the Belgian Congo. Until this State became independent he paid contributions to the Belgian social security authorities. When he applied for a Belgian retirement pension, this was refused.

The Court considered that the nationality criterion of the Regulation could not be supposed to be fulfilled when the employee concerned had, during the period in which he performed his occupational activities and paid contributions, the nationality of a Member State which was not yet a Member of the EC and who lost the status of national of that State before the State entered the EC. The Court argued that this approach is legitimate because in this situation freedom of movement as guaranteed in EC Treaty is not involved.

6.3.   Members of the Family and Survivors

Article 2 also mentions members of the family and survivors of employed persons and self-employed persons as belonging to the personal scope of the Regulation. The terms 'members of the families' and 'survivors' are defined in, respectively, Articles 1(f) and (g). The main rule is that the meaning of these terms is to be derived from the national legislation under which the benefits are provided.

As a general principle, Articles 48 and 51 of the Treaty and the Regulations based thereupon are only applicable to migrants. However, in order to be eligible for *derived benefits*, e.g. a survivor's pension, it is not necessary that the employed person *himself* moved from one country to another. For the Regulation to be applicable, it is sufficient that the member of the family crosses the border.[18] An example of this can be found in the *Laumann* judgment.[19]

---

[16]   Court of Justice 12 October 1978, Case 10/78, [1978] *ECR* 1915.
[17]   Court of Justice 14 October 1990, Case 105/89, [1990] *ECR* 4211.
[18]   *See*, also Schulte (1988: 60).
[19]   Court of Justice 16 March 1978, Case 115/77, [1978] *ECR* 805.

This case concerns two minor orphans who were born in Germany. The children received an orphans' pension. Their father had not been a migrant worker. Their mother remarried and the new husband received child benefit in Belgium. Their orphans pension was suspended on the basis of Article 79(3) (*see*, Chapter 11 of this book). The first question concerned the applicability of the Regulation, since neither their father, nor the mother or the stepfather had moved because of their occupational activities.

The answer of the Court was that the Regulation did not only concern employed persons, but also members of their family and survivors who move within the Community. Thus, the field of application is not restricted to employees who have been employed in more than one Member State.

A second question was which benefits of the Regulation are relevant to members of the family. Could members of a family rely on all provisions of the Regulation or only to those benefits payable *qua* members of the family of the worker? The approach to this issue varied through time.

The uncertainty on this issue was caused by the *Fracas* judgment.[20]

Mr and Mrs Fracas were of Italian nationality and since 1947 they resided in Belgium, where Mr Fracas was engaged in employment. They claimed a Belgian benefit for the handicapped for their fourteen-year-old son (born in 1959). This son had been handicapped from birth and apparently suffered from one-hundred per cent invalidity.

The Belgian Law on benefits to the handicapped of 1969 granted benefits to Belgian citizens residing in Belgium on the condition that they had attained the age of fourteen and that they had a permanent incapacity to work of at least thirty per cent and did not possess resources exceeding certain limits. The European Interim Agreements of 11 December 1953 permitted the application of this Belgian law to the nationals covered by this agreement on the condition that they resided for a total of at least fifteen years after attaining the age of twenty in Belgium territory. Fracas' claim was rejected on the ground that the child did not satisfy the latter condition.

The Court held that this refusal was contrary to Community law. It arrived at this conclusion by referring to Articles 2 and 3 of the Regulation (the latter supporting the principle of equal treatment). The Court held that, with regard to the enjoyment of rights under a national regulation providing benefits for the handicapped, neither the employed person himself nor members of his family may be placed in a less favourable position as compared to the nationals of their State of residence for the sole reason that they do not possess the nationality of that State.

For the particular case of a handicapped child who, since his minority fulfils the conditions required for benefits to the handicapped as a member of the employed

---

[20]   Court of Justice 17 June 1975, Case 7/75, [1975] *ECR* 679.

person's family, equality of treatment under Article 3 of Regulation 1408/71 cannot terminate when he ceases to be a minor, if the child by reason of his handicap is prevented from acquiring the status of an employed person himself as defined in the Regulation. If this were not the case, the Court continued, a worker anxious to ensure his child the lasting enjoyment of the benefits necessitated by his condition as a handicapped person, would be induced not to remain in the Member State where he has established himself and has his employment. This would run counter to the object sought to be attained by the principle of free movement within the Community.[21]

Thus, in the *Fracas* judgment the Court did not make a distinction between benefits payable to employed persons and to persons *qua* members of the family. In the *Kermaschek* judgment,[22] the Court took another direction. It opted for the interpretation under which members of a family can only rely on provisions concerning benefits payable *qua* members.

Mrs Kermaschek was a national of the Republic of Yugoslavia. She worked in several countries, the last one of which was the Netherlands. She resigned from her last job because of her marriage to a German national. She left her residence in the Netherlands and settled with her husband in Germany. There she registered as unemployed in her place of residence and applied for unemployment benefit. Benefit was refused on the grounds that the periods of employment completed in the Netherlands could not be taken into account to satisfy the conditions for benefit.

She sought to claim unemployment benefit in Germany as a member of the family of an employed person, on the basis that she had paid contributions in the Netherlands.

The Court considered that Article 69 of the Regulation enables an employed person to claim, in the circumstances envisaged, the 'exportation' of his unemployment benefit from one Member State to another (*see*, Chapter 17 on these provisions). The present case concerned, however, a person who, although a member of the family of a national of a Member State, was not a national of that State herself. Therefore, the question arose whether and to what extent the members of the family of a national are, in the application of Regulation 1408/71 and in particular of Articles 67 to 70, to be assimilated to those nationals themselves.

The Court considered that only nationals of one of the Member States, stateless persons and refugees who are or who have been subject to the social security scheme of one or more Member States are covered in their capacity of workers. This is important because although Mrs Kermaschek worked as an employed person, she did not have the nationality of a Member State.

---

[21] *See*, for a judgment of the Court of Justice which follows the same approach, Court of Justice 16 December 1976, Case 63/76, *Inzirillo*, [1976] *ECR* 2057, also concerning a handicapped child.

[22] Court of Justice 23 November 1976, Case 40/76, [1976] *ECR* 1669.

Furthermore, the Court ruled that whereas employed perons and self-employed persons could claim the rights to benefits covered by the Regulation as rights of their own, the persons belonging to the second category, of members of the family and survivors) could only claim derived rights, acquired through their status as a member of the family of a worker.

As a result, Mrs Kermaschek could not have her periods in the Netherlands aggregated on the basis of the Regulation for the purpose of her claim to German unemployment benefit. This is because unemployment benefits do not belong to the type of benefit payable to members of a family.

In later case law (until the *Cabanis* judgment, *see* infra) the Court has no longer followed the approach that members of the family could invoke the Regulation with respect to non-derived rights. Instead it followed (the *Kermaschek* approach), for instance in the *Deak* judgment[23] and the *Zaoui* judgment.[24] As a matter of fact, Regulation 1612/68 (*see* Chapter 11) often proved useful to forbid discrimination in relation to members of the family with respect to the non-derived rights.

In the *Cabanis* judgment[25], however, the Court partially departed from the *Kermaschek* doctrine.

This decision concerned a woman of French nationality, widow of a migrant worker. She had been compulsorily insured from 1 January 1957, when the AOW (General Old Age Insurance Law) in the Netherlands came into force, as she lived in Dutch territory. During a later period, when the couple resided in France, she remained insured on the basis of this Act as her husband continued voluntarily to pay contributions. Subsequently, she was again a resident of the Netherlands, and insured on a compulsory basis, until she returned definitely to France in 1969. After her husband died in 1978, she was entitled to an old age pension on the basis of this Act, but her pension was reduced for the years she had not been insured under this Act. She was offered a voluntary insurance, but the contribution conditions for this insurance were less attractive for persons with a nationality other than Dutch. Was this discrimination allowed?

The Court considered that it had decided in the *Kermaschek* judgment that the only rights, which the members of a worker's family can claim, are derived rights, that is to say those acquired through their status as a member of a worker's family. In the light of this case law a widow or widower of a migrant worker could not invoke Article 3 of Regulation 1408/71 in order to fight the discriminatory conditions of the voluntary insurance. This Article could also be helpful, in general, when members of the family were discriminated against in comparison with the members of the family of the national worker. It requires however that this discrimination take place

---

[23] Court of Justice 20 June 1985, Case 94/84, [1985] *ECR* 1873.
[24] Court of Justice 17 December 1987, Case 147/87, [1987] *ECR* 5511.
[25] Court of Justice 30 April 1996, Case 308/93, [1996] *ECR* 2097.

on the territory of the discriminating Member State, and Mrs Cabanis was no longer on the territory.

The Court argued that the case concerned the spouse of an employed person, who has accompanied the employed person to another Member State and who decides to return with the employed person or after his decease to return to the State of origin. The impossibility for a worker's spouse who, having accompanied the worker to another Member State, decides to return to his State of origin with the worker or after the worker's death, of relying on the equal treatment rule in relation to the grant of certain benefits provided for by the legislation of the last State of employment would adversely affect freedom of movement of workers. The coordination regulation of the EU was made in order to improve this free movement. It would run counter to the purpose and spirit of those rules to deprive the spouse or survivor of a migrant worker of the benefit of application of the principle prohibiting discrimination in the calculation of old-age benefits which the spouse or survivor would have been able to claim on the same conditions as nationals, if he had remained in the host State.

The distinction drawn between rights in person and derived rights, the Court considered, renders the fundamental rule of equal treatment inapplicable to the surviving spouse of a migrant worker. The distinction may furthermore undermine the fundamental Community law requirement that its rules should be applied uniformly. This could be the case if the applicability of provisions to individuals depends on whether national law relating to the benefits in question treats the rights concerned as rights in person or as derived rights. Therefore, the Court concluded, the doctrine of the distinction between rights in person and derived rights has to be partially abandoned.

The *Cabanis* judgment would, if it were to have retroactive force, have large (financial) consequences. Therefore the Court decided to limit the retroactive effect of this judgment. It decided that persons cannot rely on this judgment to require benefits relating to periods prior to the date of delivery of this judgment, except by persons who have initiated proceedings prior to that date.

This judgment is an interesting one, and its consequences are not easy to see. It raised the question of when can members of the family invoke the new rules? Only if Article 3 is involved?

In the *Hoever and Zachow* judgment[26] the Court decided that the *Cabanis* Decision did not apply only if the discrimination clause is invoked. It considered that the *Cabanis* judgment limited the *Kermaschek* doctrine to those cases in which a member of the family of an employed person invokes provisions of Regulation 1408/71 which *apply exclusively to employed persons* and not to the members of their family. Examples of such exclusive provisions are Articles 67 - 71 of the Regulation, which concern unemployment benefits. Article 73 of the Regulation, dealing with family benefits, is not an exclusive provision. This provision aims to guarantee the benefits mentioned in the applicable legislation to members of the family residing

---

[26]   Court of Justice 10 October 1996, Case 245/94, 312/94, [1996] *ECR* I-4895.

in a State other than the competent State. Therefore the distinction between 'own rights' and 'derived rights' does apply in principle to family benefits.

As a result, the *Cabanis* judgment can be relied on in several cases by members of the family in so far as provisions of the Regulation which do *not* apply exclusively to employed persons are involved.

6.4.   Civil Servants and Assimilated Persons

The fourth category listed in Article 2 are civil servants and persons who, in accordance with the legislation applicable, are treated as such, where they are or have been subject to the legislation of a Member State to which this Regulation applies. Special schemes for civil servants are excluded from the material scope of the Regulation. Consequently, civil servants (and assimilated persons) fall under the Regulation in so far as they are (have been) subject to a national scheme falling under the material field of application of the Regulation. This means that the question of the protection of the Regulation in respect of civil servants is related to the material scope of the Regulation and therefore this subject is discussed in Chapter 7.

Chapter 7

Benefits covered by Regulation 1408/71

7.1.   Introduction

Regulation 1408/71 applies to all legislation concerning the following branches of social security (*see* Article 4(1) of the Regulation):

a.   sickness and maternity benefits:
b.   invalidity benefits, including those intended for the maintenance or improvement of earning capacity;
c.   old-age benefits;
d.   survivor's benefits;
e.   benefits in respect of accidents at work and occupational diseases;
f.   death grants;
g.   unemployment benefits;
h.   family benefits.

The European Commission has proposed in 1996 to add point 'i) early retirement benefits'.[1] In Article 1(w) these benefits are defined as 'all cash benefits, other than an early retirement benefit provided to wholly unemployed workers from a specified age until the age at which they qualify for an old-age pension or an unreduced early retirement pension, the receipt of which is not conditional upon the person concerned being available to the employment services of the competent State'. This proposal has not yet been adopted.

7.2.   The Term 'Legislation'

The material scope of the Regulation is limited to *'legislation'* concerning specific branches of social security. The meaning of this term can be found in Article 1(j) of the Regulation.

---

[1]   Com. (95) 735 def. of 10 January 1996.

This article provides that *legislation* means

'statutes, regulations and other provisions and all other implementing measures, present or future, relating to the branches and schemes of social security covered by Article 4(1) and (2) or those special non-contributory benefits covered by Article 4(2a).

This term excludes provisions of existing or future industrial agreements, whether or not they have been the subject of a decision by the authorities rendering them compulsory or extending their scope.

However, in so far as such provisions

(i)   serve to put into effect compulsory insurance imposed by the laws and regulations referred to in the preceding subparagraph; or

(ii) set up a scheme administered by the same institution as that which administers the schemes set up by the laws and regulations referred to in the preceding subparagraph,

the limitation on the term can at any time be lifted by a declaration of the Member State concerned specifying the schemes of such a kind to which this Regulation applies.'

Hence it can be seen that the scope of the Regulation is limited to statutory social security. Still, the definition is a broad one and can, therefore, cover several categories of schemes.

However, an important part of social security is excluded. In some countries a substantial part of social security benefits is not governed by statutory regulations, but by collective labour agreements. In order to be effective for all persons covered by such agreements, they need to be made compulsory or extended for some or all categories of the employees.

The second sentence of Article 1(j), quoted above, provides that the term 'legislation' excludes (collective) agreements, irrespective of whether their scope was extended by the authorities. Still, such agreements can be brought under the Regulation, if a Member State has made a declaration to this effect.

An example of collective agreements governing a substantial part of social security is the French collective agreements on unemployment benefit. These agreements have a legal basis in the French Labour Code and this law also provides the Minister with the power to extend agreements.[2] France has issued a declaration that these agreements fall within the scope of the Regulation.[3] Without such a declaration, the question raised in the case *Grisvard and Kreitz*,[4] concerning French frontier workers applying for French unemployment benefit, could not have been answered.

---

[2]   *See*, for a description in English, of the French unemployment system, Pennings (1990: 189).

[3]   *OJ L* 90 of 2 April 1987. *See* Lyon-Caen (1993: 226).

[4]   Court of Justice 1 October 1992, Case 201/91, [1992] *ECR* I-5009, *see*, Chapter 17.

But if such a declaration is not made, a collective agreement is not within the scope of the Regulation. The restrictions on the material scope of the Regulation in case of industrial benefits appeared in the *Commission* v. *France* judgment.[5]

Article 33 was relevant in this case. This states that a State which according to its own rules is authorized to deduct contributions from pensions, is also allowed to do so in the case of persons, receiving a pension from the said State whereas they reside in another Member State, who are insured for sickness benefits in the former State (*see* Section 14.9). France imposed sickness insurance contributions on supplementary pensions and early-retirement benefits. The law in question provided that the contributions were to be deducted from the benefits regardless of the place of residence of the beneficiaries.

The Commission started a procedure in order to obtain a ruling of the Court that deduction of contributions in the case of persons resident in a State other than France who are not insured under the French sickness insurance schemes, is inconsistent with Article 33 of the Regulation. The French early retirement pensions concerned[6] are special benefits, paid by the State on condition that special agreements have been made between the competent authorities and organizations of employers and employees. The supplementary pension is paid on the basis of collective agreements which are made compulsory and generally binding for particular branches of industry. The question was whether the French deduction of sickness benefit contributions was allowed.

The Court remarked that no contributions can be deducted from *statutory* old-age benefits and survivor's benefits by a Member State, if the sickness and maternity benefits payable to these persons are not at the charge of that Member State.

Section 5 of Title III of Regulation 1408/71, of which Article 33 is part, concerns only the persons eligible for pensions and benefits payable on the basis of the legislation of one or more Member States. According to Article 1(j) of Regulation 1408/71 collective agreements are not covered by the Regulation, even if they are made generally binding. This exclusion can be repealed by a declaration of the Member State concerned, but in this case no such declaration has been issued. For this reason the collective agreement in question does not fall within the scope of the Regulation and Article 33 is not applicable.[7] Therefore the deduction was not forbidden.

Article 4(2) provides that the Regulation applies to all general and special social security schemes, whether contributory or non-contributory, and to schemes concerning the liability of an employer or shipowner in respect of the benefits referred to in paragraph 1 of this article.

---

[5] Court of Justice 16 January 1992, case 57/90, [1992] *ECR* I-75.
[6] *See*, for a description of this type of benefit, Pennings (1990: 236).
[7] *See*, for a comparable ruling, Court of Justice 6 February 1992, Case 253/90, *Commission* v. *Belgium*, [1992] *ECR* 531.

The relevance of the applicability of the Regulation to employers' payments for the contingencies listed in the first paragraph of Article 4 appeared in the *Paletta* v. *Brennet* case.[8] This case concerned the obligations of the employer (under German law) to continue to pay wages during sickness of the employee.

Paletta, of Italian nationality, was an employee of Brennet, a German firm. His wife and his two children were also employed by this enterprise. In July 1989 Paletta, his wife and two children spent their holidays in Italy. During their holidays, all the four members of the family registered as ill at the Italian benefit office. This benefit office had them examined by medical doctors and they were provided with declarations stating that they were ill. The employer refused to pay wages to Paletta for this period on the grounds that he did not feel obliged to rely on the medical information on Paletta given by the Italian institution. As Paletta appeared to have been ill during his holidays in three consecutive years, Brennet was suspicious about Paletta's illness.

This case will be dealt with in more detail in Chapter 14 which concerns sickness benefits. Here we will discuss the question of whether the obligations on the employer to continue to pay wages in case of sickness on the basis of the *Lohnfortzahlungsgesetz* are subject to the provisions of the Regulation.

The Court answered this question in the affirmative. It acknowledged that in earlier judgments, such as *Rinner-Kühn*,[9] it had held that the continued payment of wages in the event of illness such as provided by the *Lohnfortzahlungsgesetz* (German Law on the continued payment of wages) fell within the concept of *pay* under Article 119 of the Treaty. It does not follow from this, according to the Court, that such payments by the employer cannot at the same time be sickness benefits within the meaning of Regulation 1408/71. The answer to the question whether a payment falls under the field of application of Regulation 1408/71 is essentially determined by the constitutive elements of that payment, and particularly by the objectives and conditions for acquiring a right to benefit and not by the name of the payment (*see*, for a similar approach, the *Hoeckx* judgment, in Section 7.4). In view of these criteria the payments concerned fall within the scope of the Regulation, as they are only granted in the event of illness and these payments suspend the payment of sickness benefits for a period of six weeks as provided for by the *Sozialgesetzbuch* (the German Social Security code).

In the *Rheinhold and Mahla* judgment[10] the question was raised whether the Regulation is applicable when a foreign employer fails to pay social security contributions; in other words, do the national rules concerning liability in this case fall under the material scope of the Regulation?

---

[8]   Court of Justice 3 June 1992, Case 45/90, [1992] *ECR* I-3423.
[9]   Court of Justice 13 July 1989, Case 171/88, [1989] *ECR* 2743.
[10] Court of Justice 18 May 1995, Case 327/92, [1995] *ECR* I-1223.

A firm, established in the Netherlands, worked in Belgium as a subcontractor for Rheinhold, a Belgian company. In 1985 the subcontractor went bankrupt and it appeared that it had not paid part of the required contributions to the social security administration. As the subcontractor did not have the funds to pay these contributions, the benefit administration asked Rheinhold to pay the bill. This claim was based on a Dutch law (Coördinatiewet Sociale Verzekering) on the basis of which the contractor is liable for paying contributions which the subcontractor has to pay because it employed workers to do the job.

The question raised was whether Regulation 1408/71 is applicable to a national regulation which - as was the case with the Dutch law - coordinates social security. The Court answered that national schemes of social security are completely subject to Community law. The scope of the Regulation is not confined to those aspects of legislation governing the particular areas of social security mentioned in Article 4(1). Thus, this Dutch coordination law is also within the material scope of the Regulation.

This consideration is not an answer to the question whether the *liability* provisions of the Dutch coordination act also fall within the material scope of the Regulation. If a provision is part of an Act which is beyond the material scope of the regulation, this does not necessarily mean, the Court ruled, that that provision is also not within the material scope. An example can be seen in the *Paletta* judgment; although labour law as such is not within the scope of the Regulation, the obligation to pay wages during a period of sickness is.

If an Act is *within* the scope of the Regulation, this does not mean that all provisions of that Act fall under the Regulation. What is decisive on the question as to whether a provision is within the material scope, is whether this provision has a direct and sufficiently relevant connection to the provisions which fall under Article 4(1) of the Regulation. The provision concerned in the *Rheinhold and Mahla* judgment does not concern an obligation of an employer established in another Member State to pay the social security contributions required on basis of the Dutch social security legislation. Instead, the provision concerns the obligation of a third party established in another Member State to pay to the benefit administration a certain amount which corresponds with the contributions not paid by an employer established in the Netherlands.

The Court acknowledged that there is a certain connection between social security obligations of the employer and responsibility of the main contractor. This connection is, however, indirect. The principle of liability laid down in the Dutch legislation is not based on the fact that there is an employer-employee relationship between the main contractor and the employees in with respect of whom the contributions are required. The liability follows, however, from the fact that the main contractor has made use of the services of the subcontractor, who has not paid the social security contributions. This contractor is, from a strict point of view, not obliged to pay the social security contributions, but has to compensate the loss in income which the benefit administration suffered because of the fact that this employer did not pay these contributions. In these circumstances this liability of third parties cannot be considered to have a direct and sufficiently relevant connection with the material scope of the

Regulation as defined in Article 4(1). This could be different if fraud on the part of the main contractor could be shown. Such fraud could exist if the main contractor were in reality the real employer of the workers for whom no social security contributions were paid. This is not the case here, and therefore the Regulation cannot be invoked in this liability case.

7.3.   Exclusion of Benefits for Victims of War

The Regulation does not apply to benefit schemes for victims of war or its consequences.[11] This exclusion became relevant in the *Fossi* judgment.[12]

> Carlo Fossi, an Italian national residing in Italy, worked in the German mines in Sudetenland (which was at that time part of the former German Reich) from 1 June 1942 to 1 July 1943. He was awarded a mineworkers' pension by the German social security institution for mineworkers as from 1 February 1970 on the grounds of total disablement, but this was suspended on the basis that he had only been employed and insured outside the territory of the present Federal Republic of Germany. Under the German Law the contested pension may be paid to German nationals, who normally reside abroad, although this discretion does not apply to aliens. Fossi wished, therefore, to rely on Article 3 of the Regulation (equality principle).

The Court considered that this law was introduced in order to facilitate the economic and social integration of refugees and persons deported under the Nazi regime. Therefore these benefits are outside the material scope of the Regulation. As a result Article 3 of the Regulation does not apply to these benefits.

Another example of such a war compensation pension is found in the *Even* judgment.[13] Gilbert Even was a French national, residing in Belgium, who wished to receive a Belgian war compensation pension. The benefit officers refused to apply this provision as Even did not have Belgian nationality. As the contested benefit did not fall within the scope of the Regulation, this discrimination could not be challenged by means of the Regulation.[14]

7.4.   The Exclusion of Special Schemes for Civil Servants

Special schemes for civil servants are also not included in the material scope of the Regulation. At the end of 1991, the European Commission issued a proposal to revise

---

[11] Article 4(4) of the Regulation.
[12] Court of Justice 31 March 1977, Case 79/76, [1977] *ECR* 667.
[13] Court of Justice 31 May 1979, Case 207/78, [1979] *ECR* 2019.
[14] *See* also Section 11.2.

the Regulation in order to include the schemes for civil servants. This proposal is still under discussion; Member States with important schemes for civil servants seem to have difficulties with the proposal.

The Court ruled in cases concerning the free movement of workers related to Article 48 of the Treaty[15] that only those jobs in the public service which were related with specific public tasks were excluded from free movement. These are tasks which directly or indirectly concern participation in public authority and comprise activities which serve to protect the general interests of the State or other public bodies.

Following this case law it could be expected that for Regulation 1408/71 the term 'civil servant' also had to be interpreted in a narrow way (and, consequently, that the material scope broadens). This would imply, for instance, that teachers are covered by the Regulation, even if they are civil servants under the national legislation.

The Court did, however, not follow this line of argument. This appeared from the *Lohman* judgment (which was already mentioned in Chapter 6)[16] and the *Vougioukas* judgment.[17]

> The national court had raised the question in the *Vougioukas* case whether Article 4(4) refers only to civil servants covered by the derogation provided for in Article 48(4) of the Treaty, as interpreted by the Court. The case concerned medical doctors, working for a Greek social security institution.

The Court answered that the subject-matter of Article 48(4) of the Treaty and Article 4(4) of the Regulation is different. Article 48(4) of the Treaty provides only that Member States may exclude nationals of other Member States from access to certain posts in the public service. Article 4(4) of the Regulation excludes special schemes for civil servants and persons treated as such from the coordination of social security schemes. The exclusion by Article 4(4) of the Regulation refers therefore to all civil servants employed by a public authority and persons treated as such. Article 4(4) comprises a broader definition of civil servants than Article 48(4).

The second question concerned the interpretation of the term 'special schemes for civil servants' in Article 4(4). The Court answered that in order to be regarded as 'special scheme for civil servants' it is sufficient that the social security scheme in question is different from the general social scheme applicable to employed persons in the Member state concerned. A further condition is that all, or certain categories of, civil servants are directly subject to it, or that it refers to a social security scheme for civil servants already in force in that Member State.

The national court had also raised the important question whether the exclusion of the special schemes for civil servants must be regarded as contrary to Articles 48

---

[15]   *See* Court of Justice 3 June 1986, Case 307/84, *Commission v. France*, [1986] *ECR* 1725.
[16]   Court of Justice 8 March 1979, Case 129/78, [1979] *ECR* 853.
[17]   Court of Justice 22 November 1995, Case 443/93, [1995] *ECR* I-4033.

and 51 of the Treaty. The problem raised by Vougioukas was that for the acquisition of the right to a pension, periods of work by a person subject to a special scheme in public hospitals in another Member State are not taken into account. The relevant Greek legislation allows such periods to be taken into account if they have been completed in comparable establishments in Greece.

The Court answered that in order to safeguard the effective exercise of the right to freedom of movement enshrined in Article 48 and 51 of the Treaty, the Council was required to set up a system to enable workers to overcome obstacles with which they might be confronted in national social security rules. The Community legislature, however, has not yet adopted the measures necessary to extend the material scope of Regulation 1408/71 to special schemes for civil servants and persons treated as such. As a result Article 4(4) leaves a considerable lacuna in the Community coordination of social security schemes.

Technical difficulties, which may have justified the exclusion of civil servants' schemes at the time when the Regulation was adopted, cannot justify indefinitely the lack of any coordination of special schemes for civil servants. Moreover, as we have seen, in December 1991 the Commission submitted to the Council a proposal for a Regulation designed to bring such schemes within the material scope. The Court concluded that, by not introducing any measure for coordination in this sector following the expiry of the transitional period provided for with regard to freedom of movement for workers, the Council has not fully discharged its obligation under Article 51 of the Treaty. This does not, however, affect the validity of Article 4(4), since, having regard to its wide discretion regarding the choice of the most appropriate measures for attaining the objective of Article 51 of the Treaty, the Council remains at liberty, for the purpose of coordinating special schemes for civil servants and persons treated as such, to depart, in some respects at least, from the mechanism currently provided for in Regulation 1408/71. Article 4(4) remains, therefore, valid.

This validity of Article 4(4) does not entail, however, that a request for aggregation is to be refused when it may be satisfied, in direct application of Articles 48 to 51 of the Treaty, without recourse to the coordination rules adopted by the Council. The Court based this consideration, as it often does, on the objective of Article 48 to 51: this would not be attained if, as a result of exercising their right to freedom of movement, workers were to lose social security advantages granted to them by the legislation of a Member State. That might dissuade Community workers from exercising their right to freedom of movement and would therefore constitute an obstacle to that freedom.

A worker is subject to precisely such dissuasion, the Court continued, if national legislation provides that only periods completed in national public hospitals may be recognized as pensionable, but not those completed in comparable establishments in other Member States. The effect of such legislation is to establish different treatment for workers who have not exercised their right to freedom of movement by comparison with migrant workers which places the latter at a disadvantage. The problem of recognition of periods completed in other Member States of the Community confronts only workers who have exercised their right to freedom of movement. The documents in this case disclosed no factor affording objective justification for that difference in treatment between migrant workers and workers who have not exercised their right to freedom of movement, and therefore the difference must be regarded, the Court concluded, as discriminatory. It is therefore contrary to the fundamental rules of the Treaty seeking to ensure freedom of movement for workers.

Accordingly, Articles 48 and 51 of the Treaty must be interpreted as precluding refusal to take into account, for the acquisition of the right to a pension, periods of employment completed by a person subject to a special scheme for civil servants in public hospitals in another Member State, where the relevant national legislation allows such periods to be taken into account if they have been completed in comparable establishments within that State.

Thus, the Court ruled that periods abroad have to be aggregated for the purpose of acquiring benefit rights in the case of civil servants, even though Regulation 1408/71 does not provide for a coordination system for civil servants' schemes.

This is an interesting judgment. It is not clear to what extent other coordination rules can also be applied to civil servants' schemes. Criteria relevant to such application are that they can be based on Article 51 of the Treaty and that there is no need for a technical elaboration of the instrument invoked.

As Article 51 requires measures in the area of social security, one could also wonder whether in the area of the non-statutory social security the *Vougioukas* judgment requires that coordination must take place where possible, despite the lack of an elaborate coordination instrument. An example is that of occupational social security.

7.5. The Exclusion of Social Assistance

Social and medical assistance is excluded from the material scope of the Regulation by Article 4(4). The term 'assistance' is less clear than it seems. It is not decisive whether or not a scheme is called 'assistance'.

In Article 1, which gives the definitions of the Regulation, no definition is given of the term *social security* or *assistance*. One of the first cases in which the interpretation of 'assistance' was questioned, was the *Frilli* judgment.[18]

> This case concerned an Italian national, who was employed in Belgium in 1966 and 1967 and who had continued to reside there. Mrs Rita Frilli received a low retirement pension in respect of that employment. On 14 May 1969 she lodged a claim for payment of the guaranteed income for old people established by the Belgian Law of 1 April 1969.
> This Belgian benefit is meant to guarantee a minimum income to the elderly who have insufficient means. As it is not called 'assistance', the question was raised whether this scheme fell under the exclusion of Article 4(4). The costs of the guaranteed income are entirely borne by the State. The guaranteed income is only

---

[18]   Court of Justice 22 June 1972, Case 1/72, [1972] *ECR* 471.

granted on request, after a means test has been carried out with regard to the person concerned. Generally speaking, all means are taken into account irrespective of their nature or origin, with the exception of certain benefits, notably benefits which fall under the category of public social assistance. Thus the legislature itself makes an express distinction between the guaranteed income and assistance allowances. From this it follows that the guaranteed income is not really subsidiary in nature.

Her claim for this benefit was refused on the grounds of the provision in the law that: 'every recipient shall either be of Belgian nationality or a national of a country with which Belgium has made a reciprocal agreement concerning this matter, or a stateless person, or a refugee recognized as such'. Mrs Frilli was a national of a country with which Belgium had not made a reciprocal agreement. She invoked the equality provision of Regulation 1408/71.

The Court had to decide whether the Belgian guaranteed income for the elderly was to be classified as a social security benefit or as social assistance.

It reasoned that although it might seem desirable, from the point of view of applying the Regulation, to establish a clear distinction between the legislative schemes which come within social security and those which come within assistance, it is possible that certain laws, because of the classes of persons to which they apply, their objectives, and the detailed rules for their application, may simultaneously contain elements belonging to both the categories mentioned and thus defy any general classification.

The Court considered, that by virtue of certain of its features, the national legislation on guaranteed income had certain affinities with social assistance - in particular where it prescribed need as an essential criterion for its application and did not stipulate any requirement as to periods of employment, membership, or contribution. Nevertheless it approximated to social security because it did not prescribe consideration of each individual case, which is a characteristic of assistance, and conferred on recipients a legally defined position giving them the right to a benefit which was analogous to the old-age pensions mentioned in the Regulation.

Regarding the wide definition of the range of recipients, such legislation in fact fulfils a double function; this consists, on the one hand, of guaranteeing a subsistence level to persons wholly outside the social security system, and, on the other hand, of providing an income supplement for persons in receipt of inadequate social security benefits.[19]

Thus when a wage-earner or assimilated worker who has completed periods of employment in a Member State, resides in that State and is entitled to a pension there, the legislative provisions giving all elderly residents a legally protected right to a minimum provision are provisions which, as regards these workers, come within the

---

[19]   As these benefits have, as the Court pointed out, a hybrid character (they have both the characteristics of public assistance and social security benefits) they are called *hybrid benefits*.

Regulations adopted in application of Article 51, even where such legislation might fall outside this classification as regards other categories of recipients.

Therefore the absence of a reciprocal agreement may not be set up against such a worker because such a requirement is incompatible with the rule of equality of treatment which is one of the fundamental principles of Community law and is enshrined, in this respect, in the Regulation.

In its considerations the Court acknowledged that there may be problems in respect of coordination. They occur where a Member State has established a benefit system covering the whole population without requirements on employment or contribution record. In that case, the coordination rules might remove the relevant benefit conditions and thus no longer provide a restriction on persons eligible. This might be disastrous to their social security system. This point was also raised by the Advocate-General. The latter asked whether one should accept that nationals from other Member States who are settled in Belgium can legally claim the advantages of the Law of 1 April 1969 subject to the conditions relating to age and inadequacy of means alone. Would it be permissible for persons who arrived in Belgium at an age close to retirement, but who never worked there, to be able to enjoy the advantages of an exercise in national solidarity? The Advocate-General answered that the effect of the very wording of the Regulation is to limit the consequences which could result from an unduly broad population in principle. Although the material scope of the Regulation is particularly extensive, this Regulation concerns only wage-earners and assimilated persons.

The Court reasoned that the difficulties which may occur as regards the Community rules as the result of the application of general systems of social protection, which have been designed for a population as a whole and which are based on requirements of nationality and residence, are inherent to the very nature of such systems. This is that they are intended to protect employed persons covered as such by social security and persons who are not covered in this way. Although these difficulties, taken as a whole, can only be resolved within the context of legislative action taken by the Community, this fact cannot adversely affect the right and duty of courts and tribunals to ensure that migrant workers receive protection wherever this proves to be possible under the principles of the social legislation of the Community, and without thereby breaking the system set up by the national legislation in question. Such is the case at least whenever a person having the status of an employed or assimilated worker within the Regulation already comes, by virtue of a prior occupational activity, under the social security system of the Member State whose legislation guaranteeing a minimum income to old people is involved.

It follows from this judgment that an important criterion for deciding whether a particular benefit is within the scope of the Regulation is that claimants have a legally defined position which gives them a right to benefit. Therefore, where the benefit administration has no discretion in granting benefit, this benefit cannot be treated as social assistance within the meaning of the Regulation.

There is another important additional criterion for deciding whether a particular benefit is covered by the Regulation. This criterion is that, to be covered by the Regulation, it is necessary that the benefit scheme concerned is related to one of the contingencies of Article 4(1) - listed in Section 7.1 as (a) - (h). This criterion appeared from the *Hoeckx* judgment.[20]

> Mrs Hoeckx, of Dutch nationality, applied in Belgium for the granting of a minimum subsistence income. She had worked for a few years in France, but at the time of the application she could no longer claim unemployment benefit. The conditions for the Belgium subsistence benefit required that one had resided in Belgium for at least five years before the date of the application; this condition applied to non-Belgians only. The question arose whether the period of stay in France could be aggregated, on the basis of the Regulation, to the Belgian period for the purpose of satisfying this benefit condition.

The Court held that in order to fall within the scope of Regulation 1408/71, the national legislation had to be connected with one of the branches of social security enumerated in Article 4(1). A branch not listed in this Article cannot be qualified as such, even if the claimant has a legally defined right to benefit. The Belgian subsistence income which was contested in this case was paid to persons without sufficient means of their own. This benefit was, therefore, of a general character and could not be brought within one of the risks of the Regulation.[21]

Consequently, the Regulation does not apply to a benefit, such as a public assistance benefit for persons in need, which is not meant to compensate for one of the contingencies listed in Article 4(1), even if recipients have a legally defined right to that benefit.

A case in which the Court followed the same approach, is the *Acciardi* judgment.[22] In this case, the Court had to decide whether a Dutch benefit, the benefit for the partially disabled and unemployed persons (IOAW), fell within the material scope of the Regulation. The Netherlands government had declared that this benefit did not fall under the Regulation as it considered this benefit as public assistance.

The Court considered that the law in question provides that this benefit depends on the income received by the claimant and his spouse, as this benefit supplements the income earned in work up to a prescribed level. This is an objectively defined criterion; if this is satisfied, one has a legal right to benefit whereas the competent institution must not take the claimant's personal circumstances into account. Therefore, the first criterion to come within the material scope of the Regulation was satisfied. The second criterion, that the benefit relates to those listed in Article 4(1), was also satisfied. For this purpose it was relevant that the Law on this benefit restricted the right to benefit to unemployed persons. Secondly, the right to benefit ended as soon as the beneficiary reached the statutory retirement age.

Thirdly, one became entitled to this benefit immediately after the expiration of the right to unemployment benefit. Finally the law imposed several conditions on the

---

[20] Court of Justice 27 March 1985, Case 249/83, [1985] *ECR* 982.
[21] *See*, on this case, also the application of Regulation 1612/68, Chapter 11.
[22] Court of Justice 2 August 1993, Case 66/92, [1993] *ECR* I-4567.

beneficiary which ensured that the beneficiary was available for work, such as registering at the employment office, actually seeking work as an employed person and accepting an offer of suitable work. All these circumstances were relevant to the decision that this benefit was an unemployment benefit and fell within Article 4(1) of the Regulation.

Conclusion. The first criterion for a benefit *not* to be excluded as social assistance is that a claimant has an enforceable right to that benefit; secondly, the benefit in question must fall within the types listed in Article 4(1).

A third criterion is that benefits such as the guaranteed income for the elderly are only within the scope of the Regulation in respect of 'employed persons and assimilated persons who have completed periods of employment under the legislation of a Member State and are resident in that State and receiving a pension'.[23] This follows from the *Newton* judgment.[24]

> Newton, a United Kingdom national, was working in France as a self-employed person when on 12 October 1980 he was the victim of a car accident. As a result of that accident Mr Newton suffered from complete tetraplegia. He returned to the United Kingdom and on 4 March 1981 applied for a mobility allowance. A mobility allowance is granted to any person suffering from physical disablement such that he is either unable to walk or virtually unable to do so, provided that such person has been in the United Kingdom for a certain period, is still present and is ordinarily resident there. Mobility allowance is a flat-rate weekly cash benefit and is not means-tested.
>
> Mr Newton was awarded the benefit, but on 4 April 1984 he went to live permanently in France. Subsequently, the adjudication officer informed Mr Newton that he no longer met the conditions as to residence and presence in the United Kingdom laid down in United Kingdom legislation.

The question was whether his benefit rights could be terminated for this reason. Newton argued that under Article 10 of the Regulation, entitlement to mobility allowance could not be withdrawn from him on the ground that he had transferred his place of residence to France.

The Court first had to consider whether this benefit was within the scope of the Regulation. It reasoned that it has held on several occasions that, whilst it may seem desirable from the point of view of applying Community regulations on social security to establish a clear distinction between social security and assistance benefits, the possibility could not be excluded that by reason of the persons covered, its objectives and its methods of application, national legislation may, at one and the same time, have links to both categories.

---

[23]   In the *Costa* judgment (Court of Justice 13 November 1974, Case 39/74, [1974] *ECR* 1251) a situation can be found where the Court did not apply this criterion, perhaps because the national court did not raise this question.

[24]   Court of Justice 20 June 1991, Case 356/89, [1991] *ECR* 3017.

In view to the broad definition of the persons entitled to the benefit in issue, such legislation has a two-fold function. On the one hand, it seeks to ensure a minimum level of income for handicapped persons who are entirely outside the social security system. On the other hand, it provides supplementary income for recipients of social security benefits who suffer from physical disablement affecting their mobility. Consequently, in the case of an employed or self-employed person who by reason of his previous occupational activity is already covered by the social security system of the State whose legislation is invoked, that legislation must be deemed to fall within the meaning of Article 51 of the Treaty and the legislation adopted in implementation of that provision, although in the case of other categories of beneficiaries it may be deemed not to. In particular, legislative provisions of a Member State of the kind in issue cannot be regarded as falling within the field of social security within the meaning of Article 51 of the Treaty and the Regulation in the case of persons who have been subject as employed or self-employed persons exclusively to the legislation of other Member States.

Thus, in these considerations, the Court made an important distinction between persons covered by the Regulation and those not covered. The latter category contains *persons who have been subject as employed or self-employed persons exclusively to the legislation of other Member States*. In other words, a distinction is made among beneficiaries within this type of benefit: some of them can rely on the Regulation and others can not.

The Court gave the following reason for this approach: if such legislative provisions were to be regarded, in the case of such persons, as falling within the field of social security within the meaning of Article 51 of the Treaty and the Regulation, the stability of the system instituted by national legislation, whereby Member States manifest their concern for the handicapped persons residing in their territory, could be seriously affected.

Regulation 1408/71 does not establish a common system of social security, but lays down rules coordinating the different national social security schemes with the purpose of ensuring freedom of movement for workers. Consequently, the Court argued, although the provisions of that Regulation must be construed in such a manner as to secure the attainment of that objective, they cannot be interpreted in such a way as to upset the system instituted by national legislation of the kind in issue in the main proceeding.

7.6.   Special Non-Contributory Benefits

In 1992, after the *Newton* judgment, Regulation 1408/71 was revised. A proposal for this revision had been presented approximately seven years earlier, but was not adopted earlier because of the discussion on this proposal. In 1992 a new Article 4(2a) was inserted in the Regulation.[25]

---

[25]   By Regulation 1247/92, *OJ L* 136 of 30 April 1992, pages 1-6.

Article 4(2*a*) reads:
'This Regulation shall also apply to special non-contributory benefits which are provided under legislation or schemes other than those referred to in paragraph 1 or excluded by virtue of paragraph 4, where such benefits are intended:
a. either to provide supplementary, substitute or ancillary cover against the risks covered by the branches of social security referred to in paragraph 1(a) to (h); or
b. solely as specific protection for the disabled.'[26]

The wording of this article is not very specific, as it refers to those benefits 'excluded by virtue of paragraph 4' and 'schemes other than those referred to in paragraph 1'. Therefore, the schemes in question are defined in a negative way only and it remains uncertain, just as in the cases discussed in the previous section, whether a benefit is excluded by virtue of Article 4(4). To solve this problem, the instrument of an Annex is used. Member States can issue declarations mentioning the schemes covered by Article 4(2*a*).[27] These declarations are listed in Annex II*a*. Belgium, for instance, has included allowances for disabled persons, guaranteed income for elderly persons and guaranteed family benefits. Some of these benefits we have already seen in the case law in the previous paragraphs.

Article 4(2*a*) means that the benefits referred to are now within the scope of the Regulation, and as a result, for instance, the equal treatment provision of Article 3 applies to these benefits.

However, not all provisions of the Regulation are applicable to these benefits. This is because the Regulation was revised in order to insert special rules which form part of the new Article 10*a*.

Exportation
Article 10*a*(1) concerns the exportation of hybrid benefits.

Article 10*a*(1) provides:
'Notwithstanding the provisions of Article 10 and Title III, persons to whom this Regulation applies shall be granted the special non-contributory cash benefits referred to in Article 4(2a) exclusively in the territory of the Member State in which they reside, in accordance with the legislation of that state, provided that such benefits are listed in Annex II*a*. Such benefits shall be granted by and at the expense of the institution of the place of residence.'

Consequently, on the basis of this provision, the special non-contributory benefits - *i.e.* those covered by Article 4(2*a*) - are treated in a special way, as the legislation of the State of residence is decisive as to whether one receives these benefits or not.

---

[26]   In the proposal (*OJ* 1985 *C* 240) another area was mentioned: (*c*) 'or benefits meant to guarantee a subsistence minimum income'. This part was not adopted.
[27]   These declarations are based on Article 5 of the Regulation.

Therefore, this provision departs more radically from the general idea of the principle of exportation of benefits (Article 51 of the Treaty) than the approach of the Court in the *Newton* judgment. From the Newton judgment it followed that hybrid benefits could not be exported by *some* categories of beneficiary. On the basis of the Article 10*a* Member States are no longer obliged to allow *any* beneficiaries to export the benefits referred to by this Article (in connection with Annex II*a*). Indeed, the United Kingdom mentioned mobility allowance in its declaration concerning Article 10*a*; this was the benefit contested in the *Newton* judgment.

Conditions for receipt
There are also provisions facilitating the receipt of this type of benefit. These are found in the subsequent paragraphs of Article 10*a*.

Article 10*a*(4) concerns the case in which the legislation of a Member State makes the granting of a hybrid benefit subject to the condition that disability or invalidity is diagnosed for the first time in the territory of that Member State. According to this provision, this condition is deemed to be fulfilled when this diagnosis is made for the first time in the territory of another Member State.

Paragraph 3 of this Article provides a rule for the case where the legislation of a Member State makes entitlement to a hybrid benefit subject to the receipt of another benefit (i.e. a benefit as listed in Article 4(1)). Where a claimant is not entitled to a benefit of the latter kind under the legislation of the Member State where he wishes to receive the hybrid supplementary benefit, any corresponding benefit granted under the legislation of any other Member State shall be treated as a benefit granted under the legislation of the first Member State for the purposes of entitlement to the supplement.

Aggregation of periods in other Member States
Article 10*a*(2) also contains rules for the aggregation of periods completed in another Member State. This article provides that the institution of a Member State under whose legislation entitlement to hybrid benefits is subject to the completion of periods of employment, self-employment or residence in the territory of any other Member State as periods completed in the territory of the first Member State.

Chapter 8

The General Rules for Determining the Legislation applicable

8.1. Introduction

An essential task of a coordination regulation is to determine the legislation applicable. The general provisions of Regulation 1408/71 on the legislation applicable can be found in the Articles 13 to 17, in Title II.

With respect to some types of benefits there are special rules for determining the legislation applicable, for example in the case of unemployment benefits. These can be found in Title III and will be discussed in later chapters.

The aim of these provisions is to prevent situations in which, as a result of cross border movement between Member States, no legislation or more than one legislation is applicable.

These rules have to determine which national social security scheme is applicable. They are of a compulsory nature and leave no choice for the person concerned between a 'better' or 'worse' scheme. As a result of these rules a worker can be insured under a scheme with less attractive conditions than the one of his State of origin or State of residence.

Most rules for determining the legislation applicable provide that the legislation of the Member State in which a person is *employed* is applicable. This includes the situation in which he resides in another Member State. This rule also applies to the situation where the undertaking or the residence of the employer by whom the person concerned is employed, is situated in the territory of another Member State.

The reason for choosing the system of the State of work is obvious. First of all, it implies that all persons employed by a certain employer are subject to the same contribution and benefit system as applies to national employees. By means of this rule, employers are not encouraged, on improper grounds, to engage or not engage foreign workers. That such tendency may exist, if this principle did not apply, can be seen from the practice of *posting*. According to the posting rules of the Regulation, discussed in Chapter 9, the social security legislation of a State remains applicable to its nationals for a limited period; by means of this method workers from Member States with lower wages and benefits are actually employed under their own national employment conditions in other Member States with better conditions. It will be clear that this is done because these workers are cheap labourers.

A second reason for the principle-of-the-work-State is that Member States usually make a connection between employment and affiliation with their national social security scheme. Contribution conditions and rates, the right to benefit and the amount of benefit are usually related to wages.[1]

Article 13(1) provides, in the first place, that, except for some specific exceptions, those falling under the Regulation are subject to the legislation of only one Member State. The text of this Article itself makes clear that the rules for determining the legislation applicable have *exclusive effect*.

This means that only one legislation is applicable at the same time. The Regulation determines which legislation. Most times the Regulation determines, as we have seen above, that the legislation applicable is that of the State of work. The State whose legislation is assigned is called the competent State. During the period that the legislation of a State is applicable on a person, that person has to pay contributions to the benefit administration of that State. In general, when a risk materialises one has to claim benefit under the scheme of the competent State. This is the so-called integration principle: benefit only from one State. If a person becomes, for instance, ill, he has to claim sickness benefit from the benefit administration of the competent State. Of course the person must fulfil the benefit conditions of the scheme of that State. Sometimes the Regulation provides assistance in satisfying the national conditions, for instance by giving rules on the aggregation of periods of insurance. The rules on aggregation are given in the chapters on the benefits in Title III of the Regulation.

It can happen, though, that even with the help of rules for aggregation of periods of insurance a person cannot satisfy the conditions for benefit under the scheme of the competent State. Even if he would have qualified for benefit in the country of residence or origin, this cannot help the person concerned. The rules for determining the legislation applicable are inexorable. Such differences between the schemes are not removed by the Regulation, as the objective of the Regulation is only coordination and not harmonisation of national schemes.

As we will see in Chapter 15, with respect to some types of benefit, the integration principle is not applied, but instead person acquire benefit rights in the countries where they worked during their career. This is the case with old age, survivors' and disability benefits.

Example. A person worked from 1970 until 1980 in Germany, and resides in this period in the Netherlands. During this ten year period, he does not pay contributions for the Dutch old age benefit scheme and he does not acquire benefit rights in the Netherlands. From 1970 until 1980 he acquires rights to a German old age pension instead.

When he starts to work again in the Netherlands, he is covered by the Dutch old age scheme again and he acquires benefit rights under this scheme. When he retires at the age of 1998, he receives a Dutch and a German old age

---

[1]   *See*, for an opinion disputing the choice for the work-State-principle, Watson (1980) and Van Limberghen (1991: 79); the latter argues that if social security is linked to employment, this offers insufficient protection to families with one income and to people in irregular work.

pension. Although during his career he has been subject to one legislation at the time only, this does not prevent him from receiving benefits from two States, on the basis of periods of insurance completed in the past.

8.2. The Exclusive and Binding Effect of Rules for Determining the Legislation applicable

The rules for determining the legislation applicable have exclusive effect.[2] This follows from Article 13: 'persons to whom this Regulation applies, shall be subject to the legislation of a single Member State only'.[3]

> On the basis of early decisions of the Court, some doubt was raised as to the character of the rules for determining the legislation applicable in the Regulation. The disputed case was the *Nonnenmacher* judgment,[4] which was given under Regulation 3.[5] In this case, a person would have been entitled to a widows' pension in the State of origin, but not under the legislation of the competent State.
> This decision concerned the case of a widow, of French nationality, whose husband was in gainful employment in the Netherlands until 1 September 1959, when he obtained a job in France. He worked in France until his death, one and a half months later. During this period he resided in the Netherlands.
> There was no question that at the time of his death he was subject to French social security legislation. Under this legislation, however, Mrs Nonnenmacher was not entitled to a widow's pension. The question at issue was whether Mrs Nonnenmacher was entitled to a pension on the basis of the Netherlands general widows and orphans insurance (AWW) scheme[6], which scheme provided that widows of residents could claim this benefit. The basic question was whether

---

[2] As we will see in Chapter 16, it can happen where a person receives child benefit, that he receives a supplement from another State. This can happen if child benefit could be claimed from two countries, for instance as the parents work in different countries. In that case the benefit rights based on the scheme of one country will be suspended; if, however, the suspended benefit is higher than the benefit actually paid, this person will receive a supplement to compensate for the difference. The rules on this subject can be found in Title III of the Regulation. The rules concerning the right to this supplement do not infringe on the exclusive effect of the rules for determining the legislation applicable of Title II. This is confirmed by the Court in the judgment of 9 December 1992, Case 119/91, *Una McMenamin*, [1992] *ECR* I-6393.

[3] In some cases, it is possible to apply more than one legislation, such as, as we will see in Section 8.4, in the case of Article 14c. These are specific, rare exceptions.

[4] Court of Justice 9 June 1964, Case 92/63, [1964] *ECR* 583.

[5] Article 12 of Regulation 3 was as follows: 'Save as otherwise provided under this Head, wage-earners or assimilated workers employed in the territory of one Member state shall be subject to the legislation of that state even if they permanently reside in the territory of another Member State of their employer or the registered office of the undertaking which employs them is situated in the territory of another Member State'.

[6] The Dutch AWW came into force exactly in the period during which her husband worked in France.

the spouse of Mrs Nonnenmacher could have been subject to two national legislations at the same time.

The Court considered that the question led to determining whether the compulsorily application of the law of the State where the worker is employed, excludes the application of the law of another Member State, including the one where the worker had his permanent residence. As Article 12 did not contain any provision which forbade the simultaneous application of several laws, the intention of the authors of Regulation 3 to impose such a restriction on the freedom of national legislators could not be assumed, except in so far as this plurality is clearly contrary to the spirit of the Treaty, and particularly to its Articles 48 to 51. These provisions aimed at ensuring as free a movement of labour as possible, and this aim involved the abolition of all legal measures which discriminate against migrant workers. It follows that in the absence of specific clauses, there was nothing against a plurality of benefits under two national laws. This was even more the case, the Court continued, when one of these laws, far from being confined to workers, was applicable to the whole population and the only qualification was residence and not the exercise of gainful activities. Consequently, the Court ruled, Article 12 of Regulation 3 did not prohibit the application of the law of a Member State other than the one on whose territory the person concerned worked, unless it compelled this person to contribute to the financing of a social security institution, which did not grant any extra benefits for the same risk and the same period. States other than the one in whose territory the insured person was employed, were free to grant or not to grant this person the right to claim benefits, even if this person was entitled to claim similar rights for the same risks and the same periods under the law of the State where this person was employed.

Thus, under Regulation 3, the Court allowed the simultaneous application of two legislations if this was advantageous to the person concerned, whereas such application was not allowed if it led to extra charges for the applicant.

The provision for determining the legislation applicable in Regulation 1408/71 (Article 13) has a slightly different wording; it provides in express terms that the legislation of a single State is applicable only. As a result the rules on determining the legislation applicable have exclusive effect, even if this is disadvantageous for the persons concerned. This is confirmed in the *Ten Holder* judgment.[7]

The *Ten Holder* case concerned a Dutch woman who was employed in Germany for some time. When she became ill, she was granted German sickness benefit, *Krankengeld*. At a certain moment, she returned to the Netherlands, and after the maximum duration of *Krankengeld* had expired, she applied for a Dutch benefit for incapacity for work (AAW benefit).

---

[7]   Court of Justice 12 June 1986, Case 302/84, [1986] *ECR* 1821.

The Court held that the legislation of the work State was to be applied in this situation, which legislation continues to be applicable until the person concerned entered employment in another Member State. The consequence of this was that Mrs Ten Holder was not entitled to the Dutch benefit. She had to rely on the German social security provisions, even though she could actually not satisfy the conditions of the benefit scheme available. Hence, 'exclusive effect' of the rules for determining the legislation applicable is neutral as to the question whether the result for the person concerned is favourable or unfavourable.

The Regulation is also important for the purpose of collecting contributions as can be seen in the *Perenboom* judgment.[8]

> In 1972, Perenboom, a youth of Dutch nationality, worked for 143 days in Germany. During this year he did not work in the Netherlands. As he resided during this year in the Netherlands, the Tax Department ruled that he was subject to the national insurance scheme.
> He was assessed on a part of the income he had earned in Germany; the number of days on which he did not work in Germany divided by the total number of days of the calender year. Contributions had to be paid on this fraction multiplied by the sum of his annual income. Perenboom objected to this decision: he was assessed on (a part of) his income in his work State as well as in his State of residence.

The Court ruled that on the basis of Article 13 of the Regulation, the employed person is subject to the legislation of a single State only. A person who is assessed on one income with the social charges resulting from the application of more than one legislation, whereas he can only be held to be insured by one of those legislations, is subject to double contribution charges. This is not consistent with Article 13. Where the social legislation of the State of residence does not apply to periods of employment in another Member State, the wages earned during this period cannot be subject to contributions, the Court ruled.

Only the competent State is authorised to impose contributions; the rules for determining the legislation applicable determine which State is the competent State. In Perenboom's case, this was the State of employment.

Binding effect

If the rules for determining the legislation applicable assign a particular national legislation, it is of essential importance that the legislation applicable does not exclude employees by opposing national conditions for affiliation with the scheme.

> Suppose that a self-employed person of Belgian nationality works in the Netherlands, but resides in Belgium. The legislation applicable is the Dutch social security law. In order to be insured for the old age benefit it is required that a

---

[8]   Court of Justice 5 May 1977, Case 102/76, [1978] *ECR* 815.

person is resident of the Netherlands. The self-employed person in this example does not fulfil this condition. The Dutch rules for determining the legislation applicable would imply that this person would not be subject to the Dutch legislation.

Article 13(2) reads that '...a person employed in the territory of one Member State shall be subject to the legislation of that State *even* if he resides in the territory of another Member State'. Article 13(2)(b) gives a corresponding rule for self-employed persons.

The word *even* has to ensure that in the example given above the Belgian self-employed person is subject to the Dutch social security legislation, even though he does not satisfy the conditions of the national system.

This phenomenon is called the *binding* effect of the rules for determining the legislation applicable. Rules have binding effect if, where the national legal system is not applicable according to the territorial criteria (conflict rules) laid down in the national legislation, the rules on determining the legislation applicable mean that the national system concerned was applicable. As a result, the rule for determining the legislation applicable overrules the national rules of conflict. It has in such case the positive effect that the person concerned is insured, even if this is against the national legislation.

The binding effect of the rules of Regulation 1408/71 for determining the legislation applicable was confirmed in the *Kuijpers* decision.[9]

The binding effect of the rules for determining the legislation applicable over-rule *conditions related to the territoriality principle*. Examples of such conditions are: residence conditions, conditions that one has to register with an organisation in a particular Member State, conditions concerning the place of establishment of the employer and conditions concerning the place where the work is performed. An example of binding effect is found in the *Kits van Heijningen* judgment.[10]

We have seen in Chapter 6, that Kits, although he was a part-time worker, was within the personal scope of the Regulation. The following question was whether he could be refused Dutch child benefit. Kits was not a resident of the Netherlands, and the only condition of the Dutch Child Benefit Act for receiving child benefit was that the insured person resided in the Netherlands. Did Article 13 of the Regulation preclude this territoriality condition?

The Court answered this question in the affirmative: Article 13(2) provides in express terms that the legislation of a Member State continues to be applicable to a person who performs activities as an employed person, even if he resides in the territory of another Member State. This provision would lose all *practical effect* if national legislation could impose conditions on residence.

---

[9] Court of Justice 23 September 1982, Case 276/81, [1982] *ECR* 3027.
[10] Court of Justice 3 May 1990, Case 2/89, [1990] *ECR* 1755.

The *De Paep* judgment[11] is a special example of rules for determining the legislation applicable which overrule national rules of affiliation. In this situation a rule for determining the legislation applicable which has so far not been discussed was relevant: this rule assigns to mariners the legislation applicable of the State whose flag the vessel flies.

Mrs De Paep, of Belgian nationality, was the owner of the ship on which her husband and her son were employed. Due to sustained damage, this ship was declared unseaworthy. Nevertheless it was taken to the new owner in the United Kingdom by the husband and the son, who remained employed by the Belgian firm. The ship was lost and the husband and the son were killed. According to the Belgian law on employment contracts for seamen, the contract of employment ends as soon as the ship is officially declared to be unseaworthy. On these grounds, the husband was no longer employed by the Belgian firm when the accident happened. In addition, to be entitled to a Belgian benefit for industrial accidents, it is necessary that the person concerned sailed under the Belgian flag. As this condition was not fulfilled, Mrs De Paep was refused benefit.

The Court considered that the provision which assigns the legislation of the State of the flag would loose practical effect, if the conditions for affiliation with the national legislation of the State in whose territory an undertaking operates are held against persons to which this Article applies. The objective of rules of conflict is not only to prevent two or more legislations from being applicable at the same time, but also to avoid the situation where no legislation is applicable at all (negative conflict of laws). In this case, we see, however, that the Belgian legislation provides that affiliation to the Belgian system ends as soon as a ship is declared to be unseaworthy. Hence the conditions for affiliation imposed by the legislation of the Member State applicable (in this case, that the insurance ends when the ship is declared unseaworthy), cannot be held against persons in the circumstances as defined by the rules for determining the legislation applicable under the Regulation.

The case law of the Court that Member States can determine the conditions for the right to benefit, but cannot determine that their own legislation or the legislation of another Member State is applicable, does not always give clear criteria to determine which national condition is overruled by the rules for determining the legislation applicable and which condition is not.

Such a problematic situation can be seen in the *Coonan* judgment.[12] Mrs Coonan, a woman of Irish nationality, entered employment in the United Kingdom after the age of 65. A condition for being insured for British sickness benefits, is that one is insured for British old age benefits. Mrs Coonan was, however, because of her age not admitted to the old age benefit scheme. As a

---

11   Court of Justice 4 October 1991, Case 196/90, [1991] *ECR* I-4815.
12   Court of Justice 24 April 1980, Case 110/79, [1980] *ECR* 1445.

result she could not participate in the sickness insurance scheme either. The question was whether the rules for determining the legislation applicable could overrule the rules for affiliation with the sickness insurance scheme.

The Court decided that this could not be the case, as the Regulation does not preclude the competence of the Member States to determine the conditions for affiliation themselves. The Court did not discuss the question of whether the conditions concerned were indirectly discriminating against migrant workers. The conditions involved are not territoriality conditions and for this reason they were not overruled by the rules for determining the legislation applicable.

8.3. The Rules for Determining the Legislation applicable for Post-active Persons

From the *Ten Holder* judgment[13], discussed in Section 8.2, it followed that an employed or self-employed person continues to be subject to the social security scheme of a Member State, until he starts to work as an employee or self-employed person in another Member State. This decision was criticised as it meant that persons could not claim specific provisions in their State of residence, for example Mrs Ten Holder who could not claim disability benefit in the Netherlands, whereas she did not satisfy the conditions for a German benefit.

This decision was also regarded as problematic for national insurance schemes from the opposite point of view, *e.g.* the Netherlands. After all, for this type of insurance the completion of periods of contribution is not (always) required, but conditions of residence apply. If Article 13 of Regulation 1408/71 was applicable, these residence requirements would be overruled by this article. This would mean that the only condition for affiliation with these insurances was removed. As a result, persons who worked for a small period in a State with such insurance schemes would also remain subject to such schemes if they went to another Member State. This was especially problematic in case of non-contributory national insurance schemes. That such an effect could occur was confirmed by the *Kits van Heijningen* judgment,[14] discussed in Section 8.2.

This case law caused some consternation over the possibility of maintaining national insurance schemes,[15] as this case law could lead to a situation where the national insurance system acquired a very large group of insured persons, who do not pay contributions. A national of an Member State who is employed in the Netherlands for a certain period, after which he moves to another Member State (not engaging in employment), may continue to build up, for instance, Netherlands old-age benefit rights (or may apply for family allowance) on the basis of the Dutch

---

[13]   Court of Justice 12 June 1986, Case 302/84, [1986] *ECR* 1821.
[14]   Court of Justice 3 May 1990, Case 2/89, [1990] *ECR* 1755.
[15]   *See*, for instance, Keunen (1987: 98 ff), Schell (1991) and Levelt-Overmars (1988).

regulations, since he remains subject to Dutch legislation. If he has no income he does not have to pay contributions; if he has a sufficient income, it appears to be difficult, in practice, to collect contributions from him while residing abroad.

At a later stage, the approach of the *Ten Holder* judgment was slightly changed, as can be seen from the *Daalmeijer* judgment.[16]

> For several years Daalmeijer worked abroad as a civil servant for the Netherlands Ministry of Defence. Being engaged in employment, he was insured for the Dutch old-age benefit (AOW). At the age of fifty-six he retired and he settled in France, together with his wife. The question was whether the period after his retirement had to be taken into account for his AOW pension. As he lived in France, he was not a Dutch resident any longer, and therefore he did not build up any AOW rights. The question was whether the residence requirement in question is allowed. If Article 13 is applicable, the Dutch legislation continued to be applicable to Daalmeijer. Therefore, it followed from this Article that the residence requirements are overruled. According to this reasoning, Daalmeijer would also have built up AOW rights during the period in France after his early retirement.

The Court ruled that Article 13 no longer applied to a person who had *permanently terminated* his working activities. This is because the objective of Article 13 is to solve conflicts of law which can occur when during a certain period the place where a person resides and the place where he works are not in the same Member State. These conflicts no longer occur with persons who have permanently terminated their working activities. The Court ruled that, although post-active persons continue to be subject to the personal scope of the Regulation, Article 13 does not apply to post-active persons. Now that Article 13 no longer applies, it is possible to impose residence requirements for the affiliation to a national scheme; so, the reduction in Daalmeijer's AOW benefit was allowed.

This decision also had consequences for another group of persons entitled to benefit. This appeared from the *Commission* v. *the Netherlands* judgment.[17]

> The European Commission objected to the Netherlands rule that workers receiving a pension granted on the basis of regulations of a branch of industry or an undertaking after early retirement, only enjoy Dutch child benefit when residing in the Netherlands. If Article 13 applies to these beneficiaries, Article 73 of the Regulation would remove this residence requirement. The Court ruled, in accordance with the *Daalmeijer* judgment, that Article 13(2)(a) does not apply to persons who have permanently terminated their working activities. Therefore, they cannot rely on Article 73 of the Regulation.

---

[16]   Court of Justice 21 February 1991, Case 245/88, [1991] *ECR* I-555.
[17]   Court of Justice 28 November 1991, Case 198/90, [1991] *ECR* I-5799.

It could also happen as a result of this case law that a post-active worker had to pay contributions in two Member States. *See*, for the solution the Court found in a particular case, Section 14.9

Prior to the *Daalmeijer* judgment, the European Commission had already taken the initiative of making provisions for solving the problems resulting from the *Ten Holder* ruling. At the time of the *Daalmeijer* judgment, the Regulation was not yet revised. The considerations of the Commission as recorded in the explanatory memorandum to the amending Regulation resemble those used in the *Daalmeijer* judgment: the *Ten Holder* judgment would be especially disadvantageous for inactive persons who had their last employment in a Member State with an insurance scheme based on completing periods of employment, who became resident in another Member State with an insurance scheme based on residence.[18]
On the grounds of these arguments, a new Article 13(2)(f) was adopted.[19]

Article 13(2)(f) reads:
'a person to whom the legislation of a Member State ceases to be applicable, without the legislation of another Member State becoming applicable to him in accordance with one of the rules laid down in the foregoing subparagraphs or in accordance with one of the exceptions or special provisions laid down in Articles 14 to 17 shall be subject to the legislation of the Member State in whose territory he resides in accordance with the provisions of that legislation alone.'

In other words, in the case of a person who is not engaged in employment and who ceases to be subject to the legislation of a Member State, without being subject to the legislation of another State, the legislation of the State of residence is applicable. Note that this is a departure from the general State of employment principle which underlies Regulation 1408/71.
The amending Regulation also amended Article 10*b* of Regulation 574/72. It now provides that the date and the conditions on which the legislation of a Member State ceases to be applicable to a person as referred to in Article 13(2)(f) of Regulation 1408/71, shall be determined in accordance with the provisions of that legislation.
As a result of these rules the following approach is to be followed:
- first it has to be determined whether a person has definitely terminated his professional activities. If this is not the case, he remains affiliated with the legislation under which his last activities as an employee or self-employed person were performed.
- if a person has definitely terminated his activities, the last legislation to which he has been subject can determine whether he is still affiliated with that system

---

[18]   Com. 90 335 final of 24 July 1990.
[19]   *OJ* 1992 *L* 206.

or not. For instance, a system can provide that persons who have worked under that scheme can remain affiliated. This is not often the case, however. A more frequent rule is that persons receiving benefit under a particular legislation, remain affiliated with that system.

- if after some time a person who has terminated his activities 'permanently' resumes his professional activities, Article 13(2)(f) is no longer applicable. The other rules for determining the legislation applicable revive in this case.

8.4.   Conflict Rules in Special Situations

There are situations which are more complicated than the one of an employee who accepts work in another Member State. The Regulation gives rules for, among other things, the following situations:

- a person normally employed in the territory of two or more Member States, is subject to the legislation of the Member State in whose territory he resides (Article 14(2)(b)(i));
- if persons work in more than one Member State and reside in neither of these States, the legislation of the Member State in whose territory the employer has his registered office or place of business is applicable (Article 14(2)(b)(ii));
- if a person is simultaneously employed in the territory of one Member State and self-employed in the territory of another Member State, the legislation of the Member State in the territory of which he is engaged in paid employment is applicable (Article 14c(a)).
- in Article 14c(b) it is provided that a person may be subject to the legislation of two Member States if he is simultaneously employed in the territory of one Member State and self-employed in the territory of another Member State. Such simultaneous application of national legislations is possible only when this is provided for in Annex VII. This Annex provides in Point I that a person who performs activities as self-employed person in Belgium and activities as an employed person in another Member State (except Luxembourg) is subject to such simultaneous application of legislations. This means that a person who works as a self-employed person in Belgium and as an employed person in the Netherlands falls under the social security system of the Netherlands as an employed person and under the Belgian system as a self-employed person.

This last rule, from Article 14c, is an exception, provided by the Regulation, to the exclusive effect of the rules for determining the legislation applicable of Title II of the Regulation. This rule was discussed in the *Van Poucke* judgment[20], in which the question was raised whether a person who works in one State as a *civil servant* and in another State as self-employed, can invoke Article 14c. The question could

---

[20]   Court of Justice 24 March 1994, Case 71/93, [1994] *ECR* I-1101.

arise, because Article 14c uses the terms 'is employed' and 'is self-employed'. It could be doubted whether the term 'is employed' is also relevant to civil servants.

> Van Poucke was working as a military doctor in Belgium and as a self-employed doctor in the Netherlands. As he worked as a self-employed person in the Netherlands he had to pay contributions for the Belgian insurance scheme for the self-employed (*see* Chapter 8). Van Poucke had the Belgium the legal status of civil servant and was therefore, in principle, not covered by the Regulation. The Belgian compulsory sickness and invalidity insurance scheme for employees was, however, extended to civil servants. As Van Poucke had the legal status of civil servant, he fell under the employees insurance scheme only with respect to the contingency of sickness and invalidity.

The Court considered that civil servants are considered as employees for the Treaty. For the purpose of the Community term 'employed person' of Article 48 of the EC Treaty, we must use the objective criteria which are characteristic for the employment relationship. It is a main characteristic for this employment relationship that a person works for another person under his supervision, and that he receives remuneration in reward. A person who performs activities as a civil servant, which fall within the scope of the Regulation, performs activities in the sense of Article 14c.

The next question was whether Article 14c had to be restricted to the branches of social security in respect of which the person concerned falls under the Regulation. The Court answered this question positively. Consequently, Van Poucke was also subject to the payment of contributions of the Belgian legislation on self-employed for his self-employed activities. The *De Jaeck* judgment[21] is relevant to the interpretation of Article 14c.

> De Jaeck, of Belgian nationality, resided in Belgium. He worked in 1984 as a self-employed person in Belgium. He was also director and sole shareholder of a limited company in the Netherlands, in which country he worked generally two days a week. Because of his activities in the Netherlands he was charged with payments of contributions to the Dutch national insurance scheme.

The question whether this was allowed depended on the question whether he was employed or self-employed in the Netherlands. If he was self-employed in the Netherlands, Article 14a(2) of the Regulation would be applicable, and it would be possible to require contribution in Belgium only. If he was employee in the Netherlands, contribution was required in both Belgium and the Netherlands (Article 14c(b)).

The Court considered that the question raised was whether a person in the situation of De Jaeck performs, for the application of Article 14a and Article 14c

---

[21] Court of Justice 30 January 1997, Case 340/94, [1997] *ECR* I-461.

respectively, activities 'as an employee' or 'as a self-employed person'. How are these terms to be interpreted? The Regulation does not give a definition of these terms.

A complication was that the case law of the Dutch Supreme Court meant that a director who was main shareholder was considered to work as an employee for the company. This meant that contributions for the national insurance schemes were to be collected from him in the same way as in the case of employees. The Central Court for Social Security on the other hand did not consider a director who was main shareholder as an employee for the employees' insurances. The question was therefore whether De Jaeck was an employee or a self-employed person.

The Court considered that it has consistently held that for the interpretation of a Community rule not only the terms used are relevant. The context of these terms and the objectives of the Regulation of which these terms form part also have to be taken into account. Article 1(a) and Article 2(1) of the Regulation are relevant to this purpose. These Articles provide that the Regulation applies to employed persons or self-employed persons to whom the social security legislation of one or more Member States has been applicable. The terms 'employed person' and 'self-employed person' of the Regulation refer in this way, the Court argued, to the definitions of these terms in the social security legislations of the Member States and not to the definitions of these terms in labour law. Although Title II uses terms 'other than employed person' or 'self-employed person', a logical and coherent interpretation of the personal scope of the Regulation and the system of conflict rules of the Regulation requires that the terms concerned of Title II of the Regulation are interpreted while taking the definitions of Article 1(a) into account.

For this purpose the approach described in Section 6.2.1. is relevant, where for national insurance schemes it is necessary to distinguish employed persons and self-employed persons from others, either by the manner a scheme is administered or financed or by the criteria given in the Annex.

The Court decided that since, according to the case law of the Dutch Supreme Court, the contributions were collected in the same way as for employees, the director who was sole shareholder can be considered as an employee as the way of financing designates him as an employee.

The Court now had to solve the problem that it had, in the *Van Poucke* judgment, answered the question whether Van Poucke could as a civil servant fall under the term 'employed person', taken Article 48 of the Treaty into account, in other words, it had used the approach in labour law. The Court retreated from this approach, now that the provisions of Title II are concerned. These provisions do not have as objective to award special rights to the persons referred to in these provisions, which the Member States could withhold in particular cases, the Court argued. They only have as objective to decide which national legislation is applicable and cannot serve to decide under which conditions there is a right or obligation to participate in a scheme of social security. It cannot be assumed that the Community legislator has given to the terms 'employed person' and 'self-employed person' an autonomous Community meaning, inspired by labour law definitions with respect to the rules for determining the legislation applicable. The Court acknowledged that it used in the *Van Poucke* judgment the term 'employed person' in the sense of Article 48 of the Treaty, in order to decide whether the activities as civil servant were also activities as an employed person in the sense of Article 14*c*. This case concerned, however, an interpretation problem concerning Title II specifically. This argument is not relevant here.

The national court had also raised the question, whether, if Article 14*c* is applicable to an insured person who works only a few days a week in its territory, Community law prohibits the Member State from taking into account the contributions paid by this insured person concerning his work done on the other days of the week in the other Member State. The Court remarked that it follows from Article 14*c* that the person concerned is obliged to pay the contributions which are required on the basis of each of the legislations. According to Article 14*c* (b) in the cases mentioned in Annex VII the legislation of each of these States is applicable only as far as the activities concerned are performed in its territory. Consequently, no provision of the Regulation obliges a Member State to take account of the contributions paid by the person concerned in the other Member State.

For some situations there appeared to be no rules for determining the legislation applicable. An example of such a situation is the *Aldewereld* judgment.[22]

> The case concerned a person of Dutch nationality, who was recruited by an enterprise established in Germany. Immediately after his recruitment he was sent to Thailand. After some time Aldewereld received a request to pay contributions to the Dutch national insurance scheme. If he had been working in Germany, this payment could not have been required because of the effect of the rules for determining the legislation applicable. How was this problem to be solved now he was not working in the territory of the European Union?

The Court answered that the sole fact that an employee is employed outside the territory of the Community does not prevent the applicability of Community rules on the free movement of workers, on condition that the employment relationship remains sufficiently narrowly linked with that territory. In the case of Aldewereld there was such a link, because this employee from the Community was engaged by an enterprise of another Member State. As a result he was linked to the social security system of that State. But which system did the rules for determining the legislation applicable assign as applicable?

In general, the Court argued, the place of residence of the employed person and the place where the employer is established are the only connecting factors with the legislation of that State. These factors also have to be used in this case, as the Regulation does not contain rules with respect to this situation. The State of residence is only of subordinate significance as a criterion for determining the legislation applicable within the framework of the Regulation. This criterion is used only if the legislation of the State of residence is linked with the employment relationship.

---

[22]   Court of Justice 29 June 1994, Case 60/93, [1994] *ECR* I-2991.

When the employed person does not reside in one of the Member States where he works, usually the legislation of the place of establishment of the employer is applied. In the case of Aldewereld the legislation of the State of residence of the employed person could not be applied, because this legislation did not have any points of connection with the employment relationship. This is the case with the legislation of the State where the employer is established.

The argument of the Court meant that the German legislation was applicable and that, as a result, the Netherlands could not require payment of national insurance contributions.

If a person performs normally activities as an employed person in two Member States during a particular period, Article 14 (2)(b)(i) and (ii) is applicable. This article states that a person normally employed in the territory of two or more Member States shall be subject to the legislation of the Member State in whose territory he resides, if he pursues his activity partly in that territory or if he is attached to several undertakings or several employers who have their registered office or places of business in the territory of different Member States. If he does not reside in the territory of one of the States where he performs his activities, the legislation of the State where the registered office or place of business of the enterprise employing him is situated is applicable.

This Article creates some borderline disputes with the rules on posting, discussed in the following Chapter. In case of posting, a person is temporarily engaged in work in another Member State. It can happen that periods of posting consist of short periods, interspersed with periods of work in the State of origin. When does this situation amount to 'normally working in two Member States'? It will depend on the factual circumstances whether we will call this a posting or an Article 14(2) situation. In any case, if a person works each week for some hours in another Member State for a period of more than twelve months, this can no longer called 'posting'.

8.5.   The Rules for the Special Non-Contributory Benefits

Rules are given in Article 4(2a) on a special type of benefits, *see* Section 7.6. For these benefits, there is a special rule for determining the legislation applicable, Article 10a(1).

Article 10a(1) provides:
'Notwithstanding the provisions of Article 10 and Title III, persons to whom this Regulation applies shall be granted the special non-contributory cash benefits referred to in Article 4(2a) exclusively in the territory of the Member State in which they reside, in accordance with the legislation of that state, provided that such benefits are listed in Annex IIa. Such benefits shall be granted by and at the expense of the institution of the place of residence.'

This is a special rule for the special non-contributory benefits - *i.e.* those covered by Article 4(2*a*). They are treated in a special way, as the legislation of the State of residence is decisive as to whether one receives these benefits or not.

Chapter 9

The Rules on Posting in Regulation 1408/71

9.1.   Posting on the Basis of Article 14

If the legislation of the State of employment were applicable also to employees who go to work in another Member State for a short period only, this would impede the free movement of workers. Therefore an exception is made to the main rule, that the legislation of the State of employment is applicable. The exception can be found in Article 14(1) of the Regulation.

> This Article provides that a person employed in the territory of a Member State by an undertaking to which he is normally attached who is posted by that undertaking to the territory of another Member State to perform work there for that undertaking shall continue to be subject to the legislation of the first Member State, provided that the anticipated duration of that work does not exceed twelve months and that he is not sent to replace another person who has completed his term of posting.

Posting is possible for a maximum period of twelve months. If the duration of the work to be done extends beyond the duration originally anticipated, owing to unforeseeable circumstances, and exceeds twelve months, the legislation of the first Member State continues to apply with another maximum period of twelve months. In this case the competent authority of the Member State in whose territory the person concerned is posted has to be asked for its consent. A condition for posting is that a person must not be sent in order to replace another person who has completed his term of posting.

For the purpose of posting, the employer and employee can apply for a so-called E 101 form from the competent authorities in the Member States. Extension has to be applied by means of the E 102 form.

The Regulation does not give a definition of the term 'posting'. The text of Article 14 seems to mean that posting is possible only with employees who have worked for some time for an enterprise and who subsequently start to work for that enterprise in the territory of another Member State.

The Court ruled, however, that the provisions on posting apply also in the case of an employed person who has not worked in the State where the enterprise is established, but who is recruited exclusively to be sent abroad.[1] The Court requires, however, an organic link between the undertaking and the employed person and that the enterprise normally performs its activities in the territory of the first Member State. When satisfying these criteria temporary employment agencies can also use the posting system set out in Article 14.

In Decision 128[2] the Administrative Commission gave an interpretation of the term 'posting' in the Regulation. The Decision ruled that there must be an organic link between the sending undertaking and the employed person. In order to accept such a link, it is important, the Decision provided that that the undertaking pays wages to the employed person and has the power to dismiss. In 1996 a new decision was made by the Administrative Commission[3], Decision 162, which gives more stringent criteria in order to decide on the organic link. The latter Decision requires that the sending undertaking must, among other things, be responsible for recruiting, the contract of employment, dismissal and decision on the type of activities the employee has to perform. The number of criteria is not limited.

The rules on posting can also be applied to a temporary employment agency, on condition, as we have already seen, that there is an organic link. In Decision 162 a condition is added to this criterion, which is that in case of an undertaking whose activity consists of the temporary posting of manpower to other enterprises, it is required that this enterprise normally posts employees to users in the territory of the sending Member State. A temporary employment agency is therefore not allowed to concentrate itself on posting employees to another Member State, if it wishes to rely on the posting articles of the Regulation.

There can also be other situations than that of workers for temporary employment agencies, in which persons are recruited especially for posting. This can be the case, for example, in case of a business which posts its employees to the enterprises of the business. In this case also it is necessary that the enterprise which posts the employee performs substantial activities in the territory of the sending Member State and normally employs its employees in that State.

> For instance, an undertaking working in Britain, which wants to recruit Portuguese workers, cannot open an office (letter box company) in Portugal, with the sole objective of employing the Portuguese workers by means of this office in Britain and of using the posting system of Article 14 of the Regulation, in order to benefit from the lower Portuguese social security contributions.

The posting provisions apply, in principle, for twelve months. If the employee returns for a short period to the sending State, in order to work in that State, and subsequently returns, it is straightforward to extend the maximum period of posting (twelve calender months) with the period of interruption. In case of a temporary

---

[1] Court of Justice 17 December 1970, Case 35/70, *Manpower*, [1970] *ECR* 1970, 1251.
[2] *OJ* 1986 *C* 141.
[3] *OJ* 1996 *L* 241/28.

employment agency, which will often have to deal with periods of interruption of posting, this would lead to an extremely untransparent and complex situation. Therefore it is provided with respect to workers recruited especially for being posted abroad, that the temporary interruption of the activities of the employee are not considered as periods of interruption for the purpose of the rules on posting.

It is possible that the undertaking to which an employed person has been posted, posts this worker on its turn to another enterprise in the receiving State or even to a third Member State. Decision 162 provides that the rules on posting do not apply in this case.

Decision 162 contains some supervision rules. The competent authority of the sending State has to inform the borrowing employer and the employed person 'suitably' on the conditions they have to satisfy. The posted employee and his employer have to inform the competent authority of the sending State of some aspects of posting. The competent authorities of the sending State and the State of employment have to elaborate the required supervision measures. Such supervision measures are important, because some Member States have an interest in posting as many workers as possible. This is positive to their unemployment figures. The problem is that Decision 162 is not binding, so that we do not know whether these recommendations will have effect. Because of the conflicting interests of the Member States it did not seem possible to make a stronger rule in the Regulation itself.

A question often heard is whether one must have worked a certain period for the posting enterprise after a period of posting, before one can be posted again by that enterprise. Article 14(1) does not give a solution to this problem. It seems to be logical that such requirement exist, given the rules on the limitation of the duration of posting and the limitation to the extension of the period. The Decisions and the Regulation do not provide such rules.

Another problem is that persons without a posting declaration (E 101 form) also go to work abroad. This often happens. The posting rules of the Regulation also apply in this case, as a posting declaration is not a necessary condition for posting.

The *Calle Grenzshop* judgment[4] concerned a situation in which the employer and employee thought that the employee worked under a posting construction. It appeared that, in fact, on this situation Article 14(2) was applicable (*see,* Section 8.4).

Calle operated a business in Germany, near to the German-Danish border, which retails food, alcoholic drinks and gifts. It employed almost exclusively Danish workers who are resident in Denmark. Those employees include Mr Wandahl, who has worked for Calle since 1979, initially as a salesman, and since 1981 as a manager. Neither Wandahl nor the other Danish employees were the subject of any notification by Calle to the German social insurance institutions. By decision of 21 December 1987 the German benefit administration claimed from Calle payment of social insurance contributions

---

[4]   Court of Justice 16 February 1995, Case 45/93, [1995] *ECR* I-269.

with respect to Mr Wandahl. Mr Wandahl had a posting declaration issued by the Danish Minister for social security that he fulfilled the conditions for posting since 1 January 1985. The question was whether such a declaration was binding. Mr Wandahl worked in the disputed period for the enterprise for ten hours a week in Denmark and for thirty hours a week in Germany.

The Court ruled that this situation cannot fall within the posting provisions of the Regulation since the duration of the work performed by the person concerned in Denmark for the undertaking to which he is normally attached exceeds 12 months. On the other hand, that situation does fall within Article 14(2)(b)(i) which provides that a person normally employed in the territory of two or more Member States is to be subject to the legislation of the Member State in whose territory he resides, if he pursues his activity partly in that territory or if he is attached to several undertakings or several employers who have their registered offices or places of business in the territory of different Member States.

9.2. Article 17 Agreements

Another important exception from the main rules for determining the legislation applicable is laid down in Article 17. This article states that 'two or more Member States, the competent authorities of these States, or the bodies designated by these authorities may by common agreement provide for exceptions to the provisions of Articles 13 to 16, in the interest of certain categories of persons or of certain persons'. This provision allows the making of agreements on, for instance, employed persons who are posted by their employer for a duration exceeding twelve months, because of their special knowledge or proficiency, or because of specific objectives of the undertaking or organization concerned.[5]

Is it also possible to make an Article 17 agreement to repair situations with retroactive effect. This may be necessary if no legislation or the wrong one has been applied to a person and this has to be corrected. This question raised in the *Brusse* judgment.[6]

> Brusse, a Dutch national, was a correspondent for *de Volkskrant* in London. As soon as he was employed there in 1964, he should have become subject to United Kingdom legislation. However, Brusse did not join the United Kingdom system, and voluntarily continued to pay contributions for the Dutch social security benefits. In 1977, his situation came to the attention of the United Kingdom authorities. They contacted the Dutch authorities and agreed that

---

[5]   The Administrative Commission recommends that competent bodies of the Member States make agreements on the basis of Article 17, *see* Recommendation 16 of 12 December 1984, *OJ C* 273 of 24 October 1985.
[6]   Court of Justice 17 May 1984, Case 101/83, [1984] *ECR* 1285.

Brusse was to remain under the Dutch legislation until the beginning of 1978. After this date, he was to become subject to United Kingdom legislation. Subsequently, the employer asked the Dutch competent benefit administration to pay family allowance to Brusse until the end of 1977. This administration refused on the grounds that according to the Dutch child benefit Act, persons are insured only if they are residents, or if they have to pay income tax on income from work as an employed earner in the Netherlands. The question was whether an agreement on the basis of Article 17 can with retroactive effect withdraw a person from the legislation of a Member State.

The Court considered that Title III of the Regulation intended to designate the legislation of one Member State as applicable. However, in some cases the application of this might lead to administrative complications. Hence the special provisions given in Articles 14 to 16. In addition, Article 17 allows a deviation from this provision, and it is up to the Member States to apply it, provided that it is in the interest of the employed person. This can also be with retroactive effect. The decisive criterion is, as we can seen in the judgment, whether it is in the interest of the employed person that the agreement is made.

Chapter 10

The Equal Treatment Provisions of Article 48 and Regulation 1408/71

10.1. Introduction

One of the most important principles which underlies the EC Treaty, is the prohibition of discrimination on grounds of nationality. This principle is as a general rule laid down in Article 6 of the Treaty.[1] As regards social policy more specifically, Article 48(2) of the Treaty provides that freedom of movement for workers entails the abolition of any discrimination based on nationality between employed persons of the Member States as regards employment, remuneration and other conditions of employment. For social security, the principle of equal treatment is explicitly confirmed in Article 3 of Regulation 1408/71. Alongside Regulation 1408/71, Regulation 1612/68 can be relevant to combatting unequal treatment on the basis of nationality in social security, see Chapter 11.

Given this number of provisions forbidding discrimination on the basis of nationality, the question arose whether they can all be applied simultaneously, and if not, what order would be followed.

The Court ruled in the *Masgio* judgment[2], that Article 7 of the Treaty (now Article 6) can only pertain to those issues not covered by specific anti-discrimination rules of the Treaty. Consequently, social security rules which are suspected of discrimination will have to be considered on the basis of Articles 48 to 51 of the Treaty and Article 3 of Regulation 1408/71.

10.2. The Equal Treatment Provision of Article 48 of the Treaty

Two judgments of the Court of Justice concerning family benefit are important to demonstrate how the Regulation itself must not infringe upon the equal treatment provision of the EC Treaty. These decisions concerned residence requirements in national legislation which appeared to be disadvantageous to migrants. The first is the *Pinna* case.[3]

---

[1]   Before the Treaty on the EU came into force, this was Article 7.
[2]   Court of Justice 7 March 1991, Case 10/90, [1991] *ECR* I-1119.
[3]   Court of Justice 15 January 1986, Case 41/84, [1986] *ECR* 1.

The then Article 73(2) of Regulation 1408/71 made a distinction between France and the other Member States with respect to child benefit. The provision concerned provided that the State-of-employment principle was applicable to States other than France, whereas the State-of-residence principle applied to France. As a result, persons employed in France received for their children residing, for example, in Greece, child benefit in accordance with the Greek rules (they received the Greek amount). The other Member States were to apply their own child benefit rates for the persons employed in their country, regardless of where the children resided.

The Court declared that Article 73(2) was invalid in so far as it precluded the award to employed persons subject to French legislation of French family benefits for members of their family residing in the territory of another Member State.

The Court considered that Article 51 of the EC Treaty provides for coordination, not the harmonisation, of the legislation of the Member States. As a result, Article 51 leaves in being differences between the Member States' social security systems, and, consequently, in the rights of workers employed in the Member States. Nevertheless, the achievement of the objective of securing free movement for workers within the Community, is facilitated if conditions of employment, including social security rules, are as similar as possible in the various Member States. That objective will, however, be imperilled and made more difficult to realise if unnecessary differences in the social security rules are introduced by Community law. It follows, the Court added, that the Community rules on social security introduced pursuant to Article 51 EC Treaty must refrain from adding to the disparities which already stem from the absence of harmonisation of national legislation.

The then Article 73 of the Regulation created two different systems for migrant workers depending on whether they are subject to French legislation or to the legislation of another Member State. Accordingly, it added to the disparities caused by national legislation and, as a result, impeded the achievement of the aims set out in Articles 48 to 51 of the Treaty. More specifically with regard to the assessment of the validity of Article 73(2) itself, it must be stated that the principle of equal treatment prohibits not only overt discrimination based on nationality but all covert forms of discrimination which, by applying other distinguishing criteria, in fact achieve the same result. That is precisely the case, the Court reasoned, when the criterion set out in Article 73(2) is used to determine the legislation applicable to the family benefits of a migrant worker. Although as a general rule the French legislation employs the same criterion to determine the entitlement to family benefits of a French worker employed in French territory, that criterion is by no means equally important for that category of worker, since the problem of members of the family residing outside France arises essentially for migrant workers.[4]

---

[4]   *See*, for a more detailed discussion of child benefits, Chapter 16.

The *Pinna* judgment is an example of a successful appeal to the indirect discrimination principle. This was different in the *Lenoir* decision.[5]

Until his retirement, Lenoir lived and worked in France only, where he was entitled to a supplement for sole wage-earners and a school allowance for his children. After his retirement he went to live in England, but in this State he was not entitled to these French benefits. Lenoir could not rely on the provision of the Regulation on the export of family allowances as provided for in Article 77 of the Regulation, since family allowances are (according to Article 1(u)(ii) Regulation 1408/71) periodical cash benefits granted exclusively by reference to the number of and the age of the members of the family. In this case it was not disputed that the French benefits which Lenoir wished to claim did not exclusively depend on the number or age of the children, but also, among other things, on the income of the parents. Neither was it disputed that the term 'family allowances' had a limited meaning (it did not cover the school and sole wage-earner allowances). Instead, it was uncertain whether the limitation of Article 77 to family allowances was valid. The Advocate-General reasoned that this provision resulted in indirect discrimination on grounds of nationality, since it would be migrant workers in particular who would be affected by this Article. Restrictions on the export of family benefit restricted the freedom of movement of workers, as required by Article 51 EC Treaty.

The Court considered that Article 51 EC Treaty only provides for coordination of social security systems of the Member States and not for harmonisation. Article 51 does not remove the differences between social security systems; neither are differences between the rights of persons there employed affected. However, as the Court ruled already in the *Pinna* decision, Community regulations are not to create new disparities alongside those which exist because of the lack of harmonisation of national legislations. This decision does not mean, however, that all disparities are prohibited. The Court ruled that Articles 7 (now 6) and 48 of the Treaty do not pertain to possible disparities in treatment of employed persons which may ensue from the differences between the *national* legislations, on the condition that these regulations hold for all persons who are subject to these regulations on the grounds of objective criteria and irrespective of the nationality of the persons concerned.

The provision questioned in the *Lenoir* case had the objective of enabling the export of family benefit for pensioners (Article 77). This rule applied to all residents of the Member States and it was based on objective conditions. From this it followed that if a Member State has a family benefit scheme, the benefits on the basis of this scheme have to be paid regardless of the place of residence of the persons concerned. On the other hand, benefits other than family benefits or benefits with conditions which are not mentioned in Article 1(u)(ii), such as school benefits, are usually directly linked to a particular social situation existing in the state which established

---

[5]   Court of Justice 27 September 1988, Case 313/86, [1988] *ECR* 5391.

that scheme. Under these circumstances, the Court argued, it cannot be said that such a national regulation, which links the payment of benefits to residence requirements, creates new disparities or that it implements criteria which result in discrimination on grounds of nationality.

A final judgment, discussed in this section, is the *Roviello* decision,[6] in which the Court ruled that a provision of an Annex to the Regulation was contrary to Article 48 Treaty. On the basis of the rule in the Annex, only periods of employment completed in Germany were taken into account for the calculation of the German occupational disablement pension. Although the disputed rule did not make a distinction on grounds of nationality, it mainly applied to migrant workers from other Member States who consecutively worked in those Member States and in Germany. The Court ruled that this condition was incompatible with the principle of equal treatment as guaranteed by the Treaty.

Article 48(3) allows for restrictions on the freedom of movement of workers only which can be justified on the basis of public order, public safety and public health. Apart from these situations explicitly mentioned in the EC Treaty, impediments to the free movement cannot be justified, the Court ruled in the *Masgio* judgment.

In the *Bachman* judgment[7] the Court was asked to consider a ground of justification based on the public order exception in Article 48 of the Treaty.

> This case concerned benefits which do not fall under the Regulation, *i.e.* supplementary pensions. Mr Bachmann, of German nationality, took out, before he went to Belgium where he entered into a contract of employment, private voluntary insurance against illness and disability from a German private company. Bachmann wished to deduct the contributions concerned on these insurances from his Belgian income taxes. The Belgian legislation did not allow this; according to Article 54 of the Tax Law, such contributions could only be deducted when paid to Belgian companies. In the proceedings before the Court, the Belgian Government argued, in order to justify these provisions, that they did not make a distinction between Belgian workers and workers of other Member States, who continued their insurances taken out abroad.

The Court did not accept this argument; it will mainly be migrant workers who have taken out insurance before coming to Belgium. This rule was liable to be especially disadvantageous to workers who were nationals of another Member State.

Belgium argued furthermore that the pensions, interests and capital which were received as a result of this insurance were not taxable under Belgian Law. This was also the reason why Belgian law did not allow the deduction of contributions on taxes; no deduction of contributions and no tax liability on benefits. However, it might occur that after they had returned to their home State, these people would have to pay taxes on the sums they received from this insurance. According to the Belgian Government,

---

[6]   Court of Justice 7 June 1988, Case 237/78, [1988] *ECR* 2805.
[7]   Court of Justice 28 January 1992, Case 204/90, [1992] *ECR* I-249.

this violation of the free movement of workers is not the result of Belgian law, but due to a lack of harmonisation of tax legislations of the Member States. Again, the Court ruled that this argument could not be accepted. In practice, it will be mainly the nationals of other Member States who return to countries where tax is paid on these amounts; these nationals are unable to compensate for the fact that they cannot deduct the contributions from income tax. This is indeed the result of a lack of harmonisation. It can, however, not be held that Article 48 of the Treaty is not relevant just because of this lack of harmonisation. The Belgian argument that a national could solve the problem by cancelling the insurance bought in another Member State, was not accepted, since this would involve efforts and costs to the person concerned which would be a violation of the right of free movement.

All these arguments did not alter the fact that the rule constituted indirect discrimination which was prohibited by Article 48 of the Treaty. However, the abolition of any discrimination is subject to limitations justified on grounds of public order. The Court considered that it was essential to the Member States to maintain the coherency of their tax legislation. This coherency required that if the Member State had, on the basis of Community law, to allow the deduction of contributions from taxes, it must also be able to impose taxes on the sums paid by the insurance, even when the payments take place in another State. There were problems of a practical nature, however, in finding out how much is paid in another State; it would also be problematic to oblige insurances companies to deduct taxes. Of course, the obligation on an insurance company to deduct taxes could be realised by demanding a guarantee, but this again results in extra costs for the worker, which will be added to the contributions. Moreover, this opens the possibility of double tax levy on these sums, so that, because of the higher contribution rates, the insured persons will no longer be interested in foreign insurances. A solution to this would only be possible by means of a (conclusive system of) bilateral agreements or by means of harmonisation initiatives by the Commission. In the present state of Community law, the coherency of the tax legislation could not be ensured by less restrictive provisions than those of the Belgian legislation. Consequently, they were not incompatible with Article 48 of the EC Treaty.

Apparently the Court, with an eye on the disruptive consequences of a radical application of the prohibition of indirect discrimination provisions, hesitated to apply Article 48 radically in a clear case of suspected indirect discrimination.

10.3.   Article 3 of Regulation 1408/71

10.3.1. Prohibition of Direct and Indirect Discrimination

Article 3 of Regulation 1408/71 reads:
'Subject to the special provisions of this Regulation, persons resident in the territory of one of the Member States to whom this Regulation applies shall be

subject to the same obligations and enjoy the same benefits under the legislation of any Member State as the nationals of that State'.

There are important restrictions on the possibility of invoking Regulation 1408/71. These restrictions have been discussed in previous chapters. One of these is that in order to rely on the Regulation, it is necessary that the person concerned has undertaken activities in a State other than the State of origin. This restriction was found, for example, in the *Petit* judgment.[8]

> Mr Petit had filed in a petition to the Labour Court in French. The Belgian law on languages to be used in legal proceedings prescribed the Dutch language in a case like this. The use of another language would make the case of the person concerned inadmissible. Mr Petit had Belgian nationality and had never been employed in a state other than Belgium.

The Court considered that it has consistently held that the rules of the Treaty ensuring the free movement of workers and the Regulation 1408/71 were not applicable to activities all elements of which are restricted to the territory of a single Member State only.

Furthermore, Article 3 of Regulation 1408/71 can be applied only to persons who are subject to the personal scope of the Regulation. *See*, the *Buhari Haji* judgment.[9]

> Buhari was born in 1914 in Nigeria, and had British nationality until 1964. In 1964 he obtained Nigerian nationality. From 1937 until 1986 he worked in Belgian Congo and until the declaration of independence of this State, he paid social security contributions to the Belgian social security administration and in 1986 he applied for a Belgian pension. According to the Belgian regulation the old age pension is paid to persons who are in the territory of a State which has conclude a reciprocity agreement with Belgium. A Belgian court concluded that the national rules involved discrimination on basis of nationality.

The Court, however, ruled that Buhari could not invoke Article 3, because he did not fall under the personal scope of the Regulation as he did not have the nationality of one of the Member States.

The principle of equality of treatment under EC law is to be broadly interpreted. Not only direct discrimination on grounds of nationality is prohibited, but all rules which, by applying seemingly neutral criteria lead to discriminatory effects, so-called indirect discrimination. As regards the coordination Regulation, the suspicion of indirect discrimination will especially arise when benefit conditions can be fulfilled much more easily by nationals of the Member State in question, than by subjects with

---

[8]   Court of Justice 22 September 1992, Case 153/91, [1992] *ECR* I-4973.
[9]   Court of Justice 14 October 1990, Case 105/89, [1990] *ECR* 4211.

another nationality, or when benefit entitlement ends much sooner for foreign beneficiaries than for the nationals of that Member State.

If such effects occur there is still only a *suspicion* of discrimination; this can be refuted if objective grounds for justification can be presented.

In several decisions, the Court pointed out that the costs of the measure or implementation problems are not reasons which are a basis for objective justification.

An example of a case in which national rules were challenged for causing indirect discrimination is the *Toia* judgment.[10]

The French Social Security Code provided for an allowance for women with children; this benefit was paid to persons aged at least sixty-five, with French nationality who were of insufficient means. In addition the claimant must have brought up at least five dependent children for at least nine years before their sixteenth birthday. Those children must be of French nationality on the date on which entitlement. Diamante Palermo (née Toia), of Italian nationality, was the mother of seven children. She was resident in France and applied for this benefit. Benefit was refused on the grounds that five of the children had possessed Italian nationality from birth. The French institute argued that the purpose of this benefit was to increase the birth rate in France.

The Court considered that the condition in question was capable of leading in fact to the result that a mother of foreign nationality might benefit from the allowance in only exceptional cases. Therefore the condition concerning the nationality of children must be regarded as indirect discrimination, unless it was justified by objective grounds. The reason presented by France could not be such a justification. The benefit in question was an old-age benefit of a non-contributory nature; secondly, Regulation 1408/71 did not make any distinction between the social security schemes according to whether those schemes did or did not pursue objectives of demographic policy. As an old-age benefit was involved, the Court continued, the condition concerned could not be regarded as a rule designed to prevent the overlapping of similar benefits under the legislation of different Member States.

The Court concluded that no other arguments to show that the condition concerning the nationality of children was based on an objective difference had been advanced before the Court. It must be inferred that the condition in question constituted indirect discrimination between nationals of Member States subject to social security schemes covered by Regulation 1408/71.

However, rules suggesting indirect discrimination are not always forbidden by the Court, *see* the *Coonan* judgment.[11]

Una Coonan was an Irish woman who settled in Great Britain at the age of sixty-three. At that time she had not attained Irish retirement age, whereas she was

---

[10]   Court of Justice 12 July 1979, Case 237/78, [1979] *ECR* 2645.
[11]   Court of Justice 24 April 1980, Case 110/79, [1980] *ECR* 1445.

above the retirement age as defined in the United Kingdom legislation. She engaged in paid employment in Britain. The United Kingdom social security system provided that if a worker continued to be employed as such beyond pensionable age under that legislation, he was entitled thereafter to cash sickness benefits *only* if he would have been entitled to a particular kind of retirement pension under national legislation in the event of his ceasing to work. Since that entitlement to a retirement pension could derive only from affiliation to a national social security system during the period prior to retirement, it necessarily followed that a person, whether of United Kingdom or of foreign nationality, who, before reaching pensionable age, had never completed qualifying periods in that Member State or who had completed only an insufficient number of qualifying periods in that State to be entitled to a pension, did not fulfil that condition. If that person continued to work in the United Kingdom, he could not therefore claim, in the event of illness, to receive cash benefits which the legislation awards to workers.

That situation could be remedied only if affiliation in another Member State before pension age in the United Kingdom was treated as equivalent to affiliation in the latter Member State. The issue between the parties in this case amounted in substance to the question whether or not Community law provided for such equivalence.

As far as Regulation 1408/71 was concerned the question, the Court argued, amounted in substance to asking whether that Regulation gives an employed person in the claimant's situation the right to be affiliated to the social security scheme of the Member State to which he goes to work for the first time, even though he is refused that right on the basis of national provisions only. It is for the legislature of each Member State to lay down the conditions creating the right or the obligation to become affiliated to a social security scheme or to a particular branch under such a scheme. This only holds provided always that in this connection there is no discrimination between nationals of the host state and nationals of the other Member States. Consequently, if national legislation makes affiliation to a social security scheme conditional in certain circumstances on prior affiliation by the person concerned to the national social security scheme, Regulation 1408/71 does not compel Member States to treat as equivalent insurance periods completed in another Member State and those which were completed previously on national territory.

The Court did not consider the question whether indirect discrimination was involved in this case, although the Advocate-General had argued that in the case of the United Kingdom provisions there was indirect discrimination. The European Commission had considered that as United Kingdom nationals could be confronted with this rule it would be unjust to declare the United Kingdom legislation void for the benefit of nationals of other Member States. The Advocate-General did not follow this argument: it was up to the Member States to seek solutions for such problems and the argument as such was not a ground for refuting the suspicion of indirect discrimination.

In the *Coonan* case, the United Kingdom legislation which excluded persons above retirement age from sickness benefit, did, in my opinion, certainly raise the suspicion of discrimination. The Court, however, in this case did not go into the issue of discrimination, but only mentioned the powers of the Member States to provide the conditions for affiliation. Sometimes, the problem with the doctrine of indirect discrimination is that a broad interpretation of this term means that many differences between the social security schemes of Member States will come under debate on the grounds that the differences are not allowed as they affect, in particular, nationals of other Member States. A prohibition of such differences on this basis is, however, against the approach of the Court that Article 51 of the Treaty does not affect the variation between the social security schemes of the Member States. As can be seen, the Court is anxious to find a way between the indirect discrimination concept and the latter approach. On the other hand, an unpredictable interpretation of the concept of indirect discrimination is problematic, since this will result in uncertainty in respect of national rules as to when these involve indirect discrimination, and when they do not. One could even argue that in the *Coonan* case the solution could have been given without really affecting the powers of the national legislator to establish the conditions of affiliation, as, in order to take away the indirectly discriminatory character of the United Kingdom rules, it was simply enough to assimilate foreign periods of insurance or foreign benefits to their United Kingdom equivalents. It is, therefore, not completely clear why the Court chose to follow the approach it did.

Provisions of Regulation 1408/71 may mean that migrant workers are better off than workers who never left their country of origin. This is a problem that mainly occurs as a result of the effects of the calculation rules set out in the Regulation for long-term benefits which are discussed in Chapter 15. Such effects are not precluded by the Community anti-discrimination provisions: they are merely the result of the fact that the Regulation provides for co-ordination only, and not for harmonisation.[12]

If a scheme is accused of indirect discrimination, grounds of objective justification can be presented in order to show that there is no indirect discrimination. In several judgments the Court ruled that arguments related to costs and implementation problems cannot constitute objective grounds of justification, *see,* for instance, the already mentioned *Masgio* judgment.

Article 51 of the EC Treaty does not affect the differences between the social security systems of the Member States; neither does this Article interfere with the rights of persons employed in these States. From this it follows that if nationals of different Member States are affected by a rule of a foreign social security system with disadvantageous effects, these cannot be compensated on the basis of the equal treatment principle. *See,* for example, the *Kenny* judgment.[13]

Kenny, of Irish nationality, resided in Great Britain. As, in Ireland, he had been sentenced to a term in prison, he was imprisoned during a visit to Ireland. While in prison, he became ill and he was taken to hospital. After his return to Great Britain, he applied for a United Kingdom sickness benefit for this period. United

---

[12] Court of Justice 13 October, Case 22/77, *Mura*, [1977] *ECR* 1699.
[13] Court of Justice 28 June 1978, Case 1/78, [1978] *ECR* 1489.

Kingdom law on this issue excludes imprisoned persons from sickness benefit. Although this law provides that one is ineligible for benefit in case of imprisonment, traditionally this had the meaning of *imprisonment in Great Britain*. The extension of this rule to imprisonment in a foreign country would be a deviation from the original interpretation. On the other hand, if it was not for the coordination Regulation, the possibility of applying for United Kingdom sickness benefit while abroad would not have existed. Although a broad interpretation of the term *imprisonment* seemed most obvious, it was argued that there might be a considerable difference between rules of penal law and prosecution of Member States. It was therefore possible that a fact in one State could lead to suspension of benefit received from another State, whereas the same fact in the other State would not cause suspension. Is this indirect discrimination?

The Court was asked whether a Member State had the right to assimilate facts in the territory of another State to corresponding facts in the national territory, if these facts, when occurring in the national territory, mean that there is no right to benefit.

The Court ruled that the national legislation is allowed to impose conditions, provided that no discrimination is made. The prohibition on discrimination on nationality does not pertain to possible differences in treatment resulting from the differences between the legislations of Member States, provided that these legislations are based on objective criteria and do not take into account the nationality of the person concerned.

10.3.2. Members of the Family and Survivors

In Section 6.3. the *Cabanis* judgment was discussed.[14]

The Dutch benefit administration offered the widow of a French employee voluntary insurance, in order to repair periods she had not been insured for the Dutch statutory old age insurance. The contribution rules were less attractive for foreigners than for Dutch claimants. The question was whether this was allowed.

The Court considered that it had decided in the *Kermaschek* judgment that the only rights which the members of a worker's family can claim, are derived rights, that is to say those acquired through their status as a member of a worker's family. In the light of this case law a widow or widower of a migrant worker could not invoke Article 3 of Regulation 1408/71 in order to challenge the discriminatory conditions of the voluntary insurance.

The distinction drawn between rights in person and derived rights, the Court considered, renders the fundamental rule of equal treatment inapplicable to the

---

[14]   Court of Justice 30 April 1996, Case 308/93, [1996] *ECR* 2097.

surviving spouse of a migrant worker. The distinction may furthermore undermine the fundamental Community law requirement that its rules should be applied uniformly. This could be the case if the applicability of provisions to individuals depends on whether the national law relating to the benefits in question treats the rights concerned as rights in person or as derived rights.

Therefore, the Court concluded, the doctrine of the distinction between rights in person and derived rights has to be partially abandoned. As a result members of the family and survivors can also invoke Article 3 of the Regulation, *see* for further discussion, Section 6.3.

Chapter 11

The Equal Treatment Provisions of Regulation 1612/68

11.1.   Introduction

Regulation 1408/71 forbids discrimination on the basis of nationality for those who are within the personal scope of this Regulation and with respect to the benefits within the material scope. Thus, not every person and every benefit is covered under the equal treatment provision of this Regulation.

The equal treatment provision of Regulation 1612/68[1] may be useful in some cases because of the restricted scope of Regulation 1408/71. Regulation 1612/68 is based on Article 48 of the Treaty.

The anti-discrimination rule is found in Article 7(2) of Regulation 1612/68. This article reads:
'(1) A worker who is a national of a Member State may not, in the territory of another Member State, be treated differently from national workers by reason of his nationality in respect of any conditions of employment and work, in particular as regards remuneration, dismissal, and should he become unemployed, reinstatement or re-employment;
(2) He shall enjoy the same social and tax advantages as national workers.'

11.2.   The Personal Scope of Regulation 1612/68

The term 'employee' in Regulation 1612/68 is different from that in Regulation 1408/71. The meaning of 'employee' in Regulation 1612/68 is related to that of Article 48 of the Treaty, which Article requires that persons in order to be called 'employee' perform a substantial economic activity.

Regulation 1612/68 concerns only employees *stricto sensu, i.e.* those with a contract of employment, performing an economic activity. In addition, the employee must be in the territory of the State against which he invokes Article 7(2). In case

---

[1]   *OJ 1968 L 257.*

of alleged discrimination, his position is compared with that of national employees of the State in which territory he is.

The personal scope of Article 7(2) Regulation 1612/68 does not cover persons seeking work; neither does it contain the self-employed.

The Court considered that *students/ex-employees* can invoke Article 7(2) of Regulation 1612/68, *provided* that there is a 'demonstrable relationship' between the character of employment previously engaged in and the studies attended. Not every student or formerly employed person can rely on the equal treatment provision of Article 7(2) of Regulation 1612.[2]

A third category, alongside persons seeking work and ex-employees, is that of students in training, *see* the *Brown* judgment.[3]

> Brown could not rely on the protection provided by Article 7(2), as his training was regarded as an obligatory part of his technical studies; the status of employed persons ensued from the fact that he was admitted to university in order to do these studies. Under such circumstances his employment activities were ancillary to his status as a student and therefore he could not, in order to claim a scholarship for the costs of living, derive protection from the equal treatment clause of the Regulation with respect to social advantages, nor to Article 7 (now Article 6) EC Treaty in general.

If Article 7(2) of Regulation 1612/68 was interpreted literally, this would mean that the right to equal treatment in the field of social advantages would be granted exclusively to employed persons, and not to the members of his family who are living with him. The Court followed a broader interpretation of this provision; in the *Cristini* decision[4], the Court ruled that survivors can also derive rights from this article. The Court emphasised that this interpretation was based on the argument that if a Member State could refuse advantages to the members of his family and/or his relatives on grounds of their nationality, the employed person might leave the Member State in which he had his residence and in which he was employed. This would be against the objectives and the spirit of freedom of movement. This extension of the personal scope of Article 7(2) of Regulation 1612/68 to the members of the family and relatives is therefore based on the objectives of freedom of movement for workers.

Not only the rights of survivors are protected; in the *Castelli* judgment[5] and *First Frascogna* judgment,[6] the Court ruled that this applied with respect to relatives in the ascending line of the worker; in the *Deak* judgment[7] (*see* below) with respect to descendants.

---

[2] Court of Justice 21 June 1988, Case 39/86, *Lair*, [1988] *ECR* 3161.
[3] Court of Justice 21 June 1988, Case 197/85, [1988] *ECR* 3205.
[4] Court of Justice 30 September 1975, Case 32/75, [1975] *ECR* 1085.
[5] Court of Justice 12 July 1984, Case 261/83, [1984] *ECR* 3199.
[6] Court of Justice 6 June 1985, Case 157/84, [1985] *ECR* 1739.
[7] Court of Justice of 20 June 1985, Case 94/84, [1985] *ECR* 1873.

Family members and relatives, however, do not have a right *of their own* to equal treatment on the basis of Article 7(2): there is only the obligation to grant social benefits to members of the family if this can be regarded as a social advantage *pertaining to the employed person*. In determining this, it is important whether the employed person actually supports the family members in question. This approach in respect of members of the family, is not the same as the 'doctrine of derived rights' which was developed with respect to Regulation 1408/71.

In two aspects there is a limitation of the applicability of Regulation 1612/68 to members of the family. One of these can be seen in the *Zaoui* case.[8]

> Zaoui was of Algerian nationality and was married to a French woman. He was in receipt of a disablement pension and applied for supplementary benefit from the *Fonds national de solidarité*. The benefit was refused because he did not have French nationality.

As we have seen in Chapter 6, Zaoui did not fall within the personal scope of Regulation 1408/71, since the benefit concerned was, under the then case law, not a benefit meant for members of a family. However, according to the Court he could not rely on Regulation 1612/68 either, because the Community provisions on freedom of movement cannot be applied to situations which are not those for which Community law was established. Such a situation not governed by Community law existed, without doubt, in the case of employed persons who have never made use of their right to freedom of movement within the Community. Consequently, to involve Article 7(2), it is necessary that the employee, from whose position the member of the family will derive rights to the Regulation, has made use of the free movement of workers.

> In the *Deak* case[9] Belgium unemployment benefit for youths was claimed by a boy of Hungarian nationality, who was living with his mother in Belgium. The Court ruled that in accordance with Article 7(2) of Regulation 1612/68 the persons concerned were not to be subject to nationality conditions. This was despite the fact that Hungarian children of Belgian employees were not entitled to this benefit and could not invoke the Regulation if these workers had never undertaken cross border activities.

In the *Taghavi* judgment[10] the Court followed a different approach.

> Mrs Taghavi had Iranian nationality, was married to an Italian and lived in Belgium; she wanted to claim the grants for invalid persons on the basis of Belgian law, which stated that, with the exception of some special cases, only

---

[8]   Court of Justice 17 December 1987, Case 147/87, [1987] *ECR* 5511.
[9]   Court of Justice 20 June 1985, Case 94/84, [1985] *ECR* 1873.
[10]   Court of Justice 18 July 1992, case 243/91, [1992] *ECR* I-4401.

Belgians living in Belgium were entitled to these benefits. Can she rely on Article 7(2) of Regulation 1612/68?

The Court considered that the spouse of a *Belgian* employee, not being national of a Member State of the Community, is not entitled to this benefit. In that case there is no 'social advantage' for national employees which is not paid to foreign workers. Equal treatment of members of the family on the basis of Article 7(2) is applicable only, if national employees with members of the family having a foreign nationality can also claim equal treatment with respect to their members of the family.

In the *Schmid* judgment[11], given after the *Taghavi* judgment, the Court seemed to have amended its approach in the *Taghavi* judgment slightly.

The judgment concerned the claims of Suzanne, the daughter of Mr Schmid, who claimed a Belgian benefit for an adult handicapped person. Schmid and his daughters were of German nationality. A condition for entitlement to this benefit is, among other things, that the claimant must have Belgian nationality and must reside in Belgium. The daughter had never worked as an employed person, since she had been handicapped from birth. She was refused benefit as she had never been subject to the Belgian social security system as an employee, neither to the system of another Member State and she did not have Belgian nationality.

The Court reasoned that the right to a social advantage must not depend on conditions of nationality, as this was contrary to Article 7(2). This is also the case if the national rule applies for descendent members of the family (children) of national workers, This is because the condition that one must have the nationality of the State of work can be fulfilled easier by the children of national workers than by the children of migrant workers.

Thus, in this case the members of the family of a migrant workers could invoke Article 7(2) even when this leads to entitlement to benefit, to which foreign members of the family of national workers were not entitled. What is the difference between the *Taghavi* and *Schmid* judgments? Is discrimination against children not allowed, where unequal treatment of spouses is not contrary to Article 7(2) if the spouse of national workers are denied national benefit? The Court did not discuss this issue explicitly.

In Section 18.1 we will discuss the *Kziber* judgment, which ruled that the children of *Moroccan* workers residing in the territory of the EU are to be treated equally with nationals of Member States of the EU. The extent of equal treatment given to these Moroccan workers is larger than that given in the *Taghavi* judgment, which is an odd result, as the *Kziber* judgment concerned nationals of a third State.

Conclusion. Regulation 1612/68 is useful in the area of social security if a person is discriminated against on basis of nationality, and the person or the benefit concerned are beyond the scope of Regulation 1408/71,

---

[11] Court of Justice 27 May 1993, Case 310/91, [1993] *ECR* I-3011.

With respect to the scope of Article 7(2) of Regulation 1612/68 it is unclear whether migrant workers may be better of than national workers. The approach of the Court in the *Taghavi* and *Schmid* judgments respectively is not consistent.

11.3. The Material Scope of Regulation 1612/68

For some time, it was not clear whether the term *social advantages* in Article 7(2) was restricted to those advantages which are directly connected with the status of employee, or whether the term has a broader meaning.[12] The present approach of the Court of Justice was started in the *Cristini* judgment.[13] In this judgment the Court ruled that French reduced railway fares for large families also fall within the scope of Article 7(2). This reduction did not have anything to do with the employment of workers, but its objective was to support large families.

Since this judgment, the Court consistently held that, because of the objective of Article 48 of the Treaty, *i.e.* to promote the mobility of workers, the term *social advantages* pertains to social security benefits and public assistance benefits.

Social advantages in the sense of Article 7(2) of Regulation 1612/68 are all those which, 'whether or not linked to a contract of employment, are generally granted to national workers primarily because of their objective status as workers or by virtue of the mere fact of their residence on the national territory and the extension of which to workers who are nationals of other Member States therefore seems suitable to facilitate their mobility within the Community'.

The question whether social security or public assistance benefits are within the material scope of Article 7(2) of Regulation 1612/68 remained unanswered for some time, since the Court appeared to apply the anti-discrimination provision of Regulation 1408/71 in those cases where this question arose. In the 1980s and later case law, however, we can see that the Court consistently, in questions of discrimination concerning family members of workers, applied Regulation 1612/68. This, for instance, can be seen in the *Castelli* judgment[14], which concerned the granting of the Belgian guaranteed income for the aged to an Italian mother who was staying with an Italian worker in Belgium; in the *First Frascogna* judgment[15], which concerned a non-contributory French old-age benefit to a mother of Italian nationality staying with an Italian worker in France. In a proposal by the Commission to amend

---

[12] A restrictive interpretation of this provision can be found in Court of Justice 11 April 1973, Case 76/72, *Michel S.*, [1973] *ECR* 457. In this decision the Court ruled that the advantages under the Belgian law concerning social reintegration of disabled persons, which were claimed by a mentally disabled son of an Italian worker, were not subject to Regulation 1612/68. Social advantages were related to employment and therefore they must be to the benefit of the workers themselves and not the members of their family.

[13] Court of Justice 30 September 1975, Case 32/75, [1975] *ECR* 1085.

[14] Court of Justice 12 July 1984, Case 261/83, [1984] *ECR* 3199.

[15] Court of Justice 6 June 1985, Case 157/84, [1985] *ECR* 1739.

Regulation 1612/68, Article 7(1) is reformulated, so that the obligation of equal treatment would also explicitly pertain to the field of social security.[16]

The proposed amended Article 7(1) reads:
'A worker who is a national of a Member State may not, in the territory of another Member State, be treated differently from national workers by reason of his nationality in respect of any conditions of employment and work, especially with respect to health, safety and hygiene, and with respect to remuneration, dismissal, *social security*, occupational re-integration or re-employment if he has become unemployed or if he is the victim of total or partial incapacity for work.' (italics added).

Public assistance is also covered by Regulation 1612/68. As we have seen in Chapter 7, in the *Hoeckx* judgment, the Belgian public assistance benefits were not within the material scope of Regulation 1408/71; however, Mrs Hoeckx successfully claimed that on the basis of Article 7(2) of Regulation 1612/68 the nationality criteria in the Belgian law had to be removed.[17]

In Section 7.3 we discussed the *Even* judgment, as the benefit disputed in this case was not considered to fall under the material scope of Regulation 1408/71. The reason for this was that Article 4(4) of that Regulation provides that the Regulation does not apply to benefit schemes for victims of war or its consequences.

The second question was whether such a benefit came within the field of application of Article 7(2) of Regulation 1612/68. The Court answered that Regulation 1612/68 aims to achieve freedom of movement for workers within the Community. It follows from the provisions of this Regulation and from the objective pursued that the advantages which this Regulation extends to workers who are nationals of other Member States are all those which, whether or not linked to a contract of employment, are generally granted to national workers, primarily because of their objective status as workers or by virtue of the mere fact of their residence on the national territory and the extension of which to workers who are nationals of other Member States therefore seems suitable to facilitate their mobility within the Community.

The main reason for establishing the disputed benefit was the services which Belgian nationals had rendered in wartime to their own country and its essential objective was to give those nationals an advantage by reason of the hardships suffered for that country. The Court considered that such a benefit could not be considered as an advantage granted to a national worker by reason primarily of his status as worker or resident on the national territory. The Court concluded that, for this reason, this benefit did not fulfil the essential characteristics of the 'social advantages' referred to in Article 7(2) of Regulation 1612/68. Consequently, he could invoke neither Regulation 1408/71 nor Regulation 1612/68.

---

[16]   Com 90 180 final, *OJ* 1989 *C* 100, p. 6. Latest version *OJ* 1990 *C* 119/10.
[17]   Court of Justice 27 March 1985, Case 248/83, [1985] *ECR* 982; *see* also Court of Justice 27 March 1985, Case 122/84, *Scrivner*, [1985] *ECR* 1029.

11.4.   The Relationship between Regulation 1408/71 and Regulation 1612/68

In Section 6.3 we have discussed the *Cabanis* judgment. In this judgment the Court partially departed from the 'derived rights' doctrine concerning Regulation 1408/71. This means that in some cases Regulation 1408/71 is now applicable where previously Regulation 1612/68 had to be invoked. Mrs Cabanis could not have invoked Regulation 1612/68 as this Regulation requires a comparison of employees residing in the same territory. As she was no longer residing in the Netherlands, she could not invoke Regulation 1612/68, and the judgment of the Court was very useful to her.

Although members of the family can now in more instances invoke Regulation 1408/71, enough reasons remain for maintaining Article 7(2) of Regulation 1612/68. This is because the derived rights doctrine still applies with respect to those benefits especially meant for employees and self-employed persons. The *Deak* judgment is important for members of the family claiming unemployment benefits. Moreover, not all types of benefit fall under Regulation 1408/71; exceptions are, for instance, study grants and public assistance.

Chapter 12

Residence Requirements

12.1. Introduction

Residence requirements are problematic in relation to international movement. Therefore coordination regulations contain rules on this issue. Regulation 1408/71 has different instruments to attack resident requirements. There is, however, no general prohibition of residence requirements.

On the one hand, rules for determining the legislation applicable (Article 13) overrule residence requirements, in so far as they prevent the affiliation of workers to a certain social security system of a Member State which is designated as being applicable (Chapter 8). This involves the elimination of territorial requirements in national rules for affiliation to a social security system.

Residence requirements, as a part of national rules of substance, have also to be dealt with. These require, for instance, that a worker has resided for a minimum period in the territory of the State in question in order to qualify for benefit.

There can also be residence requirements for the payment of the benefit. Article 51(b) of the EC Treaty requires that the Council must make rules on the payment of benefits even if the worker is not in the territory of the State which would be obliged to make the payment of benefit in order to promote the free movement of workers. This rule is elaborated in Article 10 of Regulation 1408/71 for some types of benefit (*see* the following section).

Residence requirements can lead to the suspicion of indirect discrimination. If it is required that a person has resided for a certain period in a certain country in order to be eligible for benefit (minimum residence requirements), this requirement may give rise to such a suspicion. In such a case it must be considered whether there are objective justifications for these conditions.

As we have seen in Section 10.3.1., it is difficult to predict whether reliance on the prohibition of indirect discrimination will be successful. Therefore a regulation cannot confine itself solely to an anti-discrimination approach in order to deal with residence requirements. If it restricted itself to such an approach the social security position of migrant workers would often be problematic. In the first place, it would be unclear whether objective reasons exist for not taking foreign periods of insurance into account. Such grounds of justification could vary from State to State. In the second place, once it is decided that exclusion of foreign periods of insurance is indirectly discriminating against migrant workers, there can still be problems of how to take the foreign periods into account. For this reason, Regulation 1408/71 gives several specific rules. If, however, these rules do not provide for specific situations or are lacking in scope, the antidiscrimination rules of the Regulation may be useful to invoke.

12.2.　Article 10

Article 10 of Regulation 1408/71 concerns the elimination of residence requirements for specified categories of benefits

> Article 10 reads:
> 'Save as otherwise provided in this Regulation invalidity, old-age or survivors' cash benefits, pensions for accidents at work or occupational diseases and death grants *acquired* under the legislation of one or more Member States shall not be subject to any reduction, modification, suspension, withdrawal, or confiscation by reason of the fact that the recipient resides in the territory of a Member State other than that in which the institution responsible for payment is situated.' (italics added).

The scope of Article 10 is limited to the benefits mentioned in this Article, the invalidity, old-age and survivors' benefits. This Article allows the payment of benefits in the territory of another State.

From the very beginning, it was clear that Article 10 pertains to benefits to which a person had already acquired entitlement and where the person wished to have this benefit paid in another Member State. This was different to the question whether this Article is useful for the purpose of *acquiring* a right to benefit. Can Article 10 overrule residence requirements in the conditions for acquiring benefit rights?

In the *Camera* judgment, the Court made a ruling following which it could no longer be disputed that Article 10 also applies to conditions for acquiring the right to benefit.[1]

> Mrs Camera was an Italian worker who was engaged in paid employment in Belgium during 1964 and 1965. In 1965 she suffered from incapacity for work and she was granted Belgian sickness benefit. She went back to Italy where she did not go for a physical examination; following a later examination she was attested to be capable of work. Subsequently, she applied for a Belgian invalidity benefit (the benefit payable after entitlement to sickness benefit expired) and for the purpose of this benefit she was attested to be suffering incapacity for work by a Belgian institution. However, the benefit was refused, as she did not meet the condition in Belgian law which requires that the applicant actually resides in Belgian territory at the time the application for invalidity benefit is made.

---

[1]　Court of Justice 10 June 1982, Case 92/81, [1982] *ECR* 2213.

The Court ruled that Article 10 is to be interpreted in the sense that the benefit institution of the competent State is not to stipulate territorial conditions to invalidity benefits in its national legislation.

At first sight this judgment appears to deviate significantly from the text of Article 10. It fits, however, well with the system of the Regulation, as migrant workers cannot be, at the moment of materialisation of the risk, such as invalidity, in all the Member States where they have worked earlier. Under that interpretation the worker would not be entitled to benefit in the States where he did not reside at the time of materialisation of the risk, which would be an unfortunate result. Therefore the *Camera* interpretation of Article 10 fits with the system of Regulation 1408/71.

This point of view was confirmed in the *Van Roosmalen* judgment[2], which concerned a Duch AAW (General Disablement Benefits Act) benefit.

The AAW stated that a person can only apply for this benefit when he had been incapable of working for fifty-two weeks continuously *while residing in the national territory*.

In the judgment, the Court again emphasised that the principle as laid down in Article 10 of the Regulation not only means that the person concerned, even after having removed his place of residence to another State, maintains his right to benefit acquired on the basis of the legislation of one or more Member States. It also means that he cannot be deprived of his right on the sole ground that he does not reside on the territory of the State under whose legislation the benefit is payable.

12.3. Residence Requirements and Transitional Advantages

As a result of the *Camera* judgment, the question whether residence requirements can be imposed on *transitional advantages* in the Dutch old age benefit (AOW) became relevant.

The AOW-insurance provides for a benefit, the amount of which is based on insurance between the fifteenth and 65th birthday. All residents acquire an entitlement of 2% of this benefit in each calender year. As this insurance, established in 1957, would not lead to complete benefits before 2007, a special transitional rule was introduced. This rule was that persons who were at the time of introduction of the Act over fifteen years old and below 65, were considered to have been insured between their fifteenth year and the coming into force of the Act.

---

2   Court of Justice 23 December 1986, Case 300/84, [1986] *ECR* 3097. *See* also Section 6.2.2.

For this transitional rule, residence requirements applied. Whether these were allowed, was questioned in the *Winter-Lutzins* case.[3]

> Apart from national rules, Annex VI of the Regulation provides that if the person concerned was older than fifteen before 1957 and had resided or been employed *in the Netherlands* during that time, the periods lying before 1957 were considered periods of insurance for the purpose of the transitional advantages. Mrs Winter could not benefit from this rule as she lived in Germany in the period concerned.

The question was whether the residence conditions were contrary to Article 10. The Court ruled that the residence requirement in the transitional provisions of the AOW was not precluded by Article 10. Since the rule which overrules residence requirements of Article 10 cannot be totally applied to a scheme in which the residence condition is the only condition for acquiring entitlement (i.e. national insurances), the effect of Article 10 can be restricted as is done in Annex VI. Mrs Winter did not have any tie with the Netherlands before 1957, and therefore she could not benefit from the rules in Annex VI which assimilate periods of residence abroad to those periods in the Netherlands.

12.4. Residence Requirements and Hybrid Benefits

In Sections 7.5 and 7.6 the problem of the so-called hybrid benefits was discussed. With respect to these benefits the question arose as to whether they fall under the Regulation, and also whether they are to be paid in a State other than the competent state. In addition, there was the question whether the right to these benefits can be acquired if the applicant does not live in the competent State.

Before the Regulation was revised in 1992[4], the answer to this question was positive, as is seen in, for example, the *Biason* judgment.[5]

> In this case an Italian national, who enjoyed a French invalidity pension, which she had acquired as being an employed person during the time she was employed in France, received a supplement to this pension from the *Fonds National de Solidarité*. The Court ruled as follows: an insured person who is entitled to an invalidity pension, the right to which he acquired as an employed person in a Member State where he resided, and who under the provisions of this pension enjoys a supplementary benefit, continues to enjoy this benefit when he moves

---

[3]   Court of Justice 2 May 1990, Case 193/88, [1990] *ECR* 1623.
[4]   *See* Section 7.5.
[5]   Court of Justice 9 October 1974, Case 24/74, [1974] *ECR* 999.

to another Member State, in so far as this benefit falls within the material scope of the Regulation.[6]

The case law was revised in the *Newton* judgment.[7] This judgment was already discussed in Chapter 7: a person can rely on the Regulation for the export of a hybrid benefit payable under the legislation of a Member State only when the person concerned has been employed under the legislation of this State. Subsequently, Article 10*a* was added to the Regulation.

Article 10*a*(1) reads:
'Notwithstanding the provisions of Article 10 and Title III, persons to whom this Regulation applies shall be granted the special non-contributory cash benefits referred to in Article 4(2a) exclusively in the territory of the Member State in which they reside, in accordance with the legislation of that state, provided that such benefits are listed in Annex II*a*. Such benefits shall be granted by and at the expense of the institution of the place of residence.'

Now that Article 10*a* has been added to the Regulation, the State-of-residence principle is applied to all claimants of benefit which fall under Article 4(2a). The Article 4(2a) benefits are mentioned in Annex II*a*.

12.5.   Export of Unemployment Benefits

With respect to the export possibilities for benefits there is an exception for unemployment benefits. This is related to the existing link between, on the one hand, the right to unemployment benefit and, on the other hand, the condition of being available to the national labour market. The starting-point of Regulation 1408/71 is that the unemployed person is only entitled to unemployment benefit if he continues to be at the disposal of the employment services to which he is registered. Nevertheless, Regulation 1408/71 also contains a restricted export possibility for this type of benefit. An unemployed person who enjoys unemployment benefit in a certain Member State has the right to move to another Member State for the purpose of finding work and con· tinues to be entitled to the benefit of the afore-mentioned State for three months; we will discuss this in more detail in Chapter 17.

---

[6]   *See* also Court of Justice, 5 May 1983, Case 139/82, *Piscitello*, [1983] *ECR* 1427, an Italian woman who enjoyed an Italian public pension, wanted to keep this right after she went to Belgium, where she settled with her daughter. Since the Regulation does not contain special provisions for this type of benefit, the Court considered that it is to be assumed that the overruling of the residence requirements by Article 10 also pertains to this benefit.
[7]   Court of Justice 20 June 1991, Case 356/89, [1991] *ECR* 3017

Chapter 13

The General Rules against Overlapping

If an employee or a self-employed person has worked in several countries, it is possible that he has acquired benefit rights with respect to the same contingency. This can happen even though the rules for determining the legislation applicable assign one national scheme as exclusively applicable. In addition, it can happen that a person can be entitled, for instance, to a survivors' benefit in one State and unemployment benefit in another. Article 12 of the Regulation gives rules on this issue.

Article 12 provides:
'1. This Regulation can neither confer nor maintain the right to several benefits of the same kind for one and the same period of compulsory insurance. However, this provision shall not apply to benefits in respect of invalidity, old age, death (pensions) or occupational disease which are awarded by the institutions of two or more Member States, in accordance with the provisions of Article 41, 43 (2) and (3), 46, 50 and 51 or Article 60 (1) (b).
2. Save as otherwise provided in this Regulation, the provisions of the legislations of a Member State governing the reduction, suspension or withdrawal of benefits in cases of overlapping with other social security benefits or any other form of income may be invoked even where such benefits were acquired under the legislation of another Member State or where such income was acquired in the territory of another Member State.
3. The provisions of the legislation of a Member State for reduction, suspension or withdrawal of benefit in the case of a person in receipt of invalidity benefits or anticipatory old-age benefits pursuing a professional or trade activity may be invoked against such person even though he is pursuing his activity in the territory of another Member State (..).'

Article 12 (1) prohibits a situation whereby, as a consequence of the application of the Regulation, benefits of the same kind have to be paid for one and the same period. As follows from the wording of this article, and will be discussed further in Section 15.1, this prohibition does not apply in the case of some long term benefits, such as invalidity, old-age and survivors' benefits. Regulation 574/72 elaborates which benefits have priority in case of concurrence.

An example is Article 8 of Regulation 574/72 which provides that if an employed or self-employed person or a member of his family is entitled to claim maternity benefits under the legislation of two or more Member States, those benefits shall be granted exclusively under the legislation of the Member State in whose territory the confinement took place or, if the confinement did not take place in the territory of one of these Member States, exclusively under the legislation of the Member State to which the employed or self-employed person was last subject.

In addition, there are special rules concerning family benefits. As children usually have two parents, rules against overlapping of the benefits derived from each of the parents are necessary. Articles 10 and 10a if Regulation 574/72 give rules on this topic, which will be discussed in Chapter 16.

Article 12 (2) concerns the fact that national social security schemes may have their own rules against overlapping. An example is that within a national scheme a person should not receive a full unemployment and sickness benefit at the same time. Neither should a person receive a full sickness and disability benefit at the same time.

The second section of Article 12 extends the effect of national rules against overlapping to social security benefits and income which an employee or self-employed person may receive from another Member State. This is also the case if the national rules against overlapping are exclusively focused on benefits and income in its own territory. This extension applies other than the exceptions given in the Regulation, *see* for the discussion for those concerning the long-term benefits, Section 15.7.

Chapter 14

Sickness and Maternity Benefits

14.1.   Introduction

There are considerable differences between the schemes of sickness and maternity benefits of the Member States. On the one hand, there is the difference between national insurance schemes (in which all residents are insured, regardless of occupational activities) and employees' insurance schemes. There is the difference between schemes which directly pay the bills for medical services (dentists, hospitals or general practitioners) and schemes under which the person insured first pays the bill himself and can then claim reimbursement. However, in spite of these differences, cases on this issue before the Court of Justice are relatively rare. Perhaps this is due to the fact that benefits for employees who are engaged in employment are treated more pragmatically by the benefit administration than long-term benefits. Furthermore, there is less money involved with these short-term benefits.

Sickness and maternity benefits are within the material scope of the Regulation by virtue of Article 4(1)(a). The meaning of this term was explained in the *Jordens-Vosters* judgment.[1]

> Mrs Jordens received a disability benefit and a benefit in kind on the basis of the Netherlands Law on the Disability Benefits. The question was whether this benefit was covered by the rules on sickness benefit in the Regulation, despite the fact that the rules are found in the Disability Benefits Act.

The Court held that the type of social legislation under which these provisions are regulated is irrelevant. Consequently, the term 'sickness and maternity benefits' applies to medical and surgical provisions even if these are set out in legislation on invalidity benefits. The term only applies to the specific provisions and not to the whole legislation which contains such provisions.

A second question on the meaning of the terms in Article 4, was whether the term 'sickness benefit' comprises the compulsory payments by employers in the case of sickness, for instance payments on the basis of the German *Lohnfortzahlungsgesetz*. The answer to this question is positive, as was already discussed in Chapter 7.

---

[1]   Court of Justice 10 January 1980, Case 69/79, [1980] *ECR* 75.

Article 19 uses the terms 'benefits in kind' and 'benefits in cash'. The Regulation does not give a definition of these terms. The term 'benefits in kind' refers in principle to the meaning of this term in the national legislation of the organisation which provides the benefit concerned.[2]

In order to be a 'benefit in kind' it is not necessary that the benefit is really 'in kind', it can also be a restitution for medical costs.[3] A cash payment can, therefore, sometimes be a benefit in kind.

It follows from the *Dekker* judgment[4] that a scheme which pays sickness benefit contributions for retired persons, is not a benefit in kind for the purpose of the co-ordination rules on sickness benefit.

14.2. Aggregation Rules

The legislation on sickness and maternity benefits of some Member States has conditions on waiting periods before a claimant is entitled to sickness benefit. In Belgium, for instance, there is a qualifying period of six months. In such a case it is important that the time spent in another Member State can be taken into account in order to satisfy this condition. To this end, the Regulation contains rules for aggregation of periods for acquiring a right to sickness benefits (Article 18).

Article 18 rules:
'the competent institution of a Member State whose legislation makes the acquisition, retention or recovery of the right to benefits conditional upon the completion of periods of insurance, employment or residence shall, to the extent necessary, take account of periods of insurance, employment or residence completed under the legislation of any other Member State as if they were periods completed under the legislation which it administers.'

If, for example, an employee has been insured under the Dutch statutory Act on Insurance for Medical Costs of Sickness, and he starts to work in Belgium, the Netherlands' periods count towards satisfying the Belgian conditions.

14.3. Disability Existed Already before the Start of the Insurance

In the *Klaus* judgment[5] the question was raised whether a Member State is allowed to ignore the periods of insurance abroad for the purpose of refusing benefit on the ground that a person was already ill before he became insured under the system of

---

[2]   *See,* Decision 92 and 109 of the Administrative Commission.
[3]   Court of Justice 30 June 1965, Case 61/65, *Vaassen-Goebels*, [1965] *ECR* 257.
[4]   Court of Justice 1 December 1965, Case 33/65, [1965] *ECR* 1135.
[5]   Court of Justice 26 October 1995, Case 482/93, [1995] *ECR* I-3551.

the Member State or that his sickness could be expected within a certain period after becoming insured under that system. The Dutch rules provide that benefit can be refused partially or completely if the disability already existed at the commencement of the insurance. The purpose of this rule is to avoid abuse of benefits, as the Dutch sickness benefit does not contain a rule that specific types of sickness can be excluded from insurance.

> Mrs Klaus worked from December 1985 until July 1987 as a nurse in the Netherlands and was insured on the basis of the Dutch Sickness Benefits Act. In June 1987 she stopped her activities because of back complaints, and her insurance was terminated. After a period of work in Spain, she returned to the Netherlands after two years on 20 October 1989 and started working for a temporary employment agency. After two weeks of work, she had to stop working because of back problems. It appeared that Mrs Klaus had been incapable of working on 20 October 1989. The Dutch benefit administration argued that she had again become insured under the Dutch system at that date, and therefore benefit was refused on the ground that she was already ill at the start of her benefit insurance.

The Court considered that, according to Article 51 of the Treaty, the Council has to take measures which are necessary in the area of social security in order to realize the freedom of movement of workers. One of these provisions is Article 18(1) of Regulation 1408/71. This provision prevents the competent body from considering the date on which the national system covers the person as the beginning of its own insurance. If the statutory scheme of the competent Member State makes the grant of sickness benefits dependent on the condition that the disability for work must not already exist at the moment of affiliation, the competent institution must also take account, in accordance with Article 18, of the period completed in other Member States on the basis of periods of affiliation with a statutory scheme, as if these were fulfilled on the basis of the statutory scheme applied by that Member State.[6]

14.4. Overruling of Residence Requirements

14.4.1. Article 19

A second element of coordination, viz. the overruling of conditions on residence, is established in Article 19.

---

[6] *See* also Court of Justice 26 October 1995, Case 481/93, *Moscato*, [1995] *ECR* I-3525, discussed in Section 15.3.3.

Article 19 reads:

An employed person or self-employed person *residing* in the territory of a Member State other than the competent State, who satisfies the conditions of the legislation of the competent State for the entitlement to benefits, shall receive in the State in which he is resident:

a. *benefits in kind* provided on behalf of the competent institution of the place of residence in accordance with the provisions of the legislation administered by that institution as though he were insured with it. According to Article 36 of Regulation 1408/71 the costs are at the expense of the competent State. In order to prevent problems, the State providing benefit is to ask the permission of the competent State for certain kinds of benefits, *see* Article 17(7) of Regulation 574/72.

b. *cash benefits* provided by the competent institution in accordance with the legislation which it administers.

Consequently, benefits in kind are granted according to the legislation of the State of residence, but the costs are at the expense of the competent State. However, cash benefits are granted in accordance with the legislation of the competent State. The competent State is the State assigned by the rules for determining the legislation applicable, mostly the State of employment, but it can also be a State assigned by the rules on posting.

The question was raised whether this rule only applied to persons active in employment, or also to persons who are no longer professionally active. This was dealt with in the *Twomey* ruling.[7]

Mrs Twomey, a United Kingdom national, was employed as a home help in London from May 1986 to 3 July 1987. On 19 July 1987, she settled in Ireland and on 23 February of the following year, she applied to the United Kingdom benefit administration for sickness benefits. The claim was rejected on the grounds that United Kingdom law precludes payment of the benefits where the claimant does not reside in the United Kingdom. The question was whether Article 19 applies to a person who goes to live in another Member State and becomes ill in that State. In this case the British authorities argued that Article 13(2)(a) no longer applied to Mrs Twomey as she was no longer employed in the United Kingdom.

The Court disagreed with this point of view: it followed from the *Ten Holder* judgment (*see* Chapter 8), that a person remains covered by the legislation of the competent State unless one resumes activities in a new State (or one stops working definitely). The United Kingdom argued that the scope of Article 19 is limited to persons falling ill whilst employed. It pointed out that a wider interpretation of Article 19, bringing within the scope of that provision any person falling ill at the time when

---

[7]   Court of Justice 10 March 1992, Case 215/90, [1992] *ECR* I-1823.

they were not in any kind of employment, would jeopardise the cohesion of the system applicable to unemployed persons. An unemployed person seeking employment in the territory of a Member State other than the competent State is entitled to unemployment benefits for three months (Article 69 - *see* Chapter 17), whereas sickness benefit would be paid to him without any limitation in time. If the objectives of Article 51 of the Treaty are achieved by this provision in relation to unemployment benefit, it cannot be argued that those objectives require more favourable provisions in relation to sickness benefits.

The Court replied that the difference in treatment can be explained by the fact that the scope of Article 19 differs from that of Article 25. Whilst the latter provision is applicable to unemployed persons temporarily seeking employment in a Member State other than the competent state, Article 19 applies to workers who reside in a Member State other than the competent state. The Court concluded that a restrictive interpretation of Article 19 could not be justified.

14.4.2.   *Claiming and Supervision Procedures*

Benefits in kind are granted by the competent body of the State of residence according to the legislation applied by that body. This implies that the administration of the State of residence decides whether a person is ill or not in order to be entitled to a benefit in kind.

Benefits in cash are, on the contrary, granted according to the legislation of the competent State (mostly the State of employment). The State of residence is, however, responsible for the medical investigation; the benefit administration of the State of residence must send the results of the examination to the benefit administration in the State of employment. The benefit administration can, however, ask a doctor of its own choice to give a second opinion on the situation of the claimant. If the State of employment does not make use of this possibility, this State is bound by the examination of the State of residence. These rules can be found in Article 18 of Regulation 574/72.

Article 18 of Regulation 574 states that:
'1 In order to receive cash benefits under Article 19(1)(b) of the Regulation an employed or self-employed person shall, within three days of commencement of the incapacity for work, apply to the institution of the place of residence by submitting a notification of having ceased work or, if the legislation administered by the competent institution or by the institution of the place of residence so provides, a certificate of incapacity for work issued by the doctor providing treatment for the person concerned. (..)
4 The institution of the place of residence shall subsequently carry out any necessary administrative checks or medical examination of the person concerned as if he were insured with that institution. As soon as it establishes that the person concerned is fit to resume work, it shall forthwith notify him

and the competent institution accordingly, stating the date on which his incapacity for work ceased. (..)

5 In all cases the competent institution shall reserve the right too have the person concerned examined by a doctor of its own choice.'

In the *Rindone* judgment,[8] it was questioned whether the State of employment is bound by the opinion of the physician of the State of residence, when the first State does not conduct its own examination. Article 18(4) of Regulation 574/72 states that the institution of the place of residence carries out the administrative checks and medical examination as if the claimant were insured with that institution. As soon as it establishes that the person concerned is fit to resume work, it has to notify him and the competent institution accordingly. The problem was that this provision does not mention the commencement of incapacity for work, which was questioned in this case.

The Court considered that Article 18 provides that the State of residence determines the termination of incapacity for work; it is only logical that this institution also determines the commencement of the incapacity. An inconsistent rule pertaining to the commencement of incapacity for work could not be justified, since in both cases the institution of the place of residence has to consider comparable factual situations. The competent institution (*i.e.* of the State of employment) only has the opportunity of checking the findings. A different solution would be problematic for the employed person with regard to the proof that he was ill and this would be an impediment to freedom of movement for workers.[9]

This decision also considered the fact that there is no rule for a situation in which the person concerned does not observe the three-day term prescribed by Article 18(1) under which he has to receive a certificate of incapacity for work from a doctor in his place of residence, or where the State of residence does not send this report to the competent State within three days.

The Court considered that in the first case the supervising doctor of the place of residence is no longer able to diagnose incapacity for work. In that case, the employed person has to bear the consequences himself. In respect to the second situation, the Court considered that the claimant should not lose out because of a delay on the part of the administration.[10]

Subsequently, the question was raised as to whether an employed person can be required to go to the competent State in order to be examined in that State. The Court considered that Article 18(5) is not be interpreted in the sense that the employed

---

[8]   Court of Justice 12 March 1987, Case 22/86, [1987] *ECR* 1339.

[9]   For *industrial accidents* and *occupational diseases* the Court also ruled that the Member State which is to pay the benefits, must recognise the medical diagnosis of an occupational disease, even when this took place in another Member State and according to the legislation of this state; *see* Court of Justice 11 March 1986, Case 28/85, *Deghillage*, [1986] *ECR* 991.

[10]   The Court referred to the decision of 6 October 1982, Case 302/81, *Eggers*, [1982] *ECR* 3443, in which it was decided that the principle that procedural mistakes are not to be held against the applicant and may not have a negative influence on him, is to be regarded as a general legal principle.

person is under an obligation to return to the competent State for examination. The Court argued that such an obligation would be contrary to the respect owed to the state of health of the person employed. If the competent institution wishes to examine the sick person itself, it will have to send one of its physicians or ask a doctor in the country in question to do so.

This case law also applies to a situation in which the *employer* is under the obligation to pay sickness benefit. *See,* the *Paletta* ruling.[11]

> Paletta, his wife, and his children, of Italian nationality, became ill during their holidays in Italy. They were employed by the same employer; this employer refused to continue payment of their wages during the required six weeks under the German General Law on Continuation of Payment of Wages on the grounds that he was not bound by the medical report of a foreign country, the reliability of which he seriously doubted. Paletta argued that since the employer did not make use of the possibility as provided in Article 18(5) of Regulation 574/72 (the right to a second opinion by a physician of his own choice), he was bound by the medical results of the institution of the place of residence, with regard to the establishment of incapacity as well as its duration.

The first question was whether the continued payment of wages in case of illness due on the basis of the German law was a sickness benefit within the meaning of Regulation 1408/71. The reply to this was positive.[12]

The next question was whether Article 18 of Regulation 574/72 was relevant to sickness benefits paid by the employer. The Court considered that Article 1(o)(iv) of Regulation 1408/71 states that the employer is to be regarded as the competent institution as defined in this Regulation with respect to benefits under Article 4(1). Consequently, Article 18 of Regulation 574/72 applies. This result corresponds with the objective of Article 18, viz. to remove problems in the furnishing of proof by the employed person and the promotion of the free movement of workers. Consequently, the employer is bound by the certificate of the State of residence if he does not avail of the right to a second opinion by a physician of his own choice.

Brennet (the employer), the Netherlands Government and the German Government, as well as the Commission, had argued that the employer may not always be able to make effective use of the possibility of a second opinion. In addition, the medical report is not sent directly to the employer, but via the administration of sickness benefits, which causes delay. Another problem is that the employer often does not know in which place the employed person resides and he does not know any physicians in that place. The possibility which is offered by Article 18(5) is, consequently, often not a realistic one. In answer to these objections the Court considered that problems of implementation are not to impede the interpretation of

---

[11] Court of Justice 3 June 1992, Case 45/90, [1992] *ECR* I-3423.
[12] *See* Chapter 7.

an objective of Regulation 1408/71. This decision was very controversial in German literature.[13]

After the ruling of the Court of Justice the German Court awarded the claim of Paletta; this was maintained on appeal. The employer subsequently applied for a revision procedure. The Court concerned asked for a new preliminary ruling, which led to the *Second Paletta* judgment.[14] The national court had asked to what extent the national court had to take account, when applying Article 18 of Regulation 574/72, of abuse on the part of the claimant. The Court answered that the persons concerned cannot invoke Community law in case of abuse or deceit. National courts can, on the basis of objective data, take account of abuse and deceit of the claimant and deny him having recourse to Community law. Whether such abuse or deceit is involved, has to be determined with a view to the objectives of the provisions in question. The German court had referred to German case law, which implied that the employee has to provide proof that he is ill (alongside with the medical evidence) where the employer has shown circumstances which raise serious doubt of his alleged disability.

The Court of Justice did not follow this case law; the German case law is incompatible with the objectives of Article 18 of Regulation 574/72. For the employee who has become disabled in a State other than the competent State it would lead to difficulties of proof which Community law wished to avoid. This provision does not, however, preclude the employer from providing evidence on the basis of which a national court can determine whether abuse or deceit is involved. In case of a positive answer to this, the employee who invokes Article 18 of Regulation 574/72, cannot be considered ill.

In other words, in case of deceit one cannot invoke Article 18, but the proof of deceit has to be provided by the employer.

14.4.3. Members of the Family

Members of the family of employed or self-employed persons residing in the territory of a Member State other than the competent one, are entitled in the same way as employed persons to *benefits in kind* under the legislation of the place of residence and *cash benefits* under the legislation of the competent State.

If, however, the members of the family have a right to benefit in kind or cash benefits in their own right on the basis of legislation of the Member State in the territory of the State of residence (because they are subject to, for instance, a national health scheme)[15], these benefits are at the expense of the State of residence.[16]

---

[13]   *See* Schulte (1995).
[14]   Court of Justice 2 May 1996, Case 206/94, [1996] *ECR* I-2357.
[15]   This is the case, for instance, in the Netherlands and in the United Kingdom.
[16]   Article 19 of Regulation 1408/71. This State will also levy the contributions for these provisions.

In addition, employed or self-employed persons and members of their family are not only entitled to benefits in kind in the territory of the State of residence, but, if they stay in the territory of the State of employment, they are also entitled to benefits in kind from that State (Article 21).

This rule does not apply to members of the family of frontier workers (Article 20), *see* following section.

14.5. Frontier Workers and Members of the Family

14.5.1. Frontier Workers

Frontier workers are, *see* Article 1(b), persons who are employed in one State while residing in another State and who return to their State of residence at least once a week.

A frontier work can choose between the benefits in kind in his State of residence and those of the State of employment. This can result in a kind of freedom of choice for frontier workers. This is not only important in the case of differences between the benefits in kind, but also for financial differences (such as legislations requiring claimants to pay part of the costs).

14.5.2. Members of the Family

Members of the family of frontier workers are entitled only to benefits in the State of residence. They are only entitled to benefits in kind in the competent State (*i.e.* the State of employment of the frontier worker), on condition that there is an agreement between the States concerned or, in its absence, on prior authorization of the competent institution. In urgent cases such prior consent is not necessary.

The European Commission has presented a proposal to give the members of the family of frontier workers the possibility to obtain benefits in kind according to their own choice, in the State of residence or the State of employment, just as in the case of frontier workers.[17]

14.6. Temporary Stay outside the Competent State

In case of a temporary stay in another Member State it is possible to rely on the provisions of the Regulation in order to obtain benefits in case of sickness or accidents in that Member State. This can, for example, be the case during holidays.

Article 22 mentions three situations in which employed or self-employed persons and the members of their family, who satisfy the conditions of the legislation of the

---

[17]   Com. (95) 284 def. of 26 June 1995.

competent State for entitlement to benefit, are entitled to benefits in kind on behalf of the competent institution by the institution of the place of stay or residence, in accordance with the legislation which it administers. The length of the period during which the benefits in kind are provided is determined by the legislation of the competent State. Persons in these situations are also entitled to cash benefits provided by the competent institution in accordance with the legislation applied by this institution. By agreement between the competent institution and the institution of the place of stay or residence, such benefits may be provided by the latter institution on behalf of the competent State in accordance with the legislation of the competent State. These rules mean that in case of sickness it is possible to invoke the Regulation in the case of a *temporary stay* in another Member State.[18] This help is possible in the following three situations exclusively:

a. an employee requires immediate benefits during a stay in the territory of another Member State; this also involves tourists. This article does not impose additional requirements on persons who are in this situation;

b. an employee, having become entitled to benefits chargeable to the competent institution, is authorized by that institution to return to the territory of the Member State where he resides, or to transfer his residence to the territory of another Member State. This situation often occurs in the case of migrant workers who fall ill and of whom it is presumed that they will not recover quickly and who, therefore, want to recover in the State of origin;

c. an employee who is authorized by the competent institution to go to the territory of another Member State to receive there the treatment appropriate to his condition. The authorization may not be refused when the treatment in question is among the benefits provided for by the legislation of the Member State in whose territory the person concerned resides, and where he cannot be given such treatment within the time normally necessary for obtaining the treatment in question in the Member State of residence taking account of his current state of health and the probable course of the disease.[19]

The period during which benefits are provided, shall, however, be that laid down under the legislation of the Member State in whose territory the members of the family are resident.

14.7. Calculation of Benefits

According to the national legislation concerned, sickness benefits can be related to wages or can be at a flat-rate level. In this regard, Article 23 provides for the

---

[18] In Article 1(i) of Regulation 1408/71 *stay* is defined as temporary residence (whereas *residence* is defined as habitual residence).

[19] Article 22(2) Regulation 1408/71, as revised by Regulation 2793/81 *OJ L* 275 of 29 September 1981. *See*, for a judgment relating to the earlier version, Court of Justice 16 March 1978, Case 117/77, *Pierik* [1978] *ECR* 825.

calculation of *cash benefits*: the competent institution of a Member State, whose legislation provides that the calculation of cash benefits shall be based on average earnings or on average contributions, shall determine such average earnings or contributions exclusively by reference to earnings or contributions completed under the said legislation.

If the legislation of a Member State provides that the calculation of cash benefits shall be based on standard earnings, it shall take account exclusively of the standard earnings or, where appropriate, of the average of standard earnings for the periods completed under the said legislation.

Finally this article provides that if the legislation states that the amount of cash benefits varies with the number of members of the family, the members of the family of the person concerned who are resident in the territory of another Member State are also taken into account as if they were resident in the territory of the competent State.

14.8.   Categories of Persons not in Employment

14.8.1. *Unemployed Persons and Members of their Family*

Article 25 applies to an unemployed person who was formerly employed or self-employed and to whom Article 69(2) applies (this provision concerns the possibility to search for work in another Member State for a certain period).

Article 25 provides that this person is entitled, for the period provided for by Article 69[20], to *benefits in kind* provided on behalf of the competent State by the institution of the State in which he seeks employment, in accordance with the legislation applied by the State of residence. He is entitled to *cash benefits* provided by the competent institution in accordance with the legislation applied by this institution. During this period, unemployment benefits (payable under Article 69) will be suspended as long as cash benefits are received.

A frontier worker who is wholly unemployed or an unemployed person who is available for work to the employment services in the territory of the Member State in which he resides, or who returns to that territory (within the meaning of Article 71 - *see* Chapter 17), is entitled to benefits in kind and in cash in accordance with the legislation of the State of residence as if he had last been employed in that state. The costs of such benefits are met by the institution of the State of residence.

If the unemployed person satisfies the conditions of the legislation of the Member State which is responsible for the costs of unemployment benefits for entitlement to sickness and maternity benefits, his members of the family are entitled to these benefits, irrespective of the Member State in whose territory they reside or are staying.

---

[20]   Principally no more than three months, or otherwise to be extended in case of special circumstances; *see* Chapter 17.

14.8.2. *Pensioners and Members of Their Family*

In case of pensioners who are entitled to draw pensions under the legislation of *two or more* Member States, of which one is that of the Member State in whose territory he resides, the Regulation applies the principle that the pensioner has to receive medical care in the State of residence, on condition that he is entitled to such benefits under the legislation of the latter Member State. They are paid at the expense of that institution as though the person concerned were a pensioner whose pension was paid solely under the legislation of the latter Member State.

A pensioner who is entitled to a pension under the legislation of two or more Member States and who is *not* entitled to benefits under the legislation of the Member State in whose territory he resides, nevertheless receives such benefits for himself and for members of his family if he had been entitled to such benefit in the State where he receives a *pension*. This is true only if he were entitled to medical care in the situation where he had been resident in the territory of that State (Article 28).

There are the following *priority rules* in relation to this. *Benefits in kind* are provided by the institution of the place of residence as though the person concerned were a pensioner under the legislation of the State in whose territory he resides and were entitled to such benefits. Where the pensioner is entitled to these benefits under the legislation of a single Member State, the costs are borne by the competent institution of that State. Where the pensioner is entitled to the said benefits under the legislations of two or more States, the costs thereof are borne by the competent institution of the Member State to whose legislation the pensioner has been subject for the longest period of time. If this does not provide a solution, the costs are to be borne by the institution administering the legislation to which the pensioner was last subject.

Cash benefits are provided at the expense of the competent institution and according to the rules as described in the above paragraph. However, by agreement between the competent institution and the institution of the State of residence, these benefits may be paid for by the latter State on behalf of the former, in accordance with the legislation of the competent State.

Finally there is a special rule for pensioners residing in the territory of a Member State under whose legislation the rights to receive benefits in kind is not subject to conditions of insurance or employment and where no pension payable by the State of residence. This concerns persons who are entitled to pension from another country, while residing in a country with national health systems. In such a case, the costs of benefit in kind provided to him and to the members of his family are borne by the institution in accordance with the aforementioned *priority rules*. This applies to the extent that the person entitled and his family members would have been entitled to such benefits under the legislation administered by the said institution if they resided in the territory of the Member State where that institution is situated (Article 28*a*).

This provision provides that Member States who have a national health system for medical costs can charge their expenses with regard to pensioners residing in their territory and who do not receive a pension from this country to another Member State. In such a case, the Member State which pays the pensions must also pay for the benefits in kind during the period of retirement.

Family members who do not reside in the same country as the person receiving pension, and where the pensioner is entitled to sickness or maternity benefits under the legislation of the Member State, receive the benefits under the following conditions. The benefits in kind are provided by the institution of the place of residence of the members of the family in accordance with the provisions of the legislation administered by this institution. The costs are borne by the institution of the pensioner's place of residence. Cash benefits are provided for by the competent State in accordance with Article 27 or in accordance with the priority rules mentioned above.

14.9. Levying Contributions on Pensioners

If a Member State owes a pension to a pensioner and this Member State also insures this person for sickness benefit, this Member State can withhold contributions from the pension for the person concerned (Article 33).

Deducting contributions from the pension is possible only if the Member State who deducts the contributions is also liable for paying benefits. This Article was subject of the *Commission v. Belgium* judgment.[21] This ruling concerned a Belgian scheme, which provided that sickness benefit contributions could be deducted in case of *each* payment of a Belgian pension. Belgium also deducted contributions from pensions granted to persons residing in other Member States, who were not insured under the Belgian sickness insurance. The Court decided that the Belgian scheme was not allowed.[22]

Article 33 was applied analogously in the *Noij* ruling.[23]

This case concerned an employed person of Dutch nationality who worked in Belgium for twenty-five years, and acquired a right to a retirement pension. The right to family benefit and medical benefits were connected to this Belgian pension. After Noij moved to the Netherlands, he was assessed for Netherlands national insurance contributions (contributions amounting to twenty-three percent of his pension), whereas he was already covered in Belgium for (the main part of) the risks insured under the Dutch scheme.

The problem was, however, that the Court had just before this ruling delivered the *Daalmeijer* decision (*see* Chapter 8), which ruled that Article 13 was not applicable to persons who have permanently terminated their working activities.

---

[21] Court of Justice 28 March 1985, Case 275/83, [1985] *ECR* 1097.

[22] *See* also Court of Justice 16 January 1992, Case 57/90, *Commission v. France,* [1992] *ECR* I-75. This ruling concerned a scheme comparable with the Belgian one, but was not within the material scope of the regulation.

[23] Court of Justice 21 February 1991, Case 140/88, [1991] *ECR* 387.

131

The consequence of this for Noij was that Article 13 did not preclude the applicability of two or more legislations simultaneously. Therefore the contribution levies imposed by the Netherlands were allowed.

Luckily for Noij, this was not the last word in this case. The Court referred to Article 33. Although in fact this Article pertains to sickness and maternity benefits, it was considered by the Court as an expression of a more general principle, namely that the promotion of freedom of movement of workers is not to be subject to impediments. This would be the case with the contribution levies imposed on Noij. Therefore, Noij did not have to pay contributions for national insurance.

In the meantime, as we have seen, the Regulation was amended; Article 13(2) now contains a subparagraph (f). In the *Noij* case, this Article could not be applied, since it was not yet in force. Now that the new article is in force, it can be assumed that the person concerned would be subject to the legislation of the State of residence.

Since this situation is likely to cause all kinds of complications, simultaneous to the adoption of the amended Article 13, a new Article 17*a* was adopted,[24] which provides that: 'the recipient of a pension due under the legislation of a Member State or of pensions due under the legislation of several Member States who resides in the territory of another Member State may at his request be exempted from the legislation of the latter state provided that he is not subject to that legislation because of the pursuit of an occupation.'

On the basis of this article contribution charges from two countries at the same time can be prevented.

---

[24]   *OJ* 1991 *L* 206/2.

Chapter 15

Invalidity, Survivors' and Old-Age Pensions

15.1.   Introduction

Regulation 1408/71 treats long-term benefits in a way different from short-term benefits. The reason for this is that the State in which territory a person, who has worked in several countries, has become disabled or reaches pension age, will prefer not to be solely responsible for the costs of this type of benefit. Much more money is involved with long-term benefits than with short-term benefits. In other words, *the integration principle* is not easily applicable in the case of long-term benefits. According to this principle only one pension is awarded to a migrant worker and this is calculated in accordance with the rules of one Member State.

> Application of the integration principle to long-term benefits would involve, for instance, the following situation. Suppose that a claimant has first worked in Member State *A* and then in Member State *B*. In State *B* old-age pensions are higher than in State *A*. When he applies for pension in State *B* he would receive a higher pension than if he would have to apply for benefit in State *A*. An employee who worked in the reversed order for the same duration in both countries, would receive a lower pension. Also the benefit charges would be divided unequally over the States.

These phenomena also occur in the case of short-term benefits, but the financial consequences for long-term benefits are much more serious.

Consequently, the integration principle was not deemed appropriate for coordinating these types of benefit. Instead, for the coordination of old-age, disability and survivors' pensions the partial pensions method is used, which means that the pension to be paid consists of a number of pensions, based on the periods of insurance completed in the Member States where this person has been employed. The Member States where this person has been insured have to pay the costs of the pensions related to the periods completed under their respective legislations. This form of coordination is called the *partial pension* method.

There are, however, exceptions to and complications caused by the partial pension method. In order to understand these, it is important to know that there are two types of schemes for disability and survivors' benefits.

1.   The first type consists of *benefits based on the length of insurance* (the so-called Type B schemes). With respect to these benefits there is a relationship between the duration of periods of work or insurance completed by the insured person

and the amount of benefit. In this system, it is not required that a claimant is insured at the moment the insured risk materialises. In other words, the periods of insurance are 'stored' and can be claimed at a later date when the risk actually occurs, even when the claimant has become to be insured under the scheme of another State. If the risk materialises he can claim a pension based on the periods completed under the legislation of the former Member State.

2. The second type of benefit was developed in some Member States in the second half of the 20th century; the so-called insurance *schemes based on the materialisation of the risk* (the so-called Type A schemes). Such schemes were established for invalidity benefits and in some States for widows' benefits also. The following Member States have this type of schemes for invalidity: the Netherlands, Belgium, the United Kingdom, Ireland, France and Spain.[1]

An important characteristic of these schemes is that the amount of benefit is not dependent on the duration of the insured periods. An insured person is entitled to benefit under these schemes as soon as the risk occurs, even when the insured period has been short.

On the other hand, a person is entitled to benefit under such a scheme only if he is insured, in principle, at the very moment the risk materialises; in other words, periods of insurance which were completed in the past are no longer relevant if the risk materialises at a time when he is no longer insured under such a scheme.

In some Type A schemes one has to serve waiting days before one is entitled to a right to benefit. Such waiting days do not alter the character of the scheme, as there is still no relationship between insured periods and the amount of benefit.

As regards Type A schemes, coordination rules have to solve two problems for migrant workers. The first problem concerns, in particular, the interaction with the Type B schemes. Coordination rules have to find a solution for the case in which workers were consecutively insured under a Type B scheme (of country *X*) and a Type A scheme (of country *Y*). Without coordination rules, in such a case the following problems would occur. Suppose this employee worked initially under a Type B scheme, and, subsequently, under a Type A scheme. If he suffers incapacity for work under the latter scheme, the sum of benefits he will receive would be too high. This is because in a Type B scheme, the acquired pension rights are 'stored' and can be applied for at a later period. Meanwhile, a person who begins to suffer incapacity while insured under a Type A scheme, receives the full pension.

In the reversed case, an employee is first insured under a Type A scheme, and subsequently under a Type B scheme. In that case the employee concerned is, unfortunately, not entitled to benefit under the Type A scheme. This is because one is only entitled to such a benefit where one is insured at the moment the risk occurs. In that case the claimant will receive benefit under the Type B scheme only. As the person concerned will not have completed a full career under that scheme, his benefit will be lower than if he had not crossed the border.

---

[1] The schemes based on materialisation of the risk are enumerated for each Member State in Annex IV(A) of Regulation 1408/71.

In order to solve these problems Regulation 1408/71 creates the system which will be described in the following sections. This is applicable if an employed or self-employed person has worked in at least two Member States. A distinction is made between the case in which a worker has been insured exclusively under Type A schemes (Section 15.3) and the case in which he has been subject to at least one Type B scheme (Section 15.4)

15.2. The Structure of the Coordination of Long-Terms Benefits

Disability and survivors benefits may be Type A schemes or Type B schemes. Old-age benefits are always of the latter type.

Chapter 2 of the Regulation concerns disability benefits and Chapter 3 old-age benefits.

Part I of Chapter 2 deals with employees who have been subject exclusively to Type A schemes (discussed in Section 15.3 below), so this may be relevant to disability benefits and survivors benefits.

Part II of Chapter 2 of the Regulation concerns employed persons and self-employed persons who have been subject to at least one Type B scheme. Invalidity benefits of this type of scheme are for a large part dealt with in the same way as old-age benefits. Therefore, the section of the Regulation which deals with schemes of which at least one has been a Type B scheme refers to Chapter 3 of the Regulation, concerning old-age benefits, for the coordination rules.

As a result of the application of the partial pension principle, a person can be entitled to benefits from several States. According to the main rule, if a person applies for an invalidity, old-age or survivors' pension in all the other Member States where he has been insured, the amounts of the relevant benefits are calculated. As the sum of these benefits may be too high, rules against overlapping may have to be applied. These rules are discussed in Section 15.7.

15.3. A Person has been Exclusively Subject to Type A Schemes

15.3.1. Introduction

An employed person or self-employed person who has been *exclusively* subject to Type A schemes is, if he suffers incapacity for work, entitled only to benefit from a single Member State (Article 39(2)). Primarily, this is the State where this person is insured at the moment at which he suffers incapacity for work.

Article 39(1) provides that the institution of the Member State whose legislation was applicable at the time when incapacity for work occurred has to determine whether the person concerned satisfied the conditions for entitlement to benefit.

In other words, if he has been insured only in Type A schemes, he cannot claim benefits on the basis of the legislation of another State (even if the latter provides for higher benefits). This rule is in accordance with the *integration principle*. When

135

this method is followed, there is no reimbursement of benefit costs to the other States where the person concerned was insured. As will be clear, this is an exception to the partial pension principle.

On its turn, an exception to the integration principle may apply (Article 40(2)), if a person has been insured under a Type B scheme for a very short period: if he suffers incapacity for work while subject to a Type A scheme, he can be treated as if only Type A schemes are involved, even if he has been subject to a Type B scheme. This is the case if he satisfies the following conditions: he satisfies the conditions for the right to benefit under the Type A scheme, without taking account of periods not completed under Type A schemes. The second condition is that he is not entitled to benefit under a Type B scheme. The third condition is that he does not assert any claims to old-age benefits (the reader is reminded that the present section, Section 15.3, deals with disability and survivors' benefits only).

This rule has to prevent persons who worked for a very short period under a Type B scheme, from being affected by the negative consequences of that short periods of insurance.

15.3.2. After-Effect

It may happen, of course, that, even after aggregation rules is applied, an employed person or self-employed person cannot satisfy the conditions of a particular scheme under which he happened to be insured at the moment he begins to suffer incapacity for work (we are still talking about Type A schemes). In that case it has to be investigated whether he is entitled to benefit on the basis of the legislation of an other Member State (which must, now we are talking about persons who have been exclusively subject to Type A schemes, be a Type A scheme): if this is the case (for this purpose the aggregation rule can be applied), he receives benefit from that State.

> For example, an employed person has been insured in the United Kingdom, the Netherlands and Belgium. If he becomes incapable of work, he is primarily only entitled to invalidity benefits from Belgium.
> If he has not been insured during the number of days required by the Belgian legislation, even after aggregation of his Dutch and United Kingdom periods, the Netherlands and the United Kingdom have to investigate successively whether he is entitled to benefit under their legislation (Article 39(3)).

15.3.3. Rules of Aggregation

As was discussed above, in some schemes based on materialisation of the risk, waiting periods have to be completed before one is entitled to benefit. The aggregation rule of Article 38 of the Regulation is relevant in respect to this condition: periods of work or residence completed under other Type A schemes are taken into account as if they had been completed under the legislation of the State with these conditions.

Article 38 appeared to be important also for other reasons. Under Dutch law, it is provided that the benefit administration has to ignore disability of a claimant if his state of health made the onset of incapacity for work within a period of less than six months plainly forseeable. In the *Moscato* judgment[2], the question was raised whether such rules were contrary to Regulation 1408/71.

Moscato, who was an Italian national, was employed from 1981 until 1985 by an enterprise in the Netherlands, while he remained to live in Belgium. When his employment relationship was terminated due to a restructuring of the enterprise, he received Belgian unemployment benefit until 13 November 1987. From 13 November 1987 he worked for a temporary employment agency in the Netherlands. On 9 february 1988 he stopped working because of psychological problems. From this date until 8 February 1989 he received a Dutch sickness benefit. He was, however, refused a Dutch disability benefit, as his state of health before the start of his last professional activities in the Netherlands made that his disability could have been expected to materialise within six months.

The Court considered that the rules of aggregation for the periods of insurance, residence or work, laid down, in particular, in Article 38(1) of the Regulation, constitute one of the basic principles governing the Community coordination of social security schemes of the Member States. These have to ensure that the exercise of the right to free movement of employees does not have as effect that the employee loses advantages in the area of social security to which he would have been entitled if he had spent his working life in one Member State only. Consequently, where the legislation of the competent State makes the grant of invalidity benefit subject to the condition that at the time when the insurance became effective the claimant's state of health has been such as to make it forseeable that incapacity for work would shortly occur, the competent institution has to take account, in this situation, according to Article 38, also of the periods of affiliation with the statutory scheme of another Member State. Article 38 does not allow the competent institution to consider only the date of the start of its own insurance as the beginning of the insurance of the employee involved; the precedent periods have to be taken into account.

15.4. One has been Subject to the Legislation of Two or More Member States of Which at least One is Not a Type A scheme

If an employed person or self-employed person has been subject to at least one Type B scheme, the *partial pension* method is applied. This applies to invalidity, survivors' and old-age pensions. Each Member State where the person concerned has been employed has to investigate whether he is entitled to benefit (Article 40).

---

2   Court of Justice 26 October 1995, Case 481/93, [1995] *ECR* I-3525.

15.4.1. Aggregation of Periods of Insurance

Just like in the case of coordination of Type A schemes, the Regulation requires the aggregation of insurance, work or residence periods for the purpose, if necessary, of satisfying the entitlement conditions of Type B scheme. These rules can be found in Article 45(1). Aggregation is relevant only to the acquisition, retention and recovery of the right to benefits and *not* to the calculation of benefits. The calculation of benefit has to be done according to the rules of Article 46 (*see*, Section 15.6). For the calculation of the amount of the benefit the periods are taken into account only which have been satisfied under the scheme of the State where they have been fulfilled and not the foreign periods. Thus the aggregation rules only help to fulfil the conditions for the waiting period.

15.4.2. Adjustment of Insurance in Type A and Type B Schemes

If a person has worked first under a Type A scheme and then under Type B scheme, and he becomes disabled, the Regulation has to solve the problem, that under the national rules of the Type A scheme he is not entitled to benefit. It is a characteristic of Type A schemes that one must be insured under that scheme at the time of materialisation of the risk.

Article 45(5) is made for this purpose. This provision rules that the condition that a claimant must be insured at the time of materialisation of the risk is regarded as having been satisfied in the case of insurance under the legislation of another Member State in accordance with provisions which have been determined for each Member State involved in Annex VI. In this way a fictitious insurance is created for Type A schemes.

For example, Annex VI, Point J (4) provides for the Netherlands that an employee or self-employed person, who has been insured on the basis of a Dutch Disability Act, is considered to be still insured at the time of the materialisation of the risk for the purposes of Chapter 3,

(i) if he is insured for the same risk under the legislation of another Member State or,

(ii) failing that, in the case where a benefit is due under the legislation of another Member State for the same risk.

Consequently, in order to claim benefit under the Dutch scheme a person must be insured for the same risk in another Member State or receive a disability benefit in that Member State.

A subsequent question was whether additional national conditions were allowed for granting a right to benefit. The Dutch system required that a person must have earned a certain amount of income in the last year before he became disabled, in order to be entitled to a General Disability benefit (AAW benefit).

This can lead to the following problem. Suppose a person has been insured in the Netherlands, and subsequently he started to work in German for a long period. After that period he stops working and lives on his savings. After some time he becomes disabled. Under German law this is no problem, as under its Type B scheme he has acquired a right to disability benefit. As a result, he also satisfies the conditions of the Annex for creating a fictitious insurance for a Dutch disability benefit.

The Annex rules that the type of Dutch benefit to which one is entitled, depends on the status at the time of materialisation of the risk: if one is an employee, one receives the benefit relevant to employees (WAO scheme), and if one is not, a general disability benefit payable to residents (AAW-benefit) is the relevant one. In the *Drake* case[3] the person concerned was no longer an employee at the time of materialisation of the risk and therefore he was entitled to AAW benefit only. The AAW benefit requires that a claimant received an income out of work in the year before he became disbled. In the *Drake* judgment the person concerned did not satisfy this income requirement. The problem was that Drake has always been insured under the WAO, which did not have this income requirement. Only because of the rules in Annex VI his legal status was changed to that of an AAW benefit recipient.

The Dutch national court asked the Court whether the Annex can legitimately reduce the scope of Article 45(4), in the sense that the Annex introduced a new criterion, *i.e.* the status of the person concerned at the moment of materialisation of the insured contingency.

The Court answered that there is no difference in status between the provisions of Regulation 1408/71 and those of Annex VI. All these provisions have been made on the basis of Article 51 of the Treaty. The only relevant question is whether the rules of the Annex are consistent with Article 51. Article 48 to 51 of the Treaty preclude that migrant workers lose by exercising the right to free movement advantages in the area of social security which are guaranteed by the statutory legislation of a Member State. This problem does, however, not occur in this situation. A person who has been exclusively economically active in the Netherlands and who has stopped working before the insured contingency occurs, finds himself in the same situation as a person who has exercised his right to free movement. The requirement in the AAW Law is therefore allowed, the Court ruled.

15.5. Determining Incapacity for Work

In the area of invalidity insurance there can be large differences in the definition of 'disability'. Thus it can happen that a person who has worked in various Member States, is not entitled to benefit in all these States, as he is not considered disabled by all these countries.

---

[3]   Court of Justice 20 September 1994, Case 12/93, [1994] *ECR* I-4337.

A provision which was made in order to solve these problems is Article 40(4). This provides that a decision taken by an institution of a Member State concerning the degree of invalidity of a claimant shall be binding on the institution of any other Member State concerned, provided that the concordance between the legislations of these States on conditions relating to the degree of invalidity is acknowledged in Annex V to the Regulation. In this Annex, only some concordances between the legislation of some Member States are given. Belgium, Italy and Luxembourg made such arrangements with some other Member States. Thus, this possibility is not used by many Member States.

15.6. Calculation of the Amount of Pensions

15.6.1. Introduction

This section concerns the calculation of disability benefits if at least one Type B scheme is involved. The chapter of the Regulation which gives these rules is the chapter on old-age pensions. This section is not only relevant to disability schemes (when at least one Type B scheme is involved) but also to old-age and survivors' pensions.

If a person has been insured under at least one Type B scheme, every Member State where this person has been insured must make in principle two calculations.

1. First, all Member States in whose territory a claimant has been insured, have to make a calculation of the *national pension* first. A national pension is a pension acquired by virtue of the national legislation alone. In other words, a pension is a national pension if it is not necessary to invoke the provisions of the Regulation for the purpose of acquiring a right to this pension and for the calculation of its amount.
2. Subsequently, the Member States have to calculate the amount of the pension in accordance with the rules of the Regulation (which will be discussed below).

In some specified cases, the competent State may waive the second calculation. This is the case when the result of the calculation of the pension in accordance with Article 46 of the Regulation (*i.e.* in accordance with the second calculation) is equal to or lower than the national pension.

The situations in which the calculation is not required, can be found in an Annex to the Regulation.

15.6.2. The Rules of the Regulation for Calculating Pensions

In order to calculate the pension in accordance with the rules of the Regulation (*i.e.* calculation 2 mentioned in the previous section), two steps have to be taken (Article

46(2)). Firstly, the so-called theoretical amount has to be calculated. Secondly, the proportioned pension.

The *theoretical amount* has to be calculated for each Member State where the person concerned has been insured separately. Each State where a person has been insured, has to calculate the pension to which an employed person or self-employed person would be entitled if he has completed his full career of periods of insurance and of residence (also in other Member States) under the legislation of that State. For the purpose of this calculation the State concerned has to apply the legislation which is in force at the moment.

In other words: each Member State where the employed person or self-employed person can claim benefit has to make a calculation of the amount of benefit this person would receive applying the fiction that he has been insured during his full working life in that State. This amount is calculated on the basis of all (both national and relevant foreign) periods of insurance in accordance with the national rules for calculation of the State which makes the calculation. The number of theoretical amounts is the same as the number of Member States where the person concerned has been insured.

For Type A schemes, the theoretical amount is the same as the amount to which the person concerned is entitled to by virtue of application of the national legislation alone (therefore no calculation of periods of insurance is made). For this type of scheme, *the national pension* is the same as the theoretical amount (*see*, Article 46(2)(a)).

The question arose how the theoretical amount was to be calculated for benefits from Type A schemes, if the person concerned suffers incapacity for work while being insured under the other type of scheme. This problem arose as the amount of benefit of some Type A schemes is a percentage of the wages last earned; are these the wages last earned while insured under this type of scheme or at the moment of materialisation of the risk? In the *Weber* judgment[4] the Court held that the competent State has to take the wages last earned into account (the wages earned in the State where he had his last employment).

After the theoretical amount is determined, each Member State involved calculates the *proportioned pension*. This is the pension which is calculated taking account of the relationship of the duration of periods of insurance in that State to the total length of periods of insurance in all Member States in which the person concerned has been insured. In other words, the proportioned pension from a particular State where a migrant worker has been subject to its legislation is to be calculated by multiplying the theoretical amount of that State by the result of the ratio of periods of insurance in that State to the full career of that person.

Example. A person worked twenty years in the Netherlands and ten years in Germany. He becomes disabled in Germany. His theoretical amount in the

---

4   Court of Justice 29 November 1984, Case 181/183, [1984] *ECR* 4007.

Netherlands is 70% of the last earned wages (suppose NLG 50,000), thus NLG 35,000. The pro rata fraction is 2/3 (as 20 years out of 30 were spent in the Netherlands). The pro rata amount for the Netherlands is, therefore, 2/3 times NLG 35,000. The national income would have been NLG 0, as he was not insured at the moment of materialisation of the risk, so under the national rules he would not have been entitled to benefit. For Germany the pro rata amount is 1/3rd of the German theoretical amount.

The third step is to compare the national benefit and the pro rata benefit. The highest amount is applied, *see,* Article 43(3). In the example given above the highest amount for the Netherlands is the pro rata amount. Suppose that the situation was reversed: the first period was worked in Germany and the second in the Netherlands. In that case the national pension was NLG 35,000 and the pro rata pension 2/3 times NLG 35,000. Consequently, the national pension is highest. This is a general rule: when the Type A Scheme is the last scheme a person has been subject to, the national pension is always the highest.

The sum of the pensions calculated in this way for the Netherlands and Germany may be higher than what is deemed justified from the point of view of the national legislations concerned. In order to solve this problem, rules against overlapping of benefits are to be applied, see the following section.

15.7. The Rules Against the Overlapping of Benefits

In principle the Community legislator will be better equipped for giving rules against overlapping than the national legislators. The rules given in the Regulation could, however, not stand the test by the Court. We will describe the history of the overlapping rules shortly[5] and then describe the present rules.

15.7.1. History of Community Rules against Overlapping

The Community provision against overlapping could be found in the former Article 46(3) of Regulation 1408/71. This stated that the person concerned shall be entitled to an amount not exceeding the total sum of benefits calculated with the provisions of Article 46(1) and(2), *within* the limit of the highest theoretical amount of benefits.

The highest theoretical amount is the highest of the amounts which Member States have to calculate applying the fiction that the migrant person concerned had been insured during his total career solely under the national legislation of that State.

When the said limit is exceeded, any institution which made the calculation shall adjust its benefit. Therefore, each State reduces benefit by an amount corresponding

---

[5]   We will not describe the full history in this book, as it is no longer relevant to the present rules. For the history under Regulation 3, we can refer to the first edition of this book.

to the proportion which the amount of the benefit concerned bears to the total of the benefits determined in accordance with the provisions of Article 46(1).

Only the rules on overlapping given in Article 46(3) could be applied to benefits which were determined in accordance with Article 46. In other words, the national rules for this purpose were not applicable.[6]

However, this attempt at giving a Community rule against overlapping of benefits was not successful. In the *Petroni* judgment[7] the Court decided that Article 46(3) was partially void.

> Mr Raffaele Petroni, an Italian national, worked for seventeen years as a miner in Belgium and for seven years as an employed person in Italy. From 1 January 1973 he was awarded an old age pension in Belgium, calculated solely under Belgian legislation. In addition, he received an Italian pension. The sum of the Italian and Belgian benefits was higher than the highest theoretical amount. Therefore, the Belgian institution, relying upon Article 46(3) (*old*), reduced the Belgian pension correspondingly. Both pensions were calculated on the basis of non-overlapping periods of insurance. The Belgian court asked whether Article 46(3) was in conformity with Article 51 of the Treaty.

The Court pointed out that the Regulations concerning the coordination of social security have as their basis, their framework and their bounds Article 48 to 51 of the Treaty. The aim of Articles 48 to 51 would not be attained if, as a consequence of the exercise of their right to freedom of movement, workers were to lose advantages in the field of social security guaranteed to them in any event by the laws of a single Member State.

The Court considered that Article 51 of the Treaty essentially deals with the case in which the laws of one Member State do not, by themselves, allow the person concerned the right to benefits by reason of the insufficient number of periods completed under its laws, or only allow him benefits which are less than the maximum. To remedy this situation it provides, in respect of a worker who has been successively or alternatively subject to law of two or more Member States, for aggregation of the insurance periods completed under the laws of each of such States.

The aggregation and proportionment could not, therefore, be carried out if their effect was to diminish the benefits which the person concerned might claim by virtue of the laws of a single Member State on the basis solely of the insurance periods completed under those laws, always provided that this method could not lead to a duplication of benefits for one and the same period.

Article 46(3) appeared to be a rule which limits overlapping. The Council, in the exercise of the powers which it holds under Article 51 concerning the co-ordination of the social security schemes of the Member States, had the power, in conformity with the provisions of the Treaty, to lay down detailed rules for the

---

[6] As was provided in Article 12(2), last sentence (*old*) of Regulation 1408/71.

[7] Court of Justice 21 October 1975, Case 24/75, [1975] *ECR* 1149.

exercise of rights to social benefits which the persons concerned derive from the Treaty. However, a limitation on the overlapping of benefits which would lead to a diminution of the rights which the persons concerned already enjoy in a Member State by virtue of the application of the national legislation alone is incompatible with Article 51.

The Court ruled, therefore, that Article 46(3) was incompatible with Article 51 of the Treaty to the extent to which it imposed a limitation on the overlapping of two benefits acquired in different Member States by a reduction of the amount of the benefit acquired under national legislation alone.

The ruling that the Community rule against overlapping was incompatible with Article 51 was based on the consideration of the Court that the legislative powers of the Council, as derived from this article, are limited. This interpretation followed from a reading of this article whereby it only provides the powers and duty of the Council to ensure aggregation of periods of insurance and exportation of benefits. The wording of this article does, however, not contain such a limitation. The enumeration of measures in this article is likely to be an enunciative, and not a limitative one.

The second argument of the Court was that it followed from Articles 48 to 51 of the Treaty that these have to ensure that an employed earner does not lose advantages in the field of social security as a result of cross border movement. This argument meant, in the interpretation of the Court, that a migrant person must not lose benefit rights acquired by virtue of national law alone, even if the sum of all his benefits exceeds the amount to which he would have been entitled on the basis of national law alone. Although in the *Petroni* judgment the Court did not state that it is acceptable that cross border movement leads to a more favourable position than in the case of a person staying in one State, it seems to accept this conviction.

The consequence of the *Petroni* judgment was that Article 46(3) was void, as far as rights acquired on the basis of national law alone were infringed. As a result, this article could no longer preclude the application of national rules against overlapping which are (also) aimed at reducing the overlap with foreign benefits of the same kind. This conclusion was confirmed in the *Greco* judgment.[8]

15.7.2. *The Rules against Overlapping of Benefits in Regulation 1248/92*

15.7.2.1. General

In the previous section we saw that the Council did not have the authority, on the basis of Article 51 of the Treaty, to make regulations which reduced, in the case of the overlapping of two or more benefits from more than one Member State, benefits which were acquired by virtue of the national legislation alone. It was now up to the national legislators to give rules against overlapping. As such rules may give

---

[8]   Court of Justice 13 October 1977, Case 37/77, [1977] *ECR* 1711.

undesirable results, the Council issued Regulation 1248/92 to regulate the application of national rules against overlapping of benefits.[9]

The present Article 46 implies that the employed person or self-employed person is entitled to a pension calculated by virtue of the national legislation alone or in accordance with the rules of Article 46 of the Regulation, as was discussed in Section 15.6. The person concerned is entitled to the highest amount, but national rules against overlapping can be applied. This article provides expressly that where that is the case, the comparison to be carried out shall relate to the amounts determined *after* the application of the national provisions against overlapping of benefits. In addition conditions are given for the application of rules against overlapping; these are discussed below. These rules apply only to the benefits discussed in this chapter; in Chapter 13 the general rules on overlapping in other cases were discussed.

15.7.2.2. The General Conditions on Overlapping

The objective of the present Regulation is to restrict the application of national rules against overlapping of benefits. These rules constitute the following part of the Regulation: Articles 46a, 46b and 46c.

In Article 46a general rules on the applicability of rules against overlapping can be found.

This article defines first of all what is meant by *overlapping of benefits of the same kind*. According to this article, this term has the following meaning: all overlapping of benefits in respect of invalidity, old age and survivors calculated or provided on the basis of periods of insurance and/or residence completed by one and the same person. Thus, it is relevant that periods are concerned which are completed by one and the same person. All overlapping of benefits that *do not* satisfy this definition is regarded as overlapping of benefits of a different kind.

Example. Survivors' and disability pensions are not benefits of the same kind.

In case of overlapping of benefits of the *same* kind, or of a *different* kind or of *other income* (in other words: in all cases of overlapping) the following rules apply (article 46a).

- Account shall be taken of the benefits acquired under the legislation of another Member State or of other income acquired in another Member State *only* where the legislation of the first Member State provides for the taking into account of benefits or income acquired abroad. In other words, national rules against overlapping are only applicable if they make an express reference to foreign benefits.

---

[9]   *OJ* 1992 *L* 136, p. 7.

- If this condition is satisfied, account has to be taken of the *gross* benefits, *i.e.* before deduction of taxes, social security contributions and other individual levies or deductions.
- The third condition is that national rules against overlapping must not take account of benefits which are awarded on the basis of voluntary insurance or continued optional insurance.
- If the rules against overlapping of benefits of only one Member State are applicable on account of the fact that the person concerned receives benefits of a similar or different kind payable under the legislation of other Member States or other income, the rule is as follows: the benefit payable under the legislation of the first Member State may be reduced only within the limit of the amount of the benefits payable under the legislation or the income acquired within the territory of other Member States. Thus, the effect of rules against overlapping of benefits is limited to the amount of the foreign benefit or income.

15.7.2.3.Overlapping of Benefits of the Same Kind

The second set of rules is found in Article 46c.

This article states that the rules against overlapping are not applicable to benefits calculated in accordance with Article 46(2) of the Regulation. As a consequence, national rules against overlapping are applicable only to specific types of pensions acquired by virtue of the national legislation alone. These specific types consist of the following two categories.

- The first type is that of pensions payable under a Type A scheme.
- The second type consists of benefits, the amount of which is determined on the basis of a credited period deemed to have been completed between the date on which the risk materialised and a later date (in other words, a scheme with notional periods). These schemes provide for benefits under the condition that, when a claim is made, it is also possible to have specific periods counted, although the person concerned did not work in these periods (*e.g.* periods in which he raised children, or in which he served periods of military service).

It is provided by the Regulation that, in respect of these two cases, rules against overlapping can be applied in case of overlapping of benefits of the same kind.[10]

15.7.2.4.Overlapping of Benefits of the Same Kind with Benefits of a Different Kind

Finally, Article 46c gives special provisions in case of overlapping of one or more benefits of the same kind with one or more benefits of a different kind. The rule is as follows. If the receipt of benefits of a different kind entails the application of

---

[10] Except where an agreement has been concluded between two or more Member States providing that one and the same credited period may not be taken into account two or more times

national rules against overlapping against two or more benefits acquired by virtue of the national legislation alone, the amounts which would not be paid in strict application of the provisions concerning overlapping of benefits of the Member States concerned shall be divided by the number of benefits subject to reduction, suspension or withdrawal.

In other words, the provision requires that where rules against overlapping were applied, the average of the various reductions resulting from the application of the rules against overlapping has to be taken.

Example. An employee is entitled to a disability benefit of 200 and a survivors' pension of 100. A national rule against overlapping requires that these benefits must not overlap with unemployment benefit. In this case, if the rules of the Regulation did not apply, the amount of the disability benefit would be 120 and that of the survivors pension would be 20.

The rules of the Regulation involve that the unemployment benefit is divided by the number of pensions (two) and that half the unemployment benefit is deducted from each pension. The amount of the disability pension is thus 160, the amount of the survivors pension 60 and the amount of the unemployment benefit 80.

The second element of Article 46c concerns the concurrence of benefits of the same kind with pensions calculated in accordance with Article 46(2). In case of such a pension, the benefit(s) of a different kind from other Member States and all other income from other Member States shall be taken into account only in proportion to the periods of insurance and/or residence which were taken into account to calculate the said benefit in accordance with Article 46(2).

Example. Suppose that a German widow receives a Belgian survivors' benefit and a German and Belgian disability pension (based on insurance of ten years in Belgium and 15 years in Germany). The pro rata part is 3/5 in Germany and 2/5 in Belgium. If this woman receives an income of 1,000 per month, 3/5th part will be deducted from the German benefits and 2/5th from the Belgian benefits.

If the receipt of benefits of a different kind or of other income entails the rules against overlapping of one or more benefits acquired by virtue of the national legislation alone and of one or more benefits referred to in Article 46(2), the following rules apply.

a. With respect to national benefits: in case of benefits acquired by virtue of the national legislation alone, the amounts which would not be paid in strict application of the national overlapping provisions shall be divided by the number of benefits subject to reduction, suspension or withdrawal. In other words, in this case the unpaid part is averaged by the States from which the person concerned receives benefits.

b. In case of benefit(s) calculated in accordance with Article 46(2), the rules against overlapping shall be taken into account only in proportion to the periods of insurance and/or residence which were taken into account to calculate the said benefit in accordance with Article 46(2).

In some cases, as we have seen, the Regulation provides for the division of reductions in benefits. Article 46c limits this opportunity; this concerns the overlapping of a national benefit with benefits of a different kind and the reduction of such benefits plus benefits calculated in accordance with Article 46(2). If, in these cases, the legislation of a Member State provides that, for the application of rules against overlapping of benefits, account is taken of benefits of a different kind in proportion to the periods of insurance referred to in Article 46(2)(b), the division mentioned before shall not apply in respect of that Member State.

A remarkable situation occurs with the overlapping of a Belgian old-age pension and a Dutch old-age pension. This appeared in the *Van Munster* judgment.[11]

The Belgian Royal Decree no. 50 on retirement and survivors' pensions provides that persons are entitled to the family rate of an old-age pension only if the spouse is not entitled to an old-age pension of her own right. The problem arose in the case of an employee who received both a Belgian and a Netherlands pension. Under the Dutch Old Age benefit scheme both the man and the woman are entitled to a pension of their own after retirement at the age of 65. If one member of the couple is already over 65 and the other is below 65, the older one receives a supplement of 50% of the old-age benefit. If the other person also reaches the age of 65, this supplement is withdrawn and both persons receive their own benefit. The total amount granted under the Netherlands legislation does, however, not change. The result is, however, that the man, who first received a Belgian old-age pension at the family rate, is now granted the rate for a single person only, as his spouse received a Dutch pension of her own when she became 65.

The Court considered that if a national statutory scheme is applied on a migrant in the same way as on employees who remained in the same country, this can have unexpected consequences. These are hard to reconcile with the aim of the Articles 48 to 51 of the Treaty. They are caused by the circumstance that the rights to a pension of migrant workers fall under two separate statutory schemes. The differences are the result of the fact that one of the two pension schemes grants a higher benefit to the employee whose spouse does not receive an old-age or comparable pension. Under the other scheme each of the spouses receives, after reaching retirement age, half the pension of an equal part, by which the total family income does not rise.

The Court was not able to solve the problem. It considered that, taking account of the considerable difference between these statutory schemes, the principle laid down in Article 5 of the EC Treaty of loyal cooperation between the competent authorities of the Member States, requires that they apply all the available means in order to realize the aim of Article 48 of the Treaty.

---

[11] Court of Justice 5 October 1994, Case 165/91, [1994] *ECR* I-4661.

The Court thus asks the Member States to solve the problem. It added to this that it is up to the national court to interpret the national rules which he has to apply as much as possible conform the requirements of Community law.

In this decision a confrontation of the principle of equal treatment of men and women and the principle of free movement can be seen. The Dutch old age benefit scheme was drafted as it is in order to realize the principle of equal treatment. If the Dutch scheme had given the pension exclusively to the man, the problem did not arise. The Court could, however, not go so far as to solve this problem in the framework of the interpretation of coordination rules, as it cannot harmonise national law.

15.8. Recalculation of Benefits

Sometimes it is necessary to recalculate the amount of benefit. This is, for instance, relevant in case of a rise of the costs of living or rises in the wages level. Another reason for recalculation of benefits is a change in the exchange rate. Furthermore, the extent of disability can change, or it is possible that a person starts to gain income. The question arises when the recalculation has effect for foreign benefits, in other words when the calculation of Section 15.6 has to be done again.

To this question Article 51 of the Regulation is relevant. This article provides that if, by reason of an increase in the cost of living or changes in the level of wages or salaries or other reasons for adjustment, the benefits of the States concerned are altered by a fixed percentage or amount, such percentage or amount must be applied directly to the benefits determined under Article 46, without the need for a recalculation in accordance with that article. In other words, if the pensions are adjusted on the basis of social-economic factors, the percentage or amount does not lead to a recalculation. Thus, if the amount of a foreign pension is raised in order to take account of the costs of living, the other Member State cannot annihilate this rise by recalculating its own benefit.

If, however, the amount of the pension is changed because of changes in the personal circumstances, such as the level of invalidity or the family situation, a recalculation on the basis of Article 46 is possible.

The limitation of Article 51 on the recalculation of pensions is mostly to the advantage of the beneficiaries. This limitation applies, however, only, as provides Article 51, if pensions are determined 'according Article 46'. Does this limitation apply also if benefits are calculated on the basis of national legislation alone?

The Court answered this question in the affirmative in the *Cassamali* judgment[12] and the *Bogana* judgment.[13] It considered that such a national benefit is essentially determined in accordance with Article 46, exactly because a comparison has to be made with a benefit calculated on the basis of the pro rata method. Article 51(1) opposes, therefore, a recalculation of these benefits.

---

[12]   Court of Justice 20 March 1991, Case 93/90, [1991] *ECR* I-1401.
[13]   Court of Justice 18 February 1993, Case 193/92, [1993] *ECR* I-755.

This interpretation of the Court is a broad one of Article 51, as it does not follow from the wording of this article. The judgment is, however, consistent with the spirit of this article. This is to prevent benefit administrations from making new recalculations any time when in other countries a benefit is changed because of altered exchange rates or indexes.

15.9.   Acquisition of Pensions Rights by the Unemployed

In Chapter 17 we will see that for some unemployed the unemployment benefit scheme of the State of residence is assigned as the relevant scheme. This raised the question in which country they acquire rights to disability or old age pensions: in the State of employment or the State of residence? This will be discussed in Section 17.6.

15.10.   The Relationship between International Conventions and Regulation 1408/71

According to Article 6 of Regulation 1408/71, the Regulation has, in principle, priority over provisions of social security conventions binding two or more Member States. Provided that none of the exceptions mentioned in Article 6 and 7 apply, the provisions of the Regulation replace the provision of such international social security conventions. Article 7 provides that the Regulation does not affect obligations arising from Conventions adopted by the International Labour Conference (the ILO) which, after ratification by one or more Member States, has entered into force, or obligations arising from the European Interim Agreements on Social Security concluded between the Member States of the Council of Europe.

The question arose, however, whether this is also true in those cases where the application of such international conventions would be more favourable than the application of Regulation 1408/71.

The first time the Court had to answer this question was in the *Walder* case.[14] In that judgment the Court held that it was clear from Article 5 of Regulation 3 and Article 6 of Regulation 1408/71 that the principle that the provisions of social security conventions concluded between Member States were replaced by Regulation 3 was mandatory in nature. This principle did not allow for exceptions save for the cases expressly stipulated in the Regulation. The Court added that the fact that social security conventions concluded between Member States were more advantageous to persons covered by Regulation 3 was therefore not sufficient to justify an exception to this principle, unless such conventions were expressly preserved by the Regulation.

---

[14]   Court of Justice 7 June 1973, Case 82/72, [1973] *ECR* 599.

This *Walder* judgment led to much criticism.[15] In the *Rönfeldt* judgment[16], the situation and the answer of the Court was different.

Rönfeldt was a German national and resident. From 1941 to 1951 he paid contributions for a German retirement pension. Subsequently, he worked in Denmark until 1971 and he paid contributions for a Danish old-age pension. After he returned to Germany, he had to pay German contributions again.

The problem in Rönfeldt's case was that the ages for retirement pension entitlement were different between Germany and Denmark. In Denmark, the retirement age was sixty-seven, and in Germany this age was sixty-five. In addition, under the German scheme an early retirement pension could be claimed at the age of sixty-three, but for that pension it was required that one had completed thirty-five years of insurance. Therefore, he was refused early retirement benefit.

Article 45 of Regulation 1408/71 was relevant to this issue; this states that where the legislation of a Member State makes the acquisition of the right to benefits subject to the completion of periods of insurance, the competent institution shall take account of periods of insurance under the legislation of another Member State. Article 46 provides, however, that each Member State has to calculate the amount of its benefit taking account of the total amount of insured periods completed under its legislation. Consequently, Regulation 1408/71 requires only that periods of insurance have to be aggregated for the purpose of *acquiring* a right to benefit but not for the *calculation* of a right to benefit.

The Convention concluded between Germany and Denmark of 1953, however, provided that periods of insurance completed under the legislation of Denmark also had to be counted, not only for the establishment of a right, but also for the calculation of the German pension.

Article 6 of Regulation 1408/71 provided, as we have seen, that the Conventions concluded between Member States were replaced by the Regulation at the date it came into force.[17] This would have the effect that the Germany-Denmark convention which provided that the Danish periods would be counted for the calculation of the pension, was no longer applicable.

The Court considered that because of Article 6 Rönfeldt lost advantages which had been awarded to him by a bilateral convention. This loss of benefit rights was not compatible with Articles 48 and 51 of the Treaty. It had already pointed out in the *Petroni* judgment[18] and *Dammer* judgment[19] that the purpose of these articles

---

[15]   David O'Keeffe and Henry G. Schermers (1982: 117-122) wrote: 'This surprising, and it is submitted, grossly inequitable decision flew in the face of established case-law.'

[16]   Court of Justice 7 February 1991, Case 227/89, [1991] *ECR* I-323.

[17]   *I.e.* 1 April 1973 when Denmark entered the European Community (note that Denmark entered the EC only after Rönfeldt had returned to Germany. It is therefore not far fetched to say that his 'acquired' rights would be affected if the bilateral convention no longer guaranteed his rights.

[18]   Court of Justice 21 October 1975, Case 24/75, [1975] *ECR* 1149.

would not be achieved if employed persons exercising their right to free movement lost advantages to which they would have been entitled by virtue of national law alone. This case law had to be interpreted, according to the Court, as meaning that benefits awarded by virtue of national law also comprise benefits to which one is entitled by virtue of international conventions in force between two or more Member States and which are integrated in their national legislation. The latter rules have to be applied if they are more advantageous than the application of Community law. Another interpretation would involve a substantial restriction on Articles 48 and 51 as it would place a person who exercises the right to free movement in a less advantageous position.

It was feared that the *Rönfeldt* judgment would apply in all cases where bilateral Conventions are involved and this would lead to complicated situations. Bilateral and multilateral agreements are so numerous, so complicated and so varied that it would be unrealistic to require social security bodies to calculate for each migrant worker not only his benefit rights in accordance with national law and Community law, but also in accordance with international conventions.

In the *Thévenon* judgment[20] the Court clarified its position in the *Rönfeldt* ruling.

Thévenon was a French national, who has been compulsorily insured as an employee, first from 1964 to 1977 in France and subsequently in Germany. The German social assistance administration considered that the periods of insurance completed by Thévenon in France had to be taken into account for the calculation of the German pension, in accordance with the rules of the General Treatment on social security between France and Germany (1950).

The Court remarked that according Article 9 of this Treaty the periods completed under both schemes were taken into account for the calculation of the amount of benefit if a German or French employee has worked in both countries under one or more schemes of invalidity insurance. Regulation 1408/71 does not take periods abroad into account for the calculation of the amount of benefit. The Treaty thus provides for a more attractive result than the regulation.

The Court considered that it had already ruled in the *Walder* judgment that from Article 6 and 7 of the Regulation follows that Community regulations replace the provisions of treaties concluded between Member States. These provisions have a compulsory character, and do not allow for exceptions apart from those mentioned in the Regulation explicitly. Neither do exceptions apply if these treaties would lead to higher benefits than on the basis of the Regulation.

The *Rönfeldt* judgment concerned, according to the Court, a situation in which at the moment when Mr Rönfeldt returned to Germany, Denmark had not yet entered the EU. The Treaty between these two countries had not yet been replaced by Regulation 1408/71. Therefore it had to be investigated if, and if positively, how,

---

[19] Court of Justice 14 December 1989, Case 168/88, [1989] *ECR* 4553, *see* Chapter 16.
[20] Court of Justice 9 November 1885, Case 475/93, [1995] *ECR* I-3813.

the periods completed in Denmark before Regulation 1408/71 applied to Denmark had to be taken into account for the calculation of the pension in the other Member State.

The answer given to this question in the *Rönfeldt* judgment does not apply in the situation of Mr Thévenon, who had not exercised his right to free movement before the coming into force of Regulation 1408/71. This meant that at the time Mr Thévenon went to work abroad the French-German Treaty, as far as its personal and material scope are concerned, was already replaced by Regulation 1408/71. This employee cannot hold that he had lost social security advantages to which he would have been entitled on the basis of the German French Treaty.

As a result of this judgment it is not necessary to investigate in all cases whether the application of the rules of a Treaty between two Member States leads to a more advantageous result than Regulation 1408/71.

Chapter 16

Family Benefits and Child Benefits

16.1.   Introduction

Since 1989 the self-employed are also under the personal scope of the provisions on family benefits.[1]

Article 1 of Regulation 1408/71 defines what is meant by 'family benefits' and 'family allowances'. By 'family benefits' the Regulation means (*see* Article 1(u)(i)) all benefits in kind or in cash intended to meet family expenses, under the legislation provided for in Article 4(1)(h). 'Family allowances' pertain, according to Article 1(u)(ii), to periodical cash benefits which are exclusively granted by reference to the number and, where appropriate, the age of the members of the family. We can also call these 'child benefit'.

The term 'family allowances' was considered in the *Lenoir* judgment.[2] Until his retirement, Lenoir had always resided and worked in France, where he was entitled to a benefit for sole-wage earners and a school benefit for his children. After his retirement he settled in England. In this country, the disputed French benefits were not paid. The Court considered that family allowances are (according to Article 1(u)(ii) of Regulation 1408/71) only those periodical benefits which are granted exclusively by reference to the number or the age of the children. The benefits in the *Lenoir* case were not exclusively based on the number or the age of the children, but also, among other things, on the income of the parents, and, consequently, they did not come within the definition of family allowances. Otherwise, the Regulation would have enabled Lenoir to export his benefits.

The *Hoever and Zachow* judgment[3] also concerned the meaning of the term 'family allowances'.

The case concerned payment of child-raising allowance (*Erziehungsgeld*). This is a non-contributory benefit forming part of a set of family-policy measures. The German Law provides that (1) any person who is permanently or ordinarily resident in the territory to which the Law applies, (2) who has a dependent child in his household, (3) who looks after and brings up that child and (4) has no, or no full-time, employment, is entitled to this child-raising allowance.

---

[1]   As a result of Regulation 3427/89, *OJ* 1989 *L* 331/1.
[2]   Court of Justice 27 September 1988, Case 313/86, [1988] *ECR* 5391.
[3]   Court of Justice 10 October 1996, Case 245/94, [1996] *ECR* I-4895.

According to Paragraph 1(4) of the Law, a national of a Member State of the EC who does not reside in Germany but who is employed within the scope of that Law and who fulfils conditions 2 to 4 is also entitled to this benefit.

A person is employed in the sense of this provision if s/he works for not less than fifteen hours a week, that being the maximum period of minor employment provided for in the German Sozialgesetzbuch.

Both Mrs Hoever and Mrs Zachow, like their husbands, were German nationals and lived at Kerkrade in the Netherlands. Since June 1990 Mrs Hoever had been working for 10 hours a week in Aachen, in Germany. When her son was born, she took 18 months' child-raising leave. Mrs Zachow had not been employed in Germany. Their husbands both had full-time employment in Germany.

On 30 May 1991 and 28 December 1987 respectively, Mrs Hoever and Mrs Zachow applied for child-raising allowance for their sons. The Land Nordrhein-Westfalen rejected those applications, on the grounds that, by reason of her limited number of working hours, Mrs Hoever was not an employed person and that Mrs Zachow resided and had her habitual place of abode in the Netherlands.

The question was whether the benefits concerned constitute 'family benefits' within the meaning of Article 4(1)(h) of Regulation 1408/71. The German Government maintained that the child-raising allowance does not have the same purpose as a 'family benefit' within the meaning of Article 1(u), since the child-raising allowance is intended, by conferring a personal right, to remunerate the particular parent who both takes on the task of raising a child and personally fulfils the conditions for grant of the allowance. The Court did not accept this argument. The aim of this type of benefit is to meet family expenses within the meaning of Article 1(u)(i) of the Regulation. First, child-raising allowance is paid only where the family of the person concerned comprises one or more children. Furthermore, its amount varies partly according to the age and number of the children, and also according to the parents' income. Second, this type of benefit is intended to enable one of the parents to devote himself to the raising of a young child. Third, the link between child-raising allowance and child-raising leave cannot remove the allowance from the scope of Article 1(u)(i) and 4(1)(h) of the Regulation, since it must be granted to the recipient, wether or not he is an employed person. Consequently, a benefit such as the child-raising allowance must be treated as a family benefit within the meaning of Article 4(1)(h) of the Regulation. We will also discuss this judgment in Section 16.3.

16.2. Which Benefit Level Applies?

Family benefits and family allowances constitute a special type of benefits. Unlike, for instance, invalidity or unemployment benefits, it is not primarily the situation of the employed or self-employed person himself which is relevant. Instead, the situation of the members of his family is relevant (although whether the worker is insured is relevant to the question whether benefit is payable for his dependants). This type of benefits is intended to meet family expenses and this is why the relationship between this benefit and the actual living standards and domestic situation of the claimant is much more relevant than in the case of other benefits.

This specific character is reflected in national conditions for entitlement to this kind of benefit: the majority of national schemes do not contain conditions as to the completion of periods of insurance in order to be entitled to these benefits. This is why the aggregation rule of the Regulation rarely applies to this type of benefit.

On the other hand, this type of benefit raised another problem, namely the question whether this type of benefit is to be paid at the rate of the State of residence, or at that of the State of employment. In other words, should the amount of benefit be fixed at that payable in the State where the children reside or at that of the State where the employed person works?

The question whether the rate of the State of employment or the rate of the State of residence is to apply for these benefits is not so easy as it seems. The application of the State-of-employment rate seems to ensure equal treatment of workers who are employed in the same State. However, this equality exists to a relative extent only. If the differences between the living standards of the Member States are taken as a starting-point, one might as well, on the basis of the equality principle, argue for unequal treatment, that is for a calculation of child benefit in accordance with the rate of the State of residence.

The coordination Regulation does not, however, have the objective of creating equality in every respect - various examples of which we have seen in the previous chapters - but of creating equality of treatment between foreign workers and domestic workers in a Member State. Article 51 Treaty, the basis of the coordination Regulation, also requires a guarantee of the export of benefits, and not equal treatment in every situation. As a result the Regulation opts for the level of the State of employment.

The Court of Justice decided in the *First Pinna* judgment[4], discussed in Chapter 8, that the provision of the Regulation which required the State-of-residence level for France was void. This case law prompted the Council to make a uniform regulation for all Member States in 1989,[5] according to which the new Article 73 applies for all Member States the State-of-employment principle.

16.3.   Overruling of Residence Requirements

As we have seen in the preceding section, Article 73 provides that an employed or self-employed person who is subject to the legislation of a Member State is entitled, in respect of the members of his family who are residing in another Member State, to the family benefits provided for by the legislation of the former State, as if they were residing in that State. With the phrase 'as if they were residing in that State',

---

4   Court of Justice 15 January 1986, Case 41/84, [1986] *ECR* 1.
5   Regulation 3427/89, *OJ* 1989 *L* 331/1.

Article 73 overrules residence requirements in national schemes. The question of the scope of this provision was dealt with in the *Bronzino* judgment.[6]

> Bronzino, of Italian nationality, was engaged in employment in Germany. In this State he applied for family benefit for his children. The German law required that children between sixteen and twenty-one years of age be registered as unemployed persons in the territory to which the family benefits law is applicable. Bronzino's children were registered with the Italian employment services. Therefore, the German institution refused to pay benefit, because the children did not satisfy the residence condition. Is Article 73 to be interpreted as meaning that when the child benefit law requires the member of the family of the employed person to be available to the employment services of the competent State, this requirement must be regarded as being fulfilled when this family member is available to the State of residence?

Germany argued that the disputed benefit and the requirement were intended to meet the problem of high unemployment. If this requirement on residence could not be imposed, insufficient account would be taken of the difficult situation on the labour market.

The Court first had to consider the question whether these benefits could be regarded as family benefits (or were they a type of unemployment benefits?). It ruled that Article 73 applies to family benefits which are intended to cover the financial expenses for maintaining a family. This is the objective of the German law on child benefit. Article 73 is intended to prevent a Member State from refusing family benefits on the grounds that the children of an employed person are residing in a Member State other than the competent State. Otherwise the employed person concerned would be impeded in his right to free movement. This is why it is to be assumed that the condition that a person must be available to the employment services of the State that grants the benefit, is within the scope of Article 73; consequently, this condition is also fulfilled, if the member of the family is available to the employment services of the State of residence. Germany had also argued that if Article 73 is applicable to these benefits, the German employment services were deprived of the possibility to free themselves from the obligation to pay benefits by assigning a job to the person concerned. The Court replied that this argument might be valid for unemployment benefits, but not for family benefits.

In Section 16.1 we discussed the *Hoever and Zachow* judgment.[7] The problem was whether the ladies were also entitled to the child-raising benefit outside the territory of Germany. The Court considered that if, as in this case, the grant of child-raising allowance - which is a family benefit - were subject to the condition that the spouse of a worker, who is not resident in Germany, must be employed within the territory to which the German Law concerned applies, the worker could be deterred

---

[6]   Court of Justice 22 February 1990, Case 228/88, [1990] *ECR* 531.
[7]   Court of Justice 10 October 1996, Case 245/94, [1996] *ECR* I-4895.

from exercising his right to freedom of movement. Consequently, it would be contrary to the purpose and spirit of Article 73 of the Regulation to deprive a worker's spouse of a benefit to which he would have been entitled if the spouse had remained in the State providing that benefit. It follows, the Court summarized, that, where an employed person is subject to the legislation of a Member State and lives with his family in another Member State, that person's spouse is entitled, under Article 73, to receive a benefit such as child-raising allowance from the State of employment.

16.4. Priority rules

16.4.1. Introduction

One of the consequences of the specific character of family benefits and family allowances, *i.e.* that these are granted on behalf of dependent persons, is the concurrence of entitlements to child benefit when both parents are working. The Regulation contains a number of provisions to prevent the overlapping of benefits for the same child for the same period.

First we will discuss the situation in which both parents are employed as employee or self-employed (in different Member States, *see* Section 16.4.2.).

Subsequently, we will deal with the situation that a person lives in a State, where the right to child benefit is based exclusively on residence, As that State would often be responsible for the charges of benefit, a special rule is made for this situation (*see,* Section 16.4.3.).

After this, we will discuss the situation that a child lives in a State other than the State of his parents.

16.4.2. Both Parents are Engaged in Work

Article 76 contains a provision which prevents the double payment of family benefits when Article 73 (or Article 74 - Article 74 concerns child benefit for the self-employed) applies. This article means that if one parent works in State x and the other is employed in State y, where the children live, Article 76 gives priority to the legislation on child benefits of the State where the children live. The right to child benefit based on the legislation of State x is suspended in this case.

Example. The father works in Germany and the children live with the mother in Belgium. If the mother works as well, the Belgian child benefit legislation has priority to the German legislation.

16.4.3. One of the Schemes Involved does not Relate Entitlement to Occupational Activities

The coordination Regulations contain a second type of priority rules for family allowances, namely Article 10(1)(a) of Regulation 574/72. This article provides for rules in the case of overlapping of, on the one hand, entitlement to family benefits or family allowances on the basis of Article 73 (or 74) of Regulation 1408/71, and on the other hand, the entitlement to child benefit which is due on the basis of a scheme of a Member State which does not require that claimants have completed periods of insurance or employment in order to be entitled to these benefits. An example of the second type of schemes is found in the United Kingdom and in the Netherlands. In case of overlapping of a scheme which requires periods of insurance and employment and schemes without such requirements, Regulation 574/72 provides that the right to benefit due under the schemes without requirements is suspended.

> *Example*. A woman living in the Netherlands is not engaged in paid employment, while her husband is employed in Germany. On the basis of Article 73 of the Regulation, he applies for German child benefit for his two children living in the Netherlands. His wife is entitled to Dutch child benefit. According to Article 10(1)(a) of Regulation 574/72, there is only an entitlement to child benefit in accordance with the legislation of the Member State where the husband is working, *i.e.* Germany.

The situation is different, however, if in this example the parent with whom the child resides, is engaged in employment. In this case, the right to family benefit on the basis of Article 73 or 74 is suspended: family allowances are only paid in accordance with the legislation of the Member State where the member of the family resides. In the same example: if the mother accepts a job, the Dutch child benefit legislation has priority.

Article 10 of Regulation 574/72 reads:
'1.a Entitlement to benefits or family allowances due under the legislation of a Member State, according to which acquisition of the right to those benefits or allowances is not subject to conditions of insurance, employment or self-employment, shall be suspended when, during the same period and for the same member of the family, benefits are due in application of Articles 73, 74, 77 or 78 of the Regulation, up to the sum of those benefits.
b. However, where a professional or trade activity is carried out in the territory of the first Member State:
(i) in the case of benefits due under Articles 73 or 74 of the Regulation to *the person entitled to family benefits or to the person to whom they are paid*, the right to family benefits due under these Articles shall be suspended up to the sum of family benefits provided for by the legislation of the Member State in whose territory the member of the family is residing. The cost of

the benefits paid by the Member State in whose territory the member of the family is residing shall be borne by that Member State;

(ii) in the case of benefits due under Articles 77 or 78 of the Regulation, *to the person entitled to these benefits or to the person to whom they are payable*, the right to these family benefits or family allowances due in application of those articles shall be suspended; where this is the case, the person concerned shall be entitled to the family benefits or family allowances of the Member State in whose territory the children reside, the cost to be borne by that Member State, and, where appropriate, to benefits other than the family allowances referred to in Article 77 or Article 78 of the Regulation, the cost to be borne by the competent State as defined by those articles.'
(italics added)

In the *Kromhout* judgment[8] the question was whether Article 10 of Regulation 574/72 is also applicable when one of the spouses is not subject to the personal scope of the Regulation. In this case the mother was no longer employed.

The Court considered that here the question was whether Article 10 of Regulation 574/72 is applicable when the spouse, who is also entitled to family or child benefit for the same child, is not subject to the scope of the Regulation. In order to give an answer to this question, the objective of the Community rules on family benefits and family allowances needed to be clarified. As appeared from the definitions of these benefits in Article 1 of the Regulation, family benefits or family allowances have the objective of providing compensation to workers for family expenses, by making society share in these costs. In accordance with this objective, the rules against overlapping are to prevent the concurrent compensation of these expenses, which would lead to an unfair overcompensation for the family of the employed person. This provision is explained on the basis of the principle that the payment of social benefits of the same kind during the same period and for the same situation is to be prevented. In this case, it cannot be denied that the family receives a too large compensation for child costs. Therefore, this rule of Article 10 is applicable whenever a child, in respect of whom family benefits or family allowances are due is, as a member of the family of one of the recipients of such benefits or allowances, a person covered by the Community legislation on social security for employed persons. There is no need to ascertain whether the other recipient who is also entitled to family benefits or family allowances in respect of the same child is also covered by that legislation. It is relevant to the application of this provision that the child is within the personal scope of the Regulation.

Article 10 provides that 'the right to family benefits due under these Articles shall be suspended *up to the sum* of family benefits provided for by the legislation of the Member State in whose territory the member of the family is residing.' This means that the sum by which the suspended benefit exceeds the benefit actually paid, has also to be paid.

---

8   Court of Justice 4 July 1985, Case 104/84, [1985] *ECR* 2205.

Example. In State *x*, where the mother lives with the children, the child benefit is 100, and in State *y*, where the father worked is 80. The family receives 80 from State *y* and 20 from State *x*.

The wording from Article 10 was derived from earlier case-law of the Court, the *Ferraioli* judgment.[9] The Court decided in this judgment that as a general rule migrant workers may not lose benefit rights acquired on the basis of national legislation alone. The rules against overlapping of benefits form an exception to this principle, but the reduction of benefits must not be more than the beneficiary actually receives. The wording of Article 10 aims to ensure that no higher amount is to be suspended than a person receives on the basis of the legislation assigned by the Regulation.

Benefits must also be supplemented when the right to child benefit is not based on national law alone. This was decided in the *Beeck* judgment.[10]

Beeck, of German nationality, lived in Denmark and was engaged in employment in Germany. Each day he returned to his home, and consequently he was considered a frontier worker. He applied for child benefit in Germany, but this was refused on the basis of Article 10 of Regulation 574/72, since his wife received child benefit on the basis of Danish Law.

The Court considered that an employed person who is subject to the legislation of a Member State and whose family members reside in the territory of another Member State, is entitled to family allowances provided for by the regulation of the first State, as if they resided in the territory of this State. This is to be seen from Article 73 read with Article 13(2)(a) which states that a worker who is engaged in employment in the territory of another Member State, is subject to the legislation of that Member State, even when he resides in the territory of another Member State. He was therefore entitled to benefit in Germany.

In this case the German benefit was suspended, on the basis of the Regulation. The German benefit was higher than the Danish child benefit. Therefore Beeck applied for a supplement. The German benefit was, however, not a benefit Beeck would have received on the basis of national law alone, as the German law did not provide for benefits outside the territory of Germany. Still, the Court decided that a supplement has to be paid, even though no national benefits were *stricto sensu* involved. A complicated question was raised in the *Una McMenamin* case.[11]

Mrs Una McMenamin was a frontier worker who worked as a teacher in Northern Ireland (UK) and resided with her husband and her four children in Ireland. Her husband was employed in Ireland. The Irish legislation confers

---

[9] Court of Justice 23 April 1986, Case 153/84, [1986] *ECR* 1401.
[10] Court of Justice 19 February 1981, Case 104/80, [1981] *ECR* 503.
[11] Court of Justice 9 December 1992, Case 119/91, [1992] *ECR* I-6393.

entitlement to child allowance on the person with whom the child normally lives. If the child lives with its father and its mother, the law provides that it is the child's mother who is entitled to the allowance. When Mrs McMenamin applied for benefit the adjudication officer decided that she was entitled only to a supplement, namely the amount necessary to bring the family allowances payable to her under the corresponding Irish legislation up to the level of child benefit under the United Kingdom law.

The Court considered that the national court raised the issue of the application of Articles 13 and 76 of Regulation 1408/71 and of Article 10(1)(b)(i) of Regulation 574/72 to a situation which is characterised by the fact that under the legislation of the State of residence the frontier worker, who is entitled to allowances paid by the State of employment, is also entitled to allowances paid by the State of residence in whose territory only her spouse is working.

The problem was that according to Irish law the father was not entitled to child benefit. The Court considered that the phrase 'the person entitled to the family benefits, or the person to whom they are paid' within the meaning of Article 10 of Regulation 574/72 has to be interpreted as encompassing in particular, apart from the spouse, a person who is not or is no longer married to the person entitled to benefits in pursuance of Article 73 or that person himself if the overlapping entitlement to family allowances arises because that person is also working in the State of residence. The legislature chose to define that group of persons by their common characteristic, namely their status as persons entitled to family allowances in the state of residence, rather than by giving an exhaustive list. The principle that may be deduced therefrom is as follows: 'where a person having the care of children exercises a professional or trade activity in the territory of the State of residence of those children, the allowances payable by the State of employment in pursuance of Article 73 are suspended up to the amount of the allowances of the same kind actually paid by the State of residence, irrespective of who is designated as directly entitled to the family allowances by the legislation of the State of residence'.

Consequently, in this case the right to child benefit of the mother from United Kingdom is suspended, and the latter State has to pay a supplement if the Irish benefit is lower than the British benefit.

16.4.4. *Children Residing in a State Other than the Parents' State of Employment*

In the *Dammer* judgment[12] a lacuna was discovered in the provisions of Regulation 1408/71. It appeared that the Regulation did not contain provisions for a situation in which the child resides in a State other than the States where the parents work.

---

[12]   Court of Justice 14 December 1989, Case 168/88, [1989] *ECR* 4553.

Mr Dammer worked in Belgium, and Mrs Dammer worked in Germany, whereas they both lived with their child in the Netherlands. Mr Dammer applied for child benefit in Belgium. This application was refused because Dammer's wife, in accordance with an application filed on 2 September 1987 at the German institutions, received child benefit for her child since March 1987. Are the parents, who both can rely on Article 73, to choose the State in which they make their application?

The Court considered that as the provisions of the Regulation did not give any guidance, the principles underlying Article 51 of the Treaty are to be considered. As the Court consistently held, especially in the *Petroni* judgment,[13] the objectives of Articles 48 to 51 of the Treaty would not be attained if employed persons, as a result of exercising their right to free movement, would be deprived of advantages in the field of social security, which are guaranteed by the legislation of the Member State where they reside. In the present case, the Court sought an analogous solution. The employed person is entitled to a supplement amounting to the difference between the two benefits at the expense of the competent institution of the Member State which was the first to award a right to benefit. In the Member State where the person at a later date acquired a right to benefit, benefit is thus suspended, in so far as the amount of that benefit is higher than the amount in the first State. The result of this case law is that the costs of child benefit (apart from a supplement) are borne by the Member State which is the first to award benefit.

Subsequently, Regulation 574/72 was revised and the new Article 10(3) provides, that, where family allowances under the legislation of two Member States are due for the same period and the same member of the family by virtue of Article 73 and/or Article 74 of the Regulation, the Member State whose legislation grants the highest benefit, pays the full amount, whereas the other Member State refunds, within the limits of the amounts provided for in that legislation, half this amount.[14]

This is a better rule than the one designed by the Court, as in the approach of the Court the State which was the first to pay, had to bear the highest charges. The new Regulation gives a better division of costs.

16.5. Family Allowances for Pensioners and Orphans' Allowances

16.5.1. Introduction

The Regulation has a special rule for family allowances for pensioners (Article 77). The benefits concerned were family allowances for persons receiving pensions for old age, invalidity or an accident at work or occupational disease, and increases or supplements to such pensions.

---

[13] Court of Justice 21 October 1975, Case 24/75, [1975] *ECR* 1149
[14] The new article was inserted by Regulation 1945/93, *OJ* 1993 *L* 181/1.

16.5.2. The Rules for Determining the Legislation applicable for Pensioners

The main principle for benefits payable for dependents of pensioners is that these are granted in accordance with the legislation of one Member State only. The rules are given in Article 77(2). This article does not, however, preclude that supplements are paid by other Member States.

Article 77 provides that benefits are granted irrespective of the Member State in whose territory the pensioner or the children are residing.

a If the pensioner draws a pension under the legislation of one Member State only, this is in accordance with the legislation of the Member State responsible for the pension. In other words, the State responsible for the pension also has to pay the allowance for the children.

b Where the pensioner draws pensions under the legislation of more that one Member State, the following rules apply.

i He will receive family allowances in accordance with the legislation of the State in which he resides on condition that he is entitled to family allowances (in the sense of pensions discussed in the previous section) under the legislation of that State.

ii If he is not able to satisfy the conditions of the State of residence for obtaining family allowances, the legislation applicable is that of the Member State to which he has been subject for the longest period of time. Again, a condition is that he is entitled to family benefits under such legislation. If no right to benefit is acquired under that legislation, the conditions for the acquisition of such right under the legislations of the other Member States concerned shall be examined in decreasing order of the length of periods of insurance or residence completed under the legislation of those Member States.

These rules designate for ever the legislation under which the pensioner or orphan is to derive his rights. Consequently, if the right to benefit ends in accordance with the appointed legislation, he cannot make an application for benefit under the legislation of another Member State.

16.5.3. The Rules against Overlapping applicable to Family Benefits for Pensioners and other Allowances

Article 79(3) provides that the rights to benefits, due only under the national legislation or under the provisions of Articles 77 and 78, are suspended if the children become entitled to family benefits or family allowances under the legislation of a Member State by virtue of the pursuit of a professional or trade activity. In other words, if a pensioner receives family allowances and later, for the same child, benefit is paid because a parent of this child is employed, the family allowances of the pensioner are suspended; the same is true with respect to orphans' benefits. In such a case, according to this article, the persons concerned are considered as members of the family of an employed or self-employed person.

As can be expected, the rules for determining the legislation applicable and the provisions against overlapping, which are relevant to the kind of benefits discussed in this chapter, have to take into account the principle that benefit rights acquired by virtue of national legislation alone must not be reduced. The relevance of this principle for family allowances was clarified in the *Rossi* judgment.[15]

> Claudino Rossi, an Italian national, worked in Belgium in the mines and iron industry from 1948 to 1958. As he suffered from an occupational disease, he was granted a Belgian pension for permanent invalidity. He was the father of two children for whom he received family allowances in Belgium until 28 February 1973, at which date he returned to Italy with all his family. The Belgian benefit administration suspended his family allowance with effect from 1 March 1973 - applying the provisions of Article 79(3). This was done on the grounds that the claimant's wife was pursuing a professional activity in Italy such as to confer an entitlement to family allowances under the Italian legislation. The applicant's wife applied for child benefit in Italy, but Italy refused to grant this benefit on the grounds that the father was the head of the family, a capacity which could not be transferred to the mother, since the father was not an invalid nor unemployed.

The question addressed to the Court was whether the Belgian institution must assume responsibility for paying family allowances even if a right exists in Italy by virtue of the pursuit of a profession or trade by a member of the family of the person receiving a pension, but where such a right is imperfect owing to a particular feature of Italian legislation.

The Court observed that the rule against overlapping of Article 79(3) has a purpose, and is applicable, only if entitlement to benefits actually arises and is acquired according to the legislation of the State in which the professional activity is pursued. Therefore, under Article 79(3) the suspension of the entitlement to family allowances in respect of the dependent children of a father who is in receipt of a pension under the legislation of a Member State is not applicable if the mother has not actually become entitled to those same allowances under the legislation of another Member State by virtue of her pursuit of occupational activities. It is appropriate that the rule against overlapping of benefits contained in Article 79(3) should be applied only partially and that the difference between these amounts should be granted in the form of a supplement.

In the *Patteri* judgment[16] the Belgian benefit institution questioned the obligation (as developed by the Court) to grant supplements. It argued before the Court that the Council was not authorised to make regulations for such supplements. Belgium

---

[15]   Court of Justice 6 March 1979, Case 100/78, [1979] *ECR* 831.
[16]   Court of Justice 12 July 1984, Case 242/83, [1984] *ECR* 3171.

argued that Article 51 of the Treaty only gave power to the Council to make a Regulation which ensures the export of benefits and to ensure that periods of work and insurance are aggregated. Consequently, Article 77 could be no more than a rule for determining the legislation applicable and could not provide that persons became entitled to benefits to which they were not entitled under the national legislation (Belgian family allowances were subject to the territoriality requirement). In other words, Belgium claimed that the Council was not authorised to make a rule for determining the family allowance legislation applicable which has binding effect and thus the Court could not interpret the Regulation in such a way.

The Court ruled that both measures mentioned in Article 51, *i.e.* (a) aggregation of periods and (b) guarantee of payment of benefits, are only two instruments belonging to a package of measures to be used by the Council in order to promote the freedom of movement of workers. Ensuring the freedom of movement for workers is the fundamental principle of Article 51 of the Treaty. Therefore, the strict interpretation proposed by Belgium could not be followed.

A broad interpretation of the rights acquired under national legislation can be found in the *Athanasopoulos* judgment.[17]

> In Germany, ten proceedings were brought against the benefit administration, by various non-German Community nationals. All these persons were residing in other Member States, but had at one time been employed in Germany. They all claimed to have the right to receive family allowances for children or to receive a supplement equal to the difference between the amount of the German allowances and the amount of the family allowances provided for by the legislation of the Member State in the territory of which they were residing.

One of the questions which were raised was whether a supplement still had to be granted by the Member State of first residence where the right to the benefits in that State had only been acquired after the transfer of residence by the beneficiary and where it had been acquired with regard to children born after this transfer. The Court replied in the affirmative to this question. Again it referred to the objective of Regulation 1408/71, namely the free movement of workers. If workers had to keep their residence in a Member State in order not to lose part of the amount of the benefits to which they would be entitled to in that State, the free movement of workers would be impeded.

A further problem emerged because national legislation provided that the amount of the benefits could be reduced in accordance with the *national* income of the beneficiary and of the members of the family. The Court considered if it is the legislation of the Member State which has to pay the benefits by virtue of Article 77 and Article 78 which provide such a possibility of reduction, the texts of these Articles authorise such a reduction where the beneficiary resides in a State other than that Member State. If it is the legislation of the Member State from which the

---

[17]   Court of Justice 11 June 1991, Case 251/89, [1991] *ECR* I-2797.

supplement is claimed which contains such a provision, this provision may also be applied because the amount of benefits actually received from the Member State of new residence has then to be compared to the amount of benefits which would have been received if the beneficiary had not transferred his residence. The Member State which has to pay the benefits or the supplements, has to apply the national rules as if the beneficiary and the members of his family who reside in the same Member State as he does, were to reside within the territory of the first Member State and obtained there the income they realise in the State of residence.

Another requirement for suspension is that it involves benefits of the same kind. This requirement was clarified in the *Laumann* judgment.[18]

> Gert and Anja were the minor children of Hubert and Waltraud Laumann, who were divorced and of whom Hubert had deceased. They received an *orphans' pension*, but on the basis of Article 79(3) the right to benefit was suspended, because the husband of the mother (who had remarried) received family allowances in respect of the children who lived with him in Belgium.

The Court considered that, whilst Article 78 includes both family allowances and orphans' pensions, those two types of benefits are of a clearly different kind. In the system established by Regulation 1408/71, family allowances accrue from an actual occupation (even if the worker is no longer engaged in such occupation) and the direct and sole recipient is the worker himself. On the other hand, the direct and sole recipient of the orphans' pension is the orphan himself and the pension, like other survivors' benefits, constitutes protection arising from a prior occupation, pursuit of which ceased on the death of the employee. It would be contrary to the objectives of the Community provisions against the overlapping of benefits in the field of social security if the grant of a benefit to one dependant could be adversely affected by a benefit paid to another dependant. Consequently, Article 79(3) which provides that 'the right to benefit due under' Article 78 shall be suspended 'if the children become entitled to family allowances or family benefits' must be interpreted to mean that the 'rights to benefits' must exist in favour of one and the same recipient. The right to the benefits referred to in Article 79(3) of Regulation 1408/71 is to be suspended, in order to prevent duplication of benefits only in so far as that right overlaps with benefits of the same kind acquired by virtue of the pursuit of a professional or trade activity.

16.5.4. Orphans' Benefits

'Orphans' benefits' mean family allowances and, where appropriate, supplementary or special allowances for orphans and orphans' pensions except those granted under insurance schemes for accidents at work and occupational diseases. In the *Baldi*

---

[18]   Court of Justice 16 March 1978, Case 115/77, [1978] *ECR* 805.

judgment the term *orphan* was under discussion.[19] In this case a benefit was under dispute which had been granted because Baldi's wife had deceased. The Court considered that the term 'orphan of the deceased worker' in the sense of Article 78(2) cannot apply to the case in which a child becomes an orphan after the death of a family member who did not have the status of a worker.

> Article 78(2) provides that orphans' benefits are granted in accordance with the following rules, irrespective of the Member State in whose territory the orphan is resident:
> (a) for the orphan of a deceased employed or self-employed person who was subject to the legislation of one Member State only in accordance with the legislation of that State;
> (b) for the orphan of a deceased employed or self-employed person who was subject to the legislation of several Member States:
>   i in accordance with the legislation of the Member State in whose territory the orphan resides provided that, taking into account, where appropriate, the provisions of Article 79 (1) (a), a right to one of the benefits referred to in paragraph 1 is acquired under the legislation of that State;
> or
>   ii in other cases in accordance with the legislation of the Member State to which the deceased had been subject for the longest period of time, provided that, taking into account, where appropriate, the provisions of Article 79 (1) (a), the right to one of the benefits referred to in paragraph 1 is acquired under the legislation of that State; if no right is acquired under that legislation, the conditions for the acquisition of such right under the legislations of the other Member States shall be examined in decreasing order of the length of periods of insurance or residence completed under the legislation of those Member States.
> However, the legislation of the Member State applicable in respect of provision of the benefits referred to in Article 77 for a pensioner's children shall remain applicable after the death of the said pensioner in respect of the provision of the benefits to his orphans.

The *Gravina* judgment considered orphans' benefits.[20]

> The five plaintiffs were children of an Italian worker who died in the Federal Republic of Germany in 1973. After the widow and the plaintiffs transferred their residence to Italy in 1974, the German benefit administration ceased payment of survivors' pensions. These pensions were acquired by virtue of national law alone. The article applicable was Article 78(2)(a) of Regulation 1408/71, quoted above.

---

[19]   Court of Justice 14 March 1989, Case 1/88, [1989] *ECR* 667.
[20]   Court of Justice 9 July 1980, Case 807/79, [1980] *ECR* 2205.

The judgment considered the meaning of this provision: does this mean that a right to benefit based on national law alone can be lost?

The Court considered, in view of the problems with interpretation, that Article 78 is to be considered in the light of Article 51 of the Treaty. It repeated its rulings in the *Rossi* judgment that a migrant worker and his dependants could not be deprived of the benefit of a part of the legislation of a Member State. Consequently, the provisions of Article 78(2) may not be interpreted in such a way that, by the substitution of benefits provided by the new State of residence for the benefits previously acquired under the legislation of another Member State alone, the orphans of a deceased worker who was subject to the legislation of more than one Member State are prevented from receiving the greatest amount of those benefits. Where the residence of the orphans is transferred to the territory of another Member State where a right to benefit exists, it is necessary to compare the amount of the benefits actually received with the actual amount of benefits which they would have continued to receive in the other Member State. If this amount of the new benefit is less than that of the benefits previously acquired, the orphans are entitled to a supplement equal to the difference between these two amounts.

The approach of the *Athanasopoulos* judgment was followed in the *Marzio and Mario Doriguzzi-Zordanin* judgment, which also concerned orphans' benefits.[21]

> The judgment concerned the children of a migrant worker, of Italian nationality, who died on 29 August 1983, after having completed periods of insurance both in Germany and Italy. The children continuously resided in Italy. They received an Italian orphans' pension for the periods of insurance completed in Italy by the father. To this pension a fixed sum per month was added by way of family supplement. In accordance with the *Athanasopoulos* judgment, they received a supplement to this benefit from Germany; this supplement represented the difference between the orphans' pension which should have theoretically been awarded in Germany, on the basis of the periods of insurance completed in that Member State, and the total benefit, including the family supplement paid in Italy. Because the applicants considered that the family supplement was not an element of the orphans' pension but an autonomous benefit, they claimed that the supplementary benefit paid by the German benefit administration should be calculated without taking into account the family supplement.

The question as to which benefits were to be taken into account was asked of the Court of Justice. The Court observed that according to the Court's consistent case law Article 78(2)(i) implies that when the amount of the benefits received in the State of residence is lower than the benefits provided for by the legislation of another Member State, the orphan is entitled to a supplement of the difference. However, the orphan cannot claim more benefits under the legislation of another Member State than those to which he would have been entitled if he had resided in that territory.

---

[21]   Court of Justice 19 March 1992, Case 188/90, [1992] *ECR* I-2039.

This result can only be achieved if the institution of the latter State may take into account the benefits awarded by the State of residence for maintaining the orphan, whatever their name or designation. Because the national systems of assistance to orphans differ considerably, the term 'orphans' benefits' in Article 78(1) relates to any benefit provided for by the national legislation destined to maintain orphans, whatever their name.

Conclusion. It can be concluded that family allowances and orphans' pension are subject to the integration principle, instead of to the partial pension principle. With respect to these benefits, the provisions of the Regulation cannot result in a reduction of benefits, if these are exclusively granted on the basis of the legislation of a Member State. In any case supplements amounting to the difference between the benefit actually paid and the suspended benefit must be paid.

It is interesting to see that the term *rights acquired by virtue of the national legislation alone* plays a role in both family allowances and old-age and invalidity pensions. The Court considered the supplementary technique which the Court had initially designed for the old Article 46(3) for the latter type of benefit to be insufficient to protect claimant's rights. For child and orphans' benefits, however, the principle is applied in such a way that benefits can be suspended, provided that a supplement is paid, if the integration principle would result in an amount of benefit which is less than the amount to which the person concerned was previously entitled.

Chapter 17

Unemployment Benefits

17.1.   Introduction

Unemployment benefits are a complicated type of benefit, as administrations are more inclined to doubt that a claimant is and remains entitled to this type of benefit, than if other types of benefit are involved. Beneficiaries of unemployment benefit are required to terminate their unemployment as soon as possible by seeking work actively. For this purpose, supervision by the employment office is essential; this supervision can mostly, but not always, be best given in the State of employment. The possibilities to receive unemployment benefits in another Member State are therefore more restricted than in the case of other types of benefits.

What is meant by 'unemployment benefits'? The Court considered that unemployment benefits are those benefits which replace wages lost by unemployment. The objective of the benefits is to provide an income for the costs of living of the employee.[1] These comprise not only benefits in cash after the start of a period of unemployment, but also training benefits in case of actual imminent unemployment.[2] Training benefits granted during periods of unemployment can also fall under the term 'unemployment benefit'.

Not all elements which are part of an Unemployment Benefits Act fall under the term 'unemployment benefits' of the Regulation. The Court considered, for example, in the *Mouthaan* judgment[3], that the rules on guaranteeing the continued payment of wages in case of inability of the employer to pay these, do not fall under the term 'unemployment benefit', because this provision does not have the character of compensating loss of wages after the start of the unemployment period.

With respect to the coordination rules of unemployment benefits, three types of situations can be distinguished:
1.   A person lives in the competent State. Before he started to live in that State, he resided in another Member State. Thus in this case there is unity of the State of residence and the competent State. *See*, for the rules in this situation, Section 17.2.

---

[1]   *See* Court of Justice 8 July 1992, Case 102/91, *Knoch*, [1992] *ECR* I-4341.
[2]   Court of Justice 4 June 1987, Case 375/85, *Campana*, [1987] *ECR* 2387.
[3]   Court of Justice 15 December 1976, Case 39/76, [1976] *ECR* 1901.

2. A person works in one country and resides in another country, while he returns at least once a week to the State of residence (this concerns a frontier worker). This situation is dealt with in Section 17.3.
3. A third situation concerns a person for whom the competent State and the State of residence are not the same, whereas the person concerned is not a frontier worker. *See*, for this situation, Section 17.4.

17.2.   The Unemployed Person Lives in the Competent State

The competent State is the country which is assigned by the rules for determining the legislation applicable. This will often be the State where the person concerned has lately been employed, but that need not always be the case. In case of posting or an Article 17 agreement another State can also be the competent State.

If the employee becomes unemployed in the competent State, and if he lives in that State, he will be paid only the unemployment benefits payable under the legislation of that State (the principle of integration). He cannot apply for the benefits from States where he has worked before. If necessary, he can invoke the rules for aggregation found in the Regulation (Article 67) in order to satisfy the conditions in the competent State.

Article 67 makes a distinction according whether a national scheme requires periods of work or periods of insurance. The Court of Justice has given an interpretation of this section, which clarifies this provision; this interpretation was given in the *Frangiamore* judgment.[4]

This interpretation means that periods of insurance fulfilled in another Member State are aggregated with the periods in the competent State if the rules of the State where benefit is claimed require that claimants have fulfilled periods of insurance. Periods of employment in another Member State (which would, in the latter State, not lead to affiliation with an unemployment insurance) are also relevant to the claim in a State which requires periods of insurance, on condition that these periods are considered in the latter State as periods of insurance. This also applies in the reverse situation: if someone fulfils periods of insurance in another country, these count as periods of insurance in the country where benefit is claimed, even if they would not be periods of insurance according to the national scheme of the latter State.

Example. Jobs of less than eighteen hours a week are not insured in Germany for unemployment insurance. In the Netherlands there are no thresholds for insurance. If a person has first worked in Germany, and then starts to work in the Netherlands, and needs the aggregation of periods in Germany for his claim in the Netherlands, the periods in Germany count for this purpose, even if these concern work for less than eighteen hours a week.

---

[4]   Court of Justice 15 March 1978, Case 126/77, [1978] *ECR* 724.

This can be shown in a scheme:

A person worked in State A before he became unemployed	A person applies for benefit in State B and this State requires periods of insurance
suppose: he fulfilled periods of insurance under system A, which would also count as such in B	in that case these are aggregated for the claim in B
suppose: he fulfilled periods which are not periods of insurance according to A, but they are according to B	in that case these are aggregated for the claim in B
suppose: he fulfilled periods which are periods of insurance according to A, but not according to B	in that case these are aggregated for the claim in B

A second question which arose is whether periods of employment which were completed under the legislation of another Member State can only be taken into account if these periods are considered as periods of insurance under the legislation under which they were completed *for the same branch* of social security. Does such a condition exist alongside the conditions of Article 67(1)? This question was raised in the *Warmerdam* case.[5]

> Mrs Warmerdam, a woman of Dutch nationality, had worked as from 17 March to 8 August 1975 in Scotland as a potter under a contract of employment. Because of her low income she was not insured for most of the social insurance contingencies, including unemployment. Before she went to Scotland (to accompany her husband who went for a training period in this country) she had worked in the Netherlands and qualified for unemployment benefit.
> After her husband completed his training, she returned to the Netherlands and applied for unemployment benefit. She was refused this benefit on the grounds that she had not been insured for unemployment benefit in Great Britain.

The Court considered that Article 67(1) does not require, in order for aggregation by the competent State of periods of employment completed in another State, that those periods have to be considered by the legislation under which they were completed for the same branch of social security as periods of insurance. As a consequence, the Netherlands had to take into account the periods completed in Great Britain although these were not periods of insurance under the United Kingdom

---

[5] Court of Justice 12 May 1989, Case 388/87, [1989] *ECR* 1203.

legislation, as these periods would have been periods of insurance, if they had been completed in the Netherlands.

A further question concerned the interpretation of the term 'periods of insurance'. The Netherlands unemployment insurance scheme requires that claimants must have worked at least one day in a number of weeks during the period of reference (at present at least one day in the 39 weeks lying in the 52 weeks before the start of the unemployment period). These days have to be work in an employment relationship, but the Dutch law does not specify whether these periods are to be called 'periods of insurance' or 'periods of work'. Thus the question rose whether the Dutch system requires 'periods of insurance'.

The Court answered that 'periods of insurance' in the sense of Article 1(r) are periods of contributions or of work which are considered as periods of insurance under the legislation under which they are completed, or which are acknowledged by that legislation as periods assimilated with periods of insurance. The term 'periods of work' refers only to periods in which work was done which are, under the system under which they are performed, not considered as periods which give the right to affiliation with a system of unemployment insurance. Thus, the Court gave a very broad definition of the term 'periods of insurance'.

The use of aggregation rules applicable to unemployment benefits is, however, subject to an important restriction. Article 67(3) provides that application of the aggregation provisions is subject to the condition that the person concerned has last completed periods of insurance or periods of employment in accordance with the provisions of the legislation under which the benefits are claimed.

This condition is, however, not applicable to frontier workers who are completely unemployed and to employed persons, other than frontier workers, who make themselves available for work in the State where they reside or who return to that territory; a special rule applies to them which will be discussed in the following sections (Section 17.3 and 17.4).

According to the condition in Article 67(3), a French national who, for instance, worked a few years in the Netherlands and who, after he has become unemployed, goes to the United Kingdom, cannot claim British unemployment benefit.[6] This is due to the fact that he did not complete periods of work in the United Kingdom immediately before he became unemployed; he is therefore unable to rely on the rules for aggregation set out in Article 67 of the Regulation. In order to be able to have the aggregation rules applied it is necessary that one became unemployed in the State where one claims benefit. There are no conditions on the duration of periods completed in the competent State before one can ask to have the aggregation rules applied. This interpretation is confirmed in the *Van Noorden-Assedic* judgment.[7]

---

[6]   The unemployed person can rely on Article 69, which enables him to obtain benefit in the State where he seeks work for a period of three months, *see* Section 17.4 below.

[7]   Court of Justice 16 May 1991, Case 272/90, [1991] *ECR* 2543. Until July 1986, France aggregated all periods in other Member States (including when not required by the Regulation) but from this date changed its policy.

Consequently, apart from some exceptions discussed below, under Community law an unemployed person is not entitled to unemployment benefits on the basis of the national legislation of a State other than the one in whose territory he became unemployed.[8] In the *Gray* case the Court was asked whether this rule was compatible with Article 51 of the EC Treaty.[9] It was argued that the contested rule constitutes an impediment to the free movement of employed persons because it leads to a financial disadvantage for employed persons who have been engaged in one Member State and who immediately after they have become unemployed start to seek work in another Member State.

The Court considered that Article 51 of the Treaty does not prohibit the Community legislator from imposing conditions to the rules which it establishes in order to ensure freedom of movement. As regards unemployment benefits the Community legislator found it necessary to impose some conditions to guarantee that unemployed persons seek work in the State where they last worked (which means that the expenses for these unemployment benefits are to be born by that State). These conditions have to ensure that benefit is paid only to persons actually seeking work. The Court concluded, that by making these conditions, the Council correctly exercised its powers of discretion. Consequently, these provisions were upheld.

17.3.   Frontier workers

The condition that a person must have been last employed in the Member State where he claims benefit is not applicable in the case of two categories of employees: the first is that of completely unemployed frontier workers.

Frontier workers are persons who pursue their occupation in the territory of a Member State and reside in the territory of another Member State to which they return as a rule daily or at least once a week.[10]

The meaning of the term 'frontier worker' was considered in the *Bergemann* case.[11]

Bergemann was a woman of Dutch nationality who worked and resided in the Netherlands. She married a man of German nationality, resigned and moved to the Federal Republic immediately after her marriage; this took place during her maternity leave. In Germany, she applied for German unemployment benefit. However, she was refused the right to benefit as she did not satisfy the German benefit conditions and she was not able to rely on Article 67 of Regulation 1408/71, since her last employment was not in Germany. Instead, she wished

---

[8]   Court of Justice 9 July 1975, Case 20/75, *D'Amico*, [1975] *ECR* 891.
[9]   Court of Justice 8 April 1992, Case 62/91, [1992] *ECR* 2039.
[10]   Article 1 (b) of the Regulation.
[11]   Court of Justice 22 September 1988, Case 236/87, [1988] *ECR* 5125.

177

to have Article 71(1)(a) applied, which concerned frontier workers. The question was, of course, whether she qualified as *frontier worker*.

Article 1(b) defines *frontier worker*: a frontier worker means 'any employed or self-employed person who pursues his occupation in the territory of a Member State and resides in the territory of another Member State to which he returns as a rule daily or at least once a week.' This term presupposes a regular movement across the border. The Court ruled that an employee who moves to another Member State but who does not return to the prior State (like Mrs Bergemann), is not a frontier worker.[12]

For *partially or intermittently unemployed* frontier workers the competent State is the last State of employment (Article 71(1)(a)(i)). The rationale for this rule is a logical one; as the person is still employed it follows that he is covered according to the State-of-employment principle.

A frontier worker who is *wholly unemployed* receives benefits in accordance with the provisions of the legislation of the Member State in whose territory he resides 'as though he had been subject to that legislation while last employed' (Article 71(1)(a)(ii)). This rule determines as legislation applicable that of the State of residence; apparently this rule presumes that the person concerned moved his place of work but not his place of residence to another State. For frontier workers wishing to be available to the employment services in the State of employment this rule is unsatisfactory, as it implies that these persons are deprived of the rights they acquired by virtue of the legislation of the State of employment. This latter point raised the question of whether this would be accepted by the Court of Justice; *see*, the *Miethe* judgment.[13]

Miethe, of German nationality, moved in 1976 to Belgium, but he remained at work as a salesman in Germany and obtained a license for this work in Germany. In Germany he could stay with his mother-in-law, which he did regularly, and which he continued to do when he became unemployed in 1979 and started seeking work in Germany. In Germany, he also applied for unemployment benefit but his application was not successful.

The question relevant in this case was whether the rule given in Article 71(1)(a)(ii) for determining the legislation applicable (for wholly unemployed frontier workers) had exclusive effect. Does this rule, which meant that the State of residence was the competent State, really mean that it is not possible for the persons concerned to obtain benefit from the State of employment even if the person concerned does satisfy the benefit conditions of the latter State?

---

[12] Whether or not a person is a frontier worker is to be decided by the national court (Court of Justice 27 May 1982, Case 227/81, *Aubin*, [1982] *ECR* 1991).
[13] Court of Justice 12 June 1986, Case 1/85, [1986] *ECR* 1837.

The Court replied that the said article is an exception to the general rule of Article 13 of the Regulation, which is that employed persons are subject to the legislation of the State of employment. According to Article 71(1)(a) the principle of the State of residence applies. This provision is different from Article 71(1)(b); the latter provision gives unemployed persons who are *not* frontier workers the opportunity to choose.

For the *wholly unemployed frontier worker*, however, there is no such right to choose; Article 71(1)(a) is unequivocal on this. A wholly unemployed frontier worker cannot receive benefit from the legislation of the State of employment as this would mean that such employed person would have the right to choose. Another interpretation of this article would ignore the objective of coordination, according to the Court. Consequently, a wholly unemployed frontier worker is only entitled to unemployment benefit from the State of residence. We will consider this judgment also in Section 17.4.

The Commission has proposed[14] that frontier workers should have the same rights as the other category of Article 71, *see* Section 17.4 below. This implies that they can chose between the State of residence and the State of employment. This proposal has not yet been adopted.

17.4. Persons other than Frontier Workers who do not Live in the Competent State

The second category to which Article 71(1) applies, by subparagraph (b), is that of persons other than frontier workers. First, we will quote the text of this article.

Article 71 (b) provides:
'1. An unemployed person who was formerly employed and who, during his last employment, was *residing* in the territory of a Member State other than the competent State shall receive benefits in accordance with the following provisions: [subparagraph *a* left out].

b.i An employed person, other than a frontier worker, who is *partially*, intermittently or wholly unemployed [..] and who remains available to this employer or to the employment services in the territory of the competent State shall receive benefits in accordance with the provisions of that State as though he were residing in its territory; these benefits shall be provided by the competent institution.

b.ii An employed person, other than a frontier worker, who is wholly unemployed and who makes himself available for work to the employment services in the territory of the Member State in which he *resides*, or who *returns* to that territory, shall receive benefits in accordance with the legislation of that State as if he had last been employed there; the institution of the place of residence shall provide such benefits at its own expense.

---

[14]   Com. (95) 734 def. of 10 January 1996.

However, if such an employed person has become entitled to benefits at the expense of the competent institution of the Member State to whose legislation he was last subject, he shall receive benefits under the provisions of Article 69.' (italics added).

On the basis of this article, wholly unemployed persons other than frontier workers have the right to choose: they can opt either for unemployment benefit in accordance with the legislation of the Member State to which they were last subject or for benefit in accordance with the legislation of the Member State where they live or to which they return. An important condition for obtaining benefit from either of these two legislations is that the unemployed person is available to the Member State from which he wishes to receive unemployment benefit.

This provision concerns persons who do not live in the competent State (and who are not frontier workers). Usually the State of employment is the competent State. It can, however, also be a State other than the State of employment, for instance the State assigned by an Article-17-Agreement. *See,* on Article 17, Chapter 9. This appeared from the *Van Gestel* judgment.[15]

The case concerned a Dutch person, who was employed by an enterprise whose seat was in the Netherlands, where he himself resided. With a view to his temporary transfer to an affiliated company in Belgium, Van Gestel moved to Belgium at the end of October 1988, and began working there. Since Van Gestel wished to remain subject to Netherlandsh social security, the Belgian Minister for Social Afairs and the Dutch Secretary of State of Social Affairs reached an agreement on the basis of Article 17 of the Regulation, that should continue to remain subject to the Netherlands social security legislation during his employment in Belgium, until 30 November 1991. As a result of a reorganisation Van Gestel was dismissed on 31 October 1990. In the Netherlands he was paid compensation for severance. Subsequently, he applied for a Belgian unemployment benefit. This was rejected as he did not satisfy the conditions laid down in the Belgian law.

The problem was that Article 71 uses the terms 'an unemployed person who was formerly employed and who, during his last employment, was *residing* in the territory of a Member State other than the competent State (..)'. In fact, Article 71 is relevant to a person who does not reside in the State of employment, whereas Van Gestel resided in his State of employment. According to Article 13(2)(a) of the Regulation the State of employment is the competent State. Does the agreement on the basis of Article 17, which assigned the Netherlands as the State where Van Gestel was insured, mean that the conditions of Article 71 were satisfied?

The Court answered this question in the affirmative. This interpretation is corroborated by the purpose of this article, which is to gurantee to migrant workers

---

[15]   Court of Justice 29 June 1995, Case 454/93, [1995] *ECR* I-1707.

unemployment benefit under the most favourable circumstances for seeking work. These provisions are designed tp enable the migrant worker to receive unemployment benefit in his State of residence.

From the case law of the Court it appears that it is decisive for the application of Article 71 that the person concerned has his residence in a State other than the one where he was subject to the legislation during his last activities. This decisive element implies that Article 71 is applicable even when the employee has lived continuously or not during his last employment in the territory where his employer is also established. By the application of Article 71 an employee can receive unemployment benefit from the Member State where he has not paid contributions during his last employment. This effect was desired by the Community legislator, who wished to give the employee the best chance to return to the labour market.

The provision concerning non-frontier workers who return to the State of residence relates to persons whose State of residence is so far away from the State of employment, that they cannot go at least once a week to the State of residence. This means that they must have a place to stay in the State of employment, whereas it is still clear that this place to stay is different from the place of residence. In other words, the ties with the State of origin are strong enough to call that State the State of residence. An example of this category of workers is that of seasonal workers who work in a State far away from the State of origin.

The wholly unemployed non-frontier workers, in this sense, have the opportunity to choose: they can choose to receive unemployment benefit from the State where they were last employed or receive benefit from the State of residence. The key issue is that they are available to the employment services in the State where they apply for benefit.

In the *Miethe* judgment, discussed in Section 17.3, it was decided that *if* Miethe were a frontier worker, the legislation to be applied was that of the State of residence and no other. Subsequently, however, the Court considered whether Miethe was really a frontier worker. The Court recalled that the objective of Article 71 was to ensure that a migrant worker could receive unemployment benefits under those conditions which were most favourable to his search for a new job (this includes assistance to his efforts to be re-integrated into the labour market). Thus, in Article 71(1)(a)(ii) it is tacitly presumed that those conditions are most favourable in the State *of residence*. The objective of this Article cannot, however, be attained in the case where a wholly unemployed person, although he satisfies the criteria as a frontier worker, has such connections in the State of employment both personally and professionally that he will have the best chance to find work again in that State. Such a person is not a frontier worker within the meaning of Article 71. It is for the national Court to decide whether an employed person who resides in another State than one in whose territory he is employed, nevertheless has the best chances for re-integration in the State of employment. In the case of an affirmative answer to this question, he falls under Article 71(1)(b).

The Court decided in the *Di Paolo* judgment[16] that Article 71 must not be given a broad interpretation. The Court considered that Article 71(1)(b) makes some exceptions to the requirements of Article 67(3). The Court argued that the transfer of liability for payment of unemployment benefits from the Member State of last employment to the Member State of residence is justified for certain categories of workers who retain close ties with the country where they have settled and habitually reside. It would, however, no longer be justified if, by an excessively wide interpretation of the concept of residence, the point were to be reached at which all migrant workers who pursue an activity in one Member State while their families continue habitually to reside in another Member State were given the benefit of the exception contained in Article 71. It follows from these considerations, the Court continues, that the provisions of Article 71(1)(b)(ii) must be interpreted strictly.

The concept of 'the Member State in which he resides' must, therefore, be limited to the State where the worker, although occupied in another Member State, continues habitually to reside and where the habitual centre of his interests is also situated. The expression 'or who returns to that territory' means that the term 'State of residence' does not necessarily exclude a situation where the person concerned has a temporary place of residence in another Member State. The duration and the durability of the place of residence of the person concerned before his departure, the duration and objective of his absence, the nature of the activities performed in the other Member State, and the intention of the person concerned as appears from all circumstances are relevant to defining the centre of interests.

In this way, as the Court made clear in the *Di Paolo* judgment, the term 'resided' in the first section of the opening sentence of Article 71 refers to a temporary stay in a Member State where the employed persons had his last employment; the expression 'resided' in part (b)(ii) refers to the habitual place of residence which the person concerned had during his last activities abroad and which he maintained and where his habitual centre of interests is situated.

An example of the application of the latter criteria can be seen in the *Reibold* judgment[17] which concerned an employed person who for the duration of two academic years worked in a job in another Member State; the job was part of an exchange programme of universities. In deciding on the applicability of Article 71(1)(b)(ii) the Court noted that from the outset it was clear that the duration of this job was to be limited within the habitual framework of the exchange programme, and that the activities of the person concerned were interrupted every three months by lengthy holiday periods during which he stayed in the accommodation which he had kept in the State of origin.

As we saw above, according to Article 71(1)(b) some categories of unemployed person can choose between applying for unemployment benefit in his State of employment or in his State of residence. Of course, he has to be available to the employment services of the State for whose unemployment benefits he applies. This was confirmed

---

16 Court of Justice 17 February 1977, Case 76/76, [1977] *ECR* 315.
17 Court of Justice 13 November 1990, Case 216/89, [1990] *ECR* 4163.

in the *Aubin* judgment.[18] The Court considered that the rationale for this rule, which is also relevant for its interpretation, lies in the ninth consideration of the Preamble of Regulation 1408/71: its objective is to ensure the right to unemployment benefits for employed persons in those circumstances which best facilitate the search for work.

The choice between the State of employment and State of residence is made - exclusively - by the wholly unemployed employee by making himself available in the State where he applies for benefit.

In the *Naruschawicus* judgment[19] the question arose which conditions applied to the availability of employees.

Naruschawicus, a woman of Belgian nationality, worked from 1 June 1981 until 20 April 1991 full-time under a contract of employment for the Belgian army in Germany. During this period she lived in Germany but because of her status as civil servant she kept her legal place of residence in Belgium.

When she became unemployed she remained to live in Germany, and applied for unemployment benefit at the office in Liège, which was competent on the basis of her statutory place of residence. She was subject to the supervision of the unemployed exercised by that office by going regularly from Germany to Liège. After benefit was initially awarded, it was refused retroactively.

The question was whether the employee can receive benefit on the basis of Article 71(b)(ii) when he registers as seeking work at the offices for unemployment of that State, even if he is, because of distance, available to a lesser extent for applying for vacancies offered by that office.

The Court remarked that Article 71 does not define when the condition of availability is satisfied. It remarked, however, immediately, that the fact that the employed person concerned lives in the territory of a State other than the competent State, does not preclude the application of that provision, but is exactly a condition for the application of that provision. As a result, the conditions which have to be satisfied in order to be considered as available, cannot have as a direct or indirect result that the employed person has to change his place of living. In the light of these considerations it must be concluded that such an employed person remains available for the employment services in the territory of the competent State, when he registers as a person seeking work at those service and is subject to the supervision of the competent services of that State.

17.5. Does a Special Rule for Aggregation Apply with respect to Article 71?

In the *Warmerdam* judgment, *see* page 175, the question was raised which aggregation rules apply if a person makes a choice of the State of residence. Mrs Warmerdam

---

[18]   Court of Justice 27 May 1982, Case 227/81, [1982] *ECR* 1991.
[19]   Court of Justice 1 February 1996, Case 308/94, [1996] *ECR* I-207.

was not insured in the United Kingdom, where she worked, and now she applied for benefit in the State of residence, the Netherlands. The Court considered that, if Article 71(1)(b)(ii) applies, such as in the *Warmerdam* case, the competent institution has, on the basis of Article 67(1), to take account of periods of employment, which are fulfilled in another Member State, only, if these are, according to the legislation applied by that State, considered as periods of affiliation with the system of legislation of that State. It is, therefore, relevant whether the periods in the United Kingdom would have been taken into account, had they been completed in the Netherlands. No special rule applies in case Article 71 is involved.

17.6.   The Consequences of a Change of Choice of State

Suppose that an unemployed person applies for unemployment benefit on the basis of Article 71(1)(b)(ii) *after* he has already received unemployment benefit in the State of employment for some period. Is it possible for him to apply for benefit in his State of residence, and, in case of an affirmative answer, how is benefit to be calculated in this case? This question rose in the *Knoch* judgment.[20] The case concerned a German woman, who was refused German unemployment benefit on the ground that she had already applied for United Kingdom unemployment benefit.

The Court considered that a wholly unemployed person not being a frontier worker, and who during his last activities resided in the territory of another Member State than the competent State, does not lose the remainder of unemployment benefits of the State of residence if he earlier received unemployment benefits from the State of employment. Subsequently, the question had to be answered how the United Kingdom benefit, already received by Mrs Knoch, was to be considered in relation to the application of the German benefit rights. There are considerable differences between the regime of United Kingdom unemployment benefits and the German regime: the United Kingdom benefits are flat rate and are paid over a period which is the same for all claimants; the German benefits are wage-related and the duration of payments depends on the employment record of the claimant.

The Court reasoned that the German benefit administration has to take account of the periods of insurance during which Mrs Knoch had been subject to the United Kingdom legislation. The periods during which benefits were paid could be deducted from the total number of benefit days she would have been entitled to under German law. The competent organisation of a Member State whose legislation makes the acquisition and the duration of unemployment benefits dependent on the completion of periods of insurance, has to deduct the number of *days* during which benefits were actually paid (i.e. the United Kingdom period) from the number of days acquired under the other regime.

---

[20]   Court of Justice 8 July 1992, Case 102/91, [1992] *ECR* I-4341.

17.7.   Acquisition of Pension Rights by the Unemployed

Article 71(1)(a)(ii) provides that a frontier worker who is wholly unemployed shall receive unemployment benefits in accordance with the provisions of the legislation of the Member State in whose territory he resides as though he had been subject to that legislation while last employed. As this provision departs from the general rule that the legislation applicable is that of the State of work, is was unclear which legislation was applicable to building up pension rights (such as old age pension) during his period of unemployment.

This question was brought before the Court in the *Rebmann* judgment:[21] do periods during Rebmann's unemployment have to be regarded as falling under the legislation of the State of residence or of the legislation of the State of work? Or does a frontier worker have the opportunity to choose? The Court held that the legislation of the State of employment was decisive.

The Regulation was, however, amended. The present Regulation contains a provision on this subject, Article 45(6). This provision states that a period of full employment of a worker to whom Article 71(1)(a)(ii) or (b)(ii), first sentence, applies shall be taken into account by the competent institution of the Member State in whose territory the worker concerned resides. The legislation shall be applied in accordance with the legislation administered by that institution, as if that legislation applied to him during his last employment. If the period of full employment in the country of residence of the person concerned can be taken into account only if contribution periods have been completed in that country, this condition shall be deemed to be fulfilled if the contribution periods have been completed in another Member State.[22] Thus, as the result of this rule, the legislation of the State of residence is decisive.

17.8.   The Calculation of Unemployment Benefit

Article 68 provides with respect to wage-related unemployment benefits:
'(1) The competent institution of a Member State whose legislation provides that the calculation of benefits should be based on the amount of the previous wage or salary shall take into account exclusively the wage or salary received by the person concerned in respect of his last employment in the territory of that State. However, if the person concerned had been in his last employment in that territory for less than four weeks, the benefits shall be calculated on the basis of the normal wage or salary corresponding, in the place where the unemployed person is residing or staying, to an equivalent or similar employment to his last employment of another Member State.'

---

[21]   Court of Justice 29 June 1988, Case 58/87, [1988] *ECR* 3467.
[22]   This provision was inserted by Regulation 2195/91 of 25 June 1991.

The principle expressed in this provision is that the benefit administration has to take account of the wages received by the unemployed person during his last employment in the State where these activities were performed. In case, however, the last employment in that territory had been for less than four weeks, the benefits have to be calculated on the basis of the normal wage or salary corresponding, in the place where the unemployed person is residing or staying, to an equivalent or similar employment to his last employment in the territory of another Member State. This is provided by the second sentence of Article 68(1).

There is, however, one category of workers which cannot satisfy the conditions of Article 68, which is the category of frontier workers, because in their case the competent State is not the State of last employment, but the State of residence. In case of a strict application of Article 68 a frontier worker would never receive unemployment benefit based on his actual wages; in all cases he would receive benefit on the basis of the fictitious wage he would have earned in the State of residence for that work. As frontier workers tend to seek work in a region with higher wages, the effect of Article 68 would be disadvantageous for them. The calculation of benefit for frontier workers was relevant in the *Grisvard and Kreitz* judgment, concerning French frontier workers in Germany.[23]

> Grisvard and Kreitz applied for benefit, after they had worked in Germany, in France. The French benefit institution calculated unemployment benefits on the basis of the French rules; it took the income of these employed persons in Germany as the wages relevant to this calculation. However, only the income below the German maximum for the calculation of benefit was taken into account. The frontier workers concerned disputed the application of maxima for taking the wages into account.

The Court considered that the first sentence of Article 68 expresses the principle that unemployment benefit has to be calculated on previously earned wages; the second sentence of this provision only concerns the exceptional case in which the employed person did not have his last employment for at least four weeks in the State of residence. As this situation occurs often in the case of frontier workers, this would mean that this provision, which was only meant for exceptional cases, would be the normal rule for frontier workers. The Court considered that the general situation will be that the level of remuneration in the State of employment is often higher than in the State of residence. As a result, the rule that unemployment benefit payable to frontier workers could never be calculated on the basis of the remuneration in the State of employment would discourage frontier work and would violate the principles underlying Regulation 1408/71 and the Treaty.

The Court argued that Article 68(1) must be seen in the light of Article 51 of the Treaty and the objectives underlying this article. This provision must be interpreted as follows: in the case of a wholly unemployed frontier worker the

---

[23]   Court of Justice 1 October 1992, Case 201/91, [1992] *ECR* I-5009.

competent institution of the State of residence, of which the national legislation provides that the calculation of benefit depends on earlier earned wages, must calculate this benefit by taking account of the wages received by the unemployed person in the last employment in which he worked in the State of employment.

The question arose as to whether the maxima for the wages relevant for the calculation of the State of employment could be applied. The Court argued that Article 71(1)(a)(ii) provides clearly that the legislation of the State of residence has to be exclusively applied and thus precludes the legislation of the State of employment (including maxima). This interpretation, which follows from the opening sentence of this provision, is consistent with the objective of this provision, which is that the unemployment benefit regime for frontier workers is adjusted to employed persons who had been in their last employment in the State of residence. Such an assimilation could be endangered if unemployment benefits for frontier workers were subject to an ceiling which was part of the regime of another Member State, whereas this ceiling is never applicable to non-migrant workers in the State of residence. It was therefore not to be applied.

17.9. Export of Unemployment Benefits

Article 51 of the Treaty provides that the Council has to take measures to guarantee the payment of social security benefits in another Member State. The opportunity to export unemployment benefit exists to a limited extent only. This is due to an important characteristic of this type of benefit, which is that the unemployed beneficiary should remain available to the country where he is entitled to benefit; the rationale for this is that a characteristic of unemployment benefits is that they are payable only to persons who do their best to find work again. This basic rule implies, in the first place, that the benefit administration is able to check whether the beneficiary indeed does his best to seek work. In the second place, beneficiaries must be really available for work. Under the present circumstances these requirements cannot always be realised in a Member State other than the State where the person concerned is entitled to benefit. This is due to differences in languages, education etc. As regards the first requirement, there seems to be, often even within national borders, a difficult relationship between employment offices (placement services) and benefit officers. It will be even more difficult to realise a satisfying supervisory structure with regard to migrant job seekers outside the country.

The territoriality principle is removed to some extent for unemployment benefits. Article 69 offers the opportunity for unemployed persons to seek work during a restricted period in another Member State while retaining entitled to benefit.

If Article 69 applies, benefit is paid by the institution of the State where the person concerned is seeking work. The costs of benefit are refunded by the competent institution of the Member State where the person concerned was in his last employment and to whose legislation he had been subject.

In order to invoke Article 69, the employed person must have been registered as a person seeking work and have remained available to the employment services of the competent State for at least four weeks after becoming unemployed. Furthermore, he must register as a person seeking work with the employment services of the Member State to which he goes and be subject to the control procedure of that State.

Entitlement to benefit in a Member State other than the competent State exists for a maximum period of three months[24] from the date when the person ceased to be available to the employment services of the State which he left. The person must return within that period or he will lose all entitlement to national benefits. In exceptional cases, the time limit for return may be extended by the competent services.[25] Thus, the extension is possible only in case of exceptional circumstances. In the *Coccioli* case the Court was asked about the position of a person who, as he was ill, did not apply for an extension until the three-month-period had expired.[26]

The Court replied that Article 69(2) does not provide that a request for extension must necessarily be made before the expiration of the period. In fact, amongst the 'exceptional cases' capable of justifying an extension of the period may be cases of such a nature that they prevent not only the return of the unemployed person to the competent State within the period prescribed, but equally the lodging of a request for extension before the expiration of that period. Therefore, an extension is permissible even where the request is made after the expiration of the period.

The second question asked of the Court was whether the competent employment services are acting within the limits of their discretion in rejecting an exceptional case for extension of the period on the grounds that there was no likelihood of placement for the unemployed person and return within the prescribed period was impossible as a result of sudden illness. The Court's answer was that Article 69 confers on a person who avails himself of this provision an advantage as compared with a person who remains in the competent State. This is the case inasmuch as, by the effect of Article 69, he is free for the period of three months of the duty, which is the counterpart of the grant of unemployment benefits, to keep himself available to the employment services of the competent State and to be subject to the control procedure organised therein, even though he must register with the employment services of the Member State to which he goes. It is for the authorities concerned to check whether the use made by the worker of the right conferred upon him by Article 69 was in conformity with the objective for which it was instituted. The Court concluded that the answer to be given to the question is that Article 69 does not restrict the freedom of the competent services of the Member States to take into consideration all factors which they regard as relevant and which are inherent both in the individual situation of the workers concerned and in the exercise of effective control.

This means that the Court interpreted Article 69(2) in a manner which gives broad discretion to the benefit services.

---

[24] The total duration of his benefit must not be longer than if he had stayed in the competent State.
[25] Article 69(2) last sentence.
[26] Court of Justice 20 March 1979, Case 139/78, [1979] *ECR* 991.

Article 69(2) provides that if the unemployed person does not return before the expiry of the prescribed period he loses all entitlement to benefits under the legislation of the competent State. This latter provision has been seriously under discussion. This is because it is possible that an unemployed person could be entitled to a long benefit period but for his late return. One might have expected that the Court would not accept that he should lose the remainder of his benefit rights on the basis of the Regulation. The Court had established, as we have seen in the preceding two chapters (*see*, the *Petroni* judgment[27]), the principle that benefit rights acquired by virtue of national law alone must not be infringed on the basis of the regulation. This issue was brought to the Court in the *Testa* case.[28]

Mr Testa, an Italian national resident in Italy, worked in the Federal Republic of Germany. At his request the German unemployment office allowed him to seek employment in Italy. He returned one day late and he was refused the remaining period of benefit. The Court was asked whether Article 69(2) can lead to loss of benefit rights acquired on the basis of national legislation alone.

The Court considered that Article 69 is not simply a measure to coordinate national law on social security, but it establishes an independent body of rules in favour of workers claiming the benefit thereof which constitute an exception to national legal rules and which must be interpreted uniformly in all the Member States. In giving a worker the right to go to another Member State to seek employment there, Article 69 confers on a person availing himself of that provision an advantage as compared with a person who remains in the competent State inasmuch as he is freed for a period of three months of the duty to keep himself available to the employment services of the competent State. As part of a special system of rules which gives rights to workers which they would not otherwise have, Article 69(2) cannot therefore be equated with the provisions held invalid by the Court in the *Petroni* judgment to the extent to which their effect was to cause workers to lose advantages in the field of social security guaranteed to them in any event by the legislation of a single Member State.

The third question of the German national court was whether Article 69(2) is compatible with basic rights guaranteed under Community law. The national court stated that the interpretation of Article 69(2) as given above might be regarded as being incompatible with Article 14 of the German Basic Law which article gives a protection of the right to property (including social security benefit rights).

The Court answered that the question of a possible infringement of fundamental rights by a measure of the Community institutions can only be judged in the light of Community law itself, since fundamental rights form an integral part of the general principles of law. One of the fundamental rights which is protected under Community

---

[27]   Court of Justice 21 October 1975, case 24/75, [1975] *ECR* 1149.
[28]   This judgment concerned three joined cases; Court of Justice 19 June 1980, Cases 41/79, 121/79 and 796/79, *Testa, Maggio and Viale*, [1980] *ECR* 1979.

law in accordance with the constitutional concepts common to the Member States and in the light of international treaties for the protection of human rights on which Member States have collaborated, is the right to property. In order to determine whether Article 69(2) might infringe the fundamental rights guaranteed in this manner by Community law, consideration should first be given to the fact that the system set up by Article 69 is an optional system. The system applies only to the extent to which such application is requested by a worker, who thereby foregoes his right of recourse to the general system applicable to workers in the State in which he became unemployed. The consequences laid down by Article 69 of failing to return in good time are made known to the worker, in particular by means of an explanatory sheet (E 303/5) written in his own language which is handed to him by the competent employment services. His decision to opt for the system under Article 69 is therefore made freely and with full knowledge of the consequences.

Finally, it must be emphasised that the second sentence of Article 69(2), which provides that in exceptional cases the three-month period laid down by Article 69 may be extended, ensures that the application of Article 69(2) does not give rise to disproportionate results. As the Court ruled in its *Coccioli* judgment, an extension of the period is permissible even when the request is made after that period has expired. Whilst the competent services of the States enjoy a wide discretion in deciding whether to extend the period laid down by the Regulation, in exercising that discretionary power they must take account of the principle of proportionality which is a general principle of Community law. In order to apply this principle correctly in cases such as this, in each individual case the competent services and institutions must take into consideration the extent to which the period in question has been exceeded, the reason for the delay in returning and the seriousness of the legal consequences arising from this delay. The Court concluded that, even supposing that the entitlement to the social security benefits in question may be held to be covered by the protection of the right to property, as it is guaranteed by Community law - an issue which it did not seem necessary to settle in the context of these proceedings - the rules laid down by Article 69 did not involve any undue restriction on the retention of entitlement to the benefits in question.

17.10. New Proposals Concerning Unemployment Benefits

Many years ago the European Commission issued a proposal to make the possibility of exporting unemployment benefits easier. This proposal has never been adopted.[29]

This proposal provided that unemployed persons would retain their right to unemployment benefits in accordance with the national legislation of the competent State, provided that they return to the territory of that State (a) either within the period determined in Article 69 (*i.e.* three months), (b) or, after the expiry of this period, but before the expiry of the period during which, under the legislation of that Member

---

[29]   Com. (80) 312 final, *see* also *OJ* 9 July 1980, 169/22.

State, the worker may leave the territory of the said State without thereby forfeiting his right to benefits.

This proposal was, however, not adopted by the Council and it was replaced by a new proposal.[30] The new provisions serve to enable unemployed persons to keep their entitlement to benefit for a duration longer than three months, if an unemployed person goes to another Member State to seek work. This proposal envisages in the first place, according to the Commission, giving unemployed persons better opportunities to seek work in another Member State. In addition, the proposal is meant to be useful for the unemployed person who transfers his place of residence to another Member State because of a change of the place of employment of his spouse, or who wishes to return to a Member State with which he has maintained or acquired special ties.

In order to reduce the risk of abuse, however, special rules are made with a view to the administrative supervision of the unemployed.

The proposal states that the supervision will take place by the State in which territory the unemployed person seeks work, in accordance with the statutory rules of that State and in cooperation with the institutions competent to grant benefit.

With respect to the benefits it is proposed that these are to be paid by the institution of the Member State where the unemployed person is seeking work at the charge of the institution of the Member State where the unemployed person was last employed. It is proposed that the right to benefit is maintained after the first period of three months, but, in order to avoid abuse, the total duration of the grant of benefit must be no more than the periods or amounts of the legislation of the Member State where the unemployed person is seeking work. In addition, this period must be no longer than the periods or be higher than the amounts which are foreseen in the statutory legislation of the competent State. As a result the proposal contains two maxima. The Commission supposes that only persons who are really motivated to seek work abroad will invoke the proposed rules. As a result of these rules they are only entitled to the lowest amount and the shortest period of unemployment benefit as provided in the two schemes involved.

It is also proposed that *frontier workers* are entitled to the same rights as the other category mentioned in Article 71, *i.e.* that they can choose between unemployment benefit in the State of employment or State of residence, depending on for which employment services they are available.

---

[30]   Com. (95) 734 def. of 10 january 1996.

17.11. Proposals Concerning Early Retirement Benefits

The Commission has also made a proposal to make preretirement benefits subject to the Regulation.[31] With a view to these benefits it is proposed that a new chapter will be inserted into the Regulation, Chapter 6*Bis*. This chapter provides that Article 67 and 68 of the Regulation also apply on preretirement benefits (Article 71*a*).

In addition, the proposal provides that the person who is entitled to an early retirement benefit who resides in that State maintains the right to this benefit if he transfers his place of residence to another Member State. This provision thus gives the right to export preretirement benefits for persons who are entitled to these benefits in the competent State and who transfer their place of residence to another Member State. This proposal has not yet been adopted.

---

[31]   Com. (95) 735 def. of 10 January 1996.

Chapter 18

Association Agreements of the EU with Coordination Provisions

18.1. Association Agreements with the Maghreb States

The EU can also conclude treaties with States not belonging to the European Union, which are relevant to coordination of social security. Examples of such treaties are the Association Treaties with Algeria[1], Morocco[2] and Tunisia[3] respectively. In these treaties provisions are included which aim to achieve the principle of equal treatment on the basis of nationality. These treaties also include some provisions on the aggregation of periods of insurance or residence and on the payment of benefits.

For example, Article 41 of the Treaty EC-Morocco provides:
'1. Subject to the provisions of the following paragraphs, workers of Moroccan nationality and any members of their family living with them shall enjoy, in the field of social security, treatment free from any discrimination based on nationality in relation to nationals of the Member States in which they are employed.
2. All periods of insurance, employment or residence completed by such workers in the various Member States shall be added together for the purpose of pensions and annuities in respect of old age, invalidity and death and also for that of medical care for the workers and for members of their families resident in the Community.[4]
3. The workers in question shall receive family allowances for members of their families who are resident in the Community.[5]
4. The workers in question shall be able to transfer freely to Morocco, at the rates applied by virtue of the law of the debtor Member States or States, any pensions or annuities in respect of old age, death, industrial accident or occupational disease, or of invalidity resulting from industrial accident or occupational disease.

---

[1] Regulation 2210/78, *OJ* 1978 *L* 263.
[2] The cooperation Treaty was approved by Regulation 2211/78 of 26 September 1978 and published in *OJ* 1978 *L* 264.
[3] Agreement of 25 April 1976, *OJ* 1978 *L* 265.
[4] Thus, no benefit can be obtained for members of the family residing in Morocco.
[5] Thus, no family allowances can be obtained for persons residing in Morocco.

5. Morocco shall accord to workers who are nationals of a Member State and employed in its territory, and to the members of their families, treatment similar to that specified in paragraphs 1, 3 and 4.'

Article 42 reads:

'1. Before the end of the first year following entry into force of this Agreement, the Cooperation Council shall adopt provisions to implement the principles set out in Article 41.
The Cooperation Council shall adopt detailed rules for administrative cooperation providing the necessary management and control guarantees for the application of the provisions referred to in paragraph 1'.

Comparable provisions are found in Article 39 of the Cooperation Agreement EC-Algeria and Article 40 of the Cooperation Treaty EC-Tunisia.

These Cooperation Treaties are relevant to social security, as the Court of Justice has ruled that the equal treatment provisions of the Treaties have direct effect, *see* the *Kziber* judgment.[6]

The Belgian Office National de l'Emploi refused to grant unemployment allowances to Miss Bahia Kziber, a Moroccan national, as she did not possess Belgian nationality. She lived with her father, a Moroccan national, who was a pensioner in Belgium where he had worked as a wage-earner.

The first question was whether Article 41(1) of the Agreement has direct effect. The Court considered that a provision of an agreement concluded by the Community with non-Member countries must be regarded as being directly applicable when, regard being had to its wording and to the purpose and nature of the agreement itself, the provision contains a clear and precise obligation which is not subject, in its implementation or effects, to the adoption of any subsequent measure.

Article 41(1) of the Agreement satisfies those criteria, the Court considered, as it lays down in clear, precise and unconditional terms a prohibition of discrimination, based on nationality, against workers of Moroccan nationality and the members of their families living with them in the field of social security. The fact that Article 41(1) states that the prohibition of discrimination applies only subject to the provisions of the following paragraphs may not be interpreted as divesting the prohibition of discrimination of its unconditional character in respect of any other question which arises in the field of social security.

Subsequently, the Court had to decide what was meant by 'social security'. The Court answered to this question that the concept of social security in Article 41(1) of the Agreement must be understood by means of analogy with the identical concept in Regulation 1408/71. Article 4 of that Regulation lists unemployment benefits among the branches of social security.

---

[6]   Court of Justice 31 January 1991, Case 18/90, [1991] *ECR* 199.

As regards the concept of 'worker' in Article 41(1) of the Agreement, it encompasses both active workers and those who have left the labour market after reaching the age required for the receipt of an old-age pension or after becoming subject to the materialization of one of the risks creating entitlement to allowances falling under other branches of social security.

Finally the Court considered that Article 41(1) is to be interpreted as meaning that it precludes a Member State from refusing to grant unemployment benefit provided by its legislation in favour of young persons in search of employment, to a member of the family of a worker of Moroccan nationality living with him, on the ground that the person in search of employment is of Moroccan nationality.

In the *Yousfi* judgment[7] the following question arose.

Yousfi was the son of a Moroccan national who was employed in Belgium. Yousfi was born in Belgium and he resided there. While he was working as an employed person in Belgium, Yousfi suffered from an industrial accident on 31 July 1984. He applied for a Belgian allowance for the handicapped. This benefit was payable, on the basis of Belgian law, to persons with Belgian nationality alone. Yousfi's application was refused for this reason.

The Court was asked as to the extent of the non-discrimination provision which is laid down in Article 41(1). It follows from the *Kziber* judgment, the Court considered, that the personal scope of this provision comprises both active employed persons and those who have left the labour market because they reached retirement age or because they have become subject to one of the contingencies which create entitlement to benefits under the other branches of social security. In Sections 2 and 4 of Article 41 old age pensions and industrial accidents' benefits are explicitly mentioned with respect to the right to aggregation of periods of insurance and the possibility of export of benefit to Morocco. Therefore, the term 'employed person' of Article 41(1) also applies to a Moroccan national, such as Yousfi.

Allowances for disabled people fall within the material scope of Regulation 1408/71 and belong to social security within the meaning of Article 41(1) of the Agreement. Consequently, Article 41(1) of the Agreement must be interpreted in such a way that it precludes that a Member State refuses benefit for the disabled people on the basis that the person concerned has Moroccan nationality.

The *Krid* judgment[8] concerned discrimination against an Algerian widow in France. The Court decided that Article 39 of the Agreement with Algeria prohibited this discrimination.

It has not yet been decided whether the provisions on coordination of these Agreements also have direct effect. Some of these provisions, such as aggregation of periods of work or insurance are in principle applicable as they need no technical implementing provisions. We have seen an example of the application of the rules

---

[7]   Court of Justice 20 April 1994, Case 58/93, [1994] *ECR* I-1353.
[8]   Court of Justice 5 April 1995, Case 103/94, [1995] *ECR* I-719.

on aggregation of periods on the basis of Article 51 even though there was no regulation governing this issue, in the *Vougioukas* judgment[9], which concerned the specific benefits for civil servants. Whether the Court will also follow this approach with respect to the Agreements with Morocco, Algeria and Tunisia is not clear yet.

18.2.   The Agreement with Turkey

The EU has also concluded an agreement with Turkey, on the basis of which an Association Council can make coordination regulations. So far Decision 3/80 on the application of social security schemes of the Member States of the European Communities to Turkish workers and members of their families has been adopted.[10] This decision has not been implemented by the contracting parties. Its purpose is coordination of social security schemes of the Member States for Turkish nationals and not coordination of the Turkish social security scheme and that of the EU.

In the *Taflan-Met* judgment[11] the question arose whether widows who wished to claim Netherlands survivors' benefit in Turkey can rely on this regulation.

> Taflan-Met was a Turkish national, residing in Turkey, and who was the widow of a Turkish worker who was in gainful employment in various Member States, including the Netherlands. After her husband's death, she applied for widows' pension in the Member States where her husband had worked. The competent Belgian and German institutions granted the application. The application was, however, rejected by the Netherlands authorities on the ground that her husband had died in Turkey, whereas, under the Netherlands legislation, the insured person or his successors are entitled to claim benefit only if the insured risk materialises at a time when the person concerned is covered by that legislation. Decision 3/80 could be helpful to her, as this regulation contains rules analogous to Regulation 1408/71. These rules would create the fiction that her husband was insured at the time of materialisation of the risk (*see*, for the corresponding provisions of Regulation 1408/71, Chapter 15).

The first question sought to establish whether Decision 3/80 has entered into force. The Court considered that as this decision contains no provision on its entry into force, the question is whether such effect can result from the Agreement on which that decision is based. The Agreement provides in Article 6, which forms part of Title I, 'Principles', that 'to ensure the implementation and the progressive development of the Association, the Contracting parties shall meet in a Council of Association, which shall act within the powers conferred upon it by this Agreement'. It follows from this provision that decisions of the EEC-Turkey Association Council are

---

[9]   Court of Justice 22 November 1995, Case 443/93, [1995] *ECR* I-4033.
[10]   *OJ* 1983 *C* 110, p. 60.
[11]   Court of Justice 10 September 1996, Case 277/94, [1996] *ECR* I-4085. *See* Verschueren (1997).

measures adopted by a body provided for by the Agreement and empowered by the Contracting Parties to adopt such measures. By virtue of the Agreement, the Contracting Parties agreed to be bound by such decisions. The binding effect of decisions of the Association Council can, therefore, not depend on whether implementing measures have in fact been adopted by the Contracting Parties. In those circumstances, in the absence of any provision on its entry into force, it follows from the binding character which the Agreement attaches to decisions of the EEC-Turkey Association Council that Decision 3/80 entered into force on the date on which it was adopted, that is to say, 19 September 1980.

The second question was, whether the provisions of Decision 3/80, and more specifically Article 12 and 13 thereof, have direct effect in the territory of the Member States and are therefore such as to entitle individuals to rely on them before the national courts. The Court answered that a provision of an agreement concluded by the Community with non-member countries must be regarded as being directly applicable when, regard being had to its wording and the purpose and nature of the agreement itself, the provisions contain a clear and precise obligation which is not subject, in its implementation or effects, to the adoption of any subsequent measures. The purpose of Decision 3/80 is, just like Regulation 1408/71, to coordinate the Member States' social security schemes. However, the practical application of Regulation 1408/71 necessitated the adoption of implementing measures, set out in the voluminous Regulation 574/72. Decision 3/80 refers in terms to certain provisions of Regulation 1408/71 to the specific situation of Turkish workers who are or have been subject to the legislation of one or more Member States and of members of their families residing in the territory of one of the Member States. However, comparison of Regulations 1408/71 and 574/72, on the one hand, and Decision 3/80, on the other, shows that the latter does not contain a large number of precise, detailed provisions, even though such were deemed indispensable for the purpose of implementing Regulation 1408/71 within the Community. Consequently, it must be held, according to the Court, that, by its nature, Decision 3/80 is intended to be supplemented and implemented in the Community by a subsequent act of the Council. On 8 February 1983 the Commission submitted a proposal for a regulation implementing Decision 3/80.[12] However, that proposal has not yet been adopted by the Council. It follows from these considerations, the Court ruled, that, even though some of its provisions are clear and precise, Decision 3/80 cannot be applied so long as supplementary implementing measures have not been adopted by the Council.

18.3. Association Agreements with Middle and East European Countries

After the previous communist regimes in East and Middle Europe collapsed in 1989 and the countries in this part of the world had started to develop a market economy, the EU has concluded several association agreements: agreements have been adopted

---

[12]   *OJ* 1983 *C* 110, p. 1.

with Poland, Hungary, Czech Republic, Slovak Republic, Bulgaria, Romania and Russia. These agreements include provisions on social security.

The Agreement between the EC and its Member States and the Republic of Poland, for example, provides in Article 38:[13]
'With a view to coordinating social security systems for workers of Polish nationality, legally employed in the territory of a Member State and for the members of their family, legally resident there, and subject to the conditions and modalities applicable in each Member State:
- all periods of insurance, employment or residence completed by such workers in the various Member States shall be added together for the purpose of pensions and annuities in respect of old age, invalidity and death and for the purpose of medical care for such workers and such family members,
- any pensions or annuities in respect of old age, death, industrial accident or occupational disease, or of invalidity resulting therefrom, with the exception of non-contributory benefits, shall be freely transferable at the rate applied by virtue of the law of the debtor Member State or States,
the workers in question shall receive family allowances for the members of their family as defined above.

The agreements do not contain an equal treatment provision, as was the case in the Treaty with Morocco and the other Treaties discussed in the previous sections. This provision was not inserted because of the far reaching consequences of such provision arising from the *Kziber* judgment.

---

[13]   The agreement is published in *OJ* 1993 *L* 348.

Chapter 19

Some Conclusions on the Development of Coordination Law

The case law of the Court on coordination is considered to be far-reaching by several authors. One example is Schulte and Zacher, who argue that the significance of Regulation 1408/71 has changed considerably over the years.[1] The personal scope of this Regulation for employed persons was extended to include self-employed persons as well. The material scope was given an extensive interpretation by the Court, so that hybrid benefits (having elements of public assistance benefits) are also included. Consequently, the Regulation had some harmonisation effects: it is sometimes regarded as a substitute for a common system.[2] In other words, it is argued that Regulation 1408/71 has changed from a Regulation which strictly coordinates social security schemes for workers to a more extensive instrument, which has been expanded in order to attain harmonisation effects as well.

The approach of the Court is, in general, suitable for realizing a strict application of the principle of freedom of movement. For this, the Court of Justice follows an approach which is much more radical and principles-oriented than is known in most continental schemes. Because of the inability of the Community legislator to make much progress in the area of social security and the tendency of Member States to escape Community rules, this approach of the Court has been of paramount importance for realizing freedom of movement of workers.

In the previous chapters it was seen that for the Court of Justice the principle of freedom of movement of workers is a starting-point for its rulings on preliminary questions on Regulation 1408/71. This is an important element for a proper understanding of the Court's case law; although coordination by its definition intends to solve problems related to cross-border movement, there may be a considerable difference between solving such problems and promoting freedom of movement. For example, coordination rules may be made strictly for solving problems relating to cross-border movement (from the point of view of the benefit administration); such an approach is very keen not to affect national schemes and the fundamental principles of these schemes at all. In such a strict approach, the various attempts of the Community legislator to establish, for example, a Community rule against overlapping of benefits would be approved of, and even be preferable, since such a rule would

---

[1]   Schulte and Zacher (1991).
[2]   Zacher (1991: 14-15).

result in a Regulation which is more systematic and more comprehensive than a scheme in which national rules against overlapping are applied without many restrictions. The principle of freedom of movement of workers can involve considerably more than simply making coordination rules. For example, it can be argued that workers must be encouraged to accept employment in another Member State by providing them with better benefits than workers who never worked in another Member State. Article 51 of the Treaty, the basis of Regulation 1408/71, speaks of such 'measures as are necessary to provide freedom of movement of workers' and it does not impose a choice between these options. It only requires the Council to make rules when gaps occur in the Regulation, as appeared in the *Dammer* judgment[3] or the *Labots* judgment.[4]

The difference between, on the one hand, coordination from a national point of view and, on the other hand, coordination from the perspective of promotion of freedom of movement, is mainly determined by the question whether employed persons are allowed to be better off after migration. The Court consistently opted for an approach in which freedom of movement is encouraged; as a result of this, employed persons are allowed to be in a more advantageous position than if they had stayed at home. The Court considered this explicitly in some rulings; for instance in the *Chiechelski* judgment[5], the Court pointed out that according to Articles 48 and 51, the Coordination Regulations are meant to provide a more favourable position for migrant workers than would be the case if only national law were applied. This approach, that migrant workers could be in a more favourable position, goes considerably further than the principle that the most favourable alternative is to be chosen. The first approach favours employed persons over non-migrants (and may result in inequality); the second applies the most favourable arrangement to an employed person where there is a choice between alternatives.

In its later judgments, the Court expressed itself in a more reticent manner. In the *First Mura* judgment,[6] the Court considered that the differences in the situations in favour of migrant workers do not result from its interpretation of Community law, but rather from the lack of any common social security system, or of any harmonisation of national schemes. This difference in the Court's argument is not very convincing and it maintains the result that migrant workers are better off.

This approach led to the case law on the rules against overlapping of long-term pensions (Chapter 15). This case law is not problematic primarily on the grounds that it results in advantages for migrant workers, but rather as it provoked reactions by the Member States which were disadvantageous to the coordination objective.[7] Consequently, the very concept of favouring migrant workers appears to be problematic for proper coordination. The case law in question resulted in a much less

---

[3]   Court of Justice 14 December 1989, Case 168/88, [1989] *ECR* 455.
[4]   Court of Justice 13 July 1966, Case 4/66, [1966] *ECR* 293.
[5]   *See* Chapter 15, Court of Justice 5 July 1967, Case 1/67, [1967] *ECR* 223.
[6]   Court of Justice 13 October 1977, Case 22/77, [1977] *ECR* 1699.
[7]   Schuler (1988: 565).

transparent interaction of national schemes than previously existed under the Community Regulation. The concept of favouring migrant workers is, in particular, dangerous when there are large differences between national regulations. In that case, Member States will try to escape their responsibilities under the Regulation in order to avoid the effects of case law they consider to be undesirable. The following step taken by the Community legislator, viz. repealing the Community rules against overlapping and giving rules for restricting the effects of national provisions against overlapping instead, again results in a greater complexity of the Regulation, which is not favourable to freedom of movement.

In their comments of the *Petroni* case law, several authors suggest that the Court followed the idea that coordination is allowed to a restricted extent only.[8] However, it does not follow from the Court's considerations in its judgments, that it regards its case law as an inevitable result of a particular concept of coordination. For instance, in the *First Mura* judgment the Court speaks of advantages to migrant workers over workers who have never left their country, which cannot be mitigated 'by the mere coordination at present practised'. This implies that a more far-reaching coordination is conceivable. The Court did not mention restrictions ensuing from the concept of coordination itself, but restrictions ensuing from the present wording of Article 51 of the Treaty. Therefore, a revision of Article 51 of the Treaty would have been an alternative way to provide for a legal basis for a Community rule against overlapping in Regulation 1408/71. In view of the unanimous approval of the old Article 46 of the Regulation which existed when the Regulation was adopted in 1971 (and which probably still exists), this approach would have been a realistic one.

Rulings of the Court on other issues constitute another reason why it cannot generally be held that the Court applies a restricted concept of coordination. After all, the Court has given several far-reaching decisions on the material scope of the Regulation, resulting in hybrid benefits being within the scope of the Regulation (Chapter 7). The Court has created an obligation on Member States to supplement child benefits, if beneficiaries would, by virtue of the Regulation, be deprived of a more favourable right to which they were entitled from another Member State (Chapter 16). The Court has forced France to adopt the State-of-employment principle for child benefit (Chapter 8). The Court has given a Community meaning to many concepts of the Regulation, which corresponds with the principle of encouraging freedom of movement for workers. Case law of the Court has caused Member States to adapt their legislation; sometimes a Member State was forced to do this as a result of an infringement procedure.

Nevertheless, the Court has also imposed restrictions on the interpretation of the Regulation, in those cases where a particular interpretation could have a disruptive effect. Such disruptive effects can occur especially with some non-contributory benefits under certain circumstances. The same goes for the transitional advantages of the Dutch general old-age benefits. Here we have two types of benefit which traditionally have been excluded from coordination; they are not excluded from

---

[8]   Kavelaars (1992: 85).

Regulation 1408/71, but there is a restriction on the overruling of territorial conditions. This case law, however, raises the question whether the Court was not able to leave the Community rules against overlapping unaffected. The Court based its rulings on this issue on the wording of Article 51 of the Treaty. Article 51, however, contains an enunciative number of measures to be taken by the Council. This does not take the power away for the Council to act to take away advantages for migrant workers which were considered not to be in accordance with comprehensive coordination.

In addition, it can be seen that the Court applies the principle that rights acquired by virtue of national law must not be reduced in different ways, depending on the type of benefit. For long-term pensions, this principle led to a ruling that the old Article 46(3) was partially void, even though this provision required Member States to provide the highest theoretical amount. Contrary to this, the loss of rights acquired by virtue of national law alone is allowed for child benefits, whereby the Court created an obligation to supplement the benefit designated by the Regulation if lower than the suspended benefit. In the case of unemployment benefits, the fact that the remainder of benefit rights is lost, if a worker who has been seeking work in another Member State returns too late, is accepted despite this principle. How can these differences be interpreted?

The principle that rights acquired by national law must not be reduced fits in best with schemes with a relationship between the length of insurance and the amount of benefit. As we have seen, the rights acquired under these schemes continue to exist, even when a person is no longer insured at the moment the risk materialises. For other types of benefit, such as unemployment benefit, we see that the accumulated rights lapse after some time.

The principle that rights acquired under the national legislation are not to be affected, results in the method of partial pensions. For long-term benefits the Court did not accept the infringement upon acquired rights by the Community legislator, even when entitlement to these national rights is only possible by means of the export provision of the Regulation. In view of the link between schemes with a relationship between amount of benefit and length of insurance on the one hand and the partial pension method on the other hand, the ruling that infringement on rights acquired by virtue of national law is not allowed even when reliance on the export provision is necessary is consistent with the character of these schemes.

Other types of benefits are subject to the integration principle, which means that there is no export of rights from Member States other than the competent one, except if required as a supplement. The differences between the integration principle and the method of partial pension are the reason for the differences in application of the principle that rights acquired under a national legislation alone are not to be lost.

Unemployment benefits are also subject to the integration principle, although this is done in a special way.[9] For some categories of unemployed persons there is the

---

[9] In various judgments this led to the application of the principle that the most favourable alternative was to be chosen (meaning, this time, most favourable for re-integration).

choice between the State-of-residence principle and the State-of employment principle.[10] This is different for frontier workers who are wholly unemployed: they are compulsorily subject to the State-of-residence principle. These workers are deprived of rights acquired under the legislation of the State of residence. A fundamental difference with regard to other types of benefit can be found in the possibility of exporting unemployment benefits during periods one seeks work in a foreign country; a return too late may result in loss of benefit rights acquired by virtue of a national legislation. On the one hand, as we have seen in Chapter 17, this loss can be explained by the fact that the provision was invoked before the person concerned went abroad and because the person concerned had the choice as to whether to make use of this provision of the Regulation. On the other hand, this restriction does impede the principle of freedom of movement.

Although this section tried to give an explanation for the differences in approach in the case law on Regulation 1408/71, it must be said that the result is rather complex. Below, we will discuss the possibilities for a more transparent Regulation.

If the Court gives a ruling the effects of which are not acceptable to Member States, it can be seen that the Regulation will be revised in a fairly short period. Although quick (re)action by the Community legislator must be appreciated, in this case it must be said that these revisions often lead to a much more complicated Regulation. Indeed, the old Article 46 was substituted by several articles with many paragraphs, which now cover three columns in the *Official Journal* of the EC.

The extended Regulation, which is very complex, has become a major problem and this is all the more reason to plead for a more uniform approach. In the current structure of the Regulation freedom of movement for workers is only supported to a limited extent. To workers, the way in which their social security position is governed will be anything but clear. Of course, the problems with the Regulation are clearly related to the differences between the various schemes of the Member States, but this also means that, in the present approach, more and more provisions are needed to bridge these differences. The number of these will only increase now that the Regulation has been extended to the states belonging to the Extended Economic Area. After all, is there anyone who can keep track of, for instance, the interaction of the Regulation and national rules against overlapping of benefits?

It would be useful to examine the possibilities of coming to a more uniform treatment of concepts and of benefits in the Regulation. Such provisions of the Regulation would have consequences for the national schemes, but it is unlikely that the current technique of coordination can be continued, especially in view of the increase in the number of persons covered and the proposed extension of the personal (not only employed and self-employed persons) and material (also civil service schemes) scopes. Moreover, coordination is supposed to play a part in the promotion of freedom of movement, which objective is hard to realise by means of a Regulation which is so complex.

---

[10] Cf. Article 71(b)(ii).

A possible approach to establish a more transparent Regulation would be to examine the possibility of a more effective adaption of the various sections of the Regulation; in other words, harmonisation of the provisions of the Regulation. A uniform coordination technique for the various types of benefits would be a conceivable strategy. For this purpose the integration method (in combination with the supplement principle - see Section 16.3) has good credentials. The unequal division of costs can, of course, be held against this method. However, this problem can be solved. In the previous section reasons were adduced for the differences in co-ordination techniques for the various benefits. It is, however, useful to try to overcome these differences.

This approach offers an interesting scenario in which to examine whether a general application of the integration method *in abstracto* would be desirable. Subsequently, one could endeavour to come to an agreement on this method between the various Member States. In addition, this technique could also result in recommendations which are necessary as the national legislations are adapted to new developments.

A second point of departure for designing a more transparent Regulation is to acknowledge that the scope of coordination is at present limited due to the differences currently existing between the schemes of the Member States. These are difficult to overcome at present. This is why coordination provisions need to be supported by other initiatives of the Community legislator; in the analysis of the coordination problems given above we saw that the major changes of the Court in its case-law concerned hybrid benefits and non-contributory benefits and supplements.

This must be an important clue for harmonisation initiatives which are developed aside from the Regulation. Even when we implement the subsidiarity principle (in a strict sense), it can be maintained that the problems with coordination cannot be solved by the individual Member States themselves. It is, therefore, obvious that harmonisation initiatives have to supplement the coordination Regulations, as at present coordination Regulations can hardly find solutions to problems related to subsistence benefits without such support.

Harmonisation is a problematic concept. Rich countries fear a negative effect for their schemes as a result of harmonisation. In a plea for the development of harmonisation initiatives as a solution of coordination initiatives, concern for the 'better' benefits is unnecessary. After all, the coordination of traditional benefits, which are usually the 'higher' benefits, is not under discussion. The discussion particularly concerns benefits with 'social', or rather, 'solidarity' aspects.

Initiatives involving these benefits do not lead to a decrease in the benefit level in the richer States. Instead, they involve the increase of minimum and supplementary benefits. Chapter 21 will describe the first initiatives of the Council in this field. However, it will be seen that the instrument applied is very weak. Consequently, from the discussion of coordination problems the Community legislator can derive important reasons to take stronger measures to establish sufficient subsistence benefits in all Member States. Chapters 21 ff are concerned with this discussion.

PART II

HARMONISATION

Chapter 20

Harmonisation Initiatives Outside the Framework of the EU

20.1.   What is Harmonisation?

By harmonisation is meant all international rules directed at States having as an objective or requiring that these States adjust their national law to these rules.

There are several aspects in which international harmonisation rules may differ. First of all, they may differ in the degree to which they oblige States to adjust their national rules.

These degrees may vary as follows[1]:

(1) the international rules are defined as *objectives* (programs);
(2) the international rules provide for a definition of social standards, in the form of *minimum* norms or limits, which are to be met by national law;
(3) the international rules aim to adjust national systems by means of framework rules; these provisions allow the continuation of differences between national schemes;
(4) the international rules require signatory parties to adopt *uniform* rules.

Forms (2) and (3) may called *minimal harmonisation* and form (4) can be called *standard harmonisation*. In case of minimal harmonisation at least specific minimum rules are to be introduced in the signatory States, but a legislator may decide to regulate a certain subject more extensively than is required by the international rule. Standard harmonisation imposes an uniform standard on the social security schemes of the States: they must not deviate from this standard. Standard harmonisation comes close to unification of social security schemes.

If national regulations of a State do not comply with the international norms, in the case of the latter three degrees this State is obliged to adjust its law. This has a much more radical effect than coordination; coordination gives rules to take away negative effects of national rules for migrants, without requiring these rules themselves to be revised. Within EU law, the technique of minimum harmonisation was used when the principle of equal treatment of men and women was to be implemented; on the basis of EU directives, national States were given a certain

---

[1] This subdivision is taken from Schuler (1988).

amount of time to adjust their regulations in order to remove discriminatory rules (*see*, on this subject, Chapter 23).

Harmonisation can also vary as regards branches of social security:

- harmonisation can be defined as determining minimum standards;
- a different type of harmonisation is not so much concerned with minimum standards, but with norms for certain aspects of the system, such as which risks are covered, which insured persons are covered;
- the third form is creating an independent social security system which one can join and which forms a substitute for national schemes.

It has to be kept in mind that harmonisation of one area of social security can have drastic effects for other fields. The effects for these other fields may even lead to a wider differentiation between national schemes as a whole. If, for instance, social security law of EU Member States is harmonised, this may lead to larger differences between the economies of these States, since there are differences between the States in the composition of the population, industrial infra-structure, supplementary benefit schemes, etc. If, on the other hand, the national budget systems are harmonised this may cause larger differences between national social security systems.

This may indicate the importance of the distinction between *absolute* and *relative* harmonisation of social security systems. Absolute harmonisation imposes a uniform regulation on all schemes. The objective of relative harmonisation is that national systems are to be composed in such a way that the internal relations between the relevant factors of the scheme is the same as in other countries.

An example of this approach can be given with respect to minimum benefits. This is actually an important subject for harmonisation initiatives, since international organisations, such as the EU and ILO, are confronted with considerable poverty problems. If the EU would define an absolute minimum benefit, a uniform level would hold for the entire Community. An example of this would be minimum old age pension of x ecu per month in all Member States. The advantage of an absolute minimum is that it would be simple to make the rules and that it has direct harmonizing effect. A major disadvantage, however, is that such a approach takes no account of the large differences in living and wages levels between Member States. This is why, for example, ILO Convention no 102 only mentions relative minimum standards. Relative minimum standards relate the minimum wage or benefit level to local factors, such as the national or regional minimum wage level or the average wages of skilled labourers in a specific country. The national minimum benefit is to be a fixed percentage of such national factors.

In Chapter 1 we briefly discussed the relation between harmonisation and coordination. We stated that the differences between these would be discussed more extensively in the present section.

It is often thought that the difference lies in the degree of interaction with national law. However, the degree of interaction of both coordinaiton and harmonisation rules and national law may vary considerably. Some coordination rules may be categorised under the second level of degree mentioned in the discussion of harmonisation above. For instance, an important coordination rule is that a national regulation must not distinguish on grounds of nationality (of signatory States). This standard not only makes discriminatory regulations inapplicable; under EU law, this may even lead to a Court decision against a Member State which has not adjusted its national rules.[2] Of course, in the present state of affairs of international law, such a decision can only occur within a specific legal order, such as the EU. This does not alter the fact that coordination can have important effects. The extent to which a rule affects national legislation is therefore not decisive for the distinction between coordination and harmonisation.

Often the distinction between coordination and harmonisation is said to lie in that coordination leaves the differences between national systems intact,[3] whereas harmonisation may remove these differences. However, many types of harmonisation mentioned above do not affect the differences between schemes. The principle of equal treatment of men and women in the EU directives is only applied to national schemes which exist at a certain period. When there are no such national social security schemes for a certain field, the equal treatment principle does not require that a particular scheme should be established. This is so even if such a scheme is important for, for instance, promoting the opportunities of women to seek employment.[4]

The difference between harmonisation and coordination, therefore, does not lie in the degree of obligations or in the question of whether a rule affects differences between national schemes, but in the objective of harmonisation, *i.e.* to change national schemes, whereas coordination is not directed at national rules as such but makes additional rules for migrant workers in order to avoid negative effects from the interaction of national law systems.

Below we will describe the harmonisation initiatives by international organisations (apart from the EU). In Chapter 21 we will discuss those of the EU.

20.2.   The International Labour Organisation

Towards the end of the nineteenth century, employers' organisations and trade unions began to take initiatives to lay down standards for labour law and social security on an international level. In establishing these standards, altruistic motives played a part, but no less important was the argument that international competition should not be allowed to turn to the disadvantage of States with better schemes. In order to prevent such disadvantages, measures were sometimes even taken which worked against the

---

[2]   See for example, the infringement procedure, Court of Justice 10 November 1992, *Commission* v. *Belgium*, Case 326/90, [1992] *ECR* I-5517, in which Belgium was held to be in breach of EC law, because it still imposes conditions of residence on nationals of other Member States who apply for certain kinds of benefits. This is contrary to Article 7(2) of Regulation 1612/68 and Article 3 of Regulation 1408/71.

[3]   For instance, Court of Justice 13 October 1977, Case 22/77, *Mura*, [1977] *ECR* 1699.

[4]   *See* the *Johnson* decision, Court of Justice 11 July 1991, Case 31/90, [1991] *ECR* 3723; and 16 July 1992, Cases 63/91 and 64/91, *Jackson and Cresswell*, [1992] *ECR* I-4973, discussed in Chapter 23.

encouragement of freedom of movement. For instance, protectionist measures were taken in border regions facing child labour or working hour regulations which were unsatisfactory on the other side of the border. In modern terminology, one would say that this was done to prevent *social dumping*.[5]

The end of the First World War effected an important break-through in the international development of standards in the field of social security. The Treaty of Versailles, which concluded this war, contains provisions for the foundation of the International Labour Organisation (ILO). Among other things, the ILO is responsible for preparing and adopting treaties and recommendations and the supervision of the observance of existing international labour standards. Besides representatives of the governments of Member States, representatives from employers' organisations and trade unions sit on every board. The creation of this organisation brought about an institutional framework for harmonisation initiatives, which contains the powers and the authority to draw up coordination and harmonisation treaties.[6]

In the Preamble to the Constitution of the ILO, the competition argument was still present: 'the failure of any nation to adopt humane conditions of labour forms an obstacle to other nations which desire to improve the conditions in their own countries'.

However, the main driving-force was the Preamble-clause: 'universal and lasting peace can be established only if it is based on social justice'. During the conference in Philadelphia in 1944, a declaration was adopted in which the objectives of the ILO were restated.[7] In this declaration, social justice is again mentioned as a starting-point; the objectives of the ILO as stated in this declaration no longer refer to the competition argument.

The harmonisation policy of the ILO can be divided into two stages. During the first stage the objective was to increase the dissemination of social law, which was still relatively new. Treaties contained rules on how to draw up insurance schemes against certain risks. For instance, as a response to the recession at the time, harmonisation treaties with regard to unemployment schemes were already adopted in 1919. The treaties which were drawn up before the Second World War were mainly concentrated on the design of employees' insurance schemes.

The second stage began after the Second World War. Efforts were made to draw up treaties which set minimum standards for social security. In 1952, Convention 102 was adopted, which gave general directions and minimum standards for the main branches of social security. These standards must apply to at least a considerable part of the population. The most important issue is today the agreement on minimum standards for social security; the design of the national schemes in which these standards are realised is of less importance.

---

[5]   Schuler (1988: 100).

[6]   *See* for a historical overview of the ILO, Tamburi (1983) and Perrin (1969).

[7]   The 'Declaration of Philadelphia' is added as an amendment to the ILO Constitution. *See*, for a recent version of the Constitution and of ILO Conventions, F. Pennings, 'Codex', in R. Blanpain (ed), *International Encyclopaedia of Laws. Social Security Law* (loose-leaf).

20.3.   The Council of Europe

The Council of Europe also aims to encourage the Member States to develop their social security systems. To this purpose, the European Social Charter was adopted in 1961.[8] In this Charter, the 'right to social security' is laid down as a basic social right. Article 12(2) of the Charter provides that the contracting parties undertake to 'maintain the social security system at a satisfactory level at least equal to that required for ratification of International Labour Convention (No. 102) Concerning Minimum Standards of Social Security'. So, the ESC relies for its basic standards on ILO Convention 102.

In addition, the Council of Europe developed initiatives for reaching a level of minimum standards higher than that embodied in ILO Convention 102. With this purpose in mind, the Council started to work on a European Code on Social Security and the accompanying Protocol. The preparations for this Code started in 1949, but were interrupted because of the simultaneous preparations for Convention 102. The Code was signed in 1964 and complies with the set-up of the latter Convention. The Code aims to improve not only social progress, but also the harmonisation of the social charges in the Member States.

Since the Code has been formulated, the process of developing standards has advanced and in the mean time a revised Code for social security was drafted. The Committee of the Ministers of the Council of Europe agreed to this revised Code in 1990.[9]

As mentioned before, the social policy of the Council of Europe became less important. Because of the large number of EU Member States associated with the Council of Europe, the Council is orientated towards the EU. In addition, the Council of Europe is devoted to the same objectives as those of the ILO and it operates as a regional organisation of the ILO.

---

[8]   *See*, on the ESC, Jaspers and Betten (1988).
[9]   *See*, for the Code, Villars (1979).

Chapter 21

Harmonisation Initiatives of the European Union

21.1.   The Power to Take Harmonisation Initiatives

An important aspect of European integration is the promotion of economic and social progress and the continuous improvement of living and working conditions. This is also stated in the Preamble to the EC Treaty:

The Preamble reads:
'-   (..) determined to lay the foundations of an ever closer union among the peoples of Europe
-      resolved to ensure the economic and social progress of their countries by common action to eliminate the barriers which divide Europe
-      recognizing that the removal of existing obstacles calls for concerted action in order to guarantee steady expansion, balanced trade and fair competition
-      anxious to strengthen the unity of their economies and to ensure their harmonious development by reducing the differences existing between the various regions and the backwardness of the less favoured regions (..)
the (signatory parties) have decided to create a European Economic Community'.

The provisions on social policy are found in Articles 117 to 122 EC Treaty, under the title *Social Policy*.

> Article 117 reads:
> 'Member States agree upon the need to promote improved working conditions and an improved standard of living for workers, so as to make possible their harmonisation while the improvement is being maintained.
> They believe that such a development will ensue not only from the functioning of the common market, which will favour the harmonisation of social systems, but also from the procedures provided for in this Treaty and from the approximation of provisions laid down by law, regulation or administrative action.'

This article refers to 'harmonisation of social systems' and therefore it is relevant to harmonisation initiatives. However, the article does not provide for legislative powers to be granted to Community bodies for the realisation of such harmonisation. It merely states a point of view. In Section 21.2 we shall pay attention to the proposed new text of this article in the draft Amsterdam Treaty.

Article 117 suggests that harmonisation will automatically take place as a result of the functioning of the market. The reason for this obscure text can be explained by the drafting process of this provision. During the negotiations on the draft EC Treaty, France strongly pleaded for a provision for harmonisation of social security in the Treaty. France considered this to be essential, since French enterprises in a unified market would suffer too much from the large financial charges imposed by French social security on these enterprises. Germany opposed this point of view, on the grounds that social security costs are only one of many factors relevant to the competitive position of enterprises on a single market. The costs for social security per worker constitute only one element of all expenses related to labour. Differences in social security expenses between Member States would, for example, be compensated by the differences in the level of wages and taxes. Elements such as infrastructure, the social climate and the tax regime are also relevant to the competitive position of an enterprise. All these factors together determine the competitive position of enterprises. If social security only were harmonised, the competitive relationships would deteriorate rather than improve. The compromise which ended this difference in opinions is laid down in the ambiguous text of Article 117.

Still, Article 117 has been useful as being a basis for harmonisation initiatives. For this purpose, the last part of Article 117 is used, which reads that harmonisation will ensue 'also from the procedures provided for in this Treaty and from the approximation of provisions laid down by law, regulation or administrative action.' This wording is linked to a provision elsewhere in the Treaty, *i.e.* Article 100, which also deals with the approximation of laws. In combination with Article 100 and/or Article 235 of the Treaty, arrangements may be made to implement the aims mentioned in Article 117.

Article 100 of the Treaty reads:
'The Council shall, acting unanimously on a proposal from the Commission, issue directives for the approximation of such provisions laid down by law, regulation or administrative action in Member States as directly affect the establishment or functioning of the common market. (..)'.

The Court of Justice has accepted this article as a basis for measures in the area of social policy.[1]

Article 235 of the Treaty reads:
'If action by the Community should prove necessary to attain, in the course of the operation of the common market, one of the objectives of the Community and this Treaty has not provided the necessary powers, the Council shall, acting unanimously on a proposal from the Commission and after consulting the Assembly, take the appropriate measures.'

---

[1] An example is Directive 75/117 on the Approximation of the Laws of the Member States with a View to the Application of the Principle of Equal Pay of Men and Women.

The Treaty on the EEA also contains provisions on social policy. Article 66 to 71 of this Treaty are worded analogously to Articles 117 to 119 of the EC Treaty. Annex XVIII mentions the provisions of the secondary EU law which apply to the EEA Member States. These include the directives on equal treatment of men and women.

The provisions on harmonisation of social policy have become somewhat problematic as they are worded in very broad terms. Especially after the adoption of the Maastricht Treaty such provisions have become regarded with suspicion. This suspicion is given a legal meaning in the *principle of subsidiarity* which was inserted in the Maastricht Treaty.

The principle of subsidiarity has several dimensions.[2] On the one hand it may mean that higher bodies do not execute tasks which can be done by lower bodies in the hierarchy. This is called *vertical* subsidiarity. In accordance with this, a decision is to be made at an hierarchic level which is as low as possible.[3] However, this does not provide criteria for its application. Is a relevant criterion for selecting a level that a measure can be implemented most effectively and/or efficiently on that level? If so, what do efficiency and effectiveness mean in this context?

The principle of subsidiarity is so vague, that there is a risk that it will be used in an opportunistic way by Member States who are in fact not in favour of measures of social policy issued by Brussels.

In the Maastricht Treaty, the principle of subsidiarity is set out in legislation.[4]

Article 3B reads:
'The Community shall act within the limits of the powers conferred upon it by this Treaty and of the objectives assigned to it therein.
In areas which do not fall within its exclusive competence, the Community shall take action, in accordance with the principle of subsidiarity, only if and in so far as the objective of the proposed action cannot be sufficiently achieved by the Member States and can therefore, by reason of the scale of effects of the proposed action, be better achieved by the Community.
Any action by the Community shall not go beyond what is necessary to achieve the objectives of this Treaty.'

This Article does not provide criteria either. After all, when can we say that measures 'cannot be sufficiently' achieved and can, therefore, 'by reason of the scale of effects', be better achieved by the Community? Is it sufficient that the internal market brings about social disruption which is difficult to solve by the Member States themselves, in view of the competitive aspects of social measures? Does this mean that, in view of the poverty in many areas of Europe, the Member States are not capable

---

[2]   Cf. *Subsidiarity: the Challenge of Change* (1991), which contains a collection of articles on this principle. *See* also Pennings (1993).

[3]   The term *hierarchy*, though, can become problematic in view of the concept of one judicial territory, which was created by the EC Treaty.

[4]   *OJ* 1992 *C* 224.

of solving these problems by themselves? It will be clear that the positions taken by the parties concerned before entering negotiations on possible measures will not be altered on the basis of this article.

A different dimension of the principle of subsidiarity concerns the relationships between the social partners; this is the dimension of *horizontal subsidiarity*. This concept requires that the Community legislator does not take measures which can also be taken by the social partners. This type of subsidiarity is an answer to the objections which may exist to vertical subsidiarity. After all, with vertical subsidiarity there is the problem that, although it might be understandable that Member States wish to rely on the principle of subsidiarity to keep as much autonomous powers as possible, this impedes the establishment of a clear social policy. In the case of social security there is no driving force for such a policy and this is why solutions for problems in adjustment (competitive problems) and a possible redistribution of means for a social policy are not, or are only slowly, developed.

Horizontal subsidiarity includes initiatives by the social partners at a Community level, as well as on a national level. The first type of action is based on a central perspective and this may result in advantages as compared to the principle of vertical subsidiarity. However, to achieve this, strong organisation of social partners on a European level will be necessary. Moreover, once these organisations have gained more influence, they still have a long way to go to free themselves from the inevitable national interests and perspectives of the participating organisations. Therefore, the principle of subsidiarity appears to be a serious impediment to developing a social Europe at sufficient speed.

The principle of subsidiarity also has aspects which are not problematic. This definitely is the case in as far as the principle requires that Community legislation is not to result in a deterioration in schemes currently existing in the Member States. Consequently, Member States are allowed to maintain a higher level than that laid down in the Community regulation. In other words, the objective of this principle is minimum harmonisation instead of standard harmonisation.

Apart from the directives on equal treatment of men and women, the EU has taken very few measures of harmonisation of social security. In fact, the only instruments adopted so far are recommendations. Recommendations constitute a group of instruments which have considerably less force than regulations and directives. However, they are not without any meaning. In order to give a better insight into this subject, it is necessary to consider the way the Court interprets non-binding (parts of) Community instruments, directives included.

A well known example of such a decision is the *Marleasing* judgment.[5] In this judgment the Court argued that the national court was to interpret national law as far as possible in the light of the wording and the objective of a directive. This interpretation method is called the 'interpretation of law in conformity with a directive'. This type of interpretation means that non-binding elements of a Community instrument can also be considered. In this way a directive can be relied on against

---

[5]   Court of Justice 13 November 1990, Case 106/89, [1990] *ECR* 4135.

an individual party (such as Marleasing) and persons who are not subject to the personal scope of the directive can rely upon it before a national court.[6] The Court has, however, not given a ruling yet in which this approach was also applied in the area of equal treatment of men and women in social security.

The duty for national courts to interpret national law in conformity with Community instruments is also relevant to *recommendations*. This can be seen in the *Grimaldi* judgment[7], in which a recommendation was involved. Recommendations do not have binding consequences for those to whom they apply. Consequently, they cannot create rights which individual persons can rely on before a national court. In order to fully answer the question of the national court, however, the Court emphasised in the *Grimaldi* judgment that the actions concerned are not to be regarded as having no legal consequences at all. The national court is obliged to take account of the recommendations in the solution of the disputes presented to it, especially when they help clarify the interpretation of national provisions which are the result of these recommendations or when they are meant to supplement binding Community rules.

21.2.   The Agreement on Social Policy and the Amsterdam Treaty

At the Summit in Maastricht no unanimity could be reached on a text with regard to social policy, because the United Kingdom did not wish to commit itself. Instead an agreement was made between the Member States without the United Kingdom.[8] This Agreement states that the Community and the Member States have as their objectives the promotion of employment, improved living and working conditions. Other objectives are proper social protection, dialogue between management and labour, the development of human resources with a view to lasting employment and combatting exclusion. To this end the Community and the Member States shall implement measures which take account of the diverse forms of national practices, in particular, in the field of contractual relationships, and which take account of the need to maintain the competitiveness of the Community economy.

The competition argument re-emerges in this wording. On the other hand, this article contains a reference to the principle of subsidiarity in the sense that the social partners are to be involved in making measures. The aspect of the principle of subsidiarity which was identified above by the term *minimum harmonisation* is also contained in the agreement: 'the provisions adopted pursuant to this article shall not

---

[6]   *See,* also Court of Justice 8 November 1990, Case 177/88, *Dekker,* [1990] *ECR* 3941.
[7]   Court of Justice 13 December 1989, Case 322/88, [1989] *ECR* 4407.
[8]   *OJ C* 224 of 31 August 1992, p. 127. *See,* also Fitzpatrick (1992), Prechal (1992), and Watson (1993).

prevent any Member State from maintaining or introducing more stringent preventive measures compatible with the Treaty'.[9]

In order to make these measures concrete, the Agreement contains the following provisions. Article 2 provides that with a view to achieving the objectives of Article 1, the Community shall support and complement the activities of the Member States in the following fields. One of them is the improvement of the working environment, in order to protect the health and the safety of the workers. Another field concerns the integration of persons excluded from the labour market. Article 2(2) reads that the Council may, by means of directives, adopt minimum requirements for gradual implementation of these objectives. However, for a number of issues unanimity of votes is required (Article 2(3)), *i.e.* in the field of social security and social protection of workers, the protection of workers where their employment contract is terminated and financial contributions for promotion of employment and job-creation. Consequently, for the main part of our subject, unanimity of votes is required, that is, unanimity of the Member States which have signed the Agreement.

Article 2(4) of the Agreement elaborates upon the role of the social partners on the following points. A Member State may entrust management and labour, at their joint request, with the implementation of directives adopted pursuant to paragraphs (2) and (3) of this article. The subjects which can be governed in these directives were listed above. Article 2(4) continues that in this case the Member State has to ensure that, no later than the date on which a directive must be transposed management and labour have introduced the necessary measures by agreement. The Member State concerned is required to take any necessary measure enabling it to be in a position to guarantee the results required by that directive.

Article 3 is concerned with the consultation of management and labour at *Community level*. According to this article, the Commission has the task of promoting the consultation of management and labour at Community level and of taking any relevant measures to facilitate their dialogue by ensuring balanced support for the parties. To this end, before submitting proposals in the social policy field, the Commission has to consult the social partners on the possible direction of Community action. Subsequently, if, after such consultation, the Commission considers Community action advisable, it shall consult management and labour on the content of the envisaged proposal.[10]

On the occasion of such consultation, management and labour may inform the Commission of their wish to initiate the process provided for in Article 4. The latter article provides in the second paragraph that the dialogue between management and

---

[9]   Article 2(5). The term 'compatible with the Treaty' is not explained in the Agreement. It can be expected that the relevance of the Treaty does not concern the level of benefits but, instead, benefit conditions. For example, certain types of subsidies for labour costs or employment measures, which have the objective of preventing unemployment or promote the re-employment of unemployed persons, will, under certain circumstances, be prohibited as causing distortion of competition by means of aids provided by the Member States.

[10]   The agreement determines that the duration of the procedure is not to exceed nine months, unless the parties concerned and the Commission agree upon a prolongation.

labour may lead, if management and labour so desire, to contractual relations, including agreements. Agreements concluded at Community level can be implemented in two ways. One way is that they are implemented in accordance with the procedures and practices specific to the social partners and the Member States. The other is that they are, in matters covered by Article 2 (listed above), implemented at the joint request of the signatory parties, by a decision of the Council on proposal of the Commission.

In June 1997, the text of the Treaty of Amsterdam was adopted. This Treaty is still to be ratified. One of the elements of the Treaty was to incorporate the Agreement on social policy into the Treaty, since the new UK government, which had come into office shortly before, was willing to accept this agreement. As a result, the Treaty proposes that Article 117 to 120 are to be replaced by a text, in which the provisions of the Agreement are laid down.

The new Article 117 reads:
'The Community and the Member States, having in mind fundamental social rights such as those set out in the European Social Charter signed at Turin on 18 October 1961 and in the 1989 Community Charter of the Fundamental Social Rights of Workers, shall have as their objectives the promotion of employment, improved living and working conditions, so as to make possible their harmonisation while the improvement is being maintained, proper social protection, dialogue between management and labour, the development of human resources with a view to lasting high employment and the combating of exclusion.
To this end the Community and the Member States shall implement measures which take account of the diverse forms of national practices, in particular in the field of contractual relations, and the need to maintain the competitiveness of the Community economy.
They believe that such a development will ensue not only from the functioning of the common market, which will favour the harmonisation of social systems, but also from the procedures provided for in this Treaty and from the approximation of provisions laid down by law, regulation or administrative action.'

As we can see, although the last sentence is the same as that of the present Article 117, the Article now also gives the power and the duty to implement measures for the improvement of living and working conditions. Following the approach of the Agreement, Article 118 gives the possibility to make directives for minimum requirements in the specified fields mentioned in the Agreement. For social security, Article 118(3) requires, just like the Agreement, unanimous voting for measures concerning social security and social protection for workers. Article 118(4) provides that a Member State may entrust management and labour, at their joint request, with the implementation of directives meant here. Here we see also the possibility of horizontal subsidiarity, which we have met in the Agreement. Article 118(5) makes clear that the provisions adopted pursuant to this article shall not prevent any Member

State from maintaining or introducing more stringent protective measures compatible with this Treaty.

Article 118b concerns horizontal subsidiarity at Community level: when management and labour so desire, the dialogue between them at Community level may lead to contractual relations, including agreements. Agreements concluded at Community level shall be implemented either in accordance with the procedures and practices specific to management and labour and the Member States or, in matters covered by Article 118, at the joint request of the signatory parties, by a Council decision on a proposal from the Commission. The Council shall act by qualified majority, except where the agreement in question contains one or more provisions relating to one of the areas referred to in Article 118(3), in which case it shall act unanimously. So we see that social security remains, on whatever level, an area where unanimous voting is required. The new Article 117 to Article 118c, therefore, probably not change much in the field of social security. There is only an explicit obligation of the Commission to encourage cooperation between the Member States, also in the area of social security:

> Article 118c reads:
> 'With a view to achieving the objectives of Article 117 and without prejudice to the other provisions of this Treaty, the Commission shall encourage cooperation between the Member States and facilitate the coordination of their action in all social policy fields under this chapter, particularly in matters relating to:
> (..)
> – social security; (..)
> To this end, the Commission shall act in close contact with Member States by making studies, delivering opinions and arranging consultations both on problems arising at national level and on those of concern to international organisations.
> Before delivering the opinions provided for in this Article, the Commission shall consult the Economic and Social Committee.'

21.3. The Recommendations Concerning Sufficient Resources and the Convergence of Social Protection Policies

In 1992, the Council adopted two recommendations in the field of social policy. One of these is the Recommendation on 'Common criteria concerning sufficient resources and social assistance in social protection.' The second Recommendation is the Recommendation of the Council on the 'convergence of social protection objectives and policies.'[11] Both recommendations are based on Article 235 of the EC Treaty, which gives general powers to the Council to make measures which are deemed necessary for the realisation of the common market. By establishing these recommen-

---

[11]   Both are published in *OJ* 1992 *L* 245.

dations, for the first time the Council expressed its opinion on the way in which national social security schemes should be constructed albeit in a broad and general way.[12]

21.3.1. *Council Recommendation on Common Criteria concerning Sufficient Resources and Social Assistance Protection Systems*

In the memorandum to this recommendation the Commission acknowledged the danger that the extent and the intensity of social exclusion will increase as a result of the establishment of the internal market, with all the consequences for competition. This increased competition will, at least in the beginning, accentuate the tensions in the labour market and the pressure on government funds and social policy.[13] At the moment, eight Member States have a 'safety net-system', which grants persons the right to a minimum income. In the other four Member States[14], this right does not exist on a national level. It does exist, however, in some regions and cities or for certain categories.

The Recommendation aims at the introduction of the right to a minimum income in countries where this does not yet exist. In so far as existing provisions are concerned, the objective is to establish common general principles and criteria for the purpose of granting this right to all persons residing in the territory of the Community.

We will now describe the most important standards of the Recommendation. The Recommendation calls upon the Member States to recognize the basic right of a person to sufficient resources and social assistance to live in a manner compatible with human dignity as part of a comprehensive and consistent drive to combat social exclusion, and to adapt their social protection systems as necessary, according to the principles and guidelines of this recommendation.

The first principle mentioned is that the right is to be based on respect for human dignity.

With regard to the personal scope, the Recommendation states that it is to be defined *vis-à-vis* individuals, having regard to legal residence and nationality, in accordance with the relevant legal provisions on residence, with the aim of progressively covering all exclusion situations in that connection as broadly as possible, in accordance with detailed arrangements laid down by the Member States.

According to the Recommendation, access to this right is to be granted to all persons who individually or within the household in which they live, do not have access to sufficient resources. This is conditional upon the fact that they are actively available for work or for vocational training with a view to obtaining work. This condition applies to persons whose age, health and family situation permit such active

---

[12] *See*, for an interesting discussion of the background of these recommendations, Cousins (1993).
[13] Recommendation 92/441 EEC, *OJ* 1991 *C* 163/3.
[14] Italy, Greece, Spain and Portugal.

availability. Where appropriate persons can be required to be available for economic and social integration measures.

Finally, the Recommendation states that access to this right must not be subject to time limits (although the right may be granted for limited but renewable periods) and it must be auxiliary in relation to other social rights.

On a more concrete level, the Recommendation contains the following guidelines with regard to minimum subsistence levels. Account should be taken of the living standards and the price-levels in the Member State concerned. For different types and sizes of household, the amount of resources is to be fixed so as to be sufficient to cover essential needs with regard to respect for human dignity.

The amounts are to be adjusted or supplemented in order to meet specific demands. In fixing these amounts, appropriate indicators must be used, such as, for example, statistical data on the average disposable income in the Member State, statistical data on household consumption, the legal minimum wage if this exists or the level of prices. Persons of working age who have the capacity to work, should still be encouraged to search for work.

Financial aid should be granted to persons whose resources taken at the individual or the household level are lower than the amounts fixed in this way in order to bring them up to these amounts.

Appropriate measures are necessary to ensure that the least privileged are informed of this right. The administrative procedures and arrangements for the examination of means and circumstances involved in claiming this right need to be simplified as far as possible. A machinery for appeals has to be organized to independent third parties, such as tribunals, to which the persons concerned should have easy access.

It is also recommended that the scope of the Recommendation be varied according to age or family situation. Account should be taken of the economic and budgetary resources of the Member States, as well as the priorities set by the authorities and the balances within the social security schemes.[15]

The measures laid down in the Recommendation are to be implemented as from 24 June 1992. The Recommendation ends with a provision which asks the European Commission to encourage and organise, in liaison with the Member States, the systematic exchange of information and experiences. The Commission is to submit reports on a regular basis based on information supplied by the Member States, describing the progress achieved and obstacles encountered in implementing this Recommendation.

In conclusion, we can see that this Recommendation contains only general standards. For example, it does not involve a right which is enforceable by individuals. Furthermore, the implementation is subject to economic factors and the Recommenda-

---

[15]   Cousins (1993: 294) points out that this reference to the availability of financial resources, of national priorities and of balances between national social protection systems was inserted into the recommendation after amendments in the Council. This is a clear example of how the subsidiarity principle has its influence on social policy issues.

tion does not eliminate the dependence of needy person on others. In several ways, ILO Treaty 102 has more far-reaching standards than this Recommendation.

21.3.2. *Council Recommendation on the Convergence of Social Protection Objectives and Policies*

The second Recommendation is concerned with the convergence of objectives of social protection.[16] Apparently, the word *harmonisation* has a meaning which is regarded as being too strong. The exact difference between convergence and harmonisation is not clear.

The Recommendation on convergence recommends that the Member States allow their general policy in the area of social protection to be guided by the following principles. This is done without prejudice to the powers of the Member States to establish the principles and organizations of their own systems in the sectors concerned. Taking account of the availability of funds, of priorities and balances within social protection systems and according to those systems' own organisational and funding procedures, social protection should attempt to fulfil the following tasks. In conformity with the Recommendation on minimum subsistence benefits (see above), a level of resources is to be guaranteed which is in keeping with human dignity. Under conditions determined by each Member State the chance to benefit from the system for the protection of human health existing in the Member State should be given to any person residing legally within its territory, regardless of his or her resources. Social integration of all persons legally resident within the territory of the Member State and the integration into the labour market of those who are in a position to exercise a gainful activity must be encouraged. Employed workers who cease work at the end of their working lives or are forced to interrupt their careers owing to sickness, accident, maternity, invalidity or unemployment, should be provided with a replacement income. This should be fixed either in the form of flat-rate benefits, or benefits calculated in relation to their earnings in their previous occupation, which will maintain their standard of living in a reasonable manner in accordance with their participation in appropriate social security schemes. In addition, the recommendation requires that the possibility of introducing and/or developing appropriate social protection for self-employed persons is to be examined.

Social benefits should be granted in accordance with the following principles. The first is equal treatment in such a way as to avoid any discrimination based on nationality, race, sex, religion, customs or political opinion, provided that applicants fulfil the conditions regarding length of membership and/or residence required to be eligible for benefits. Secondly, there is the principle of fairness, so that beneficiaries of social benefits will receive their share of improvements in the standard of living of the population as a whole, while taking account of priorities set at national level.

---

[16]   Recommendation 92/442/EEC of 27 July 1992, *OJ* 1992 *L* 245

Subsequently, the Recommendation requires that social protection systems must endeavour to adapt to the development of behaviour and of family structures where this gives rise to the emergence of new social protection needs, related in particular to changes on the labour market and demographic changes. Finally, social protection systems must be administered with maximum efficiency having regard to the rights, needs and situations of those concerned, and with maximum effectiveness in terms of organization and functioning.

The Recommendation contains specific provisions for different types of benefits. The Member States are recommended to adapt and, where necessary, develop their social protection systems, without prejudice to their powers to establish the principles and organization of their own systems in the sectors concerned in order progressively to attain the following aims and to take the necessary measures to this end.

1. *Sickness*

The role of social protection in preventing illness and in treating and rehabilitating the persons concerned is to be organized in such a way so as to meet the following objectives. Under conditions determined by each Member State, for all persons legally resident within the territory of the Member State access is be to ensured to necessary health care as well as to facilities seeking to prevent illness. The Member States are required to maintain and, where necessary, develop a high-quality health-care system geared to the evolving needs of the population, and especially those arising from dependence of the elderly, to the development of pathologies and therapies and the need to step up prevention. Where necessary the rehabilitation of convalescents, particulary following serious illness or an accident, and their subsequent return to work is to be organized. Either flat-rate benefit or benefits calculated in relation to their earnings in their previous occupation must be provided to employed persons forced to interrupt their work owing to sickness, so as to maintain their standard of living in a reasonable manner in accordance with their participation in appropriate social security schemes.

2. *Maternity*

In the field of maternity provisions, Member States must organize, for all women legally resident within the territory of the Member State, coverage of the costs of treatment necessary due to pregnancy, childbirth and their consequences, subject to participation by the woman concerned in appropriate social security schemes and/or subject to cover by social assistance. In addition Member States must ensure that employed women who interrupt their work due to maternity enjoy appropriate social protection.

3. *Unemployment*

In accordance with the provisions of the Recommendation on the minimum subsistence benefits and subject to their active availability for work, Member States must guarantee minimum means of subsistence for unemployed persons legally resident in the territory of the Member State. For the unemployed, particularly for young people arriving on the job market and for the long-term unemployed, a range of measures against exclusion must be made available designed to foster their integration into the labour market. This is also subject to their active availability for work or for vocational training with a view to obtaining employment. For employed workers who have lost their jobs either flat-rate benefits, or benefits calculated in relation to their earnings in their previous occupation must be provided. These have to maintain their standard of living in a reasonable manner in accordance with their participation in appropriate social security schemes and the unemployed persons have to be actively available for work or for vocational training with a view to obtaining employment.

4. *Incapacity for work*

In accordance with the provisions of the Recommendation on minimum subsistence level, Member States must guarantee minimum means of subsistence to disabled persons legally resident within the territory of the Member State. They must also foster the social and economic integration of persons suffering from a chronic illness or from a disability.

Employed workers forced to reduce or interrupt work due to invalidity must be provided with either flat-rate benefits, or benefits calculated in relation to their earnings in their previous occupation. These have to be adjusted where appropriate according to the degree of their incapacity, so as to maintain their standard of living in a reasonable manner in accordance with their participation in appropriate social security schemes.

5. *The elderly*

Member States must, in accordance with the provisions of the Recommendation on minimum subsistence benefits, guarantee minimum means of subsistence to elderly persons legally resident within the territory of the Member State. In addition, they must take appropriate social security measures, having regard to the specific needs of the elderly where they are dependent on care and services from outside. The Member States must also take steps to combat the social exclusion of the elderly. Having regard to specific national circumstances as regards unemployment and demographic conditions, the Member States must seek to remove obstacles to work for persons who have reached the minimum age at which entitlement to retirement pension begins. It is recommended that mechanisms be put in place to enable former employed workers who have retired with no gap in their working lives to benefit from a reasonable replacement income throughout their retirement, taking into account, where appropriate, statutory and supplementary schemes. A balance may be maintained between the interests of the working population and those who have retired. For purposes of calculating pension rights, Member States must reduce, in particular by allowing voluntary contributions, the penalty for those workers who have gaps in their careers as a result of periods of illness, invalidity or long-term unemployment, and for those who gave up work temporarily to bring up their children or, where appropriate, in accordance with national legislation, other dependants. In addition, pension schemes must be adapted to the trend of behaviour and family structures. The Member States must promote, where necessary, changes in the conditions governing the acquisition of retirement and, especially, supplementary pension rights with a view to eliminating obstacles to the mobility of employed workers. In due course, the pension schemes must be adapted to demographic changes, while maintaining the basic role of statutory pension schemes.

6. *Family*
In the field of family benefits Member States must develop benefits paid to families with the greatest child-related costs, for example because of the number of children, and/or the most disadvantaged families. The Member States must also contribute to fostering the integration of persons who, having brought up children, wish to enter the labour market and to help remove obstacles to occupational activity by parents through measures to reconcile family and professional responsibilities.

Conclusion
Similar to the Recommendation on minimum subsistence benefits, this Recommendation contains general standards which are lower than those of ILO Treaty 102. The Recommendation contains little encouragement to improve schemes, although this is one of the important considerations of the EC Treaty.

The provisions for the elderly do contain some interesting items; for example, the part that recommends wage-related pensions. In addition there is the recommendation to take account of incomplete working lives and changes in family structure (survivor's pensions also for unmarried couples?). Finally, there is the recommendation to remove obstacles for elderly persons who want to keep on working. Meanwhile, a number of proposals have been made for better adjustment of national systems.

21.4.   Harmonisation Scenarios in the EU

21.4.1. *The Thirteenth State Scheme*

The proposal for a thirteenth-country system was published by Pieters in 1989.[17] This proposal is based on the idea that a special system must be made for persons who move across borders and who are subject to more than one social security system during their careers. This scheme is to be developed in addition to existing national schemes. It should be up to the employed person and his employer to affiliate to this system. Association is voluntary, but once an employed person has joined this scheme, this cannot be revoked. This is only logical, because otherwise an additional regulation would be necessary for coordination with respect to persons having been subject to this scheme and other (national) schemes.

Voluntary affiliation to this scheme would have to be encouraged by making the new scheme attractive, that is, as good as possible. An example for this is the special scheme for EC officials. Since it is a favourable scheme, no complaints are made

---

[17]   *See* Pieters (1989a) and (1989b), Vansteenkiste (1991).

by officials employed by the European Commission on the grounds that they are not covered by the Belgian social security (which would have been applicable otherwise). Following this analogy, Pieters recommends a favourable, optimal system. It should be kept in mind, however, that an 'optimal' system need not mean that it is a system providing the highest amounts of benefits. It can also involve a scheme providing a favourable ratio between contribution and benefits: in view of the amount of contributions paid, the person receives a benefit which is relatively advantageous. The proposal does not elaborate any further on this point; it is conceivable that there will be considerable differences in opinion between the various categories of workers on the best ratio. However, if the scheme becomes popular among many categories of workers, the road to a unified social security system will be open.

This proposal was praised by various authors for its originality,[18] but it received little support. It is held against this proposal that the costs will be high, since it is argued that it is to be a scheme which is favourable for workers. Pieters suggests funding this scheme by means of wage-related contributions payable by the employer and the employed person to which national governments pay a subsidy. He believes that the contributions will be relatively low, since the scheme is particularly meant for persons on a high income. It was argued that this would result in a split into first class and second class legal positions for migrant workers, since it is doubtful whether the contributions will be low enough for workers on lower incomes as well. For that matter, people on low incomes will often have different demands with regard to social security (occupational diseases, accidents at work, early retirement, unemployment) as compared to persons on high incomes. This would also be an impediment to a Thirteenth-country scheme.[19]

21.4.2. The European Social Snake

Another proposal is aimed at the adjustment of existing schemes. Among other things, this proposal intends to prevent dismantling of or radical changes in social security schemes as a result of the Single Market. In 1989, a proposal for a European social snake was made.[20] In this scheme, the level and the extent of the protection of each state are first determined by means of one or more parameters. An example of such a parameter is the relationship between social security and the gross national product. Subsequently, the deviation of each Member State from the Community average is to be determined. For states above the average, the 'positive' difference should remain unaffected or even increase over a certain amount of time. If social protection drops to a considerable extent below the fluctuation margins allowed, consultation with the

---

[18] Feenstra (1990), Kavelaars (1992), Laske (1993).

[19] A further problem is the adjustment of these contributions to other levies, such as income taxes, which do fall under national legislations.

[20] M. Dispersyn and Pierre van der Vorst (University of Brussels) at the colloquium *1993 - Europe et protection sociale* on 9 and 10 October 1989. This is described in Busquin (1990: 562 f.f.).

Commission would be necessary. A considerable increase in protection might result in interventions in favour of the states which do not reach the Community average, in order to prevent their 'arrears' in respect of the average from increasing too much. This proposal is still being developed. The problems seem to be the following; will states with an expanding social security scheme be willing to take part in a Community fund supporting the states that lag behind? Will this be a restraint on improvement? And doesn't such a policy reward inactive behaviour?

Chapter 22

Equal Pay for Men and Women: Article 119

22.1.   Introduction

Article 119 EC Treaty sets out the principle of equal pay of men and women.

> This article reads:
> 'Each Member State shall during the first stage ensure and subsequently maintain the application of the principle that men and women should receive equal pay for equal work.
> For the purpose of this Article, 'pay' means the ordinary basic or minimum wage or salary and any other consideration, whether in cash or in kind, which the worker receives, directly or indirectly, in respect of his employment from his employer.'

It was France which took the initiative to insert this article in the draft EC Treaty of 1957. In this time some future Member States had already ratified ILO Convention 100 concerning equal remuneration for men and women for work of equal value. Three of the future Member States had, however, not ratified this Convention. Therefore the fear existed that the latter States could have competitive advantages by employing women as a cheaper labour force. This would amount to distortion of competition. Such distortion was not acceptable from the point of view of social policy, and therefore Article 119 was inserted into the Treaty. Despite this history, Article 119 proved to be important for the development of a specific part of European social security law.

In the interpretation of this article, three judgments concerning Mrs Defrenne have been of pioneering importance.

> Gabriëlle Defrenne was employed as an air hostess by Belgian Sabena (an air company). She gave up her duties on 15 February 1968 in pursuance of a provision of the contract of employment entered into by air crew employed by Sabena, which stated that contracts held by women members of the crew shall terminate on the day on which the employee in question reaches the age of forty years. She started three actions on the basis of Article 119 of the EC Treaty, which led to three Court of Justice judgments. The first concerned the Royal Decree which laid down special rules governing *pensions* for air crew of Sabena. The second case concerned the calculation method of her *allowance on*

termination of service. The object of the third case was the question of whether the differences in terms of termination of the contract of employment based on sex were allowed.

We will discuss these three judgments below. We will start with the *Second Defrenne* judgment,[1] as some essential elements of Article 119 were clarified by the Court in this judgment.

In this judgment the first question concerned the meaning of 'during the first stage' in the phrase 'Each Member State shall during the first stage ensure and subsequently maintain the application of the principle that men and women should receive equal pay for equal work'. In the preparatory process of the EC Treaty, the future Member States had agreed that this stage would expire on 30 December 1961. Just before the expiration of this period, however, the Member States made a new resolution which stated that the principle of equal treatment was to be ensured by 31 December 1964. On this new date also, not all Member States had eliminated all types of discrimination and because, since the creation of the EC, new Member States had joined the Community, it was decided that by 1 January 1973 Article 119 was to be implemented to its full extent. In the *Second Defrenne* case Mrs Defrenne wished to know whether Article 119 was self-executing. For this purpose, it was relevant to know at what time the first stage had expired.

The Court considered that Article 119 pursues a double aim. Firstly, in the light of the different stages of the development of social legislation in the various Member States, the aim of Article 119 is to avoid a situation in which undertakings established in Member States which have actually implemented the principle of equal pay suffer a competitive disadvantage in intra-Community competition as compared to undertakings established in States which have not yet eliminated discrimination against women as regards pay. Secondly, this provision is part of the social objectives of the Community, which is not merely an economic union, but which is at the same time intended, by common action, to ensure social progress and seek the constant improvement of the living and working conditions of their peoples, as is emphasised by the Preamble of the Treaty. This aim was accentuated, the Court considered, by the insertion of Article 119 in a chapter devoted to social policy. This double aim, which is at once economic and social, shows that the principle of equal pay forms part of the foundations of the Community. This explains why the Treaty has provided for the complete implementation of this principle by the end of the first stage of the transitional period. The Court argued that it follows from the express terms of Article 119 that the application of the principle that men and women should receive equal pay was to be fully secured and irreversible at the end of the first stage of the transitional period, that is, by 1 January 1962. Later resolutions were ineffective to make any valid modification of the time limit fixed by the Treaty.

Another question raised in the *Second Defrenne* case was whether Article 119 forbids a difference being made between men and women in the calculation of the

---

[1]   Court of Justice 8 April 1976, Case 43/75, [1976] *ECR* 455.

allowance at the end of the contract. The Court considered that, for the purpose of the implementation of the principle of equal pay, a distinction must be drawn within the area of application of Article 119. This distinction must be made between, firstly, direct and overt discrimination which may be identified solely with the aid of the criteria based on equal work and equal pay referred to by the article in question and, secondly, indirect and disguised discrimination which can only be identified by reference to more explicit implementing provisions of a Community or national character.

The forms of direct discrimination which may be identified solely by reference to the criteria laid down by Article 119 include particularly those, the Court considered, which have their origin in legislative provisions or in collective labour agreements and which may be detected on the basis of a purely legal analysis of the situation. This applies even more in cases where men and women receive unequal pay for equal work carried out in the same establishment or service, whether public or private. In such a situation the Court is in a position to establish all the facts which enable it to decide whether a female worker is receiving lower pay than a male worker performing the same tasks. In such a situation, at least, Article 119 is directly applicable and may thus give rise to individual rights which the courts must protect.

Another question raised was whether, given the possible economic consequences of attributing direct effect to Article 119, the retroactive effect of this judgment has to be limited. This decision might have financial results in many branches of economic life if it would have retroactive effect from the coming into force of the Treaty.

The Court decided that, although the practical consequences of any judicial decision must be carefully taken into account, it would be impossible to go so far as to diminish the objectivity of the law and compromise its future application on the ground of the possible repercussions which might result, as regards the past, from such a judicial decision.

However, in the light of the conduct of several of the Member States and the views adopted by the Commission and repeatedly brought to the notice of the circles concerned, it was appropriate to take exceptionally into account the fact that, over a prolonged period, the parties concerned have been led to continue with practices which were contrary to Article 119, although not yet prohibited under their national law. In these circumstances, the Court concluded, it was appropriate to determine that, as the general level at which pay would have been fixed cannot be known, important considerations of legal certainty affecting all the interests involved, both public and private, made it impossible in principle to reopen the question as regards the past. Therefore, the direct effect of Article 119 cannot be relied on in order to support claims concerning pay periods prior to the date of this judgment, except as regards those workers who have already brought legal proceedings or made an equivalent claim.

The Court made here a rather confusing distinction between direct (overt) and indirect (disguised) discrimination. Indirect discrimination in this case did not have the meaning it usually has, of making a distinction on seemingly neutral criteria, which has different effects for some categories. In case of indirect discrimination in the latter sense, Article 119 is directly applicable. This can be seen in the *Jenkins* judgment[2], in which the Court ruled that:

'A difference in pay between full-time workers and part-time workers does not amount to discrimination prohibited by Article 119 of the Treaty unless it is in reality merely an indirect way of reducing the pay of part-time workers on the ground that that group of workers is composed exclusively or predominantly of women.

Where the national court is able, using the criteria of equal work and equal pay, without the operation of Community or national measures, to establish that the payment of hourly rates of remuneration for part-time work which is lower than for full-time work represents discrimination based on difference of sex the provisions of Article 119 of the Treaty apply directly to such a situation.'

Mrs Defrenne was not successful in her other two cases. The *First Defrenne* judgment[3] concerned the question whether the exclusion of female air hostesses from the Sabena pension was contrary to the principle of equal pay laid down by Article 119. In answer to this question, the Court referred to the second paragraph of Article 119 which extends the concept of pay to any other consideration, whether in cash or in kind, whether immediate or future provided that the worker receives it, albeit indirectly, in respect of his employment from his employer. The Court concluded that although consideration in the nature of social security benefits is not, therefore, in principle alien to the concept of pay, social security schemes or benefits, in particular retirement benefits, directly governed by legislation without any element of agreement within the undertaking or the occupational branch concerned, which are obligatorily applicable to general categories of workers, cannot be brought within this concept, as defined in Article 119. The part due from the employers in the financing of such schemes does not constitute a direct or indirect payment to the worker.

Consequently, the pension for Sabena crew established within the framework of a social security scheme laid down by legislation (a special Royal Decree for Sabena) did not form 'pay' in the sense of Article 119. Therefore, Mrs Defrenne could not rely on Article 119.

The *Third Defrenne* case[4] concerned the question as to whether the insertion in a contract of employment of an air hostess of a clause bringing the said contract to an end when she reaches the age of forty years, constituted prohibited discrimination. Mrs Defrenne established that no such limit was attached to the contract of male cabin attendants who were assumed to do the same work. In other words, the question was whether Article 119 also applied to conditions of recruitment and working conditions, outside the scope of pay. Mrs Defrenne claimed that the condition on the automatic termination of her contract was contrary to Article 119, because she could only be remunerated in the same way as men on condition that she has the same working

---

[2] Court of Justice 31 March 1981, Case 96/80, [1981] *ECR* 911.
[3] Court of Justice 25 May 1971, Case 80/70, [1971] *ECR* 446
[4] Court of Justice 15 June 1978, Case 149/77, [1978] *ECR* 1365.

conditions. Moreover, the age-limit had disadvantageous pecuniary consequences for her end of contract allowance and pension.

The Court answered that the field of application of Article 119 had to be determined within the context of the system of the social provisions of the Treaty, which were set out in the chapter formed by Article 117 *et seq.* The general features of the conditions of employment and working conditions are considered in Articles 117 and 118 from the point of view of the harmonisation of the social systems of the Member States and the approximation of their laws in that field. There was no doubt, according to the Court, that the elimination of discrimination based on the sex of workers was part of the programme for social and legislative policy which was clarified in certain respects in a Council Regulation and a directive.[5] In contrast to the provisions of Articles 117 and 118, which are essentially in the nature of a programme, Article 119 which is limited to the question of pay discrimination between men and women workers, constitutes a special rule, whose application is linked to precise factors. In these circumstances the Court considered it impossible to extend the scope of that article to elements of the employment relationship other than those expressly referred to. It was, therefore, the Court decided, impossible to widen the terms of Article 119 to the point of, firstly, jeopardizing the direct applicability which that provision must be acknowledged to have in its own sphere and, secondly, intervening in an area reserved by Articles 117 and 118 to the discretion of the authorities referred to therein.

22.2. Article 119 and Occupational Pensions

The equal treatment rule of Article 119 of the Treaty is not only relevant in case of differences in wages between men and women, but can also apply to social security. This follows from the definition of *pay* in this article: 'any other consideration, whether in cash or in kind, which the worker receives, directly or indirectly, in respect of his employment from his employer'.

The relevance of this was already seen in the *First Defrenne* judgment where the Court pointed out that a consideration in the nature of social security benefits is not, in principle, alien to the concept of pay. Therefore, this article can be relevant to types of social security such as pension schemes which have been established on the basis of agreements within the undertaking or the occupational branch concerned. An example of such a scheme is seen in the *Weber* v. *Bilka Kaufhaus* judgment.[6]

Bilka Kaufhaus, a department store, had for several years had a supplementary pension scheme ('occupational pension') for its employees. According to the version in force from 26 October 1973, part-time employees qualified under the scheme only if they had been in full-time employment for fifteen years out of

---

[5]   Regulation of 21 January 1974, *OJ* 1974 *C* 13, p. 1, and Directive 76/207, *OJ* 1976 *L* 39, p. 1.
[6]   Court of Justice 13 May 1986, Case 170/84, [1986] *ECR* 1607.

a total of twenty. Mrs Weber did not satisfy this requirement, as she worked full-time for only eleven years.

As a preliminary issue the Court considered whether the conditions laid down by an employer for his employees to join an occupational pension scheme, such as in this case, came within the scope of Article 119 of the Treaty. Its answer was that the occupational scheme in question was indeed within the ambit of Article 119. The occupational pension scheme in question, although adopted in accordance with German legislation for schemes of this type, originated from an agreement made between Bilka and the works council representing its employees. This agreement supplemented the social security benefits payable under national legislation which generally applied, with benefits financed solely by the employer. Therefore, the benefits paid to employees under the disputed scheme constituted consideration paid by the employer to the employee in respect of his employment, within the meaning of Article 119.

However, this did not necessarily mean that this scheme, with special conditions for part-time workers, was contrary to Article 119, as these conditions were applicable to both men or women. If, however, the number of female part-time workers was disproportionate as compared to the number of male part-timers, the rule on part-timers could constitute indirect discrimination against women, unless it could be justified by objective reasons. Bilka (the employer) maintained that the exclusion of part-time workers was based on objectively justified economic grounds. It emphasised that the employment of full-time workers, by comparison with part-time workers, involves fewer ancillary costs and permits staff to be used for the whole period during which stores are open. The Court ruled that it fell to the national court to decide whether, and if so to what extent, the grounds put forward by an employer to explain the adoption of a pay practice which in fact affects more women than men, could be considered to be objectively justified for economic reasons.

To answer the question whether a specific rule is indirectly discriminatory, the following steps have to be followed.

First, it is important whether a scheme, although using neutral criteria, affects in a significant way, men rather than women (or vice versa).

If the answer is positive, it has to be decided whether the scheme is justified by objective factors not related to discrimination (grounds of justification).

If this question is also answered positively, the court has to investigate whether the means chosen by the legislator are appropriate and necessary in order to reach the objective of the scheme.

In the *Bilka* judgment, the question of applicability of Article 119 arose with respect to the exclusion of part-timers from occupational schemes. Another issue which can arise with respect to occupational schemes is the difference in retirement age for men and women respectively. For women this age was often lower than for men. As men can also invoke Article 119, this issue was brought before the Court, *see* the *Barber* judgment.[7]

> Douglas Harvey Barber, born in 1928, was a member of the pension fund established by his employer (an assurance firm). The scheme was financed wholly by the employer. It was a 'contracted out' scheme, which is a scheme which is allowed, after approval by the authorities, to replace statutory social security provisions, *i.e.* the earnings-related part of the State pension scheme.
>
> Under this pension scheme, the normal pension age was fixed, for the category of employees to which Mr Barber belonged, at sixty-two for men and at fifty-seven for women. That difference was equivalent to that which exists under the state social security scheme, where the normal pension age is sixty-five for men and sixty for women.
>
> The Guardian Royal Exchange Assurance Guide to Severance Terms, which formed part of Mr Barber's contract of employment, provided that, in the end of redundancy, members of the pension fund were entitled to an immediate pension subject to having attained the age of fifty-five for men or fifty for women. Mr Barber was made redundant with effect from 31 December 1980 when he was aged fifty-two. He was paid a redundancy payment and an *ex gratia* payment. It is not disputed that a woman in the same position as Mr Barber would have received an immediate retirement pension as well as the statutory redundancy payment and that the total value of these benefits would have been greater than the amount paid to Mr Barber.

The Court considered, first of all, whether the benefits paid by an employer to a worker in connection with the latter's compulsory redundancy fell within the scope of Article 119 of the Treaty. The Court pointed out that, as regards, in particular, the compensation granted to a worker in connection with his redundancy, it must be stated that such compensation constitutes a form of pay to which the worker is entitled in respect of his employment. It is paid to him upon termination of the employment relationship, which makes it possible to facilitate his adjustment to the new circumstances resulting from the loss of his employment and which provides him with a source of income during the period in which he is seeking new employment. It follows that compensation granted to a worker in connection with redundancy falls in principle within the concept of pay for the purpose of Article 119 of the Treaty.

The second question was interpreted by the Court as seeking to ascertain whether a retirement pension paid under a 'contracted-out' private occupational scheme falls within the scope of Article 119 of the Treaty, in particular where that pension is awarded in connection with compulsory redundancy payments. In that regard the Court referred to its judgment in the *First Defrenne* case, where it had stated that consideration in the nature of social security benefits was not in principle alien to the concept of pay. However this concept cannot encompass social security schemes or benefits,

---

[7] Court of Justice 27 May 1990, Case 262/88, [1990] *ECR* 1990.

in particular retirement pensions, directly governed by legislation without any element of agreement within the undertaking or the occupational branch concerned, which are compulsorily applicable to general categories of workers. The schemes in question in this case, however, were the result either of an agreement between workers and employers or of a unilateral decision taken by the employer. They were wholly financed by the employer or by both the employer and the workers without any contribution being made by the public authorities in any circumstances. Accordingly, such schemes form part of the consideration offered to workers by the employer. Secondly, such schemes are not compulsorily applicable to general categories of workers. On the contrary, they apply only to workers employed by certain undertakings, with the result that affiliation to those schemes derived out of necessity from the employment relationship with a given employer. Thirdly, even if the contributions paid to those schemes and the benefits which they provide were partly a substitute for those of the general statutory scheme, that fact could not preclude the application of Article 119. It is apparent that occupational schemes such as those referred to in this case may grant to their members a higher amount of benefit than the amount which would be paid by the statutory scheme, with the result that their economic function is similar to that of the supplementary schemes which exist in certain Member States, where affiliation and contribution to the statutory scheme is compulsory and no derogation is allowed. The answer of the Court to the second question was therefore that a pension paid under a contracted-out private occupational scheme fell within the scope of Article 119 of the Treaty.

In response to the subsequent questions the Court pointed out that Article 119 prohibits any discrimination with regard to pay between men and women, whatever the system which gave rise to such inequality. Therefore, it is contrary to Article 119 of the Treaty for a man who is made compulsorily redundant, to be entitled to claim only a deferred pension payable at the normal pensionable age, whereas a woman in the same position is entitled to an immediate retirement pension as a result of the application of an age condition that varies according to sex in the same way as is provided for by the national statutory pension scheme.

22.3. Limitation of the Temporal Effect of the Barber Judgment

The last subject of the *Barber* judgment concerned the effects of the judgment *ratione temporis* because of the serious financial consequences of the present interpretation.

The Court considered that it could, as it had done in the *Second Defrenne* case, *see* page 231, as an exception, and taking account of the serious difficulties which might be created by its judgment as regards events in the past, restrict the possibility of all persons concerned relying on this interpretation. With regard to this case, the Court pointed out that Article 7(1) of Directive 79/7, as we will see in Section 23.5.6, authorised the Member States to defer the compulsory implementation of the principle of equal treatment with regard to the determination of pensionable age for the purposes of granting old-age pensions. That exception had been incorporated in Article 9(a) of Directive 86/378 on the implementation of the principle of equal treatment for men and women in occupational schemes, which applied to contracted-out schemes such as the one at issue in this case (see Section 24.2.5 below). The Court considered that in the light of those provisions, the Member States and the parties concerned were reasonably entitled to consider that Article 119 did not apply to pensions paid under contracted-out schemes. In these circumstances, the overriding considerations of legal certainty precluded legal situations, which had exhausted all their effects in the past, from being called in question where that might retroactively upset the financial balance of many contracted-out pension schemes.

Therefore, the Court ruled, the direct effect of Article 119 of the Treaty may not be relied upon in order to claim entitlement to a pension with effect from a date prior to this judgment, except in the case of workers who have before that date initiated legal proceedings or made an equivalent claim under the applicable law.

The judgment led, in its turn, to many new questions. The main question was whether this judgment meant that a claimant of an occupational pension could, on the basis of Article 119, claim an *equal amount of benefit* from the date of the ruling (17 May 1990), or did it mean that only the acquisition rules for pensions had to be the same for men and women from this day.

The first interpretation had important financial consequences, because in the past the application of the principle of equal treatment in respect of pensions was not foreseen when calculating the contribution rates; the result of the alternative interpretation would be that the effects of unequal treatment in the past would still be felt for many years. A protocol was annexed to the Treaty of Maastricht with regard to this question.[8]

> This reads as follows:
> 'For the purposes of Article 119 of this Treaty, benefits under occupational social security schemes shall not be considered as remuneration if and in so far as they are attributable to periods of employment prior to 17 May 1990, except in the case of workers or those claiming under them who have before that date initiated legal proceedings or introduced an equivalent claim under the applicable national law.'

This Protocol is a statement by the Council which fits in with the second interpretation of the *Barber* judgment.[9] In the following sections, we will discuss which interpretation is followed by the Court.

---

[8]   *OJ* 1992 C 229/104.
[9]   *See*, on the status of this protocol, also Prechal (1992).

22.4. Widowers Pensions, Age Discrimination and Article 119

In 1993, the Court issued the *Ten Oever* ruling, in which the temporal effects of the *Barber* judgment were clarified.[10]

> The spouse of Mr Ten Oever was affiliated to an occupational scheme until her decease on 13 October 1988. The scheme was funded by employers and employees; at the date of her death, under the provisions of the scheme, only a widows' pension was payable. Pensions for widowers were only made payable after 1 January 1989. Mr Ten Oever applied for such a widowers' pension from the date of the decease of his wife. This pension was refused on the basis of the provisions of the pension scheme in force on the date of her decease. Mr Ten Oever claimed, on the basis of the *Barber* judgment, that his pension had to be considered as pay within the meaning of Article 119 of the EC Treaty, and that, therefore, no discrimination in the pension scheme was allowed.

The Court answered that the pension scheme did indeed fall within the scope of 'pay' within the meaning of Article 119. The second question to be answered by the Court was more difficult. This question was related to the meaning of the *ratione temporis* of the *Barber* judgment. The Court reasoned that it is a characteristic of this form of pay that there is a time lag between the accrual of entitlement to a pension, which occurs gradually throughout the employee's working life, and the actual payment, which is deferred until a particular age. The Court also took into consideration the way in which occupational pension funds are financed and thus of the accounting links in each individual case between the periodic contributions and the future amounts to be paid. On the basis of this statement, the Court ruled that equal treatment of men and women can be claimed, in the matter of occupational pensions, only in respect of benefits payable for periods of employment subsequent to 17 May 1990, the date of the *Barber* judgment. The Court opted, as can be seen in this judgment, for the second interpretation of the *Barber* judgment, and corresponds to the Protocol. As a result, Mr Ten Oever was refused benefit, as his wife had died during a period which lay before the *Barber* judgment.

It appeared from the *Ten Oever* judgment that the Court did not limit the restricted temporal effect to 'contracted-out' schemes. This is confirmed in the *Moroni* judgment.[11] In this case also the question was raised of the relationship between Article 119 and Directive 86/378. The directive gave specific rules on occupational schemes, whereas Article 8(1) provided that the equal treatment did not have to be realized before 1 January 1993. The question was, therefore, whether claimants could invoke the directive with respect to a claim based on Article 119 with respect to the payment of pensions before 1 January 1993. The Court answered that Article 119 is directly applicable to each form of discrimination which can be shown with the sole

---

[10]   Court of Justice 6 October 1993, Case 109/91, [1993] *ECR* I-4879.
[11]   Court of Justice 14 December 1993, Case 110/91, [1993] *ECR* I-6591.

criteria of equality of work and equality of payment, which criteria form part of this article. As pension ages can be determined directly with the help of the criteria of Article 119, it is no longer necessary to look at the effects of the directive. Equality of treatment with respect to occupational pensions can, however, as we can see in the *Ten Oever* judgment, only be invoked with respect to benefits due on the basis of periods of work lying after 19 May 1990.

In the *Neath* case the Court was asked whether an employer is allowed to distinguish between employers' contributions for male and female employees.[12]

> Mr Neath was employed under a 'contracted out' scheme until 27 June 1990, the date on which he was made redundant. At that time he was fifty-four years and eleven months old. According to the rules of that contracted-out scheme, male employees may not claim a full company pension until they are sixty-five years of age whilst female employees may receive a full pension at sixty years of age. The male member under 65 is entitled only to have his acquired pension rights transferred to another pension scheme or to receive a deferred pension payable on the normal retirement date.
>
> When making his choice, Mr Neath realised, on the basis of the figures given by the scheme, that if he opted to have his pension transferred, his financial position would be more favourable if the interpretation of the *Barber* judgment were that any male employee retiring after 17 May 1990 is entitled to have his pension recalculated on the same basis as his female counterpart in relation to the entire period of service. If the interpretation were that such entitlement may be claimed only in respect of periods of service subsequent to that date, he would be entitled to a smaller sum.

The Court considered that the *employees'* contributions correspond to a percentage of their salary, which is identical for men and women. The *employer's* contributions, however, vary over time, so as to cover the balance of the cost of the pensions promised. They are higher for female employees than for male employees. This variability and inequality are due to the use of actuarial factors in the mechanism for funding the scheme. In the case of the transfer of acquired rights and in the case where part of a pension is converted into capital, the fact that account is taken of different actuarial factors has the result that male employees are entitled to sums lower than those to which female employees are entitled. Essentially, the national court wanted to know whether such differences are compatible with Article 119.

The Court ruled that contributions paid by the employees are an element of their pay since they are deducted directly from their salary. The amount of those contributions must therefore be the same for all employees, male and female. This is not so in the case of the employer's contributions which ensure the adequacy of the funds necessary to cover the cost of the pension promised, so securing their payment in the future, that being the substance of the employer's commitment.

---

[12]   Court of Justice 22 December 1993, Case 152/91, [1993] *ECR* I-6935.

Therefore employees' contributions are pay in the sense of Article 119, while employers' contributions are not.

The subject of the *Smith* v. *Advel Systems* judgment[13] was the question how a transitory scheme can realize equal treatment of men and women retroactively.

> Until 1 July 1991 the pension scheme of Smith's employer provided that the normal pensionable age was 65 years for men and 60 for women. The pension scheme was amended with effect from 1 July 1991 to provide for a normal pensionable age of 65 for both men and women. The amendment applied both to benefits earned in respect of years of service after 1 July 1991 and to benefits earned in respect of years earned in respect of years of service prior to 1 July 1991.
>
> The increase of the retirement age for women meant that their pensions were decreased significantly after the date of equalization which was 1 July 1991. The national court wanted to know what scope the employer had to take measures to realize equal treatment for men and women in the past as well as for the future.

The Court answered that it was in order to comply with the *Barber* judgment that the occupational scheme concerned adopted the measure now in dispute. In order to do so, it opted for one of the two possible ways of achieving equal treatment: instead of granting men the same advantage as that enjoyed by women and thus lowering their retirement age to that for women, the scheme raised the retirement age for women to that for men, even for the past. This was done including the period prior to the *Barber* judgment, and as a result the position of women was made less favourable. In the *Second Defrenne* judgment the Court already ruled against the argument that compliance with Article 119 could be achieved otherwise than by raising the lowest salaries. A national court must set aside any discriminatory provision of national law, without having to request or await its prior removal by collective bargaining or by any other constitutional procedure. Instead, the court has to apply to members of the disadvantaged group the same arrangements as those enjoyed by other workers, arrangements which, failing correct implementation of Article 119 in national law, remain the only valid point of reference.

Application of this principle to the present case means that, as regards the period between 17 May 1990 (the date of the *Barber* judgment) and 1 July 1991 (the date on which the scheme adopted measures to achieve equality) the pension rights of men must be calculated on the basis of the same retirement age as that for women. As regards periods of service prior to 17 May 1990, the *Barber* judgment excluded application of Article 119 to pension benefits payable in respect of those periods, so that employers and trustees are not required to ensure equal treatment as far as those benefits are concerned. It follows that, as far as those latter periods are concerned,

---

[13]   Court of Justice 28 September 1994, Case 408/92, [1994] *ECR* I-4435.

Community law established no rule which would prevent retroactive reduction of the advantages which women enjoyed.

As regards periods of service completed after the entry into force, in this case of 1 July 1991, of rules designed to eliminate discrimination, Article 119 of the Treaty does not preclude measures which achieve equal treatment by reducing the advantages of the persons previously favoured. Article 119 merely requires that men and women should receive the same pay for the same work without imposing any specific level of pay.

This ruling of the Court meant that in effect men received some advantages, whereas women were finally worse off than before the *Barber* judgment. This judgment was followed in the *Van den Akker* judgment.[14]

The decision can be represented in the following figure:

	17 May 1990	July 1991	
	_____*_____	_____*_____	
unequal treatment is allowed		equal pension age for men and women (60)	new age (65)

22.5. Retroactive Effect in Other Cases of Unequal Treatment

In the previous section we discussed judgments of the Court on widowers' pensions and differences in pension age. In these judgments the Court took account of the gradual implementation of the principle of equal treatment of men and women and consequently it limited the retroactive effect of the *Barber* judgment. This limitation of the effect in time of that ruling does not, however, apply in the case of exclusion of part-time workers; in their case the effects of their exclusion have to be taken away completely, including with effect for the past, as appears from the *Vroege* judgment.[15]

Since 1975 Mrs Vroege had worked on a part-time basis (25.9 hours a week). Before 1 January 1991, the pension scheme rules of her employer provided that only men and unmarried women employed for an indeterminate period and working at least 80% of the normal full day could be members of the scheme. Since Mrs Vroege never worked more than 80% of the full day, she was not allowed to pay contributions into the scheme and was therefore unable to acquire pension rights. On 1 January 1991 new pension scheme rules came into force,

---

[14]   Court of Justice 28 September 1994, Case 28/93, [1994] *ECR* I-4527.
[15]   Court of Justice 28 September 1994, Case 57/93, [1994] *ECR* I-4541.

providing that employees of both sexes who have reached 25 years of age and work at least 25% of normal working hours can join the scheme. The pension scheme rules also provided that women who were not members before 1 January 1991 can purchase additional years of membership, provided, however, that they had reached the age of 50 on 31 December 1990. Since she had not reached the age of 50 on 31 December 1990 Mrs Vroege could not rely on that transitional provision and therefore she could begin to accrue pension rights only as from 1 January 1991. Consequently, she challenged the new pension scheme rules on the ground that since they did not give her the right to be a member of the pension scheme in respects of periods of service prior to 1 January 1991 they involved discrimination incompatible with Article 119 of the Treaty.

The question to be answered by the Court was whether the limitation in time of the effects of the *Barber* judgment also applied to part-time workers who were excluded from occupational pension schemes. The Court answered that it is important to remember the context in which it was decided to limit the effects in time of the *Barber* judgment. According to its established case law, the Court may exceptionally, having regard to the general principle of legal certainty inherent in the Community legal order and the serious difficulties which its judgment may create as regards the past for legal relations established in good faith, find it necessary to limit the possibility for interested parties, relying on the Court's interpretation of a provision, to call in question those legal relations. The Court established therefore two essential criteria for deciding to impose such limitation, namely that those concerned should have acted in good faith and there should be a risk of serious difficulties.

As regards the first criterion, the Court found first of all that Article 9(a) of Directive 86/378 provided for the possibility of deferring the compulsory implementation of the principle of equal treatment with regard to the determination of pensionable age, as did the exception provided for in Article 7(1)(a) of Directive 79/7. In the light of those provisions the Member States and the parties concerned were reasonably entitled to consider that Article 119 did not apply to pensions paid under contracted-out schemes and that derogations from the principle of equality between men and women were still permitted in that sphere.

As regards the criterion of serious difficulties, the Court also held in the *Barber* judgment that if any male worker concerned could, like Mr Barber, retroactively assert the right to equal treatment in cases of discrimination which, until then, could have been considered permissible in view of the exceptions provided for in Directive 86/378, the financial balance of many occupational schemes might be upset retroactively. These criteria were applied in the *Ten Oever* case, which confirmed the limitation of the retroactive effect of the *Barber* judgment.

It follows, in particular, from the foregoing that the limitation of the effects in time of the *Barber* judgment concerns only those kinds of discrimination which employers and pension schemes could reasonable have considered to be permissible owing to the transitional derogations for which Community law provided and which were capable of being applied to occupational pensions.

As far as the right to join an occupational scheme is concerned, there is no reason to suppose that the groups concerned could have been mistaken about the applicability of Article 119. It has indeed been clear, according to the Court, since the judgment in the *Bilka* case that a breach of the rule of equal treatment committed through not recognising such a right is caught by Article 119. Since the *Bilka* judgment included no limitation in time, the direct effect of Article 119 can be relied upon in order retroactively to claim equal treatment in relation to the right to join an occupational pension scheme and this may be done as from 8 April 1976, the date of the *Defrenne* judgment in which the Court held for the first time that Article 119 has direct effect (and which also contained a limitation of the effect of the judgment in time).

The *Fisscher* judgment[16] concerned a case comparable to the *Vroege* case, discussed above, but in this case *married women* were excluded from the pension fund. The Court reproduced most of the considerations from the *Vroege* judgment and reached the same conclusion. So in the case of married women also there is no limitation in time of the effect of *'Barber'*. An additional question which was raised in this case was, however, whether the fact that a worker can claim to join an occupational pension scheme retroactively allows the worker to avoid paying the contributions relating to the period of membership concerned. The Court answered that where discrimination has been suffered, equal treatment is to be achieved by placing the worker discriminated against in the same situation as that of workers of the other sex. It follows that the worker cannot claim more favourable treatment, particularly in financial terms, than he would have had if he had been duly accepted as a member. This means that contributions can be required retroactively.

In the Treaty of Amsterdam it is proposed that Article 119 reads as follows:
'1. Each Member State shall ensure that the principle of equal pay for male and female workers for equal work or work of equal value is applied.
2. For the purpose of this Article, 'pay' means the ordinary basic or minimum wage or salary and any other consideration, whether in cash or in kind, which the worker receives directly or indirectly, in respect of his employment, from his employer.
Equal pay without discrimination based on sex means:
a   that pay for the same work at piece rates shall be calculated on the basis of the same unit of measurement;
b   that pay for work at time rates shall be the same for the same job. (..)'

Conclusion. Article 119 is of imminent importance for occupational pensions. It has direct effect with retroactive force with the exception to a limited category of situations only. These categories are the differences in pension age and the exclusion

---

[16]   Court of Justice, 28 September 1994, Case 128/93, [1994] *ECR* I-4583.

of widowers' pensions. In the other instances, such as exclusion of part-timers and married women, it could have been clear from the *Bilka* judgment that the funds had to realize equal treatment. Therefore, in these instances the effect of the *Barber* judgment was not limited in time.

Chapter 23

Directive 79/7 concerning Equal Treatment of Men and Women

23.1. Introduction

Article 119 concerns pay alone and not statutory social security. In order to ensure that there can be equal treatment in the area of social security also, the Council has made a series of directives.

Directive 79/7 concerns the progressive implementation of the principle of equal treatment for men and women in matters of social security.[1] This directive applies to *statutory social security* schemes. The period of implementation of this directive expired on 23 December 1984.

Directive 86/378 concerns the implementation of the principle of equal treatment for men and women in occupational social security schemes.[2]

Directive 86/613 concerns the application of the principle of equal treatment between men and women engaged in an activity, including agriculture, in a self-employed capacity, and on the protection of self-employed women during pregnancy and motherhood.[3] This directive concerns the self-employed.

Finally, the Commission issued a proposal for a directive completing the principle of equal treatment of men and women in statutory social security and occupational schemes; this has not been adopted yet.[4]

Directive 79/7 will be discussed in this chapter. The other directives are studied in Chapter 24.

Directive 79/7 requires the progressive implementation of the principle of equal treatment for men and women in matters of social security. The term *progressive* expresses the idea that the directive does not apply to all parts of social security; only statutory schemes are covered by this directive and some exceptions apply (survivors' benefits and family benefits are not within the material scope). Furthermore, the period of implementation of this directive was six years; this period expired on 23 December 1984. Finally, Article 7 of the directive allows Member States to exclude some areas of the statutory social security from the scope of this directive. In order to be able to rely on this directive, one has to fall both within the personal scope of the directive and the material scope. These issues are discussed in Sec-

---

[1]   Directive of 19 December 1978, *OJ* 1979 *L* 6, p. 24.
[2]   Directive of 24 July 1986, *OJ* 1986 *L* 225.
[3]   Directive of 11 December 1986, *OJ* 1986 *L* 359.
[4]   *OJ* 1987 *C* 309.

tions 23.2 and 23.3 respectively. The heart of the directive, the equal treatment provision, is discussed in Section 23.4.

23.2.   The Personal Scope of Directive 79/7

The directive applies to the working population, including self-employed persons, workers and self-employed persons whose activity is interrupted by illness, accident or involuntary unemployment, and also to persons seeking employment, retired and invalid workers and self-employed persons (*see* Article 2).

The working population in this directive thus covers more than persons actually engaged in work; persons who worked in the past and those who will work in the (near) future (*i.e.* who are seeking work) are also covered, civil servants included. Only persons with no link with economic life (such as housewives) do not fall within the scope of this directive.

The term *working population* in Article 2 of the directive led to several preliminary references to the Court of Justice. One of these led to the *Drake* judgment.[5]

> Mrs Drake was married and lived with her husband. Over a number of years, until the middle of 1984, she held a variety of full-time and part-time jobs. In June 1984, her mother, a severely disabled person who received an *attendance allowance*, came to live with her. Mrs Drake thereupon gave up her work in order to look after her mother. Under the British legislation on invalidity benefits, an invalid care allowance was payable to persons who (among other things) were regularly and substantially engaged in caring for a severely disabled person. The invalid care allowance was not paid to married women living with their husbands. Could Mrs Drake rely on the directive in order to remove this discriminatory clause? This question was raised as it was uncertain whether she fell under the personal scope of the directive, because she did not suffer from unemployment, illness or an accident herself.

The Court pointed out that the term 'working population' in Article 2 is defined broadly to include workers and self-employed persons whose activity is interrupted by illness, accident, or involuntary unemployment and persons seeking employment. That provision is based on the idea, the Court argued, that a person whose work has been interrupted by one of the risks referred to in Article 3 belongs to the working population. Mrs Drake had given up work solely because of one of the risks listed in Article 3; she must therefore be regarded as a member of the working population for the purposes of the directive. Thus, according to this ruling, persons 'indirectly' affected by a risk as mentioned in Article 3 also belong to the field of application of this directive.

---

[5]   Court of Justice 24 June 1986, Case 150/85, [1986] *ECR* 1995.

From the *Zürchner* judgment[6] it appears that only a person who terminated her occupational activities in order to care for another person, can invoke the directive. A housewife who starts to care for another person does not fall under the personal scope of the directive.

Mrs Zürchner wished to rely on a legal aid scheme for the purpose of bringing a claim against the sickness benefit administration of her spouse as this refused to pay for her care for this spouse. Mrs Zürchner's spouse, who was in gainful employment before suffering from an accident, was not able to walk. His situation required the help of a third person, for his household care and his medical care. His spouse had taken on these tasks. The German administration refused to pay for this, as the German Law provided: 'One is entitled to care only if a person, who does not form part of the household, cannot care for the sick person to an adequate extent'. According to Mrs Zürchner this provision is contrary to the directive.

The Court was asked whether a person in the situation of Mrs Zürchner as a spouse of an invalid person also falls under the term 'working population' of Article 2 of the directive. At the time when her spouse was affected by the accident, she was not employed in gainful employment, and in this respect she was in a situation different to Mrs Drake's. It could be argued, however, that her work done for her husband which could also be done in a remunerated form, could imply that she was part of the working population. This was a difficult question for the Court, as it would mean, that housewives in general, in particular when they had to perform heavy tasks, were to be part of the working population. Mrs Zürchner argued that she had to follow training for the care she provides to her husband and that this work should by its nature and extent be assimilated with occupational work. If she did not do this work, a remunerated person would have to do it.

The Court considered that the directive does not apply to persons who are not in gainful employment, or who are not seeking work or whose work or seeking work has not been interrupted by one of the risks mentioned in Article 3 of the directive.

From these considerations it follows that the term 'occupational activity', which is implied in the term 'working population' in Article 2 of the directive, must be interpreted as requiring an economic activity, *i.e.* an activity which is done for remuneration in a broad sense. The Court argued that it has to be acknowledged that a person can be obliged to rely on a third person when he is not, or is no longer, able to do specific activities himself, such as the care for children or domestic work. This can include the education of children, household activities, or the care for personal goods or usual daily activities. The Court acknowledged that these activities require certain capabilities, are of a certain extent and would have to be done on a remunerated basis if a person, whether a family member or not, could not do them on a voluntary basis. The Court did not, however, go so far to accept that housewife's

---

[6]   Court of Justice 7 November 1996, Case 77/95, [1996] *ECR* I-5689.

activities indeed constitute occupational activities: an interpretation of the term 'working population' so as to include the member of the family who performs an unremunerated activity, which would be done by a third person if the family member could not do it, would extend the scope of the directives without any restrictions, whereas, according to the Court, Article 2 aims to restrict the personal scope.

The approach of the Court is arguably not a very principled one: it does not make clear why the personal scope of the directive has to be restricted. In fact, the directive has no other effect than removing discrimination, and there is no good reason to allow discrimination in the case of housewives. Moreover, whether a person falls under the directive or not depends on accidental circumstances: if Mrs Zürcher had a job (even a small one) or was registered at the employment office as seeking work when her husband was affected by the accident, she would have been under the personal scope.

Persons who interrupted their occupational activities in order to dedicate themselves to the care of their children are usually *not* within the personal scope of the directive. This reason for the interruption of their occupational activities is not mentioned in the list of contingencies in Article 3 of the directive and therefore they do not belong to the personal scope. This was shown by the judgment in the *Johnson* case.[7]

This judgment concerned a woman who stopped working in 1970 in order to care for her then six year old daughter. In 1980 she wanted to start working again, but because of a back ache she was unable to do so. Therefore in 1981, when she was living alone, she was awarded a non-contributory invalidity benefit. In 1982 she started to cohabitate with a man. Payment of her benefit was terminated, because at that time a woman, cohabiting with a man who claimed disability benefit, had to show that she was incapable for doing normal household activities. This condition did not apply to men.

A person may be regarded as falling within the scope of the directive as 'a person seeking employment whose search is made impossible by the materialisation of one of the risks listed in Article 3(1)(a)'. It is sufficient for this purpose that one is seeking employment. It is not relevant why the person concerned left previous employment or even whether or not that person previously carried on an occupational activity. In order to fall within the personal scope of the directive, on the basis of this capacity, however, the person concerned must prove that he was a person seeking employment when one of the risks specified in Article 3(1)(a) of the directive materialised. In this regard, it is for the national court to determine whether the person concerned was actually seeking employment at the time when he was affected by one of the risks specified in the directive. For this purpose, it is particularly relevant, the Court considered in the *Johnson* judgment, whether that person was registered with an employment organisation responsible for dealing with offers of

---

[7]   Court of Justice 11 July 1991, Case 31/90, [1991] *ECR* 3723.

employment or assisting persons seeking employment. It is, furthermore, relevant whether he had sent job applications to employers and whether certificates were available from firms stating that he had attended interviews. These criteria opened the possibility for Mrs Johnson to fall under the person scope of the directive.

A judgment in which it appeared clearly that persons who were not working or who interrupted their occupational activities for a reason other than the ones mentioned in Article 3, was the *Achterberg-Te Riele* judgment.[8]

> This judgment concerned three joined cases. One of the three applicants worked as an employed earner and terminated her activities when she married. The second has never been engaged in occupational activities and the third had worked as an employed earner, had become unemployed (and received unemployment benefit for some time) but had never sought work again. These applicants disputed the disadvantageous effect of a provision in the Dutch old-age pension law (AOW).

The Court held that the scope *ratione personae* of the directive is determined by Article 2, according to which the directive applies to the working population, to persons seeking employment and to workers and self-employed persons whose activity is interrupted by one of the risks set out in Article 3(1)(a). Although, according to this article, the directive applies to statutory schemes which provide protection against old age, including the scheme at issue, it may be inferred from Article 2 in conjunction with Article 3 of the directive that the directive only covers persons who are working at the time when they become entitled to claim an old-age pension or whose occupational activity was previously interrupted by one of the risks set out in Article 3(1)(a). It follows from this analysis that the directive did not apply to persons who had never been available for employment or who had ceased to be available for a reason other than the materialisation of one of the risks referred to by the directive. This reply was not affected if the person concerned stopped working and was not available for employment before the last date for transposing the directive.

The consequences of the limited personal scope of the directive appeared also in the *Verholen* judgment.[9] This, like in the *Achterberg* case, concerned the calculation of the old-age pension (in force until 1985). The first question in this case was if a person is not covered by the personal scope of the directive, but is insured under a national scheme falling under the material scope of the directive (*e.g.* the Dutch AOW), can he rely on the directive? The Court answered negatively to this question.

A second question in this case was whether an applicant may invoke the provisions of a directive when he is suffering from a national discriminatory rule concerning his *spouse*, who is not taking part in the proceedings. In this case the

---

[8]   Court of Justice 27 June 1989, joined Cases 48, 106 and 107/88, [1989] *ECR* 1963.
[9]   Three joined cases: Court of Justice 11 July 1991, Cases 87/90, 88/90 and 89/90, [1991] *ECR* 3757.

husband of a woman, who had, because of the contested rule, been excluded from insurance during the periods he stayed abroad, started the proceedings. This husband had been an employee and therefore he fell under the personal scope. The question was raised whether he could rely on the directive in relation to this issue.[10] The Court answered that persons who do not fall within the personal scope of a directive are not prevented from invoking it when they have a direct interest in the directive being respected with regard to the persons protected by it. In the present case, however, the applicant was only allowed to invoke a provision applicable to his wife, if his wife effectively fell within the personal scope of this directive, *see* page 261.

In the *Megner and Scheffer* case[11] the question was raised, whether persons working in small part-time jobs fall under the personal scope of the directive.

> Under the German legislation persons working less than 18 hours a week are not insured for unemployment insurance. Mrs Megner and Mrs Scheffer were employed as cleaners, whose normal working time was a maximum of two hours per working day, five days a week. They sought recognition that they were subject to compulsory insurance under the statutory sickness and old-age insurance scheme and they were under an obligation to pay contributions to the statutory unemployment insurance scheme. Their request was refused on the ground that they were in subsidiary employment (work of less than 15 hours a week, remunerated below a certain level), which, under the German legislation, is exempt from compulsory insurance. The women claimed before the Court that the national provisions relating to exemption from compulsory insurance constituted indirect discrimination against women and were therefore contrary to Article 4(1) of Directive 79/7.

The first question was whether persons in employment of the type referred to fall within the scope of the directive. The Court considered that Article 2 of the directive implies that the definition of the working population is very broad, since it covers any worker, including persons who are merely seeking employment. The German Government and the employer had argued that persons in subsidiary employment are not part of the working population within the meaning of Article 2, because the small earnings which they receive from such employment are not sufficient to satisfy their needs. The Court did not accept this argument. The fact that a worker's earnings do not cover all his needs cannot prevent him from being a member of the working population. It appears from the Court's case law that the fact that his employment yields an income lower than the minimum required for subsistence or normally does not exceed eighteen hours a week (*see* the *Ruzius-Wilbrink* judgment) does not prevent the person in such employment from being regarded as a worker within the meaning

---

[10] Under the rules at the time, a supplement was given, under the AOW, for the partner to the pensioner; this supplement was reduced for the years the partner was not insured. Therefore, the husband also had an interest in this case.

[11] Court of Justice 14 December 1995, Case 444/93, [1995] *ECR* I-4741.

of Article 48 or Article 119 of the Treaty. Furthermore, the Court referred to the *Unger* judgment, in which it ruled that the concept of 'wage-earner or assimilated worker' referred to in the coordination regulation concerned, had, like the term 'worker' in Articles 48 to 51, a Community meaning.

It is remarkable that in this judgment the Court dealt with the case law on coordination (Regulation 1408/71) and on equal treatment of men and women at the same time, although these instruments each have their own definitions of personal scope.

In the *Nolte* judgment[12], the approach from the *Megner* judgment was followed.

> According to the German social security law a disabled person is entitled to a disability insurance, if he can show that he has been subject to liability for compulsory contribution payments during at least three years out of the last five years. Small jobs are exempted from compulsory insurance. Nolte had worked from 1977 until March 1987, when she terminated her activities worked in a small job as a cleaner. Since June 1988 she was seriously ill, so that she was no longer capable of performing remunerated work. On 28 November 1988 Nolte applied for a disability benefit. This was refused on the ground that Nolte had not worked during the required period in contributory employment.

The only point in which the considerations of the Court deviate from the *Megner and Scheffel* judgment in the present judgment, is that the German Government had argued that Mrs Nolte could also not rely on the directive for another reason. This was that she had terminated employment more than one year before the start of her disability and there were no indications that she was at work at that moment. The Court remarked, however, that Nolte could claim, according to German law, a disability benefit, if the periods during which she had been working in her small job, were considered as periods of compulsory insurance. For this reason the Court decided that she fell under the personal scope of the directive. *See* also page 271.

23.3.   The Material Scope of Directive 79/7

The material scope of Directive 79/7 is defined in Article 3:

Article 3, section 1:
'a.   statutory schemes which provide protection against the following risks: sickness, invalidity, old age, accidents of work and occupational diseases, unemployment;
b.   social assistance, in so far as it is intended to supplement or replace the schemes referred to in (a).'

---

[12]   Court of Justice 14 December 1995, Case 317/93, [1995] *ECR* I-4625.

The second paragraph of Article 3 provides that the directive shall not apply to the provisions concerning survivors' benefits nor to those concerning family benefits, except in the case of family benefits granted by way of increases of benefits due in respect of the risks referred to in paragraph 1(a).

As we saw in the *Drake* judgment[13] on page 246 the Court had given Article 2 a broad interpretation, as it ruled that persons caring for an invalid person also fall under the scope of the directive (Section 23.2). In that case, the question was also raised as to whether benefits payable for care of an invalid person fell within the material scope of the directive.

The Court answered this question in the affirmative. It considered that it is possible for the Member States to provide protection against the consequences of the risk of invalidity in various ways. For example, a Member State, may, as the United Kingdom had done, provide for two separate allowances; one payable to the disabled person himself and the other payable to a person who provides care. Another Member State might arrive at the same result by paying an allowance to the disabled person at a rate equivalent to the sum of those two benefits. The Court argued that, in order to ensure that the progressive implementation of the principle of equal treatment is carried out in a harmonious manner throughout the Community, Article 3(1) must be interpreted as including any benefit which in a broad sense forms part of one of the statutory schemes referred to or a social assistance provision intended to supplement or replace such a scheme. The fact that a benefit which forms part of a statutory invalidity scheme is paid to a third party and not directly to the disabled person did not place it outside the scope of Directive 79/7. Otherwise it would be possible, as emphasised by the Commission and the Court, to remove existing benefits covered by the directive, from its scope by making formal changes to such benefits.

As can be seen from this decision, the Court does not pay too much attention to the formal aspects of a scheme. This appeared also from the *Richardson* judgment.[14]

In the United Kingdom the National Health Service Act authorizes the Secretary of State to adopt regulations providing for the payment of prescription charges in accordance with the rules laid down therein. The Act authorizes the adoption of regulations providing for exemption from those charges for certain categories of persons. Those categories of persons may be prescribed in particular by reference to age, type of condition affecting them, and the resources available to them. The Secretary of State had provided exemptions for, among other persons, a man who has attained the age of 65 years or a woman who has attained the age of 60 years. The preliminary question was whether the scheme was within the scope of the directive.

---

[13] Court of Justice 24 June 1986, Case 150/85, [1986] *ECR* 1995.
[14] Court of Justice 19 October 1995, Case 137/94, [1995] *ECR* I-3407.

The Court stated, that in order to fall within the scope of Directive 79/7, a benefit must constitute the whole or part of a statutory scheme providing protection against one of the specified risks, or a form of social assistance having the same objective. Although the way in which a benefit is granted is not decisive for the purposes of Directive 79/7, the benefit must, in order to fall within its scope, be directly and effectively linked to the protection provided against one of the risks specified in Article 3(1) of the directive. A benefit such as that provided for in the regulations concerned fulfils those conditions.

Not all types of benefit fall under the material scope of the directive. An example can be seen in the *Jackson and Cresswell* judgment.[15]

This case concerned the calculation of the United Kingdom income support. This benefit is granted to anyone aged at least eighteen whose income did not exceed a specified amount and who was engaged in no more than 24 hours a week. The applicants were single mothers with small children. One of them started vocational training, in respect of which she received a weekly allowance. The benefit officer took account of that income and withdrew her entitlement to supplementary benefit while refusing her the right to deduct from her income the child-minding expenses which she incurred in respect of her child during her period in training. The other applicant had a part-time job, and the benefit officer took account of that income and reduced income support without deducting from her income the expenses for minding her two children. The applicants argued that the refusal to take child minding costs into account was allegedly indirectly discriminating against women. However, before the Court could come to this point, the preliminary question had to be answered as to whether these benefits were within the material scope of the directive.

The Court answered that a benefit, if it is to fall within the scope of Directive 79/7, must constitute the whole or part of a statutory scheme providing protection against one of the specified risks or a form of social assistance having the same objective. Article 3(1)(a) of Directive 79/7, however, does not refer to a statutory scheme which, on certain conditions, provides persons with means below a legally defined limit with a special benefit designed to enable them to meet their needs. That finding is not affected by the fact that the recipient of the benefit is *in fact* in one of the situations covered by Article 3(1) of the directive (the applicants were (considered) unemployed).

Exclusion from the scope of Directive 79/7 is justified where, as in the case of Mrs Jackson and Mrs Cresswell, the law sets the amount of the benefits in question independently of any consideration relating to the existence of any of the risks listed in Article 3(1). The fact that the national schemes at issue exempt claimants from the obligation to be available for work, shows that the benefits in question cannot

---

[15]   Court of Justice 16 July 1992, Cases 63/91 and 64/91, [1992] *ECR* I-4973.

be regarded as being directly and effectively linked to protection against the risk of unemployment.

Thus, Article 3 is to be interpreted as not applying to benefits, such as supplementary benefit and income support, which may be granted in a variety of personal situations to persons whose means are insufficient to meet their needs as defined by statute. The answer does not depend on whether the claimant is in fact suffering from one of the risks listed in Article 3 of the directive. In other words, the Court considers *in abstracto* whether a particular scheme requires as a general condition that one is available for work; the factual circumstances of the applicant are not decisive.

In the *Smithson* judgment[16] another type of benefit did not fall under the material scope of the directive.

> The contested scheme in this case was the United Kingdom housing benefit. This was payable to persons whose actual income was below a theoretical amount as defined in the scheme. One of the factors relevant to the increase of this benefit was that one is a single person and is between sixty and eighty years of age. Furthermore, one must be in receipt of one or more social security benefits, including invalidity pension. This pension is payable until pension age (which is sixty for women and sixty-five for men).

The Court argued that, according to Article 3(1) of this directive, in order to fall within the scope of the directive, the benefit had to be part of the statutory protection against one of the contingencies listed in the directive. If the conditions of a benefit scheme were not decisive to qualify this benefit as one mentioned in Directive 79/7, then this benefit can still fall under the scope of this directive if it is directly and effectively linked to protection against one the risks listed in Article 3. Article 3 does, however, not concern housing costs. Age and invalidity of the claimant are just two of the criteria to determine the financial needs of the applicant. Even if these criteria are decisive for the increase of the benefit, this is not sufficient to bring this benefit within the material scope of this directive, the Court concluded.

23.4. The Distinction between the Material Scope of Directive 79/7 and Article 119

Now that the material scope of both Article 119 of the Treaty and the directive have been described, it can be understood that here are some borderline cases, in which it is not clear which instrument applies.

> An example of such borderline cases is a judgment of the Court which concerned the Dutch ABP-scheme. This is a scheme for pensions for civil servants and those assimilated with them. These pensions supplement the statutory basic old-age

---

[16]   Court of Justice 4 February 1992, Case 243/90, [1992] *ECR* I-467.

pensions. The level depends on the periods of insurance. They are governed by a statute. This means that they have elements of occupational pensions (Article 119), but are also based on a statutory scheme (Directive 79/7).

The judgment concerned was the *ABP v. Beune* judgment.[17] The national court sought to determine whether a pension scheme such as the APB scheme falls within the scope of Directive 79/7 or that of Article 119 of the Treaty.

The Court considered that in order to determine whether a pension scheme of the type set up by the ABP Act falls within the scope of Directive 79/7 or of Article 119, it is necessary to analyze the relative importance of the criteria referred to by the Court in its previous decisions. The Court has developed *inter alia* the following criteria: the statutory nature of a pension scheme, negotiation between employers and employees' representatives, the fact that the employees' benefits supplement social security benefits, the manner in which the pension scheme is financed, its applicability to general categories of employees and, finally, the relationship between the benefit and the employees' employment. The finding that the pension scheme is governed directly by statute is without doubt a strong indication that the benefits provided by the scheme are social security benefits. However, the fact that a scheme like the ABP is directly governed by statute is not sufficient to exclude it from the scope of Article 119. The Court has sofar in its judgments given precedence to the criterion of whether there is an agreement rather than the criterion of statutory origin. In the *Bilka* judgment, for instance, the Court stated that, even if adopted in accordance with legislation, a pension scheme based on an agreement between employer and staff representatives, and having the effect of supplementing social benefits paid under generally applicable national legislation with benefits financed entirely by the employer, is not a social security scheme, and that such a scheme provides benefits constituting consideration received by the worker from the employer in respect of his employment, within the meaning of the second paragraph of Article 119. A pension scheme set up by negotiation between both sides of the industry concerned and funded wholly by the employees and employers in that industry, to the exclusion of any financial contribution from the public purse, falls within the scope of Article 119, even when the public authorities, at the request of the employers' and trade union organisations concerned, declare the scheme compulsory for the whole of the industry concerned. However, the Court continued, the negotiation between the employers and employees' representatives must be such as results in a formal agreement.

The only possible decisive criterion is whether the pension is paid to the worker by reason of the employment relationship between him and his former employer, that is to say the criterion of employment based on the wording of Article 119 itself.

Conclusion. It follows from all the foregoing considerations that a civil service pension scheme of the type at issue which essentially relates to the employment of

---

17   Court of Justice 28 September 1994, Case 7/93, [1994] *ECR* I-4471.

the person concerned, forms part of the pay received by that person and comes within the scope of Article 119.

23.5.   The Prohibition of Discrimination in Directive 79/7

23.5.1. Introduction

Article 4 reads:
'1 The principle of equal treatment means that there shall be no discrimination whatsoever on ground of sex either directly, or indirectly by reference in particular to marital or family status, in particular as concerns:
- the scope of the schemes and the conditions of access thereto;
- the obligation to contribute and the calculation of contributions;
- the calculation of benefits including increases due in respect of a spouse and for dependants and the conditions governing the duration and retention of entitlement to benefits.
2 The principle of equal treatment shall be without prejudice to the provisions relating to the protection of women on the grounds of maternity'.

Article 4 forbids direct and indirect discrimination.

23.5.2   The Direct Effect of Directive 79/7

As directives are addressed to the Member States, it was not clear at first sight whether individuals could rely on a directive. In Chapter 1 of this book, we saw that this is indeed possible where provisions of a directive appear, as far as their subject-matter is concerned, to be unconditional and sufficiently precise. Such circumstances occur where a Member State does not implement provisions of a directive within the time-limit mentioned in that directive. In that case individuals can rely on the directive against any national provision which is incompatible with the directive, or in so far as the provisions of the directive define rights which individuals are able to assert against the state.

The question whether the equal treatment provision of Directive 79/7 has direct effect was answered in the *FNV* v. *The Netherlands* judgment.[18]

Article 13(1)(l), of the Dutch *Wet Werkloosheidsvoorziening* (Law on Unemployment Benefit) excluded workers who, being married women, were not described as main wage-earners in a family, under the rules adopted by the competent minister, from the right to benefit. The *Federatie Nederlandse Vakbeweging* (Netherlands Trades Union Federation) started a legal action in order to obtain

---

[18]   Court of Justice 4 December 1986, Case 71/85, [1986] *ECR* 3855.

a decision that the Netherlands acted unlawfully by maintaining in force or refusing to cease to apply this Article after 23 December 1984.

The question was whether Article 4 had direct effect as from 23 December 1984. The Court answered, that wherever the provisions of a directive appear, as far as their subject-matter is concerned, to be unconditional and sufficiently precise, individuals may rely on those provisions in the absence of implementing measures adopted within the prescribed period as against any national provision which is incompatible with the directive. Article 4 precludes, generally and unequivocally, all discrimination on ground of sex. The provision is therefore sufficiently precise to be relied upon. Secondly, the Court considered whether the prohibition of discrimination which it contains may be regarded as unconditional having regard to the exceptions provided for in Article 7. For this purpose, it was also relevant that, according to the wording of Article 5, Member States are to take certain measures in order to ensure that the principle of equal treatment is applied in national legislation. The Court argued that, as regards Article 7, that provision merely reserved to Member States the right to exclude certain clearly defined areas from the scope of the directive. It does not contain any condition with regard to the application of the principle of equal treatment as regards Article 4 of the directive; therefore, Article 7 is not relevant in this case. As for Article 5, which obliges Member States to take the measures necessary to ensure that any laws, regulations and administrative provisions contrary to the principle of equal treatment are abolished, it cannot be inferred from the wording of that article that it lays down conditions to which the prohibition of discrimination is subject. Consequently, Article 4(1) of the directive does not confer on Member States the power to make conditional or to limit the application of the principle of equal treatment within its field of application. It is, as far as the subject-matter is concerned, sufficiently precise and unconditional to allow individuals, in the absence of implementing measures adopted within the prescribed period, to rely upon it before the national courts as from 23 December 1984 in order to preclude the application of any national provision inconsistent with that article.

A further question concerned the consequences for individuals once the direct effect of this article is established. Article 4 precludes any form of discrimination, but what does this mean for national provisions inconsistent with this article? Are married women, not being main wage-earners in a family, entitled to this benefit? Or, from now on, are male married persons, not being main wage-earners, also no longer entitled to this benefit? The Court answered that Member States may have recourse to several methods other than the straightforward repeal of the rule that is incompatible with the directive. However, in the absence of measures implementing that article, women are entitled to be treated in the same manner, and to have the same rules applied to them, as men who are in the same situation, since, where the said directive has not been implemented, those rules remain the only valid point of reference.[19] Therefore, married women not being main wage-earner were no longer excluded from entitlement to the WWV.

Direct discrimination

'Direct discrimination' means that a distinction is made on ground of a forbidden criterion (in this directive sex). In the past, many national social security schemes of the Member States contained many provisions that were directly discriminatory on ground of sex. Usually, this was in combination with marital status. However, the fact that sex was used as a criterion in connection with marital status did not mean that such provision was not discriminatory, as *married men* were not treated in the same way as *married women*.[20] An example of such a combination is the *McDermott and Cotter* judgment.[21]

> Nora McDermott and Ann Cotter were married women who from January 1984 received unemployment benefit. On the basis of the Irish Social Welfare Act 1981 their benefit was terminated after one year on the ground that a married woman could receive unemployment benefit for a maximum of 312 days. A married man, a single man or a single woman would have received benefit for seventy-eight days more. The applicants required the annulment of the termination of their benefit after the 312 benefit days, on the ground that from 23 December 1984 they were entitled to benefit at the same rate and for the period as married men.

The Court ruled that the national rule was incompatible with the directive; individuals may rely on the directive in the absence of implementing measures adopted within the prescribed period as against any national provision which is incompatible with the directive. With regard to the argument to the effect that the multiplicity of alternatives available for the purpose of achieving equal treatment made it impossible for the directive to confer rights on individuals, the Court decided that it was sufficient to point out that the fact that directives left to the national authorities the choice of the form and methods for achieving the required result, could not constitute a ground for denying all effect to those provisions which may be relied upon before a court. Until the moment that the national government adopted the necessary implementing measures, women were entitled to have the same rules applied to them as were applied to men who are in the same situation, since in such circumstances those rules remain the only valid point of reference.

---

[19]   The approach of the FNV judgment is followed in the judgments of the Court of 11 July 1991, Case 31/90, *Johnson*, [1991] *ECR* 3723; 24 March 1987, Case 286/85, *McDermott and Cotter*, [1987] *ECR* 1453; 13 December 1989, Case 102/88, *Ruzius-Wilbrink*, [1989] *ECR* 4311, discussed in the following section.
[20]   See, for instance, Court of Justice 24 June 1986, Case 150/85, *Drake*, [1986] *ECR* 1995; 4 December 1986, Case 71/85, *FNV*, [1986] *ECR* 3855.
[21]   Court of Justice 24 March 1987, Case 286/85, [1987] *ECR* 1453.

23.5.3. Prohibition of the Effects of a Former Discriminatory Rule

Most of the cases which concerned direct discrimination, which were brought before the Court, concerned transitory rules that were related to prior discriminatory rules or situations, and in these transitory rules the effects of the prior discrimination could still be seen. On page 258 we discussed the *McDermott and Cotter* judgment. As the subsequent law adopted by the Irish legislator still had a directly discriminatory effect, the applicants had to go to court again in a second case. This led to a second preliminary reference and to the *Cotter and McDermott* judgment.[22]

> Under the Social Welfare Act 1981, a married man was automatically entitled to increases in his social security benefits in respect of a spouse and children without having to prove that they were actually dependent on him, whereas married women were required to fulfil additional conditions. Moreover, under this Act a married woman received a lower unemployment benefit than the amount for a married man, and for a shorter period.
>
> That position was altered by the Social Welfare (No. 2) Act 1985, which confined the payment of an increase in respect of an adult dependant to a situation where actual dependency can be shown, irrespective of the sex of the claimant. This law established equality of treatment for male and female claimants with regard to increases in respect of a dependent child. Regulations adopted in 1986 provided on a transitional basis that claimants who did not have a spouse actually dependent on them and therefore ceased to be entitled to an increase in respect of an adult dependant after the entry into force of the Social Welfare (No. 2) Act 1985 became eligible for a compensatory allowance. It was common ground that those provisions covered only married men, who previously received automatic increases even if they had no actual dependants.

At the hearing, the Irish government argued as a preliminary point that the prohibition of discrimination laid down in Article 4(1) of the directive applied only to circumstances in which the person, in respect of whom an increase has been granted, was financially dependent. The Court decided that this argument could not be upheld. Article 4 of the directive applied, in particular, to the calculation of benefits, including increases for spouses and dependants. From this it is clear that the article also applies to increases for non-dependent spouses. The determination of the conditions for increases of social security benefits is left, according to the Court, entirely to the Member States, with the restriction that the principle of equal treatment has to be taken fully into account. As long as the necessary implementation measures for the directive are not adopted, the application of the rules which apply to men who are in the same situation remains the only valid point of reference. Therefore, if men did not have to show, after 23 December 1984, that their spouses were actually dependent on them, and if they received the increases automatically, women have

---

22   Court of Justice 13 March 1991, Case 377/89, [1991] *ECR* 1155.

the same automatic right to increases if they are in the same circumstances as these men. Specific additional conditions are not allowed.

A further question was whether national principles of law can restrict the application of the principle of equal treatment. The Irish government had brought forward the argument that the directive should not be interpreted in such a way that it would lead to an 'unjust enrichment'. This alleged national principle means that payment to an applicant, even if it would be according to the law, does not have to take place, if that payment would lead to unjust enrichment of the person concerned to the detriment effect of the defendant. It was argued that the state could also rely on this principle; for this purpose the state must have acted in good faith and the circumstances must have changed in the course of time to such an extent that payment would be unreasonable. The Irish government argued that a radical interpretation of the equal treatment principle could have the effect that one family received the same increase twice, *i.e.* when both partners receive social security benefits in the same period. This would infringe the national principle on unjust enrichment. The Court rejected this argument; if such an application of the principle of unjust enrichment was accepted, the national authorities could use their own illegal behaviour as an argument to deprive Article 4 of its full meaning.

In the *Dik* case also[23], the contested regulation concerned the effects of older discriminatory rules.

Article 13(1)(l) of the *Wet Werkloosheidsvoorziening* (WWV), which led to the *FNV* judgment discussed above, was repealed with retroactive effect as from 23 December 1984. Article II of the Law of 24 April 1985 nevertheless provided a transitional measure to the effect that the repeal of that article was not to apply to workers whose unemployment commenced before 23 December 1984, unless they were in receipt of the benefit under the *Werkloosheidswet* (unemployment insurance act - WW) on that date. The three appellants all lost their employment before 23 December and lost their entitlement to the benefit under the WW because the maximum period for receiving that benefit had expired. After that date they were refused WWV benefit pursuant to Article 13(1), point *l* thereof.

The Court considered that the directive does not provide for any derogation from the principle of equal treatment laid down in Article 4(1) in order to authorise the extension of the discriminatory effects of earlier provisions of national law. It follows that a Member State may not maintain beyond 23 December 1984 any inequalities attributable to the fact that the conditions for entitlement to benefit are those which applied before that date. That is so notwithstanding the fact that those inequalities are the result of transitional provisions. By virtue of Article 4(1) of the directive, women are entitled as from 23 December 1984, to be treated in the same manner and to have applied to them the scheme which applies to men in the same situation. In this case that meant that if a man who lost his employment and his right to benefit

---

[23]   Court of Justice 8 March 1988, Case 80/87, [1988] *ECR* 1601.

under the WWV under 23 December 1984 and who did not obtain benefit under the WWV before that date was entitled to benefit under the WWV after 23 December 1984, a woman in the same position would also be entitled to such benefit without having to satisfy any additional condition applicable before that date exclusively to married women.

Belatedly adopted implementing measures must fully respect the rights which Article 4(1) has conferred on individuals in a Member State as from the expiry of the period allowed to the Member States for complying with it. A Member State which adopts implementing measures after the expiry of the period prescribed by the directive may fix the date of their entry into force retroactively to the date of expiry of that period, provided that the rights which Article 4(1) of the directive confers on individuals in the Member States as from the expiry of the said period are respected.

The *Verholen* judgment[24], already discussed on page 249, also concerned the effect of previous discriminatory rules.

The contested regulation was the Dutch AOW provision which provided until 1 April 1985 that married women were not insured for the general old age pension act during the periods their husbands were not insured because they were employed in another State. Although this scheme insured residents of the Netherlands, a married woman whose husband was insured abroad, was not covered by the Dutch scheme. The opposite was not the case: a married man, resident of the Netherlands, whose wife was insured abroad, remained insured. The effects of the exclusion from insurance was a reduced old-age benefit.

The Court considered that the directive must be interpreted as meaning that it did not allow the Member States to maintain the effects of prior national legislation which excluded, in certain cases, married women from the benefit of an old-age pension after the time limit for transposition laid down in Article 8. The directive does not contain exceptions to this principle which would allow the discriminatory effects of older national provisions after 23 December 1984, even if these are the effect of benefit conditions in force before this date. Arguments related to the nature of a benefit system (contributory or not[25]), were not relevant to the question whether Member States were allowed to maintain the effects of prior national legislation. Therefore, the Court followed a different approach in respect to discriminatory effects due to former legislation with respect to *statutory* old-age pensions, then it did in the case of occupational pensions, *see* the *Ten Oever* judgment (discussed in Section 22.3 above). Directive 79/7 is a different scheme than Article 119 with a different history, the Court did not allow the effects of previous discriminatory rules to continue to have an impact.

---

[24]   Court of Justice 11 July 1991, Cases 87/90, 88/90 and 89/90, [1991] *ECR* 3757.
[25]   In fact, the AOW scheme is not a contributory one, but the amount of benefit is related to the duration of insurance.

In order to invoke this rule one must, as we have seen before, fall under the personal scope of the directive at the moment one applies for this benefit. For this reason Mrs Achterberg, who wished to receive an unreduced benefit, could not rely on the directive and was still only entitled to the lower benefit.

In the *Van Gemert-Derks* case[26] the question was raised whether the withdrawal of disability benefit was acceptable in case of persons who received a widows' pension.

> The Dutch General law on disability benefits provided that the right to a disability benefit was to be withdrawn as soon as a woman became entitled to a widows' pension. A widows pension is granted after an application for this benefit is made or it may be granted *ex officio* by the benefit administration, as is provided by the General Law on widows' pensions. The substitution of a disability benefit by a widows' pension meant that the woman concerned received a lower benefit. As widows' pensions were by virtue of the text of this Law payable to women only, this rule affected only women; the disability benefit of male beneficiaries could not be withdrawn when they became a widower. However, the Dutch Court of Appeal ruled in 1988, that by virtue of Article 26 of the International Convention on Civil and Political Rights, widowers were also entitled to benefit under the General Law on widows' benefits. Consequently, the question arose as to how to interpret the disputed provision of the General Law on disability benefits.

The first question of the national court was whether Directive 79/7 still allowed national courts to apply Article 26 of the Convention. This question was raised, as application of this article could lead to different situations in the Member States. These were due to the fact that some Member States had ratified this convention and others had not. Moreover, there might be differences in the interpretation of this Convention by States who had ratified it, since there is no court to provide an overall interpretation of the Convention. Consequently, application of this article could be contrary to the development of one legal order as intended by the EC Treaty. The Court replied that as regards benefits which are not within the material scope of Directive 79/7, these benefits are governed by national and international law. A decision of a national court based on Article 26 of the Convention mentioned above does not affect the implementation of the principle of equal treatment. The second question of the national court was whether the rule of the General disability law mentioned above was contrary to Article 4 of Directive 79/7. The Court first considered that the directive did not apply to survivors' benefits; it was relevant, therefore, to see whether the disputed Dutch provision was within the scope of the directive. The Court considered that the disputed provision concerned the withdrawal of disability benefit; consequently, Directive 79/7 was applicable. A provision of national legislation, which deprived women of benefit whereas men in the same

---

[26]   Court of Justice 27 October 1993, Case 337/91, [1993] *ECR* I-5943.

situation were not deprived of this benefit, constituted discrimination within the meaning of Directive 79/7. The Dutch benefit administration argued that at present widows' benefits were granted only after an application had been received; from 1989, all beneficiaries of a general disability benefit who became widows were informed of the consequences of claiming for the widows' benefit.

The Court considered this procedure acceptable; it could not be said that the directive is infringed upon, if a widow renounced her right to a general disability benefit, on condition that she has been informed accurately and comprehensibly of the financial effects of substitution of this benefit by a widows' benefit. It is up to the national court to decide whether the widow concerned had indeed renounced her entitlement to benefit after she had been informed in this way.

23.5.4. Procedural Limitations for Realizing Equal Treatment

National law often restricts the periods for which benefit can be claimed with retroactive effect. As some Member States were late in removing discriminatory rules form their national law, the question arose to what extent national rules of procedure are contrary to the directive. This matter was dealt with in the *Emmott* judgment.[27]

> Mrs Emmott's situation closely resembled that as described in the (first) *McDermott and Cotter* judgment and concerned the same national scheme.
> As soon as the *McDermott and Cotter* judgment[28] had been delivered (24 March 1987), Mrs Emmott entered into correspondence with the Minister for Social Welfare with a view to obtain, as from 23 December 1984, the same amount of benefits as paid to a married man in a situation identical to hers. By letter of 26 June 1987 the Minister replied that, since the directive was still the subject of litigation before the Irish High Court, no decision could be taken in relation to her claim, which would be examined as soon as that court had given judgment. By order of 22 July 1988, the High Court granted Mrs Emmott leave to institute proceedings for judicial review for the purpose of recovering the benefits which had not been paid to her since 23 December 1984 in breach of Article 4(1) of the directive. However, that leave was granted without prejudice to the right of the defendants to raise the issue of the non-observance of the time-limit for initiating proceedings. The national authorities concerned did in fact plead that the applicant's delay in initiating proceedings constituted a bar to her claim.

The Court of Justice was asked whether the ruling in *McDermott and Cotter* must be understood as meaning that, in a claim before a national court made in purported reliance upon Article 4(1) of the directive, it is contrary to the general principles of Community law for the relevant authorities of a Member State to rely upon national

---

27   Court of Justice 25 July 1991, Case 208/90, [1991] *ECR* 4269.
28   Court of Justice 24 March 1987, Case 286/85, [1987] *ECR* 1453.

procedural rules, in particular rules relating to time-limits, so as to restrict or refuse such compensation. The Court held that in the absence of Community rules on the subject, it is for the domestic legal system of each Member State to determine the procedural conditions governing actions at law intended to ensure the protection of the rights which individuals derive from the direct effect of Community law. Such conditions must not be less favourable than those relating to similar actions of a domestic nature nor framed so as to render virtually impossible the exercise of rights conferred by Community law. Whilst the laying down of reasonable time-limits which, if unobserved, bar proceedings, in principle satisfies the two conditions mentioned above, account must nevertheless be taken of the particular nature of directives. It must be borne in mind that the Member States are required to ensure the full application of directives in a sufficiently and precise manner so that, where directives are intended to create rights for individuals, they can ascertain the full extent of those rights and, where necessary, rely on them before the national courts. Only in specific circumstances, in particular where a Member State has failed to take the implementation measures required or has adopted measures which are not in conformity with a directive, has the Court recognised the right of persons affected thereby to rely, in judicial proceedings, on a directive as against a defaulting Member State. Therefore, the Court argued, this is a minimum guarantee, arising from the binding nature of the obligation imposed on the Member States by the effect of directives, which cannot justify a Member State absolving itself from taking implementation measures appropriate to the purpose of each directive in due time. This is because, as long as a directive has not been properly transposed into national law, individuals are unable to ascertain the full extent of their rights. That state of uncertainty for individuals subsists even after the Court has delivered a judgment finding that the Member State in question has not fulfilled its obligations under the directive. This is also the case if the Court has held that a particular provision or provisions of the directive are sufficiently precise and unconditional to be relied upon before a national court. Only the proper transposition of the directive will bring that state of uncertainty to an end and it is only upon that transposition that the legal certainty which must exist if individuals are to be required to assert their rights is created. It follows that, until such time as a directive has been properly transposed, a defaulting Member State may not rely to an individual's delay in initiating proceedings against it in order to protect rights conferred upon him by the provisions of the directive. A period laid down by national law, within which proceedings must be initiated, cannot begin to run before that time.

In the *Steenhorst-Neerings* case[29] the Court was asked whether the *Emmott* ruling meant that legislation was also inconsistent with Directive 79/7 if it limited the retroactive effect of a claim for disability benefit to one year.

Initially the Dutch General disability benefit was payable only to men and to unmarried women. By a law of 1979, married women also became eligible for

---

[29]   Court of Justice 27 October 1993, Case 338/91, [1993] *ECR* I-5475.

this benefit, but an exception was made in respect of women who had begun to suffer incapacity for work before 1975. The Dutch court of appeal, however, decided in 1988 that this was contrary to Article 26 of the International Convention on Civil and Political Rights. This meant, that married women whose incapacity materialised before 1975, could receive disability benefit as from the date on which the 1979 Act came into force. The General disability law provided that one could not receive benefit with retroactive effect for more than one year from the date of application. The Court was asked whether the latter rule was compatible with Community law.

The Court considered that the conditions for this benefit must be the same for men and women. Moreover, the conditions for entitlement to benefit were to be governed by national law and must not be less favourable then those generally applicable for this type of benefit and must not make the exercise of rights which were derived form Community law impossible. The national court had asked this question with the *Emmott* judgment in mind; in this ruling the Court decided that, until such time as a directive has been properly transposed, a defaulting Member State may not rely to an individual's delay in initiating proceedings against it in order to protect rights conferred upon him by the provisions of the directive.

With respect to the question raised in this case, however, the Court replied that a rule of national law which limits the retroactive effect of a claim is different from the rule which was disputed in the *Emmott* case. The loss of rights following from a delay in initiating procedures before a court corresponds to the need to prevent administrative decisions from being liable to dispute in proceedings outside a restricted time period. The provision in the legislation which limits the retroactive effect of applications for disability benefit serves an objective which is totally different from time limits for initiating a procedure before a court. The legislative provision is needed to satisfy the requirements of proper administration, and, in particular, to maintain the financial balances of a pay-as-you-go system.

23.5.5. Indirect Discrimination

It is much more difficult to decide whether a regulation is indirectly discriminatory than when direct discrimination is in dispute. A rule is indirectly discriminatory, if its effects are different for either of the sexes, although it does not itself contain criteria directly related to sex. In such a case it is not relevant whether the person or body who made this regulation had the intention of discriminating on grounds of sex.

Article 4 of the directive, quoted in the first paragraph of this section, forbids indirect discrimination, in particular by reference to marital or family status. This provision lists some aspects in which indirect discrimination can occur; these include the calculation of benefits including increases due in respect of a spouse and for dependants.

From the judgments of the Court, it appears that many cases of alleged indirect discrimination concern supplements for dependants. The first case is the *Teuling-Worms* judgment.[30]

> According to the Dutch *Wet op de Arbeidsongeschiktheidsverzekering* (WAO - Law on Insurance against Incapacity for Work), the minimum benefit could be increased by means of supplements to one hundred per cent, only for beneficiaries having family responsibilities. Mrs Teuling was not entitled to benefit supplements because of the income arising from or in connection with her husband's work. Her husband died on 28 April 1984. Mrs Teuling claimed that the system of supplements, which took account of income arising from or in connection with the work of a spouse, constituted indirect discrimination against women.

In answer to this, the Court pointed out that in this case supplements were provided which were not directly based on the sex of beneficiaries, but took account of their marital status or family situation. In respect of this, it emerged that a considerably smaller proportion of women than of men were entitled to such supplements. This would be contrary to Article 4(1) of the directive, if that system of benefits could not be justified by reasons which exclude discrimination on grounds of sex. According to statistics provided to the Commission by the Netherlands Government, a significantly greater number of married men than married women receive a supplement linked to family responsibilities. This results from the fact that in the Netherlands there are at present considerably more married men than married women who carry on occupational activities, and therefore considerably fewer women who have a dependent spouse.

Can the grant of these supplements be justified by reasons which exclude discrimination on grounds of sex? In that regard, the Court continued, the purpose of the supplements at issue must be considered. According to the Netherlands Government, the disability benefits act did not link benefits to the salary previously earned by the beneficiaries but sought to provide a minimum subsistence income to persons with no income from work. Such a guarantee to persons who would otherwise be destitute is an integral part of the social policy of the Member States. Consequently, the Court considered, if supplements to a minimum social security benefit are intended, where beneficiaries have no income from work, to prevent the benefit from falling below the minimum subsistence level for persons who, by virtue of the fact that they have a dependent spouse or children, bear heavier burdens than single persons, such supplements may be justified under the directive. The Court left the final answer to this to the national court: the national court has to investigate whether supplements such as those in this case correspond to the greater burden which beneficiaries having a dependent spouse or children must bear in comparison with persons living alone. If these serve to ensure an adequate minimum subsistence

---

[30]   Court of Justice 11 June 1987, Case 30/85, [1987] *ECR* 2497.

income for those beneficiaries and are necessary for that purpose, the fact that the supplements are paid to a significantly higher number of married men than married women is not sufficient to support the conclusion that the grant of such supplements is contrary to the directive.

In the arguments of the Court, we can clearly see the three steps which have to be taken in the case of discrimination: first one must examine whether the regulation has different effects for women and men, then one must consider whether there are objective reasons for the contested regulation, and finally it has to be examined whether the regulation is necessary and adequate to achieve these aims.

The application of these criteria did not appear to be very easy. The Dutch court of the first instance[31] considered, when it reached the third step, that the disputed increases were subject to a means test; this means test did not take *all* income into account (such as other disability benefits). Therefore, this regulation was not (absolutely) necessary to ensure a minimum (in some cases beneficiaries could achieve a higher income).

On appeal, the Court of Appeal[32] followed a different approach. It considered that all categories of income, which were not taken into account by the means test, concerned disability benefits. Therefore, the court considered that obviously it had been the intention of the legislator that the means test should not affect those disability benefits; in other words, the contested benefits were to be a basic benefit and this should not be reduced to the detrimental effect of those other specific benefits. This ancillary objective is acceptable and the effects of this are not such that it cannot be said that the increases are not necessary or not adequate.

The criteria of the Court of Justice were, as can be seen in this national follow-up, not easy to apply. From the point of view that a strict application of the criteria of the Court favours a uniform application of the directive in all Member States, the approach of the first national court was the most appropriate one. Below, as we will see in the *Molenbroek* judgment, the Court later adopted a view similar to that of the Dutch court of appeal described above.

Other types of benefit conditions can also raise the question of alleged indirect discrimination. A second case before the Court concerned, again, the Dutch General disability benefit (AAW); the *Ruzius-Wilbrink* case.[33]

> Benefits on the basis of this law are, as a rule, flat rate, i.e. at the level of the minimum wage. However, for persons who earned *less* than the minimum wage before they suffered incapacity for work, benefit is calculated on a lower individual basis. As this calculation method applies only where one earned less than the minimum wage, this rule is relevant only for (low paid) part-time workers. It was, in particular, women who worked in such jobs.

---

[31]   RvB Amsterdam 29 December 1987, *RSV* 1988/173.
[32]   CRvB 19 April 1990, *RSV* 1990/323.
[33]   Court of Justice 13 December 1989, Case 102/88, [1989] *ECR* 4311.

The Court took into consideration that the national legislation at issue granted all insured persons, with the exception of those who previously worked on a part-time basis, entitlement to an allowance which corresponded to a minimum subsistence income. The amount of benefit payable to the general category was not dependent on the previous earnings of the insured persons. Certain groups of recipients of the allowance who had no earnings at all in the year before their incapacity arose or who had only very low income, such as self-employed persons working on a full-time basis whose income was less than fifteen per cent of the minimum wage, students and unmarried persons keeping house for their parents, were also entitled to that minimum subsistence income. Only the allowance granted to *part-time* workers was calculated by reference to the insured person's income. It appeared from the documents before the Court that in the Netherlands there were considerably fewer male than female part-time workers. Accordingly, the Court concluded, a provision such as the one at issue led, in principle, to discrimination against female workers in relation to male workers and must be regarded as contrary to the objective pursued by Article 4(1) of Directive 79/7, unless the difference of treatment as between the two categories of workers is justified by objective factors unrelated to any discrimination on grounds of sex. The only reason put forward by the Netherlands government in the main proceedings to justify the difference of treatment between persons who worked on a part-time basis before the onset of their disability and other beneficiaries of the allowance in question, was that it would be unjust to grant them an allowance higher than the income previously received. This could not objectively justify that difference of treatment since, in a substantial number of other cases, the amount of the allowance granted under the 1975 Law was higher than the previous income. The Court ruled that Article 4(1) had to be interpreted as precluding a provision from creating, within the framework of national legislation which guarantees a *minimum subsistence income* to insured persons suffering from incapacity for work, an exception to that principle in respect of insured persons who had previously worked on a part-time basis and from limiting the amount of the allowance to the wage previously received. This is the case where that measure affects a much larger number of women than of men, unless that legislation is justified by objective factors unrelated to any discrimination on grounds of sex.

The national courts had to decide whether there were such factors. Both the court of the first instance[34], and the Dutch Court of Appeal considered that the AAW was not a scheme to ensure a minimum subsistence income, but guaranteed an income for those who lost such income. This argument is based on the fact that for most categories it is required that they earned at least a particular amount in the preceding year. The problem was, however, that some categories did not have to satisfy this condition (such as those who were already disabled at their eighteenth birthday and students). The Court of Appeal considered that this followed from an ancillary objective of the social policy of the State, and did not affect the general character

---

[34]   RvB Groningen 10 April 1990, *RSV* 1990/314.

of the Act. For this reason the supplements were not considered to infringe on the equal treatment provision.[35]

In later judgments, the Court of Justice followed an approach in which there was indeed more room for the national legislator to elaborate its social policy. A first example is an infringement procedure: *Commission* v. *Belgium*.[36]

> Under Belgian law, the benefit rate for unemployed persons was thirty-five per cent of the previous income. A person living with another who had occupational or replacement income received only a minimum payment; after eighteen months of unemployment he could receive a supplement where the income of the other person was below a certain amount. The benefits concerned were earnings related.

The Court considered that a system with increases, which takes account of the marital and family situation and which has the effect that fewer women than men can apply for such a benefit is potentially indirectly discriminatory. This is however not the case, if there are objective factors which exclude any discrimination on grounds of sex. The Belgian government had argued that the reason that more men were eligible for an increase was due to the fact that more men were employed in occupational activities and that this constituted such an objective factor. This difference was, however, not sufficient, according to the Court, to decide that this provision is not discriminatory.

It pointed out that the chosen regulation had to correspond to a necessary objective of the social policy of a state and had to be appropriate and necessary to attain that objective. The Belgium government responded that the objective of the national scheme was to grant, within the limits of its funds, a minimum replacement income, taking account of the family situation of the claimant. Secondly, the Belgium scheme aimed to avoid an overly large drop in income in the first year and also to provide for a special provision for the long term unemployed with a dependant. The Court considered that these principles of the national system were part of its social policy and that Member States are allowed a reasonable margin of discretion in relation to their social policy. The maximum level for the earnings-related benefit and the increase for long-term unemployed persons whose incomes were below a specified minimum constituted elements which meant that the national scheme has the character of a social minimum scheme. In respect of a social minimum scheme, Community law does not prevent a Member State from taking account of the relatively higher needs of beneficiaries with dependants.

In this judgment, the Court of Justice left considerable room for discretion to the Member States in respect of social minimum schemes. The Court followed this

---

[35]   CRvB 6 June 1991, *RSV* 1992/75
[36]   Court of Justice 7 May 1991, Case 229/89, [1991] *ECR* I-2205.

approach in a preliminary reference, the *Molenbroek* case.[37] In this case, the contested national law was that on increases to the old-age pensions.

> The Dutch old age pension provided as follows. Where both partners of a couple were retired, they each received an old-age pension of fifty per cent of the statutory minimum. The old age pension Act provided for an increase for the partner of a retired person who had not yet reached pension age, if this partner had insufficient means. Thus the retired person received (as was the rule at the time of the case) seventy percent of the minimum wage and thirty per cent for the dependant. Income, if any, of the partner was deducted from the increase. It was not disputed that under this scheme, men were more likely to receive an increase for a dependant partner. This was due to the fact that, in a couple, the man is often older than his spouse. Even if the man is younger than his wife, he will often have income from occupational activity which will mean that his wife will not qualify for the increase. The conditions under which the increase were payable were far more generous than the contested regulation in the *Teuling-Worms* case, discussed on page 266 (*i.e.* there were far more elements disregarded for the means test for this minimum benefit), because the income of the pensioner himself was not taken into account. The scheme was, therefore, not strictly appropriate and necessary to guarantee a minimum income. It was therefore doubted whether this scheme could stand the test of the *Teuling-Worms* judgment.

The Court pointed out, in the *Molenbroek* judgment, that factors constitute objective justification, if the scheme corresponds with a justified objective of the social policy of the Member State whose regulation was contested. The means used by a Member State had to be appropriate to attain the objective of the social policy and had to be necessary. The Dutch old-age pension had the characteristics of a basic income payment, in the sense that it aimed to guarantee a minimum income to the persons concerned, irrespective of other income. Thus, the income of the pensioner was not taken into account in calculating the increase for the dependant. The reason for this was, the Court considered, that the objective of the national legislation was to provide a couple with an income which they would have received if they had both reached retirement age. The increases were therefore necessary to maintain the character of a basic income payment in the AOW. Under these circumstances, the fact that in some situations an increase is also paid to persons for whom the increase is, because of their other income, not necessary to guarantee a subsistence minimum, does not mean that the means chosen by the Member State are not necessary. From these considerations, it followed that the national legislation fitted in with a legitimate objective of social policy and that the increases were considered appropriate to attain this objective and necessary. They were justified by factors not linked to discrimination on grounds of sex.

---

[37] Court of Justice 19 November 1992, Case 226/91, [1992] *ECR* I-5943.

As can be seen in this judgment, the Court itself answered the question whether the Dutch scheme is discriminatory, and did not leave this question, as it has done in, for instance, the *Bilka* judgment, to the national court.

The approach in the *Molenbroek* judgment was continued in the *Megner and Scheffel* judgment.[38]

The main question in this case was whether the exclusion of persons working in part-time jobs with a low number of working hours from social security protection was compatible with Article 4 of Directive 79/7. The case concerned two women, who are employed as cleaners by a firm. Their normal working time is a maximum of two hours per working day, five days a week. They were excluded from the compulsory insurance under the statutory sickness and old-age scheme and also from the insurance for unemployment benefit. They had filed a request to the competent German benefit administrations to be covered by these acts but this request was refused on the ground that they were in subsidiary employment which, under German legislation, is exempt from compulsory insurance under the relevant statutory schemes.

This judgment has already been discussed on page 250, where the Court had do answer the question whether they fell under the personal scope of the directive. The second question was whether the exclusion of subsidiary employment from the social insurance was forbidden by Article 4 of the directive. The Court considered that it is common ground that the national provisions at issue in the main proceedings are not directly discriminatory, since they do not exclude persons in subsidiary employment from the statutory schemes at issue on the ground of their sex. Article 4(1) of the directive precludes the application of a national measure which, although formulated in neutral terms, works to the disadvantage of far more women than men, unless that measure is based on objective factors unrelated to any discrimination on grounds of sex. That is the case, according to the Court, where the measures chosen reflect a legitimate social policy aim of the Member State whose legislation is at issue, are appropriate to achieve that aim and are necessary in order to do so.

The United Kingdom and Irish Government had stressed before the Court that contributory schemes, such as those at issue, require equivalence to be maintained between the contributions paid by employees and employers and the benefits paid in the event of the materialisation of one of the risks covered by the scheme. The structure of the scheme could not be maintained in its present form if the provisions in question had to be abolished.

The German Government further explained that there is a social demand for subsidiary employment, that it considered that it should respond to that demand in the context of its social policy by fostering the existence and supply of such employment and that the only means of doing this within the structural framework

---

[38]   Court of Justice 14 December 1995, Case 444/93, [1995] *ECR* I-4741.

271

of the German social security scheme is to exclude subsidiary employment from compulsory insurance. The jobs lost would not be replaced by full or part-time jobs subject to compulsory insurance. On the contrary, there would be an increase in unlawful employment and a rise in circumventing devices (for instance, false self-employment) in view of the social demand for subsidiary employment.

The Court observed that, in the current state of Community law, social policy is a matter for the Member States; it is for the Member States to choose the measures capable of achieving the aim of their social and employment policy. In exercising that competence, the Member States have a broad margin of discretion. The social and employment policy aim relied on by the German Government is objectively unrelated to any discrimination on grounds of sex and, in exercising its competence, the national legislature was reasonably entitled to consider that the legislation in question was necessary in order to achieve that aim.

In those circumstances, the Court concluded, the legislation in question cannot be described as indirect discrimination within the meaning of Article 4(1) of the directive.

In the *Nolte* judgment[39] the problem raised and the answer given by the Court resembled that of the *Megner and Scheffel* judgment to a large extent.

We can see in these judgments that the Court applies a loser test on objective grounds for justification than it had done in its earliest judgments on this issue, such as in the *Teuling* ruling. In that ruling the Court considered that a scheme must be appropriate, necessary and proportional to its objectives in order to be objectively justified in case of a suspicion of indirect discrimination. The Dutch social security court of the first instance applied these criteria in such a tight sense, that the scheme in question was not allowed. In the *Commission v. Belgium* judgment, the Member States were given the room within their social policy objectives to decide the provisions concerning minimum benefits to some extent themselves. But this judgment concerned benefits which provided for a minimum income in households. In the *Megner and Scheffel* judgment, this room has even become larger, the social policy concerning wage related benefits is now also considered as belonging to the discretionary room of the Member States, at least insofar as part-time employment is concerned.

In the *Roks-de Weerd* judgment the Court seemed to be strict in the criteria on *indirect discrimination*.[40]

Until 1979 married women were excluded from a disability benefit on the basis of the AAW Law. The law of 3 May 1989 provided that the discrimination against married women had to be terminated; Article III of this Law determined that persons who had become disabled before 1 January 1979 and who claimed benefit after 3 May 1989 (until this date married women were excluded), must have earned a certain amount of income from work in the last year before they

---

39   Court of Justice 14 December 1995, Case 317/93, [1995] *ECR* I-4625.
40   Court of Justice 24 February 1994, Case 343/92, [1994] *ECR* I-571.

became disabled. On 8 May 1989 Mrs Roks, who had become disabled on 1 January 1976, claimed a disability benefit. Her claim was refused on the basis of Article III of the Law of 3 May 1989. The question raised was whether Article 4(1) precludes the application of national legislation which makes the grant of benefits for incapacity for work dependent on the requirement of having received some income during the year preceding the commencement of he incapacity, a condition which, although it does not distinguish on grounds of sex, affects far more women than men, even if the adoption of that national legislation is justified on budgetary grounds.

The Court argued that Article 4 precludes the application of a national measure which, although formulated in neutral terms, works to the disadvantage of far more women than men, unless that measure is based on objectively justified factors unrelated to any discrimination on grounds of sex (*see* the *Commission v. Belgium* judgment). That is the case where the measures chosen reflect a legitimate social policy of the Member States whose legislation is at issue, are appropriate to achieve that aim and are necessary to do so (*Molenbroek* judgment). Nevertheless, although budgetary considerations may influence a Member State's choice of social policy and affect the nature or scope of the social protection measures it wishes to adopt, they cannot themselves constitute the aim pursued by that policy and cannot, therefore, justify discrimination against one of the sexes. The Court added, that to concede that budgetary considerations may justify a difference in treatment as between men and women which would otherwise constitute indirect discrimination on grounds of sex, would be to accept that the application and scope of as fundamental a rule of Community law as that of equal treatment between men and women might vary in time and place according to the status of the public finances of the Member States. The Court concluded that the income requirement is not allowed if it affects far more women than men, even if the adoption of that national legislation is justified on budgetary grounds.

In the *Posthuma-van Damme and Öztürk* judgment[41] a follow-up of the *Roks-De Weerd* judgment can be found. The question of the national court was whether the income requirement was compatible with Community law and what exactly the Court had meant in the *Roks-de Weerd* judgment. The Court answered that it had held in the *Roks-de Weerd* judgment that Directive 79/7 leaves intact the powers reserved by Articles 117 and 118 of the EC Treaty to the Member States to define their social policy within the framework of close co-operation organized by the Commission, and consequently the nature and extent of measures of social protection, including those relating to social security, and the way in which they are implemented. In exercising that competence, the Member States have a broad margin of discretion. Guaranteeing the benefit of a minimum income to persons who were in receipt of income from or in connection with work which they had to abandon owing to incapacity for work satisfies a legitimate aim of social policy. Making the benefit of that minimum income

---

[41]   Court of Justice 1 February 1996, Case 280/94, [1996] *ECR* I-179.

subject to the requirement that the person concerned must have been in receipt of such an income in the year prior to the commencement of incapacity for work constitutes a measure appropriate to achieve that aim which the national legislature, in the exercise of its competence, was reasonably entitled to consider necessary in order to do so, the Court argued. That fact that that scheme replaced a scheme of pure national insurance and that the number of persons eligible to benefit from it was further reduced to those who had actually lost income from or in connection with work at the time when the risk materialized cannot affect that finding.

Conclusion. We have finally reached a stage, in which the approach of the Court will not easily lead to the conclusion that a scheme of social security is indirectly discriminating if objectives of social policy underlie the scheme. The Court has left it to the national legislators to make their instruments of social policy and does not, in case of alleged indirect discrimination, investigate the reasons given as objective justification when measures of social policy are concerned, in any case not when social policy measures are aimed at guaranteeing a subsistence income.

23.5.6.   The Article 7 Exception

Article 7 of Directive 79/7 reads:
'This Directive shall be without prejudice to the right of Member States to exclude from its scope:
(a) the determination of pensionable age for the purposes of granting old-age and retirement pensions and the possible consequences thereof for other benefits;
(b) advantages in respect of old-age pension schemes granted to persons who have brought up children; the acquisition of benefit entitlements following periods of interruption of employment due to the bringing up of children;
(c) the granting of old-age or invalidity benefit entitlement by virtue of the derived entitlements of a wife;
(d) the granting of increases of long-term invalidity, old-age, accidents at work and occupational disease benefits for a dependent wife;
(e) the consequences of the exercise, before the adoption of this Directive, of a right of option not to acquire rights or incur obligations under a statutory scheme.'

This provision led to a number of rulings, in which the differences in pension age between men and women were disputed: the cases concerned, in particular, situations in which the earlier distinction in pension age was repealed, but the effects of that distinction were still felt. An example is the *Remi van Cant* judgment.[42]

---

[42] . Court of Justice 1 July 1993, Case 154/92, [1993] *ECR* I-3811.

The Belgian Royal Decree of 24 October 1967 provided that the normal pension age for men was sixty-five, whereas the pension age for women was set at sixty. Under the terms of this Decree, the amount of pension was calculated over forty-five years of work in case of men, and forty years of work in case of women. The income earned in each of these years was divide by forty-five (men) or forty (women); the pension was the aggregated sum of these calculations. In 1990, the eligible pension ages were revised. At present the pension age is sixty for men and women alike. The amount of the pension, was, however, still calculated in accordance with the rules of the Decree of 1967 and as this method was less attractive to men than to women, Mr Van Cant brought proceedings before a Belgian court.

The Court considered that the present Belgian law was of a discriminatory character, and prohibited by the directive. It could only be denied that this law was discriminatory if Article 7(1)(a) of the directive was applicable; this article authorises the Member States to defer the compulsory implementation of the principle of equal treatment with regard to the determination of pensionable age for the purposes of granting old-age pensions. Once the differences established in national law concerning the determination of the pension age were repealed, the exception in Article 7 could be no longer invoked to justify differences in the calculation of old age pensions which had been connected with the difference in pension age.

In the *Richardson* judgment[43] the disputed regulation was a British one.

In the United Kingdom the National Health Service Act authorizes the Secretary of State to adopt regulations providing for the payment of prescription charges in accordance with the rules laid down therein. The Act authorizes the adoption of regulations providing for exemption from those charges for certain categories of persons. Those categories of persons may be prescribed in particular by reference to age, type of condition affecting them, and the resources available to them. The Secretary of State had provided exemptions for, among other persons, a man who has attained the age of 65 years or a woman who has attained the age of 60 years. The question was whether Article 7(1)(a) of the directive applies to this case. The preliminary question was whether the scheme is within the scope of the directive. The answer to this was in the affirmative (*see* page 252). Subsequently, the question was raised whether Article 7 authorizes a Member State which, pursuant to that provision, has maintained different pension ages for men and women, also to provide that women are to be exempt from prescription charges at the age of 60 and women only at the age of 65.

The Court stated that where, pursuant to Article 7(1)(a) of Directive 79/7, a Member State prescribes different retirement ages for men and women for the purposes of

---

[43]   Court of Justice 19 October 1995, Case 137/94, [1995] *ECR* I-3407.

granting old-age and retirement pensions, the scope of the permitted derogation, defined by the words 'possible consequences thereof for other benefits' contained in Article 7, is limited to forms of discrimination existing under the other benefit schemes which are necessarily and objectively linked to the difference in retirement age. That is so where the discrimination in question is objectively necessary in order to avoid disturbing the financial equilibrium of the social security system or to ensure coherence between the retirement pension scheme and other benefit schemes. The grant of benefits under non-contributory schemes to persons in respect of whom certain risks have materialised where this occurs without reference to their entitlement to an old-age pension by virtue of contribution periods completed by them, has no direct influence on the financial equilibrium of contributory pension schemes. There is here an inverse relationship between entitlement to the benefit constituted by exemption from prescription charges as provided for in the British Regulations and the payment of contributions, inasmuch as it is only once a person has reached pensionable age and is no longer liable to pay National Insurance contribution that he is exempt from prescription charges under that provision. That being so, the Court argued, it must be accepted that the removal of the discrimination would not affect the financial equilibrium of the pension system. That conclusion cannot in any way be affected by the mere fact that extending entitlement to exemption from prescription charges to men who have reached the age of sixty would increase the financial burden borne by the State in the funding of its national health system. Therefore, the discrimination at issue is not objectively necessary to ensure coherence between the retirement pension system and the British Regulations on prescription. Although the fact that the elderly will generally incur more prescription charges than younger people at a time when they will normally have less disposable income may provide some justification for exempting them from prescription charges above a certain age, that consideration does not require this benefit to be granted at statutory pensionable age and therefore at different ages for men and women.

In the *Richardson* judgment a non-contributory benefit was involved. In the *Graham* judgment[44] the questions concerned contributory benefits. The approach of the Court led to a different result in this case.

> A British scheme provided, in essence, that where a person has received sickness benefit for a period of 168 days due to incapacity for work, that person is entitled to invalidity pension for each subsequent day of incapacity for work if he or she is under pensionable age, set at 65 for men and 60 for women. For those under pensionable age, the rate of invalidity pension is the same as that of a full State retirement pension.

The Court noted first that legislation such as that at issue is discriminatory inasmuch as, first, the rate of invalidity pension for women is limited to the rate of the retirement pension to which they would have been entitled had they not opted to defer

---

[44]   Court of Justice 11 August 1995, Case 92/94, [1995] *ECR* I-2521.

payment of that pension from the age of 60, whereas that is not the position for men until they reach the age of 65. Secondly, the scheme is discriminatory as women are not entitled to invalidity allowance in addition to invalidity pension if their incapacity commenced after they reached the age of 55, whereas, in the case of men, that is the position only if their incapacity commenced after they reached the age of 60.

The question is, again, whether Article 7(1) allows this discrimination. The Court answered that the scope of the derogation to the principle of equal treatment permitted by Article 7(1) is limited to the forms of discrimination existing under the other benefit schemes which are necessarily and objectively linked to the difference in pensionable age. As regards the forms of discrimination in the present case, the Court found that they are objectively linked to the setting of different pensionable ages for men and women, inasmuch as they arise directly from the fact that that age is fixed at 60 for women and 65 for men. As to the question whether the forms of discrimination are also necessarily linked to the difference in pensionable age for men and women, the Court noted, that since invalidity benefit is designed to replace income from occupational activity, there is nothing to prevent a Member State from providing for its cessation and replacement by a retirement pension at the time when the recipients would in any case stop working because they have reached pensionable age. Further, the Court argued, to prohibit a Member State which has set different pensionable ages from limiting, in the case of persons becoming incapacitated for work before reaching pensionable age, the rate of invalidity benefit payable to them from that age to the actual rate of the retirement pension to which they are entitled under the retirement pension scheme would mean restricting to that extent the very right which a Member State has under Article 7(1)(a) to set different pensionable ages. Such a prohibition would undermine the coherence between the retirement pension scheme and the invalidity benefit scheme in at least two respects.

First, the Member State in question would be prevented from granting to men who become incapacitated for work before reaching pensionable age invalidity benefits greater than the retirement pensions which would actually have been payable to them if they had continued to work until reaching pensionable age unless it granted to women over pensionable age retirement pensions greater than those actually payable to them. Second, if women did not have their invalidity pension reduced to the level of their retirement pension until they reached the age of 65, as in the case of men, women aged between 60 and 65, thus over pensionable age, would receive an invalidity pension at the rate of a full retirement pension if their incapacity for work commenced before they reached pensionable age and a retirement pension corresponding to the rate actually payable if it did not.

The Court concluded on the basis of these considerations that the derogation from Article 7 also extends to difference between the rates of invalidity pension payable to men and women from the time when they reach pensionable age. Owing to the link between invalidity pension and invalidity allowance, which is paid in addition to invalidity pension and thus only to persons entitled to that pension, that conclusion must also apply with regard to the difference between the qualifying dates for the grant of invalidity allowance, the Court ruled.

The *Bramhill* judgment[45] concerned part (d) of Article 7.

The judgment concerned a woman, who had claimed a retirement pension and an increase in that pension for her dependent husband. Her claim for an increase was disallowed. Before the legislative reform introduced in 1984, only male pensioners were entitled to increases in retirement pension for their dependent spouses. The new Act provides that such an increase is to be granted only on condition, in particular, that the claimant's retirement pension began immediately upon the termination of a period for which she was entitled to an increase in unemployment benefit, sickness benefit or invalidity pension in respect of adult dependants. According to the explanations provided by the United Kingdom, this possibility for women to obtain an increase in old-age benefit in respect of dependent spouses in the circumstances described above was introduced in order to prevent a sharp drop in income upon retirement for women when after the 1984 legislative reform they had been entitled to receive, before retirement, increases in sickness, unemployment and invalidity benefit in respect of dependent persons. However, Mrs Bramhill was not in such a situation.

The Court considered that the essence of the questions of the national court was whether Article 7(1)(d) precludes a Member State which provided for increases in long-term benefits in respect of a dependent spouse to be granted only to men from abolishing that discrimination solely with regard to women who fulfil, certain conditions. Mrs Bramhill argued that it follows from the wording of Article 7(1)(d) that Member States may exclude from the scope of the directive only the grant of increases in benefit for 'a dependent wife' so that schemes which, like that in force in the United Kingdom since 1984, provide for increases for both husbands and wives, but on different conditions, involve discrimination which is not covered by the derogation provided for in Article 7.

The Court does not accept this view. It followed the argument of the British government, which had pointed out that rules such as in force in the United Kingdom before the amendment of the law, which allowed certain categories of married women to receive the increases in question, incontestably fell within that derogation since at that time increases in retirement pension were provided for only in respect of a 'dependent wife'. The purpose of the directive is the progressive implementation of the principle of equal treatment for men and women in matters os social security; to interpret the directive in the way contended for by Mrs Bramhill would mean that in the case of benefits which a Member State has excluded from the scope of the directive pursuant to Article 7(1)(d) it could no longer rely on the derogation provided for by that provision if it adopted a measure which, like that in question in this case, has the effect of reducing the extent of equal treatment based on sex. This would therefore be incompatible with the purpose of the directive and would be likely to jeopardize the implementation of the aforesaid principle of equal treatment.

---

[45] Court of Justice 7 July 1994, Case 420/92, [1994] *ECR* I-3191.

Conclusion. Directive 79/7 has led to a considerable number of rulings. This case law is rather complicated. In general, it can be said that in its initial judgments, the Court followed a radical approach, by giving broad interpretations to the personal and material scope of the directive and by ruling that old schemes must not remain to have discriminatory effects.

A notorious lack in protection is that women do not fall under the directive if they stopped working in order to raise children.

With respect to the case law on indirect discrimination, we can see that the Court changed its case law through time: initially it appeared to be rather tight on the nature and content grounds for objective justification. If one reconsiders the old criteria, the present approach is not completely contrary to those criteria. The Court could, however, have prevented much work and cases if it had been more clear on these. The present case law does not leave many possibilities to fight situations of alleged indirect discrimination.

Chapter 24

Equal Treatment of Men and Women: The Other Directives

24.1.   Directive 86/378 on Occupational Social Security

24.1.1. Introduction

Directive 86/378 aims to ensure the implementation of the principle of equal treatment for men and women in *occupational* social security schemes. This Directive was adopted by the Council on 24 July 1986.[1] It is an important complement to the Directive discussed in the previous chapter, because the latter concerned statutory social security only.

The implementation period of this Directive expired on 1 January 1993. Member States were allowed to defer some parts of the Directive even later. In Chapter 22 we discussed the *Barber* judgment; the Court's rulings in this case interfered with these exceptions. In 1997 Directive 86/378 was amended by Directive 96/97 in order to make the former Directive consistent with the case law on Article 119 EC Treaty.[2]

24.1.2. Personal Scope of Directive 86/378

The personal scope of this Directive is defined in approximately the same way as for Directive 79/7. This means that the Directive applies to members of the working population including self-employed persons, persons whose activity is interrupted by illness, maternity, accident or involuntary unemployment and persons seeking employment, and to retired and disabled workers (Article 3). It is plausible that the case law of the Court on the personal scope of the Directive 79/7 is also relevant for questions concerning the personal scope of this Directive. Directive 96/97 added to this personal scope the persons claiming under the persons mentioned above, as is defined in national law and/or practice.

---

[1]   *OJ* 1986 *L* 225.
[2]   Directive 96/97 can be found in the *OJ* 1997 *L* 46/20.

24.1.3. Material Scope of Directive 86/378

The object of the Directive is to implement, in occupational social security schemes, the principle of equal treatment. Article 2 defines 'occupational schemes': these are schemes not governed by Directive 79/7 whose purpose is to provide workers, whether employees or self-employed, in an undertaking or group of undertakings, area of economic activity or occupational sector or group of such sectors with benefits intended to supplement the benefits provided by statutory social security schemes or to replace them. It is not decisive whether membership of such schemes is compulsory or optional.

Some types of schemes are excluded from the scope of this Directive. These are individual contracts of self-employed persons and schemes for self-employed persons having only one member. Neither does the Directive apply, in the case of salaried workers, to insurance contracts to which the employer is not a party. Optional provisions of occupational schemes offered to participants individually to guarantee them either additional benefits or a choice of date on which the normal benefits will start, or a choice between several benefits are also excluded.

The directive does not preclude an employer granting to persons who have already reached the occupational pension retirement age, but who have not yet reached retirement age for the statutory retirement pension, a pension supplement, the aim of which is to make equal or more nearly equal the overall amount of benefit paid to these persons in relation to the amount paid to the persons of the other sex in the same situation who have already reached the statutory retirement age, until the persons benefiting from the supplement reach the statutory retirement age. This provision codifies the *Neath* judgment (*see* Chapter 22) and was inserted by Directive 96/97.

Article 4 is relevant as regards the types of contingencies for which occupational schemes provide protection. This article states that the Directive applies to occupational schemes which provide protection against the following risks: sickness, invalidity, old age, including early retirement, industrial accidents and occupational diseases and unemployment. In addition to the contingencies mentioned in Directive 79/7, Directive 86/378 also applies to early retirement schemes.

The Directive also applies, according to Article 4(b), to occupational schemes which provide for other social benefits, in cash or in kind, and in particular survivors' benefits and family allowances, if such benefits are accorded to employed persons and thus constitute a consideration paid by the employer to the worker by reason of the latter's employment.

24.1.4. The Principle of Equal Treatment

The principle of equal treatment, according to Article 5 of this Directive, requires that there shall be no discrimination on the basis of sex, either directly or indirectly, by reference in particular to marital or family status, especially as regards:
-   the scope of the scheme and the conditions of access to them;

- the obligation to contribute and the calculation of contributions;
- the calculation of benefits, including supplementary benefits due in respect of a spouse or dependants, and the conditions governing the duration and retention of entitlement to benefits.

In the Directive, a list of areas is given where provisions are supposed to be contrary to the principle of equal treatment. These include provisions based on sex, either directly or indirectly, in particular by reference to marital or family status for determining the persons who may participate in an occupational scheme.

In addition provisions based on sex for fixing the compulsory or optional nature of participation in an occupational scheme are contrary to the Directive.

They include provisions based on sex for laying down different rules as regards the age of entry into the scheme or the minimum period of employment or membership of the scheme required to obtain the benefits thereof and provisions based on sex laying down different rules, except as provided for in subparagraphs (h) and (i) - discussed below - for the reimbursement of contributions where a worker leaves a scheme without having fulfilled the conditions guaranteeing him a deferred right to long-term benefits. They also include provisions based on sex for setting different conditions for the granting of benefits or of restricting such benefits to workers of one or other of the sexes. Provisions based on sex for fixing different ages and for suspending the retention or acquisition of rights during periods of maternity leave or leave for family reasons which are granted by law or agreement and are paid by the employer are also included.

Subparagraph (h) of Article 6 provides that criteria for setting different levels of benefit are provisions which are supposed to be contrary to the equal treatment provision. An exception applies, however, in so far as it may be necessary to take account of actuarial calculation factors which differ according to sex in the case of benefits designated as defined contribution. Directive 96/97 adds to this, that in the case of funded defined-benefit schemes, certain elements may be unequal where the inequality of the amounts results from the effects of the use of actuarial factors differing according to sex at the time when the scheme's funding is implemented. In the annex to the Directive examples of such elements can be found. The annex mentions:

- conversion into a capital sum of part of a periodic pension;
- transfer of pension rights;
- a reversionary pension payable to a dependant in return for the surrender of part of a pension;
- a reduced pension where the worker opts to take early retirement.

This subparagraph concerns schemes in which a certain pension is proposed. An example is a scheme which guarantees that a person receives eighty percent of the last earned wages at pension age. In that case, different benefits may not be defined for men or women, except in so far as necessary to take account of actuarial factors which differ for the sexes. This provision applies for benefits paid from contributions. In particular if the life expectancy for men and women differs, a difference is allowed in benefits.

Subparagraph (i) concerns the criteria for setting different levels of worker contribution and for setting different levels of employer contribution in the case of benefits designated as defined contribution (sometimes these schemes are called money purchase schemes).

Article 6 (j) mentions different standards or standards applicable only to workers of a specified sex as an area which is supposed to be contrary to equal treatment, except as provided for in subparagraphs (h) and (i), as regards the guarantee or retention of entitlement to deferred benefits when a worker leaves a scheme. Thus, different standards can also continue to be applied in the case of transfer of pensions, in so far as actuarial elements referred to in (h) and (i) are concerned.

According to the obligations of the Directive, Member States shall take all necessary steps to ensure that provisions contrary to the principle of equal treatment in legally compulsory collective agreements, staff rules of undertakings or any other arrangements relating to occupational schemes are null and void or may be declared null and void or amended. Schemes containing such provisions may not be approved or extended by administrative measures.

The Directive imposes the obligation on Member States to introduce into their national legal systems such measures as are necessary to enable all persons who consider themselves injured by failure to apply the principle of equal treatment to pursue their claims before the courts, possibly after bringing the matters before other competent authorities.

This is an important rule, also found in the Directive 79/7, as the Directive concerns schemes established by employers or independent organisations which have to administer the occupational schemes. For individuals this article is necessary as otherwise there was no way for them to ensure their rights as regards these schemes; this is due to the fact that directives do not have horizontal effect.

The *Ten Oever* case law has been inserted into the Directive. It now reads that any measure implementing this Directive, as regards paid workers, must cover all benefits derived from periods of employment subsequent to 17 May 1990 and shall apply retroactively to that date (with an exception for those who have already started proceedings prior to that date). For Mmeber States entering the Union at a later date, the relevant moment is the day of accesion to the Union.

24.1.5. *The Exceptions to the Principle of Equal Treatment*

The Directive contained some exceptions where equal treatment could be deferred. Following the *Barber* judgment these exceptions could no longer be upheld. At present, they apply for the schemes for the self-employed only, as is defined in Directive 96/97.

Under the present rules, Member States may defer compulsory application of the principle of equal treatment with regard to the self-employed:
(a) determination of pensionable age for the granting of old-age or retirement pensions, and the possible implications for other benefits in the case of schemes for self-employed persons:

- either until the date on which such equality is achieved in statutory schemes;
- or, at the latest, until such equality is prescribed by a directive;

(b) survivors' pensions until Community law establishes the principle of equal treatment in statutory social security schemes in that regard;

(c) the application of the first subparagraph of point (i) of Article 6(1) to take account of the different actuarial calculation factors, at the latest until 1 January 1999.

24.2. Directive 86/613 for the Self-employed

24.2.1. Introduction

Directive 86/613 concerns the application of the principle of equal treatment between men and women engaged in an activity, including agriculture, in a self-employed capacity, and on the protection of self-employed women during pregnancy and motherhood.[3]

The purpose of this Directive is to ensure the application in the Member States of the principle of equal treatment as between men and women engaged in an activity in a self-employed capacity, or contributing to the pursuit of such an activity, as regards those aspects not covered by Directive 79/7. The period of implementation is up to 30 June 1989.

24.2.2. Personal Scope of Directive 86/613

The Directive covers self-employed workers. This term includes all persons pursuing a gainful activity on their own account, under the conditions laid down by national law, including farmers and members of the liberal professions.

Secondly, the Directive covers the spouses of the self-employed workers, not being employees or partners, where they habitually, under the conditions laid down by national law, participate in the activities of the self-employed worker and perform the same tasks or ancillary tasks.

24.2.3. Material Scope of Directive 86/613

There are, as yet, few social security schemes for self-employed workers. The Directive states that: if a contributory social security system for self-employed workers exists in a Member State, that Member has to take the necessary measures to enable the spouses of self-employed workers (defined in Section 24.2.2.) who are

---

[3]   Directive of 11 December 1986, *OJ* 1986 *L* 359.

not protected under the self-employed worker's social security scheme to join a contributory social security scheme voluntarily.

A further, weak obligation on Member States is to undertake to examine whether, and under what conditions, female self-employed workers and the wives of self-employed workers may, during interruption in their occupational activity owing to pregnancy or motherhood have access to services supplying temporary replacements or existing social services. They also have to examine whether women in these circumstances may be entitled to cash benefits under a social security scheme or under any other public social protection system.

24.2.4. *The Principle of Equal Treatment*

For the purposes of this Directive, the principle of equal treatment implies the absence of all discrimination on grounds of sex, either directly or indirectly, by reference in particular to marital or family status (Article 3).

24.3.   Proposal for a Directive completing the Principle of Equal Treatment

24.3.1. *Introduction*

This proposal[4] aims to complete the principle of equal treatment in matters of social security which were excluded from Directives 79/7 and 86/378. The objective of this draft Directive is to extend the principle of equal treatment to the provisions of statutory schemes concerning survivors' benefits and family benefits. It also intends to extend the principle to the corresponding provisions of occupational schemes (including those concerning the family benefits of occupational schemes for self-employed earners). Thirdly, its objective is the extension of the equal treatment principle to the areas excluded or deferred pursuant to article 7(1)(a) to (d) of Directive 79/7 and Article 9(a) of Directive 86/378. This Directive has not yet been adopted by the Council.

24.3.2. *Personal Scope of the Draft Directive*

The proposed Directive will apply to the working population (including self-employed persons, workers whose activity is interrupted by illness, maternity, accident or involuntary unemployment and persons seeking employment); the Directive will also apply to retired workers and disabled workers and to members of the family, survivors and other persons dependent on those referred to under the three categories

---

[4]   Com (87) 494 final, *OJ* 1987 *C* 309/11.

mentioned above, these categories of dependents to be defined by the Member States' national legislation.

24.3.3. Material Scope of the Draft Directive

Under the conditions laid down by the Directive, the principle of equal treatment would be extended to the provisions of statutory schemes concerning survivors' benefits and family benefits. The extension would also apply to the corresponding provisions of occupational schemes (including those concerning family benefits or occupational schemes for self-employed earners). The third object of extension concerns the areas in which the implementation of the principle of equal treatment was excluded or deferred pursuant to Article 7 of Directive 79/7 and Article 9 of Directive 86/378. The last category is that of provisions concerning social assistance, where they are intended to supplement the benefits referred to under the provisions of statutory schemes concerning survivors' benefits and family benefits and the parts excluded from Directive 79/7.

24.3.4. The Principle of Equal Treatment

This draft Directive gives several definitions of how equal treatment is to be implemented for the various types of benefit excluded so far. For this purpose, the Directive is subdivided into various sections.

As regards *surviving spouses' benefits*, the principle of equal treatment means that there shall be no discrimination on grounds of sex. To this end, Member States can either grant entitlement to widows' pensions on the same terms for widowers or replace widows' benefits by the creation or extension of a system of individual rights open to all surviving spouses regardless of sex.

With regard to *orphans' benefits and other survivors' benefits* the principle of equal treatment means that there shall be no discrimination on the grounds of the sex of the deceased parent or the orphan.

The second chapter of the Directive contains provisions on *family benefits*. Article 7 provides that the principle of equal treatment means that there shall be no discrimination on grounds of sex with regard to child benefit and benefits introduced to assist parents to assume their parental responsibilities. The principle of equal treatment thus completed in this area applies both to natural parents and other persons responsible for a child and thus meets the conditions (other than those which are incompatible with this principle) laid down for the grant of benefits referred to in paragraph 1 of Article 7.

A special chapter is dedicated to *retirement pensions*. This chapter provides for extension of the principle of equal treatment to areas where its implementation might be excluded or deferred under Article 7 of Directive 79/7 and Article 9 of Directive 86/378. When a pension age is determined for the purpose of granting old age and retirement pensions, it shall be identical for both sexes.

Fixing an identical age can also lead to a reduction or increase in that age for workers of a given sex. If women can retire at the age of sixty and men at the age of sixty-five, equal treatment may mean that the women may in future not retire before the age of sixty-five. In respect of such effect, Article 9 provides that provision shall be made for gradual implementation and for temporary safeguards for workers having reached the specified age, enabling them if they wish to claim their pension at the age previously prescribed.

The Directive also forbids discrimination as regards the advantages in respect of old age pension schemes granted to persons who have brought up children, or as regards the acquisition of benefit entitlements following periods of interruption of employment due to the bringing-up of children, provided that such persons have actually interrupted their employment for that purpose.

The granting of old age or invalidity benefit entitlements by virtue of the derived entitlements of a spouse, or the granting of increases in long-term benefits in respect of invalidity, old age, accidents at work and occupational disease for a dependent spouse shall be authorised solely in the case of those spouses who on the date when this Directive comes into effect have not established their own personal entitlements to these benefits.

Chapter 25

Freedom of Movement of Services and Social Security

Apart from the provisions on the free movement of workers, which were dealt with in the first part of this book, another part of the Treaty is also relevant to social security. These provisions concern competition, and can be found in Articles 85 and 86 of the Treaty. At first sight they are not relevant to social security. The relevance becomes clear, however, if insured persons argue that compulsory affiliation with statutory social security is contrary to these articles. As more and more States consider partial or full privatisation of their social security system, these provisions become more and more important. The relevant articles read as follows.

Article 85 provides:
'1. The following shall be prohibited as incompatible with the common market: all agreements between undertakings, decision by associations of undertakings and concerted practices which may affect trade between Member States and which have as their object or effect the prevention, restriction or distortion of competition within the common market (..)'.

Article 86:
'Any abuse by one or more undertakings of a dominant position within the common market or in a substantial part of it shall be prohibited as incompatible within the common market in so far as it may affect trade between Member States. (..)'.

These provisions were invoked by two artists who contested their compulsory affiliation with a scheme of statutory social security.[1] Without challenging the principle of compulsory affiliation to a social security scheme, the litigants considered that, for such purposes, they should be free to approach any private insurance

---

[1] Court of Justice 17 February 1993, Cases 159/91 and 160/91, *Poucet*, [1993] *ECR* I-637. *See* also Laigre, 'Les Organismes de sécurité sociale, sont ils entreprises?', in: *Droit social* 1993, 488. F. de Pré, 'Klein Duimpje en de Nederlandse ziektekostenverzekeringen', in: *Sociaal recht*, 1993, 138; H. Hermans and I. Tiems, 'Convergentie in de ziektekostenverzekering; mogelijkheden en belemmeringen in Europees perspectief', in: *Sociaal recht* 1995, 113; K. Mortelmans, 'Marktgerichte arbeidsongeschiktheidsregelingen onder de loep van algemene leerstukken van EG-recht', in: *Sociaal recht*, 1995, 326.

company established within the territory of the Community. In fact they argued that they should not have to be subject to the conditions laid down unilaterally by the above-mentioned organisations, which, they maintain, hold a dominant position, contrary to the rules on freedom of competition laid down in the Treaty. The question was whether social security organisations fall under Article 85 and 86 of the Treaty; for this purpose the Court had to decide whether they were enterprises within the meaning of the Treaty.

The Court answered that it is relevant that the schemes in question pursue a social objective and embody the principle of solidarity. The principle of solidarity is, in the sickness and maternity scheme concerned, embodied in the fact that the scheme is financed by contributions proportional to the income from the occupation, whereas the benefits are identical for all those who receive them. Furthermore, persons no longer covered by the scheme retain their entitlement to benefits for a year, free of charge. It follows that these social security schemes are based on a system of compulsory contribution, which is indispensable for application of the principle of solidarity and the financial equilibrium of those schemes. The management is entrusted by statute to social security funds whose activities are subject to control by the State. In the discharge of their duties, the funds apply the law and thus cannot influence the amount of the contributions, the use of assets and the fixing of the level of benefits.

The Court concluded that in the context of competition law the concept of undertaking encompasses every entity engaged in an economic activity, regardless of the legal status of the entity and the way in which it is financed. Sickness funds, and the organisations involved in the management of the public security system, fulfil an exclusively social function. That activity is based on the principle of national solidarity and is entirely non-profit-making. Accordingly, that activity is not an economic activity and, therefore, the organisations to which it is entrusted are not undertakings within Article 85 of the Treaty.

Thus, in this judgment statutory social security organisations are not considered to be an enterprise within the meaning of Article 85, and for this reason the Court did not rule that other organisations must be admitted to the management of social security. In arriving at this interpretation, it appears to be important that an organisation has an exclusively social function and that there is no making profit objective. Thus where these criteria do not apply, it may be anticipated that the Court woud allow free competition.

Chapter 26

Towards a Social Europe?

The case law of the Court of Justice had a central place in this study. We focused, in particular, on how the Court interpreted the principles underlying Regulation 1408/71 and Directive 79/7. We saw that the Court followed an approach in which the principles of freedom of movement and equal treatment were given a meaning which left no room for Community and national legislation which was inconsistent with these principles. In this, the Court followed a radical approach. It frequently explicitly pointed out that this Community legislation required a uniform interpretation, which must not allow the Member States to escape their responsibilities under Community law. By this case law, the Court has made an immense contribution to the development of a social Europe.

On the other hand, the limits of the possibilities of the Court of Justice also became clear in this study. These limits appeared especially with respect to those subjects where the differences between the Member States are very large. Thus, we regularly see that the Court deviated from its earlier case law (although not explicitly) and developed a new approach in order to respond to problems raised by the Member States. This can be seen in the *Newton* judgment[1] (which restricted the overruling of residence requirements with respect to hybrid benefits - Chapter 7), the *Winter-Lutzins* judgment[2] (Article 10 was not to apply to transitional advantages in old-age-pension law - Chapter 12), and the *Lenoir* judgment[3] (which did not go into the question of indirect discrimination - Chapter 10). Furthermore, the consequences of the *Ten Holder* judgment[4], which was considered as being problematic, were mitigated by the *Daalmeijer* judgment.[5] Examples from equal treatment law are the *Ten Oever* judgment[6] (in which a less wide-reaching interpretation of the *Barber* judgment[7] was given - Chapter 22), and the *Commission* v. *Belgium* and *Molenbroek* judgments[8] (Chapter 23), in which the Court has given a much softer application

---

[1]   Court of Justice 20 June 1991, Case 356/89, [1991] *ECR* 3017.
[2]   Court of Justice 2 May 1990, Case 293/88, [1990] *ECR* 1623.
[3]   Court of Justice 27 September 1988, Case 313/86, [1988] *ECR* 5391.
[4]   Court of Justice 12 June 1986, Case 302/84, [1986] *ECR* 1821.
[5]   Court of Justice 21 February 1991, Case 245/88, [1991] *ECR* 555.
[6]   Court of Justice 6 October 1993, Case 109/91, [1993] *ECR* I-4879.
[7]   Court of Justice 27 May 1990, Case 262/88, [1990] *ECR* 1990.
[8]   Court of Justice 7 May 1991, Case 229/89, *Commission* v. *Belgium* [1991] *ECR* 2205; Court of Justice 19 November 1992, Case 226/91, *Molenbroek* [1992] *ECR* I-5943.

of the prohibition of indirect discrimination in Directive 79/7 in the cases where minimum benefits are concerned.

It can be said that the influence of the governments of the Member States and of the Commission on the proceedings before the Court in respect to such subjects is greater than is usual in national proceedings. This influence has been given an institutionalized form in the possibility for the Commission and the Member States to express their views to the Court. Indeed, there are additional (more indirect) methods for influencing the Court, of which the Protocol to the Treaty of Maastricht on Article 119 EC Treaty (the Barber Protocol - *see* Section 22.3) is an example.

These ways of influencing the case law of the Court do not make a common policy more easy; neither do they facilitate consistent case law from the Court of Justice. Consequently, we see that Regulation 1408/71 is constantly growing in length.

The judgments of the Court mentioned above concern, in particular, areas of Community law in respect of which the Court had given earlier rulings which led to significantly higher expenses for the Member States. More specifically, the judgments often concerned *non-contributory* benefits.[9] The objections of the Member States to the possibility of exporting these benefits, as long as such benefits do not guarantee a minimum income for comparable risks in all Member States, is quite understandable. Some writers explain problems with the harmonisation of social security systems by referring to differences in traditions.[10] In my view, the problems with these judgments are not, primarily, due to discrepancies arising from different traditions in the social security systems of the Member States. The judgments mentioned concerned problems which can be regarded as due to the transitional stage of development of systems. For instance, the *Winter-Lutzins* judgment concerns transitional advantages in the Dutch old-age benefit, due to the fact that under this Act one cannot acquire a full benefit until the completion of fifty insured years, which cannot happen before the year 2007. This means that in the course of the 21st Century, these advantages will no longer be needed. Hybrid benefits concern an area of social protection which is also still in development; it may be expected that all Member States will establish subsistence benefits within time. When this process is completed, it will be easier to allow export of this type of benefit to other Member States as well. Another example is the supplements payable to persons who have dependents. These aroused the suspicion of indirect discrimination (the *Teuling-Worms* judgment[11]); these may also be expected to be of a temporary nature. After all, many organisations and authors have pointed to the need for an individual system of social security and the labour force participation rate of women is currently increasing.

These remarks are not meant to suggest that all problems will be solved overnight. The developments mentioned above do, in their turn, provoke critical

---

[9]   The *mobility allowance* in the United Kingdom, Dutch General Disability benefits at a minimum level, the transitory advantages of the Dutch (flat-rate) old-age benefits), the French school benefits in the *Lenoir* judgment.

[10]   Pieters (1989a).

[11]   Court of Justice 11 June 1987, Case 30/85, [1987] *ECR* 2497.

remarks, for example, concerning the type of employment in which the growing participation rate of women is realised. This is often precarious employment. Neither can one expect that the internal single market will lead to a satisfactory social protection system in all Member States. Consequently, the hypothesis that the problems with Community action, which were analysed in this book, are mainly due to transitional stages in social protection, does not mean that no initiatives are needed to attain a Social Europe. The hypothesis is, however, useful to indicate which measures are appropriate. This is because coordination problems appear, in particular, to be related to differences in the levels of protection. These differences will not disappear if the Community legislator does not take action. Neither can it be expected that the Court will be able to solve the problems arising from the differences between the Member States without such initiatives. One might argue that the Court should not have altered its case law on political or financial grounds. This would, however, not work well as the resistance of the Member States to such an approach would become too great. Moreover, such an approach would also lead to undesirable results. An example could be seen in the *Bachmann* judgment[12] (Chapter 10); if the Court had decided on a radical application of the prohibition of indirect discrimination, this would have led to a disruption of the fiscal regimes of the Member States involved.

The conclusion that initiatives of the Community legislator are needed in the field of subsistence benefits, accentuates, on the other hand, the criticism of the weak instruments on minimum protection described in Chapter 21. In my view, there is a need for stronger instruments. The lack of enthusiasm of the Member States to establish a European social policy is mainly at the level of principle. Most systems of the Member States reach higher standards than those contained in the recommendations discussed in Chapter 21. ILO Convention no 102, for instance, has been ratified by a considerable number of the Member States.[13] The resistance to higher and binding standards seems to be mainly due to the present feelings in the Member States in regard to the 'powers' of the Community bodies rather than to hard arguments. The United Kingdom, for instance, which has so far been the most important adversary of a European social policy, has a comprehensive social security system. An increase in Community standards would - in the present state of affairs - not lead to a radical change in the United Kingdom system. Moreover, the United Kingdom scheme is at present affected more than others by the discrepancy between its traditional nature, on the one hand, and the system of Regulation 1408/71 on the other, as can be seen from the predominance of United Kingdom cases (child benefit, sickness benefit, mobility allowances).

Consequently, a first step in the process of harmonisation and improvement of coordination could be to develop a stronger Community instrument (such as a directive) to improve the protection provided by subsistence benefits. This should establish standards no lower than are at present already reached by the Member

---

[12]   Court of Justice 28 January 1992, Case 204/90, [1992] *ECR* I-249.
[13]   *See*, for the ratifications of ILO Conventions, Pennings (looseleaf).

States. To this end, the Commission should make a study of the present state of affairs.

A new element would be that the Commission should undertake this study in relation to the benefits which proved problematic for coordination.

This would lead to the following steps. The European Commission would make, following ILO Convention no 102, and having in mind the problems in protection levels which caused practical problems for co-ordination initiatives, an analysis of the present situation. It would analyze to what extent Member States already satisfy the standards of the ILO Convention mentioned. Subsequently, the measures necessary to satisfy these conditions completely should be studied. With the transitional nature of several national benefits in mind, it could be argued that there should be (financial) support from the EU for those systemes in which the standards have not yet been reached. Finally, one should study the type of additional protection needed to find solutions in those areas where the realisation of comprehensive co-ordination has proved problematic. This last question would lead to long-term objectives.

This approach would be useful as proposals for harmonisation initiatives would be, as a result of the steps described above, suggested by the need for a solution in relation to coordination. They would not be done on the basis of the objective of establishing a Community social policy as such, which is resisted by some Member States. Consequently, this approach, in which a link is made between the problems existing for harmonisation and coordination respectively, would be in line with the subsidiarity principle, discussed in Chapter 21 of this book.

Bibliography

- Addison, J. en W. Siebert, 'The social charter of the European community: evolution and controversies.' In: ILRR 1991, 597.
- Amoroso, B. (1990), 'A Danish perspective: the impact of the internal market on the labour unions and the welfare state'. In: *Comparative labor law journal* 1990, 483.
- Berg, C. van den (1990), 'Geen Handvest; toch handvat voor Europa 1992.' In: PS 1990, 1.
- Betten, L. (ed), D. Harris, and T. Jaspers, (1989), *The future of European Social Policy*. Deventer, 1989.
- Betten, L. (1993), *International Labour Law*. Deventer, 1993.
- Borgesius, J. (1990), 'De invloed van het communautaire recht op de Nederlandse sociale verzekering.' In: SVr, *Van alle kanten bekeken*. Zoetermeer, 1990, 63.
- Brenninkmeijer, A. (1981), 'De ongelijke behandeling van mannen en vrouwen in de AAW.' In: NJB 1981, 613.
- Brinkman, O. (1992) 'Post-actieven en de aanwijsregels van Verordening (EEG) 1408/71.' In: *Migrantenrecht* 1992, 108.
- Brinkman (1994), 'De personele werkingssfeer van Verordening (EEG) nr. 1408/71'. In: *Migrantenrecht*, 1994, 86.
- Bruce, M. (1961), *The Coming of the Welfare State*. London, 1961.
- Busquin, Ph. (1990), 'De sociale Slang en het Europees programma ter bestrijding van armoede.' In: BTSZ, 1990, 557.
- Byre, A. (1992), *EC Social policy and 1992*. Deventer, 1992.
- Catala, N. and R. Bonnet, *Droit social européen*. Paris, 1991.
- Clever, P. (1989), 'Tendenzen zur Aufgabe des Territorialitätsprinzips', In: *Der Arbeitgeber*, 1989, 988-990.
- Cornelissen, R.C. (1984), *Europese coördinatie van invaliditeits- en weduwenverzekeringen*. Antwerpen, 1984.
- Cornelissen, R.C., 'Communautaire en Nederlandse jurisprudentie inzake conflictregels in het Europees sociaal zekerheidsrecht'. In: SEW, 1986, 799-823.
- Cornelissen, R. (1988), 'Invaliditeit, Ouderdom en overlijden (pensioenen), Uitkeringen bij overlijden'. In: Pieters (1988: 89 -118).
- Cornelissen, R. (1989), '[review of] Levelt-Overmars, *Halen de volksverzekeringen het jaar 2000?*'. In: SMA 1989, 197.
- Cornelissen R. (1991), 'De Nederlandse volksverzekeringen en de Europese verordeningen inzake sociale zekerheid'. In: Schell (1991: 59).
- Cousins, M. (1993), 'The EC Recommendations on Social Protection: A Case Study in EC Social Policy.' In: *Social Policy and Administration*. 1993, p. 286.
- Crijns, L. (1986), 'Het sociaal beleid van de Europese Gemeenschap'. In: F.A.J. van den Bosch en A.M. Dancot-Devriendt (ed.), *Sociaal en zeker*. Deventer, 1986, 149-175.

- Curtin, D. (1987), 'Occupational pension schemes and article 119: beyond the fringe?'. In: C.M.L. Rev. 1987, 254.
- Curtin, D. (1990), 'Scalping the Community legislator: occupational pensions and "Barber"'. In: C.M.L. Rev, 1990, 475.
- Curtin, D. (1990), 'Directives: the effectiveness of judicial protection of individual rights.'. In: C.M.L. Rev. 1990, 709.
- Driessen, M. (1992), 'Algemene achtergrondinformatie'. In: Jacobs (1992a: ix).
- Dijt, E. (1988), 'De gevolgen van het arrest Teuling-Worms.' In: SMA 1988, 769.
- Eichenhofer, E. (1993), 'Co-ordination of social security and equal treatment of men and women in employment: recent social security judgments of the Court of Justice.' In: C.M.L. Rev. 1993, 1021.
- Eichenhofer, E. en M. Zuleeg (1995), *Die Rechtsprechung des Europäischen Gerichtshof zum Arbeits- und Sozialrecht im Streit*, Schriftenreihe der Europäischen Rechtsakademie Trier, Köln, 1995.
- Feenstra, S. (1990), 'De Verordening (EEG) nrs. 1408/71 en 574/72 in het licht van 1992'. In: SMA 1990, 729.
- Fitzpatrick, B. (1992), 'Community social law after Maastricht.' In: ILJ, 1992, vol. 3, 199.
- Forde, M. (1980), 'The vertical conflict of social security law in the European Community', LIEI, 1980, 21 ff
- Fraser, D. (1973), *The Evolution of the British Welfare State*. London etc, 1973.
- Fuchs, M. (ed) (looseleaf), *Nomos Kommentar zum Europäischen Sozialrecht*. Baden-Baden.
- Gauthier, P. (1988), 'Les prestations familiales face au droit communautaire: suite du feuilleton "Pinna". In: *Droit social,* 1988, 288.
- Govers, A. (1973), 'Het Hof van Justitie en het EEG sociale zekerheidsrecht.' In: SEW, 1983, 286.
- Govers, A. (1977), 'Communautaire jurisprudentie inzake het EEG sociale zekerheidsrecht.' In: SEW, 1977, 758.
- Govers, A. (1988),'Gelijkheid van vrouw en man in het Europees recht.' In: *Geschriften VAR*, 1981.
- Govers, A.W. (1983), 'Het Hof van Justitie en het EEG sociale zekerheidsrecht.' In: SEW 1983, 286.
- Heerma van Voss, G. (1990), 'Hoe het Hof van Justitie van de EEG de AAW op haar grondvesten doet wankelen.' In: SR 1990, 108.
- Heijden, P. van der and G. Heerma van Voss (1990), 'Sociaal recht en EVRM'. In: A. Heringa et al. (ed.), *40 jaar europees verdrag voor de rechten van de mens*. Leiden, 1990, 209.
- Jacobs, A. (1985), *De rechtstreekse werking van internationale normen in het sociaal recht*. Alphen aan den Rijn, 1985.

- Jacobs, A. (ed) (1992a), *Het Nederlandse sociale zekerheidsrecht en de minimumnormen van de IAO en de Raad van Europa*. Deventer, 1992
- Jacobs, A. (1992b), 'Algemene minimum-normen'. In: Jacobs (1992a: 1).
- Jacobs, A. and H. Zeijen (1993), *European Labour Law and Social Policy*, Tilburg, 1993.
- Jaspers A. and L. Betten (ed) (1988), *25 Years European Social Charter*, Deventer (1988).
- Jorens, Y. (1992), *Wegwijs in het Europees sociale zekerheidsrecht,* Brugge, 1992.
- Kavelaars, P. (1992), *Toewijzingsregels in het Europees sociaal-verzekeringsrecht*. Deventer. Deventer, 1992.
- Keunen, F. (1987), 'Het arrest Ten Holder en de wijziging van K.B. 557', SMA, 1987, 98.
- Keunen, F. (1992), 'Coördinatie en gelijke behandelingnormen'. In: Jacobs (1992a: 131).
- Köbele, B. en G. Leutschner (ed) (1995), *Dokumentation der Konferenz 'Europäischer Arbeitsmarkt Grenzenlos mobil?' 6 bis 8 März*, Bonn, 1995.
- Köhler, P. and H. Zacher (1983), *Beiträge zu Geschichte und aktueller Situation der Sozialversicherung*. Berlin, 1983.
- Kuile, B. ter (1992), 'Pensioenrecht als kansspel. Schrijnende rechtsonzekerheid bij aanvullende pensioenen.' In: SMA, 1992, 727.
- Laske, C. (1993), 'The impact of the Single European Market on Social protection for migrant workers.' In: C.M.L. Rev. 1993, 515.
- Levelt-Overmars, W.M. (1988), *Halen de volksverzekeringen het jaar 2000?* Deventer, 1988.
- Limberghen, G. van (1991), *Pensioenen van Belgen in het buitenland*. Antwerpen, 1991.
- Loenen, M. (1986) 'Artikel 119 EEG-Verdrag en de gelijke behandeling van mannen en vrouwen in de aanvullende pensioenregelingen.' In: SMA 1986, 390.
- Lutjens, E. (1992), *Pensioenrecht*. Deventer, 1992.
- Lyon-Caen, G. and A. (1993), *Droit social international et européen*. 8th edition. Paris, 1993.
- Neal, A.C. and S. Foyn (1995), *Developing the Social Dimension in an Enlagerd European Union,* Oslo, 1995
- Nielsen, R. and E. Szyszcak (1991), *The social dimension of the European Community*. Copenhagen, 1991.
- Nielsen, R. and E. Szyszcak (1993), *The social dimension of the European Community*. Second edition. Copenhagen, 1993.
- O'Keeffe, D. (1981), 'The scope and content of social security regulation in European Community law'. In: O'Keeffe, D. and Schermers, H. (eds.) (1982), *Essays in European Law and Integration*. Leiden, 1982, 105-122.
- O'Keeffe, D. (1985), 'Equal Rights for Migrants; the Concept of Social Advantages in Article 7(2), Regulation 1612/68', YER, 1985, 93-123.

- Limberghen, G. van (1991), *Pensioenen van Belgen in het buitenland.* Antwerpen, 1991.
- Overeem, P.C.G. (1982), 'Het vrij verkeer van werklozen in EEG-verband'. In: *Ars Aequi*, 1982, 267-273.
- Pennings, F. (1990), *Benefits of Doubt. A Comparative Study of the Legal Aspects of Employment and Unemployment Schemes in Great Britain, Germany, France and the Netherlands.* Deventer, 1990.
- Pennings, F. (1992), 'Groeiende ruimte voor woonplaatsbepalingen in het EG-coördinatierecht'. In: SMA 1992, 503-518.
- Pennings, F. (1993), 'Is the subsidiarity principle useful to guide the European integration process.' In: *Tilburg Foreign law review.* 1993, vol. 2, 153.
- Pennings, F. (looseleaf), 'Codex' in R. Blanpain (ed.), *International Encyclopaedia of Laws, Social Security Law* (looseleaf).
- Pennings, F.J.L. (1993), *Grondslagen van het Europese sociale-zekerheidsrecht,* Deventer, 1993
- Pennings, Frans (1994), *Introduction into European social security law.* Deventer, 1994.
- Pennings, F. (1996a), 'Internationale aspecten van de sociale zekerheid', in: C.J. Loonstra, H.W.M.A. Staal, W. Zeijlstra (red), *Arbeidsrecht en mensbeeld,* Deventer, 1996, blz. 329-343.
- Pennings, F. (1996b), *Europees sociale-zekerheidsrecht,* Leuven, 1996.
- Pennings, F.J.L. (red.) (1996c), *Tewerkstelling over de grenzen,* Deventer, 1996.
- Fennings, F.J.L. (1997), 'De WULBZ en grensoverschrijdend verkeer van werknemers'. In: *SMA* 1997, 174.
- Perrin, G. (1961), 'Les prestations non contributives et la sécurité sociale', Droit Social, 1961, 179-183
- Perrin, G. (1969), 'De aktie van de internationale arbeidsorganisatie ten gunste van de coördinering en van de harmonisering van de wetgevingen betreffende de sociale zekerheid', BTSZ, 1969, 1165-1253.
- Pieters, D. (1987), *Europees en internationaal sociale zekerheidsrecht,* Antwerpen, 1987.
- Pieters, D. (ed.) (1988a), *Europees sociale zekerheidsrecht, commentaar.* Antwerpen, 1988.
- Pieters, D., 'Situering van het Europees sociale zekerheidsrecht'. In: Pieters (1988, 17-45).
- Pieters, D. (1989a), *Sociale Zekerheid na 1992: één over twaalf.* Tilburg, 1989.
- Pieters, D. (1989b), 'Brengt '1992' coördinatie en harmonisatie van de sociale zekerheid?'. In: NJB 1989, 831.
- Pieters, D. (1992), *Sociale-zekerheidsrechtsvergelijking ten dienste van Europa.* Deventer, 1992.
- Prechal, S. (1992), 'Bommen ruimen in Maastricht: wijziging van art. 119 EEG'. In: NJB 1992, 134.
- Prechal, S. (1990), 'Remedies after *Marshall*.' In: C.M.L. Rev. 1990, 451.

- Raepenbusch, S. van (1985), 'La jurisprudence communautaire en matière de règles anticumul de sécurité sociale.' In: CDE 1985, 251.
- Raepenbusch, S. van (1988), 'Werkloosheid'. In: Pieters (1988: 119).
- Regenmortel, A. van, and Y. Jorens (ed) (1993), *Internationale Detachering*, Brugge, 1993
- Schell, J.L.M. (1988), 'Gezins- en kinderbijslagen.' In: Pieters (1988: 147).
- Schell, J.L.M. (1991) (ed), *De toekomst van de volksverzekeringen in Europa*. Tilburg, 1991.
- Schoukens, P. (ed) (1997), *Prospects of Social Security Co-ordination*. Leuven, Amersfoort, 1997.
- Schuler, R. (1985), 'Zwischenstaatliche und gemeinschaftsrechtliche Sozialrechtsintegration im Vergleich', *Europarecht*, 1985, 113.
- Schuler, R. (1988), *Das Internationale Sozialrecht der Bundesrepublik Deutschland*, Baden-Baden, 1988.
- Schulte, B. (1982), 'Auf dem Weg zu einem europäischen Sozialrechts? - der Beitrag zur Entwicklung des Sozialrechts in der Gemeinschaft', *Europarecht*, 1982, 357 ff.
- Schulte, B. (1984), 'Das Sozialrecht in der Rechtsprechung des Europäisches Gerichtshofs'. In G. Wannagat (ed.), *Jahrbuch des Sozialrechts der Gegenwart*, Band 6, Berlin, 1984.
- Schulte, B. and H. Zacher (1991), *Wechselwirkungen zwischen dem Europäischen Sozialrecht und dem Sozialrecht der Bundesrepublik Deutschland*. Berlin, 1991.
- Schulte, B. (1988), 'Algemene bepalingen'. In: Pieters (1988: 47).
- Schulte, B. (1992), 'Armut und Armutsbekämpfung in der Europäischen Gemeinschaft - Mindesteinkommenssicherung und Sozialhilfe in EG-Sozialrecht und EG-Sozialpolitik'. In: Zeitschrift für Sozialhilfe und Sozialgesetzbuch *ZfSH/SGB*, 1992, 393.
- Schulte, B. (1992), *Europäisches Sozialrecht*. Wiesbaden, 1992.
- Schulte, B. (1995), 'Konfliktfelder im Verhältnis zwischen mitgliedstaatlichem und europäischem Recht.' In: Eichenhofer en Zuleeg (1995), 11.
- Schultz (1991), 'Grundsätze, Inhalte und institutionelle Verankerung im EWG-Vertrag.' In: *Sozialer Fortschritt*, 1991, 135.
- Steen, I. van der (looseleaf), 'Thema Grensarbeid en sociale zekerheid', in: *Internationale Sociale Verzekering*, Deventer.
- Steyger, E. (1988), 'De gemeenschappelijke arbeidsmarkt en het sociale beleid van de Gemeenschap, over discriminatie, distorsies, en ingebakken dispariteiten'. In: NJB, 1988, 249.
- Steyger, E. (1990), 'Het vervolg van de Ruzius-zaak of: hoe ver ligt Groningen van Luxemburg.' In: NJB 1990, 1405
- Stiemer, N. (1988), 'Ziekte en moederschap'. In: Pieters (1988: 69).
- *Subsidiarity: the Challenge of Change*. (1991). Proceedings of the Jacques Delors Colloquium 1991. Maastricht, 1991.

- Tamburi, G. (1983), 'L'Organisation internationale du Travail et l'évolution des assurances sociales dans le monde.' In: Köhler en Zacher (1983: 647).
- Tantaroudas, C. (1976), *La protection jurdidique des travailleurs migrants,* Paris, 1976.
- Tantaroudas, C. (1979), 'L'égalité de traitement en matière de sécurité sociale dans les règlements communautaires', RTDE, 1979, 63.
- Tegtmeier, W. (1991), 'Wechselwirkungen zwischen dem Europäischen Sozial-recht und dem Sozialrecht der Bundesrepublik Deutschland - Erfahrungen und Vorstellungen aus deutscher Sicht.' In: Schulte und Zacher (1991: 27).
- Timmermans, C. (1982), 'Verboden discriminatie of geboden differentiatie', SEW, 1982, 427-460.
- Urbanetz, H. (1991), 'Modaliteiten voor het behoud van de rechten en de berekening van de prestaties in het Europees Verdrag inzake sociale zekerheid en andere samenordeningsinstrumenten'. In: BTSZ 1991, 359.
- Vansteenkiste, S. (1991), 'The idea of the thirteenth state system: towards a competition between a federal social insurance system and the national social security systems.' In: Caixa Andorrana de seguretat social, *Colloqui international sobre seguretat social,* Andorra, 1991.
- Verschueren, H. (1993), 'Het arrest Taghavi en de tegemoetkoming van gehandicapten aan niet-EG-familieleden van EG-werknemers'. In: *MR* 1993/4, blz. 74.
- Verschueren, H. (1997), 'Na het arrest Taflan-Met: is er leven na de dood.' In: *MR* 1997, 29.
- Villars, C. (1979), *Le Code européen de sécurité sociale et le Protocole additi-onnel.* Genève, 1979
- Vogel-Polsky, E. (1990), 'Welk juridisch instrumentarium is nodig voor een sociaal Europa?'. In: SMA, 1990, 60-69
- Vonk, G. (1988), 'De Ten Holder problematiek opnieuw aanhangig bij het Hof van Justitie van de Europese Gemeenschap'. In: SR, 1988, 371.
- Vonk, G. (1991), *De coördinatie van bestaansminimumuitkeringen in de Europe-se Gemeenschap,* Deventer, 1991.
- Vonk, G. (1992), 'Migranten in Europa en het recht op gezinsbijslagen'. In: *Migrantenrecht* 1992.
- Watson, Ph. (1980), *Social Security Law of the European Communities,* London, 1980.
- Watson, Ph. (1991), 'The Community social charter.' In: C.M.L. Rev. 1991, 37.
- Watson, Ph. (1993), 'Social policy after Maastricht.' In: C.M.L. Rev. 1993, 481.
- Wiebringhaus, H. (1983), 'Die Sozialversicherung im Rahmen der Funktionen, der Möglichkeiten und der sozialpolitischen Vorhaben des Europarats.' In: Köhler en Zacher (1983: 507).

-   Zacher, H. (1991), 'Wechselwirkungen zwischen dem Europäischen Sozialrecht und dem Sozialrecht der Bundesrepublik Deutschland - Einführungsreferat aus sozialrechtlicher Sicht.' In: Schulte und Zacher (1991: 11).

Table of Cases

Index on Cases

Subject Index

List of publications in this series

1) The Social Quality of Europe - Beck/van der Maessen/Walker - 1997
    ISBN 90 411 0456 9